Improving Libra Systems with AI:

Applications, Approaches, and Bibliometric Insights

K.R. Senthilkumar
Sri Krishna Arts and Science College, India

R. Jagajeevan
Sri Krishna Arts and Science College, India

IGI Global
PUBLISHER of TIMELY KNOWLEDGE

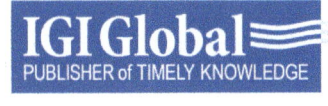

A volume in the Advances in Library and Information Science (ALIS) Book Series

Published in the United States of America by
	IGI Global
	Information Science Reference (an imprint of IGI Global)
	701 E. Chocolate Avenue
	Hershey PA, USA 17033
	Tel: 717-533-8845
	Fax: 717-533-8661
	E-mail: cust@igi-global.com
	Web site: http://www.igi-global.com

Copyright © 2024 by IGI Global. All rights reserved. No part of this publication may be reproduced, stored or distributed in any form or by any means, electronic or mechanical, including photocopying, without written permission from the publisher. Product or company names used in this set are for identification purposes only. Inclusion of the names of the products or companies does not indicate a claim of ownership by IGI Global of the trademark or registered trademark.
	Library of Congress Cataloging-in-Publication Data

CIP Pending
ISBN: 979-8-3693-5593-0
EISBN: 979-8-3693-5595-4

This book is published in the IGI Global book series Advances in Library and Information Science (ALIS) (ISSN: 2326-4136; eISSN: 2326-4144)

British Cataloguing in Publication Data
A Cataloguing in Publication record for this book is available from the British Library.

All work contributed to this book is new, previously-unpublished material. The views expressed in this book are those of the authors, but not necessarily of the publisher.

For electronic access to this publication, please contact: eresources@igi-global.com.

Advances in Library and Information Science (ALIS) Book Series

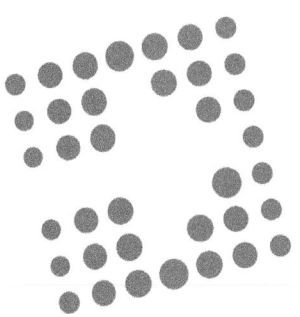

Alfonso Ippolito
Sapienza University-Rome, Italy
Carlo Inglese
Sapienza University-Rome, Italy

ISSN:2326-4136
EISSN:2326-4144

Mission

The **Advances in Library and Information Science (ALIS) Book Series** is comprised of high quality, research-oriented publications on the continuing developments and trends affecting the public, school, and academic fields, as well as specialized libraries and librarians globally. These discussions on professional and organizational considerations in library and information resource development and management assist in showcasing the latest methodologies and tools in the field.

The **ALIS Book Series** aims to expand the body of library science literature by covering a wide range of topics affecting the profession and field at large. The series also seeks to provide readers with an essential resource for uncovering the latest research in library and information science management, development, and technologies.

Coverage

- Human Side of Information Services
- Conservation
- User-Centered Technologies
- Community Outreach
- Discovery Tools
- Virtual Reference Services
- Interlibrary Loans
- Mobile Library Services
- Licensing Issues
- Partnerships in Library Communities

IGI Global is currently accepting manuscripts for publication within this series. To submit a proposal for a volume in this series, please contact our Acquisition Editors at Acquisitions@igi-global.com or visit: http://www.igi-global.com/publish/.

The Advances in Library and Information Science (ALIS) Book Series (ISSN 2326-4136) is published by IGI Global, 701 E. Chocolate Avenue, Hershey, PA 17033-1240, USA, www.igi-global.com. This series is composed of titles available for purchase individually; each title is edited to be contextually exclusive from any other title within the series. For pricing and ordering information please visit http://www.igi-global.com/book-series/advances-library-information-science/73002. Postmaster: Send all address changes to above address. Copyright © 2024 IGI Global. All rights, including translation in other languages reserved by the publisher. No part of this series may be reproduced or used in any form or by any means – graphics, electronic, or mechanical, including photocopying, recording, taping, or information and retrieval systems – without written permission from the publisher, except for non commercial, educational use, including classroom teaching purposes. The views expressed in this series are those of the authors, but not necessarily of IGI Global.

Titles in this Series

For a list of additional titles in this series, please visit: http://www.igi-global.com/book-series/advances-library-information-science/73002

Examining Information Literacy in Academic Libraries
Sabelo Chizwina (North-West University, South Africa) and Mathew Moyo (North-West University, South Africa)
Information Science Reference • copyright 2024 • 313pp • H/C (ISBN: 9798369311431) • US $230.00 (our price)

AI-Assisted Library Reconstruction
K.R. Senthilkumar (Sri Krishna Arts and Science College, India)
Information Science Reference • copyright 2024 • 363pp • H/C (ISBN: 9798369327821) • US $235.00 (our price)

Challenges of Globalization and Inclusivity in Academic Research
Swati Chakraborty (GLA University, India & Concordia University, Canada)
Information Science Reference • copyright 2024 • 301pp • H/C (ISBN: 9798369313718) • US $225.00 (our price)

Multidisciplinary Approach to Information Technology in Library and Information Science
Barbara Holland (Brooklyn Public Library, USA (Retired)) and Keshav Sinha (University of Petroleum and Energy Studies, India)
Information Science Reference • copyright 2024 • 345pp • H/C (ISBN: 9798369328415) • US $245.00 (our price)

Handbook of Research on Innovative Approaches to Information Technology in Library and Information Science
Barbara Holland (Brooklyn Public Library, USA (Retired)) and Keshav Sinha (University of Petroleum and Energy Studies, India)
Information Science Reference • copyright 2024 • 427pp • H/C (ISBN: 9798369308073) • US $285.00 (our price)

Illuminating and Advancing the Path for Mathematical Writing Research
Madelyn W. Colonnese (Reading and Elementary Education Department, Cato College of Education, University of North Carolina at Charlotte, USA) Tutita M. Casa (Department of Curriculum and Instruction, Neag School of Education, University of Connecticut, USA) and Fabiana Cardetti (Department of Mathematics, College of Liberal Arts and Sciences, University of Connecticut, USA)
Information Science Reference • copyright 2024 • 389pp • H/C (ISBN: 9781668465387) • US $215.00 (our price)

Emerging Technology-Based Services and Systems in Libraries, Educational Institutions, and Non-Profit Organizations
Dickson K. W. Chiu (The University of Hong Kong, Hong Kong) and Kevin K. W. Ho (University of Tsukuba, Japan)
Information Science Reference • copyright 2023 • 353pp • H/C (ISBN: 9781668486719) • US $225.00 (our price)

701 East Chocolate Avenue, Hershey, PA 17033, USA
Tel: 717-533-8845 x100 • Fax: 717-533-8661
E-Mail: cust@igi-global.com • www.igi-global.com

Table of Contents

Preface xvii

Chapter 1
Unravelling AI Ethics: A Bibliometric Journey Through Scholarly Publications 1
    A. Subaveerapandiyan, Bennett University, India
    S. Radhakrishnan, Debre Berhan University, Ethiopia
    Madhuri Kumari, Central University of Gujarat, India
    Arnold Chama, National Archives of Zambia, Zambia

Chapter 2
Revolutionizing Medical Libraries: The Vital Role of AI in Enhancing Discovery, Access, and Library Services for Healthcare Professional 24
    Amreen Taj, Yenepoya Pharmacy College and Research Centre, India
    Mohammed Gulzar Ahmed, Yenepoya Pharmacy College and Research Centre, India
    K. S. Ali, Yenepoya University, India
    K. R. Senthilkumar, Sri Krishna Arts and Science College, India

Chapter 3
Impact of AI in Library Operations 39
    G. Bhuvaneswari, Kumaraguru School of Business, India
    P. T. Vijaya Rajakumar, Nehru Institute of Engineering and Technology, India

Chapter 4
Harnessing the Power of AI for Information Management and User Engagement in Next-Generation Libraries 47
    Jaya K. Vijesh, Sri Krishna Arts and Science College, India

Chapter 5
Exploring the Transformative Impact of Artificial Intelligence on Research Library Management 63
    M. Sathiya, Sri Krishna Arts and Science College, India
    M. Vidya, Sri Krishna Arts and Science College, India

Chapter 6
Exploring the Top ChatGPT Libraries for Powerful Conversational AI 72
   Delma Thaliyan, Christ University, India
   Joe Joseph, Christ University, India
   V. L. Helen Josephine, Christ University, India

Chapter 7
Ethical Considerations of AI Implementation in the Library Era.. 85
   N. Rajkumar, Alliance College of Engineering and Design, Alliance University, India
   C. Viji, Alliance College of Engineering and Design, Alliance University, India
   A. Mohanraj, Sri Eshwar College of Engineering, India
   K. R. Senthilkumar, Sri Krishna Arts and Science College, India
   R. Jagajeevan, Sri Krishna Arts and Science College, India
   Judeson Antony Kovilpillai, Alliance College of Engineering and Design, India

Chapter 8
Enhanced Services of Next-Gen Libraries Through Artificial Intelligence....................................... 107
   J. Joselin, Sri Krishna Arts and Science College, India
   B. Anuja Beatrice, Sri Krishna Arts and Science College, India
   S. Indhumathi, Sri Krishna Arts and Science College, India

Chapter 9
Emerging and Innovative AI Technologies for Resource Management 115
   Balusamy Nachiappan, Prologis, USA

Chapter 10
Educational Program for AI Literacy... 134
   Mageshkumar Naarayanasamy Varadarajan, Capital One, USA

Chapter 11
E-Resources Content Recommendation System Using AI 155
   Balusamy Nachiappan, Prologis, USA

Chapter 12
Assessing Student Satisfaction With Artificial Intelligence in Education: A Study of
E-Applications in Selected Educational Institutes in Coimbatore 178
   S. Aravind, G.T.N. Arts College (Autonomous), India
   R. Kavitha, Mother Teresa Women's University, India

Chapter 13
Artificial Intelligence Journey in Enhancing Library Accessibility 186
   N. Karthick, Sri Krishna College of Arts and Science, India
   P. Nithya, PSG College of Arts and Science, India
   R. Rajkumar, RVS College of Arts and Science, India

Chapter 14
Anticipating AI Impact on Library Services: Future Opportunities and Evolutionary Prospects 195
    B. Lalitha, KPR Institute of Engineering and Technology, India
    K. Ramalakshmi, Alliance College of Engineering and Design, India
    Hemalatha Gunasekaran, University of Technology and Applied Sciences, Oman
    P. Murugesan, KSR College of Engineering, India
    P. Saminasri, KPR Institute of Engineering and Technology, India
    N. Rajkumar, Alliance College of Engineering and Design, Alliance University, India

Chapter 15
AI for Accessibility: A Case Study of Enhancing Library Services for Users With Disabilities 214
    Henry S. Kishore, Sri Krishna arts and Science College, India
    D. Solomon Paul Raj, Sri Krishna Arts and Science College, India
    K. R. Senthilkumar, Sri Krishna Arts and Science College, India

Chapter 16
Exploring the Intersection of AI and Financial Literacy: Current Insights, Hurdles, and
Prospects 226
    S. Dheepiga, Sri Krishna Arts and Science College, India
    N. Sivakumar, Sri Krishna Arts and Science College, India

Chapter 17
Implementing AI-Based Recommendation Systems for Personalized Financial Services in
Libraries 235
    N. P. Kowsick, Sri Krishna Arts and Science College, India
    K. Ramasamy, Sri Krishna Arts and Science College, India

Chapter 18
AI-Driven Language Enhancement Strategies for Libraries: Empowering Information Access and
User Experience in an English Language Context..244
    R. Visnudharshana, Sri Krishna Arts and Science College, India
    Henry S. Kishore, Sri Krishna Arts and Science College, India

Chapter 19
A Study on Advanced Applications of Mathematics and AI in Library Science 254
    S. Durga Devi, Sri Krishna Arts and Science College, India
    R. Mohanapriya, Sri Krishna Adithya College of Arts and Science, India
    N. Sarumathy, Sri Krishna Arts and Science College, India

Chapter 20
AI-Driven Libraries: Pioneering Innovation in Digital Knowledge Access 272
    K. C. Anandraj, Madurai Kamaraj University, India
    S. Aravind, G.T.N. Arts College (Autonomous), India

Chapter 21
AI Insights Deciphering India's Ascendancy Through the Digital Library: Navigating the Digital
Realm India's Odyssey Towards Information Equity and Technological Eminence 285
    B. Velmurugan, NPR College of Engineering and Technology, India
    S. Dharmalingam, Chettinad College of Engineering and Technology, India
    K. Binith Muthukrishnan, NPR College of Engineering and Technology, India
    K. R. Senthilkumar, Sri Krishna Arts and Science College, India

Compilation of References 294

About the Contributors 318

Index 324

Detailed Table of Contents

Preface xvii

Chapter 1
Unravelling AI Ethics: A Bibliometric Journey Through Scholarly Publications 1
    A. Subaveerapandiyan, Bennett University, India
    S. Radhakrishnan, Debre Berhan University, Ethiopia
    Madhuri Kumari, Central University of Gujarat, India
    Arnold Chama, National Archives of Zambia, Zambia

The rapid expansion of artificial intelligence (AI) has engendered significant societal and ethical concerns, necessitating a comprehensive examination of scholarly work in AI ethics. This study aims to present a bibliometric analysis delineating the growth trends, author collaborations, thematic evolution, and international contributions within the realm of AI ethics research from 2014 to 2023. Employing established bibliometric methodologies, this research utilizes data from the Scopus database, encompassing 1490 articles. The study investigates growth patterns, authorship trends, thematic, and global contributions in AI ethics scholarship. The result reveals an exponential surge in annual AI ethics publications, with critical thematic shifts and prolific author collaborations. Author productivity, citation metrics, institutional affiliations, and country-wise contributions elucidate the global landscape of AI ethics research.

Chapter 2
Revolutionizing Medical Libraries: The Vital Role of AI in Enhancing Discovery, Access, and Library Services for Healthcare Professional 24
    Amreen Taj, Yenepoya Pharmacy College and Research Centre, India
    Mohammed Gulzar Ahmed, Yenepoya Pharmacy College and Research Centre, India
    K. S. Ali, Yenepoya University, India
    K. R. Senthilkumar, Sri Krishna Arts and Science College, India

The study aims to analyse the discovery, access strategies, and library services at the Central Library of Yenepoya (deemed to be University) (hereafter referred to as YCL) with a specific focus on the role of AI. By identifying challenges and proposing solutions, the study employs a qualitative case study method to investigate the discovery, access, and library services at YCL. Data gathering techniques include interviews, observation, content analysis of library records, and a thorough review of relevant literature. The researcher personally observes the library operations and supplements primary data with an analysis of secondary materials. Microsoft Excel is utilized for data management and analysis. The study indicates that the Yenepoya Central Library effectively facilitates the discovery and access of e-resources, along with providing various additional services such as research support, RFID services, QR codes for materials, reference assistance, technical support, and email-based services. However, there's a need for integrating AI tools into the library services.

Chapter 3
Impact of AI in Library Operations 39
 G. Bhuvaneswari, Kumaraguru School of Business, India
 P. T. Vijaya Rajakumar, Nehru Institute of Engineering and Technology, India

Artificial intelligence (AI) is disrupting how information is processed and searched. It can help information professionals improve their services by allowing individuals to perform more effective searches. However, there are concerns about its potential to replace humans in various jobs and lead to catastrophic events. Artificial intelligence (AI) has positive and negative impacts, but its potential to improve the operations of libraries far outweigh its drawbacks. According to Robinson, it can help them achieve their goals of improving the user experience and operational efficiency. AI can help libraries establish themselves as leaders in the scholarly community. In advanced nations, such as the US, libraries have integrated the capabilities of AI by applying various cutting-edge technologies, like augmented reality and virtual reality. These innovations have greatly enhanced how individuals discover information. The chapter explores the utilization of AI within libraries and the obstacles that it encounters when it comes to implementation.

Chapter 4
Harnessing the Power of AI for Information Management and User Engagement in Next-Generation Libraries 47
 Jaya K. Vijesh, Sri Krishna Arts and Science College, India

In this era of digital transformation, libraries are evolving into next-generation knowledge hubs by harnessing the power of artificial intelligence (AI). This research explores the integration of AI to enhance information management and user engagement in libraries. The study investigates diverse AI applications, methodological approaches, and their impact on library systems. By examining intelligent systems and algorithms, the research aims to uncover how AI technologies can streamline information organization, retrieval, and dissemination, ultimately contributing to a more efficient and user-friendly library experience. Additionally, the study delves into user engagement strategies, leveraging AI to tailor services based on individual preferences and behaviors.

Chapter 5
Exploring the Transformative Impact of Artificial Intelligence on Research Library Management 63
 M. Sathiya, Sri Krishna Arts and Science College, India
 M. Vidya, Sri Krishna Arts and Science College, India

Artificial intelligence (AI) has wielded considerable influence over diverse facets of contemporary society, including the intricate dynamics of research libraries. This chapter undertakes an in-depth exploration of AI's profound impact on library functionalities, services, and user interfaces. Through an exhaustive review of scholarly works and empirical studies, the authors scrutinize how AI technologies such as machine learning, natural language processing, and data analytics are fundamentally altering the landscape of information retrieval, resource curation, and scholarly discourse within research libraries. Moreover, they delve into the nuanced challenges and prospects stemming from the integration of AI, encompassing concerns regarding privacy, algorithmic bias, and the evolving roles and responsibilities of librarians. By grasping and leveraging AI's potent influence, research libraries can adeptly navigate and thrive amidst the swiftly evolving digital milieu, thereby amplifying their support for scholarly pursuits and the dissemination of knowledge.

Chapter 6
Exploring the Top ChatGPT Libraries for Powerful Conversational AI 72
    Delma Thaliyan, Christ University, India
    Joe Joseph, Christ University, India
    V. L. Helen Josephine, Christ University, India

This research analyzes the need for top ChatGPT libraries and their usage today. It focuses on the features, benefits, and drawbacks of ChatGPT through in-depth interviews to uncover nuanced insights into library preferences and usage patterns. The findings reveal diverse perspectives among developers, highlighting preferences for libraries based on ease of integration and customization. Participants emphasize the significance of user-friendly interfaces and robust documentation in shaping positive experiences with ChatGPT libraries. Additionally, themes emerge around the need for continuous updates to address evolving AI challenges. Through in-depth insights from developers, the study elucidates the importance of user-friendly interfaces, adaptability, and efficient documentation, providing valuable guidance for developers seeking to optimize their conversational AI projects. This research contributes essential qualitative dimensions to the evaluation of ChatGPT libraries, offering actionable insights for the development community.

Chapter 7
Ethical Considerations of AI Implementation in the Library Era... 85
    N. Rajkumar, Alliance College of Engineering and Design, Alliance University, India
    C. Viji, Alliance College of Engineering and Design, Alliance University, India
    A. Mohanraj, Sri Eshwar College of Engineering, India
    K. R. Senthilkumar, Sri Krishna Arts and Science College, India
    R. Jagajeevan, Sri Krishna Arts and Science College, India
    Judeson Antony Kovilpillai, Alliance College of Engineering and Design, India

As the mixture of artificial intelligence (AI) continues to permeate several sectors, ethical considerations have ended up a focus in ensuring responsible and sustainable AI deployment. This virtual library explores the multifaceted moral dimensions related to AI implementation. The gathering of scholarly articles and studies papers delves into key moral problems, spanning troubles which includes bias and fairness, transparency, responsibility, privacy, and societal impact. The number one section of the virtual library addresses the undertaking of algorithmic bias and fairness, reading how biases in AI systems can perpetuate societal inequalities. Various methods to mitigating bias and selling fairness in AI algorithms are explored, providing insights into the improvement of more equitable AI programs. Transparency and duty are the focal factors of the second one segment, emphasizing the need for clean conversation of AI decision-making techniques and mechanisms for holding AI systems answerable for their movements.

Chapter 8
Enhanced Services of Next-Gen Libraries Through Artificial Intelligence... 107
    J. Joselin, Sri Krishna Arts and Science College, India
    B. Anuja Beatrice, Sri Krishna Arts and Science College, India
    S. Indhumathi, Sri Krishna Arts and Science College, India

In today's rapidly evolving digital landscape, next-generation libraries are embracing artificial intelligence (AI) to revolutionize their services and redefine the user experience. This chapter explores the transformative role of AI in enhancing library services, focusing on key applications and approaches. AI-powered technologies are facilitating improved information retrieval systems, personalized recommendation services, streamlined metadata management, and advanced digital preservation efforts. Additionally, AI enables intelligent cataloguing and classification, automated text analysis, and user-centric design principles. Through collaborative partnerships, in-house training programs, and agile methodologies, libraries are effectively integrating AI solutions to meet the diverse needs of patrons and ensure efficient and user-friendly services. This chapter highlights the potential of AI to elevate next-gen libraries into dynamic hubs of knowledge and innovation, poised to thrive in the digital era.

Chapter 9
Emerging and Innovative AI Technologies for Resource Management 115
   Balusamy Nachiappan, Prologis, USA

Emerging AI technologies are revolutionizing library services by the usage of presenting contemporary procedures to resource management, operational innovation, and enhancing client research. AI in libraries involves schooling the structures to perform tasks that usually require human intelligence, together with natural language processing (NLP) for advanced talents. NLP lets users look at library catalogs and databases using language processing, making record retrieval extra touchy and efficient. System mastering is every other crucial technology being applied in libraries to increase recommendation structures for customers. The structures examine client options and behavior to indicate relevant books, articles, and other resources, providing personalized tips.

Chapter 10
Educational Program for AI Literacy... 134
   Mageshkumar Naarayanasamy Varadarajan, Capital One, USA

As artificial intelligence (AI) permeates numerous factors of society, it's crucial for people to develop a foundational understanding of AI standards, abilities, and implications. Academic applications for AI literacy play a crucial characteristic in equipping beginners with the understanding, abilities, and critical wondering abilities vital to engage meaningfully with AI technologies. This comprehensive evaluation examines various forms of instructional tasks aimed in the direction of promoting AI literacy throughout high-quality age businesses and settings. This chapter gives an in-depth evaluation of the targets, methodologies, demanding situations, and excellent practices associated with each form of educational software. Furthermore, it explores the importance of integrating moral issues, social obligation, and inclusivity into AI training projects to make certain that beginners are prepared to navigate the ethical and societal implications of AI.

Chapter 11
E-Resources Content Recommendation System Using AI.. 155
   Balusamy Nachiappan, Prologis, USA

In the virtual age, the huge amount of available content material fabric poses a challenge for clients to find out applicable facts suited to their alternatives. To cope with this problem, the authors advise a practical content advice system (ICRS) that leverages superior synthetic intelligence (AI) techniques to enhance content discovery and person engagement. This tool employs a multifaceted method, incorporating collaborative filtering, content material-based totally absolutely filtering, and deep analyzing algorithms to generate customized tips. The collaborative filtering thing of the gadget analyzes user behaviors, alternatives, and interactions with content to grow to be aware about styles and similarities with exceptional users. This collaborative method helps in recommending content that aligns with a user's interests based totally on the alternatives of like-minded people.

Chapter 12
Assessing Student Satisfaction With Artificial Intelligence in Education: A Study of
E-Applications in Selected Educational Institutes in Coimbatore 178
    S. Aravind, G.T.N. Arts College (Autonomous), India
    R. Kavitha, Mother Teresa Women's University, India

This study presents a comprehensive overview of the revolution brought about by artificial intelligence in the education sector. It delves into the current landscape of artificial intelligence in education. The term "artificial intelligence" encompasses the integration of artificial intelligence (AI) into communication tools and systems, encompassing chatbots, virtual assistants, and other AI-driven platforms designed to enhance communication processes. The primary focus of this study is to investigate students' satisfaction with such AI communication technology within the educational context. Specifically, the study targets selected educational institutes in Coimbatore District, evaluating the effectiveness and reception of e-apps (electronic applications) that integrate AI into the educational communication process. Through this exploration, the researcher aims to provide valuable insights into the impact and viability of AI-driven communication technology in enhancing the educational experience.

Chapter 13
Artificial Intelligence Journey in Enhancing Library Accessibility 186
    N. Karthick, Sri Krishna College of Arts and Science, India
    P. Nithya, PSG College of Arts and Science, India
    R. Rajkumar, RVS College of Arts and Science, India

Artificial intelligence (AI) has become integral to modern library services, offering solutions for tasks ranging from information retrieval to accessibility improvements. This chapter explores the evolution and applications of AI in libraries, highlighting its role in enhancing user experiences and optimizing resource management. Case studies from libraries worldwide demonstrate successful implementations of AI for document reconstruction, metadata enrichment, and user support. Furthermore, the chapter discusses the ethical considerations associated with intellectual freedom and censorship in the digital age, emphasizing the importance of preserving open access to information while addressing challenges posed by content filtering and algorithmic recommendation systems. Overall, the chapter provides insights into the transformative potential of AI in libraries and underscores the need for ethical AI practices to ensure inclusivity and intellectual freedom for all patrons.

Chapter 14
Anticipating AI Impact on Library Services: Future Opportunities and Evolutionary Prospects 195
    B. Lalitha, KPR Institute of Engineering and Technology, India
    K. Ramalakshmi, Alliance College of Engineering and Design, India
    Hemalatha Gunasekaran, University of Technology and Applied Sciences, Oman
    P. Murugesan, KSR College of Engineering, India
    P. Saminasri, KPR Institute of Engineering and Technology, India
    N. Rajkumar, Alliance College of Engineering and Design, Alliance University, India

Artificial intelligence (AI) is an emerging field in library science, involving the programming of computers to execute tasks that typically require human intelligence. The overarching goal is to create computer systems capable of thinking and acting like humans, which holds profound implications for the field of librarianship. AI has found widespread application within libraries, with examples including expert systems for reference assistance, robots designed to assist with tasks like book sorting, and the integration of virtual reality for immersive learning experiences. While some may fear that AI implementation could distance librarians from their users, the prevailing view suggests that it will instead complement human expertise rather than replace it. By leveraging AI, libraries can enhance their service delivery, streamline operations, and adapt to the evolving demands of a digital society.

Chapter 15
AI for Accessibility: A Case Study of Enhancing Library Services for Users With Disabilities 214
    Henry S. Kishore, Sri Krishna arts and Science College, India
    D. Solomon Paul Raj, Sri Krishna Arts and Science College, India
    K. R. Senthilkumar, Sri Krishna Arts and Science College, India

This chapter examines integrating artificial intelligence (AI) technologies to enhance library services for users with disabilities, aiming to contribute to the accessibility and inclusivity of library resources. The study adopts a mixed-methods approach, combining quantitative user experience surveys with qualitative interviews to assess the impact of AI-driven tools—such as voice recognition, text-to-speech, and AI-powered search and recommendation systems—on the accessibility of library services for individuals with visual, auditory, and mobility impairments.

Chapter 16
Exploring the Intersection of AI and Financial Literacy: Current Insights, Hurdles, and Prospects . 226
    S. Dheepiga, Sri Krishna Arts and Science College, India
    N. Sivakumar, Sri Krishna Arts and Science College, India

Within the evolving landscape of artificial intelligence (AI), the significance of financial literacy remains paramount for individual and societal prosperity, impacting not only financial decision-making but also economic resilience and equitable access to opportunities. This chapter conducts a thorough examination of the intersection between AI and financial literacy, amalgamating insights from scholarly works, empirical investigations, and applied endeavors. It delves into fundamental concepts, evaluative frameworks, influential factors, and resultant ramifications of AI-driven financial literacy. Furthermore, it scrutinizes AI-enabled interventions, hurdles encountered, and prospects on the horizon within this domain. By consolidating existing insights and pinpointing areas necessitating further exploration, this review aspires to furnish policymakers, educators, and practitioners with actionable insights to propel financial literacy initiatives imbued with AI advancements, fostering inclusive financial well-being.

Chapter 17
Implementing AI-Based Recommendation Systems for Personalized Financial Services in
Libraries 235
    N. P. Kowsick, Sri Krishna Arts and Science College, India
    K. Ramasamy, Sri Krishna Arts and Science College, India

Artificial Intelligence (AI) has revolutionized various sectors, including finance and libraries. Libraries are increasingly adopting AI-based recommendation systems to provide personalized financial services to patrons. This chapter explores the implementation of AI-driven recommendation systems within library settings to offer tailored financial guidance. Leveraging advanced machine learning algorithms, these systems analyze users' financial preferences and behaviors to offer customized recommendations for financial resources and educational materials. The adoption of AI-based recommendation systems aims to enhance access to relevant financial information and empower individuals to make informed financial decisions. By leveraging AI technology, libraries can cater to the diverse needs of their patrons, fostering financial literacy and inclusion.

Chapter 18
AI-Driven Language Enhancement Strategies for Libraries: Empowering Information Access and User Experience in an English Language Context.. 244
    R. Visnudharshana, Sri Krishna Arts and Science College, India
    Henry S. Kishore, Sri Krishna Arts and Science College, India

In the rapidly evolving landscape of artificial intelligence (AI), the integration of advanced technologies becomes imperative for the enhancement of libraries, especially in the context of the English language. This research explores innovative AI-driven language enhancement strategies designed to optimize information access and elevate user experience within library settings. The study focuses on leveraging AI tools and techniques to enhance various facets of the library environment. This includes the development of intelligent language processing systems that facilitate efficient cataloging, indexing, and retrieval of diverse materials. Moreover, the research investigates natural language processing (NLP) applications tailored to English language nuances, aiming to improve the precision and relevance of search results. The user-centric approach emphasizes the implementation of AI-powered recommendation systems, personalized content suggestions, and adaptive interfaces, creating a tailored experience for English-speaking library patrons.

Chapter 19
A Study on Advanced Applications of Mathematics and AI in Library Science 254
    S. Durga Devi, Sri Krishna Arts and Science College, India
    R. Mohanapriya, Sri Krishna Adithya College of Arts and Science, India
    N. Sarumathy, Sri Krishna Arts and Science College, India

In the rapidly evolving field of information management, libraries are actively embracing the transformative potential of mathematics and artificial intelligence (AI). This chapter explores how established mathematical frameworks, such as the vector space model, together with cutting-edge natural language processing (NLP) techniques, are fundamentally altering how libraries organize information, facilitate retrieval, and ultimately, enhance user experience. The research suggests a symbiotic relationship between these seemingly distinct disciplines. By combining the strengths of mathematical models and probabilistic AI algorithms, this study aims to illuminate paths toward a more efficient and user-centric library ecosystem. This convergence has the potential to reshape resource management, information retrieval, and ultimately, transform the information landscape for library patrons, empowering them to navigate the vast ocean of knowledge with greater ease and effectiveness.

Chapter 20
AI-Driven Libraries: Pioneering Innovation in Digital Knowledge Access 272
    K. C. Anandraj, Madurai Kamaraj University, India
    S. Aravind, G.T.N. Arts College (Autonomous), India

In today's digital age, libraries are undergoing a profound transformation fueled by advancements in artificial intelligence (AI) technology. AI-driven libraries are pioneering innovative solutions to address the evolving needs of users, revolutionizing the way digital knowledge is accessed and utilized. This chapter explores the transformative potential of AI-driven libraries and their role in pioneering innovation in digital knowledge access. Through a comprehensive review of literature, case studies, and real-world implementations, this chapter examines various AI applications in libraries, including advanced search and discovery tools, virtual assistants, content recommendation systems, data analytics, and digital preservation. By highlighting best practices, challenges, and emerging trends, this chapter aims to provide insights into the transformative impact of AI-driven libraries on information management and access.

Chapter 21
AI Insights Deciphering India's Ascendancy Through the Digital Library: Navigating the Digital
Realm India's Odyssey Towards Information Equity and Technological Eminence 285
    B. Velmurugan, NPR College of Engineering and Technology, India
    S. Dharmalingam, Chettinad College of Engineering and Technology, India
    K. Binith Muthukrishnan, NPR College of Engineering and Technology, India
    K. R. Senthilkumar, Sri Krishna Arts and Science College, India

India's trajectory toward digital eminence is intricately woven into the fabric of its burgeoning digital library ecosystem. Through the lens of artificial intelligence (AI) insights, this chapter delineates the pivotal role of digital libraries in India's ascent within the global digital milieu. At the heart of this exploration lies the profound impact of digital libraries as reservoirs of knowledge, catalyzing innovation, and fostering inclusive growth. By employing a multifaceted analysis, the authors uncover the transformative potential inherent in these repositories, elucidating their capacity to democratize access to information, propel research and education, and underpin socioeconomic advancement.

Compilation of References 294

About the Contributors 318

Index 324

Preface

In the dynamic landscape of modern libraries, where tradition meets innovation, we find ourselves at the precipice of an exciting revolution. As editors of this edited reference book, *Improving Library Systems with AI: Applications, Approaches, and Bibliometric Insights*, we are thrilled to present a comprehensive exploration of the integration of artificial intelligence (AI) in the reconstruction and revitalization of libraries.

In an era marked by rapid technological advancements, libraries stand as bastions of knowledge, continually evolving to meet the changing needs of society. The infusion of AI into library systems represents a paradigm shift, offering unprecedented opportunities to enhance access, efficiency, and user experiences.

Through this book, we aim to delve deeply into the multifaceted relationship between AI and libraries, offering insights, best practices, and ethical considerations for librarians, information professionals, technologists, policymakers, and enthusiasts alike. Our objective is to provide a roadmap for navigating the intersection of tradition and innovation, ensuring that AI integration aligns with core library values of accessibility, inclusivity, and intellectual freedom.

The journey begins with an exploration of the foundational concepts of AI and its historical adoption in libraries. From there, we venture into practical applications, from digitization strategies to content recommendation systems, metadata enhancement, automatic cataloging, search optimization, and user-centric approaches. We address ethical considerations with utmost importance, emphasizing the need for responsible AI implementation and safeguarding user privacy.

Drawing from real-world case studies and best practices, we showcase the transformative power of AI in library management, predictive analytics, and collection development. We confront challenges head-on, offering strategies for overcoming technological hurdles and fostering interdisciplinary collaboration.

As we peer into the future, we envision libraries as dynamic hubs of knowledge dissemination and community engagement, augmented by AI technologies. To realize this vision, we emphasize the importance of continuous learning and skill development, equipping library professionals with the tools and knowledge needed to thrive in the AI era.

We extend our gratitude to the contributors who have shared their expertise and experiences, enriching this volume with diverse perspectives and insights. It is our hope that this book serves as a valuable resource for all those passionate about the future of libraries and the transformative potential of AI.

Let us embark on this journey together, as we navigate the ever-evolving landscape of libraries with curiosity, creativity, and a commitment to advancing the noble mission of knowledge preservation and dissemination.

Chapter 1: Unravelling AI Ethics: A Bibliometric Journey Through Scholarly Publications

Authored by Subaveerapandiyan A, S.Radhakrishnan, Madhuri Kumari, and Arnold Chama, this chapter presents a meticulous bibliometric analysis of scholarly publications in AI ethics from 2014 to 2023. Through data extracted from the Scopus database, the study delineates growth trends, author collaborations, thematic evolution, and international contributions within the realm of AI ethics research. Readers can expect insights into the exponential surge in AI ethics publications, critical thematic shifts, prolific author collaborations, and the global landscape of AI ethics scholarship.

Chapter 2: Revolutionizing Medical Libraries: The Vital Role of AI in Enhancing Discovery, Access, and Library Services for Healthcare Professional

Authored by Amreen Taj, Mohammed Ahmed, K. S. Ali, and Senthilkumar KR, this chapter focuses on the central role of AI in revolutionizing medical libraries, with a specific lens on the Central Library of Yenepoya (deemed to be University). By employing qualitative case study methods, the authors investigate discovery, access strategies, and library services, offering insights into challenges, solutions, and the need for integrating AI tools into library services to enhance efficiency and user experience.

Chapter 3: Impact of AI in Library Operations

Authored by Bhuvaneswari G and Vijaya Rajakumar P T, this chapter explores the disruptive influence of AI on library operations. The authors examine the positive and negative impacts of AI, with a focus on its potential to improve library services, user experience, and operational efficiency. Through insights from Robinson, the chapter highlights AI's role in establishing libraries as leaders in the scholarly community, despite encountering obstacles in implementation.

Chapter 4: Harnessing the Power of AI for Information Management and User Engagement in Next-Generation Libraries

Authored by Jaya Vijesh, this chapter investigates the integration of AI to enhance information management and user engagement in next-generation libraries. Readers can expect insights into diverse AI applications, methodological approaches, and their impact on library systems, along with a discussion on user engagement strategies leveraging AI to tailor services based on individual preferences and behaviors.

Chapter 5: Exploring the Transformative Impact of Artificial Intelligence on Research Library Management

Authored by Sathiya M and Vidya M, this chapter offers an in-depth exploration of AI's profound impact on library functionalities, services, and user interfaces within research libraries. Readers can expect scrutiny of AI technologies such as machine learning, natural language processing, and data analytics, along with discussions on challenges and prospects associated with AI integration.

Preface

Chapter 6: Exploring the Top ChatGPT Libraries for Powerful Conversational AI

Authored by Delma Thaliyan, Joe Joseph, and Helen Josephine V L, this chapter analyzes the need for top ChatGPT libraries and their usage today. Through in-depth interviews, the authors uncover nuanced insights into library preferences and usage patterns, offering valuable guidance for developers seeking to optimize their conversational AI projects.

Chapter 7: Ethical Considerations an AI Implementation in Library Era

Authored by N Rajkumar, Viji C, Mohanraj A, Senthilkumar KR, Jagajeevan R, and Judeson Antony Kovilpillai, this chapter explores the multifaceted moral dimensions related to AI implementation in libraries. Readers can expect discussions on key ethical issues such as bias, transparency, responsibility, privacy, and societal impact, along with approaches to mitigating bias and promoting fairness in AI algorithms.

Chapter 8: Enhanced Services of Next-Gen Libraries through Artificial Intelligence

Authored by J JOSELIN and Anuja Beatrice B, this chapter delves into the transformative role of AI in enhancing library services for next-generation knowledge hubs. Readers can expect insights into key AI applications and approaches, including improved information retrieval systems, personalized recommendation services, and streamlined metadata management.

Chapter 9: Emerging and Innovative AI Technologies for Resource Management

Authored by Balusamy Nachiappan, this chapter explores emerging AI technologies revolutionizing library services, including natural language processing (NLP) for advanced search capabilities and machine learning for recommendation systems. Readers can expect discussions on the potential impact of AI in optimizing resource management and enhancing client research experiences.

Chapter 10: Educational Program for AI Literacy

Authored by Mageshkumar Naarayanasamy Varadarajan, this chapter examines educational programs aimed at promoting AI literacy across age groups and settings. Readers can expect insights into the objectives, methodologies, challenges, and best practices associated with various educational initiatives, along with discussions on the importance of integrating ethical considerations into AI education.

Chapter 11: E-Resources Content Recommendations System Using AI

Authored by Balusamy Nachiappan, this chapter proposes a practical content recommendation system (ICRS) leveraging advanced AI techniques to enhance content discovery and user engagement. Readers can expect discussions on collaborative filtering, content-based filtering, and deep learning algorithms, along with insights into personalized recommendation generation.

Chapter 12: Assessing Students Satisfaction With Artificial Intelligence in Education: A Study of E-Applications in Selected Educational Institutes in Coimbatore

Authored by Aravind S and Kavitha R, this chapter presents a comprehensive overview of the impact of AI-driven communication technology on students' satisfaction within the educational context. Through a mixed-methods approach, the authors evaluate the effectiveness and reception of AI-driven E-Apps in selected educational institutes, shedding light on their viability and potential.

Chapter 13: Artificial Intelligence Journey in Enhancing Library Accessibility

Authored by Karthick N, Nithya P, and Rajkumar R, this chapter examines the integration of AI technologies to enhance library services for users with disabilities, aiming to contribute to accessibility and inclusivity. Readers can expect discussions on AI-driven tools such as voice recognition, text-to-speech, and recommendation systems, along with their impact on accessibility.

Chapter 14: Anticipating AI Impact on Library Services Future Opportunities and Evolutionary Prospects

Authored by Lalitha B, Ramalakshmi K, Hemalatha Gunasekaran, Muregesan P, Saminasri P, and N Rajkumar, this chapter explores the transformative potential of AI-driven libraries in reshaping information management and access. Readers can expect insights into AI applications such as advanced search tools, virtual assistants, and content recommendation systems, along with discussions on challenges and emerging trends.

Chapter 15: AI for Accessibility A Case Study of Enhancing Library Services for Users With Disabilities

Authored by Henry Kishore, Solomon Paul Raj D, and Senthilkumar KR, this chapter presents a case study on integrating AI technologies to enhance library services for users with disabilities, aiming to promote accessibility and inclusivity. Readers can expect discussions on AI-driven tools such as voice recognition, text-to-speech, and search and recommendation systems, along with insights into their impact on user experience.

Chapter 16: Exploring the Intersection of AI and Financial Literacy: Current Insights, Hurdles, and Prospects

Authored by Dheepiga S and Sivakumar N, this chapter examines the intersection between AI and financial literacy, highlighting insights, hurdles, and prospects within this domain. Readers can expect discussions on fundamental concepts, evaluative frameworks, AI-enabled interventions, and the importance of integrating ethical considerations into financial literacy initiatives.

Preface

Chapter 17: Implementing AI-Based Recommendation Systems for Personalized Financial Services in Libraries

Authored by Kowsick N P and Ramasamy K, this chapter examines the implementation of AI-driven recommendation systems within library settings to offer personalized financial guidance. Readers can expect discussions on machine learning algorithms, user behavior analysis, and the potential of AI to enhance access to relevant financial information.

Chapter 18: AI-Driven Language Enhancement Strategies for Libraries: Empowering Information Access and User Experience in an English Language Context

Authored by Visnudharshana R and Henry Kishore, this chapter explores AI-driven language enhancement strategies designed to optimize information access and elevate user experience within library settings. Readers can expect discussions on intelligent language processing systems, natural language processing applications, and personalized content suggestions tailored to English-speaking patrons.

Chapter 19: A Study on Advanced Applications of Mathematics and AI in Library Science

Authored by Durga Devi S, Mohanapriya R, and Sarumathy N, this chapter investigates the integration of mathematics and AI in modern library services, focusing on their transformative potential in reshaping resource management and information retrieval. Readers can expect discussions on mathematical frameworks, probabilistic AI algorithms, and their synergistic impact on library ecosystems.

Chapter 20: AI-Driven Libraries: Pioneering Innovation in Digital Knowledge Access

Authored by Anandraj K.C and Aravind S, this chapter explores the transformative potential of AI-driven libraries in revolutionizing digital knowledge access. Readers can expect discussions on AI applications such as advanced search tools, virtual assistants, and content recommendation systems, along with insights into real-world implementations and emerging trends.

Chapter 21: AI Insights Deciphering India's Ascendancy Through the Digital Library: Navigating the Digital Realm India's Odyssey Towards Information Equity and Technological Eminence

Authored by Velmurugan B, Dharmalingam S, Binith Muthukrishnan K, Senthilkumar KR, and Jagajeevan R, this chapter delineates the pivotal role of digital libraries in India's ascent within the global digital milieu. Readers can expect discussions on the transformative potential of digital libraries, their impact on research, education, and socioeconomic development, and the overarching goal of democratizing access to information.

As editors of *Improving Library Systems with AI: Applications, Approaches, and Bibliometric Insights*, we are honored to present this comprehensive exploration of the integration of artificial intelligence (AI) in the evolution of libraries. In a world where technology rapidly reshapes our interactions with information, libraries remain essential pillars of knowledge dissemination, adaptation, and preservation. The infusion of AI into library systems represents not only a paradigm shift but also an exciting opportunity to enhance access, efficiency, and user experiences.

Throughout this edited reference book, we have embarked on a journey to delve deeply into the symbiotic relationship between AI and libraries. From foundational concepts to practical applications and ethical considerations, each chapter offers valuable insights for librarians, information professionals, technologists, policymakers, and enthusiasts alike. We have explored diverse topics, ranging from AI-driven recommendation systems and accessibility enhancements to the transformative impact of AI on research library management.

As we peer into the future, we envision libraries as dynamic hubs of knowledge augmented by AI technologies, where traditional values of accessibility, inclusivity, and intellectual freedom are preserved and enhanced. However, this vision can only be realized through continuous learning, collaboration, and a commitment to responsible AI implementation. We emphasize the importance of equipping library professionals with the necessary skills and knowledge to navigate the ever-evolving landscape of libraries in the AI era.

We extend our heartfelt gratitude to all the contributors who have enriched this volume with their expertise, experiences, and perspectives. It is our sincere hope that this book serves as a valuable resource, guiding readers towards a deeper understanding of the transformative potential of AI in libraries and inspiring them to embrace innovation while upholding core library values.

Let us embark on this journey together, as we navigate the intersection of tradition and innovation with curiosity, creativity, and a shared dedication to advancing the noble mission of knowledge preservation and dissemination in the digital age.

K.R. Senthilkumar
Sri Krishna Arts and Science College, India

R. Jagajeevan
Sri Krishna Arts and Science College, India

Chapter 1
Unravelling AI Ethics:
A Bibliometric Journey Through Scholarly Publications

A. Subaveerapandiyan
https://orcid.org/0000-0002-2149-9897
Bennett University, India

S. Radhakrishnan
https://orcid.org/0009-0005-4468-8980
Debre Berhan University, Ethiopia

Madhuri Kumari
https://orcid.org/0000-0002-3205-0323
Central University of Gujarat, India

Arnold Chama
https://orcid.org/0000-0003-2845-4242
National Archives of Zambia, Zambia

ABSTRACT

The rapid expansion of artificial intelligence (AI) has engendered significant societal and ethical concerns, necessitating a comprehensive examination of scholarly work in AI ethics. This study aims to present a bibliometric analysis delineating the growth trends, author collaborations, thematic evolution, and international contributions within the realm of AI ethics research from 2014 to 2023. Employing established bibliometric methodologies, this research utilizes data from the Scopus database, encompassing 1490 articles. The study investigates growth patterns, authorship trends, thematic, and global contributions in AI ethics scholarship. The result reveals an exponential surge in annual AI ethics publications, with critical thematic shifts and prolific author collaborations. Author productivity, citation metrics, institutional affiliations, and country-wise contributions elucidate the global landscape of AI ethics research.

DOI: 10.4018/979-8-3693-5593-0.ch001

1. INTRODUCTION

The rapid advancement of Artificial Intelligence (AI) in the 21st century has led to transformative changes across various industries, driving innovation and technological progress. This progress also brings ethical challenges that must be addressed. As AI becomes increasingly integrated into our lives, concerns about privacy, bias, accountability, and its impact on society are growing.

This article presents a comprehensive bibliometric analysis of scholarly publications on AI ethics to shed light on the research landscape and provide valuable insights. By examining growth trends, regional contributions, authorship patterns, and critical themes in AI ethics research, this study aims to enhance our understanding of this crucial field. The intersection of AI and ethics has become a focal point for researchers, policymakers, and practitioners worldwide, making it essential to explore influential works, key contributors, and emerging trends in AI ethics.

2. LITERATURE REVIEW

2.1 Current Landscape of AI Ethics Research

The current landscape of AI ethics research reflects a dynamic exploration of AI technology's applications across various domains, including education, business, medicine, and daily life (Zhang & Aslan, 2020). AI Ethics research is paramount for organizations to fulfill social responsibility, drive economic growth, and demonstrate ethical commitments to stakeholders, serving as strategic planning tools and mechanisms for legal compliance (Dennis & Aizenberg, 2022).

Bozkurt et al. (2021) delineate three primary research clusters within AI studies in education: AI-related issues, pedagogical concerns, and technological exploration. These encompass adaptive and personalized learning facilitated by AI algorithms, human-AI interaction in educational contexts, and AI integration in higher education. Notably, the oversight of ethics investigations within AI studies underscores the critical need for comprehensive ethical inquiry in the field (Bozkurt et al., 2021).

Micheli et al. (2022) underscore the importance of contextual considerations—social, legal, cultural, and institutional—in AI and data governance discussions, emphasizing potential conflicts within these contexts. Meanwhile, Zohny et al. (2023) raise ethical concerns regarding AI's capacity to generate plagiarism-evading content, prompting reflections on authorship, academic integrity, and the role of generative AI in ethical analysis.

2.2 Key Ethical Concerns in AI Development

Ethical concerns pervade the development and deployment of artificial intelligence (AI) technologies, touching upon various aspects of human rights, societal values, and the broader ethical implications of AI systems. Scholars have extensively examined these concerns across different domains, shedding light on potential risks, challenges, and opportunities inherent in AI development.

2.2.1 Human Rights and Privacy

One of the primary ethical concerns in AI development revolves around the potential infringement of fundamental human rights. Dennis and Aizenberg (2022) highlight the risks posed by AI technologies in human resources, including issues related to employment discrimination, privacy violations, and the erosion of personal autonomy. AI systems deployed in recruitment, hiring, and performance evaluation processes may perpetuate biases, reinforce systemic inequalities, and undermine individuals' right to fair treatment and equal opportunity.

Moreover, the proliferation of AI-driven surveillance technologies raises profound privacy concerns, as AI-enabled systems collect, analyze, and process vast amounts of personal data without adequate safeguards for privacy and data protection. The indiscriminate use of facial recognition, biometric identification, and predictive analytics algorithms exacerbates privacy risks and threatens individuals' right to privacy and autonomy in public and private spaces (Habbal et al., 2024; Kavoliūnaitė-Ragauskienė, 2024; Williamson & Prybutok, 2024).

2.2.2 Accountability and Transparency

Another critical ethical concern in AI development pertains to accountability and transparency in algorithmic decision-making processes. As AI systems become increasingly autonomous and opaque, questions arise regarding the accountability of AI developers, operators, and users for the decisions and actions of AI systems. The lack of transparency in AI algorithms and decision-making mechanisms complicates efforts to understand, interpret, and challenge algorithmic outcomes, particularly in high-stakes domains such as criminal justice, healthcare, and financial services (Felzmann et al., 2020; Kumar & Suthar, 2024; Rodgers et al., 2023).

Furthermore, the black-box nature of many AI algorithms hinders accountability mechanisms and undermines public trust in AI technologies. Without clear mechanisms for accountability, individuals affected by AI-driven decisions may face challenges in seeking recourse, remediation, or redress for algorithmic biases, errors, or discriminatory outcomes (Misra et al., 2023; Pokrovskaya, 2024).

2.2.3 Socioeconomic Impacts and Equity

AI development also raises profound concerns about its broader socioeconomic impacts and implications for equity and justice in society. Heilinger (2022) underscores the importance of integrating AI justice perspectives into ethical frameworks to address systemic inequalities, power asymmetries, and distributional consequences of AI technologies. The deployment of AI systems in labor markets, education, healthcare, and public services may exacerbate existing disparities, marginalize vulnerable populations, and widen the digital divide.

Moreover, the automation of jobs, the gig economy, and the rise of AI-driven decision-making processes pose challenges to labor rights, worker protections, and economic justice. Without adequate safeguards and policies to mitigate these risks, AI technologies have the potential to exacerbate socioeconomic inequalities, deepen social divisions, and erode trust in institutions and governance systems (Aloisi & De Stefano, 2023; George et al., 2023; Nissim & Simon, 2021).

Ethical concerns in AI development encompass a wide range of issues, including human rights, privacy, accountability, transparency, socioeconomic impacts, and equity. Addressing these concerns requires a multidisciplinary approach, informed by ethical principles, legal frameworks, and stakeholder engagement to ensure that AI technologies are developed, deployed, and governed in a manner that upholds human dignity, promotes social justice, and advances the collective well-being of society (Aizenberg & van den Hoven, 2020; Banerji & Feroz, 2024; Fukuda-Parr & Gibbons, 2021; Mizrahi, 2024; Rodrigues, 2020).

2.3 Ethical Frameworks and Guidelines for AI Technologies

Mazurek (2023) advocates for the establishment of moral standards and legal frameworks to govern the creation and deployment of generative AI, focusing on accountability, fairness, and transparency. Pflanzer et al. (2023) delve into the ethical, political, and governance implications of AI integration, addressing concerns such as political authority, policy-making processes, and the legal ramifications of AI systems in various sectors.

Mao and Shi-Kupfer (2023) shed light on international influences on Chinese AI governance discourse, revealing a cautious approach towards international initiatives. Despite governmental reservations, public discourse in China highlights concerns over algorithmic bias and privacy, indicating potential for international collaboration and ongoing societal engagement in AI governance discussions.

3. METHODOLOGY

This study endeavors to conduct a comprehensive bibliometric analysis of scholarly publications pertaining to AI ethics from 2014 to 2023. Its primary aim is to discern the developmental trajectory, thematic evolution, collaborative dynamics among authors, and the global impact of such publications. Employing established bibliometric methodologies, this research seeks to provide insights into the trends and thematic nuances prevalent in the domain of AI ethics.

3.1 Objectives of the Study

This research is structured around several key objectives:

- Analysis of Growth and Thematic Trends: To elucidate the growth patterns and thematic evolution within AI ethics scholarly publications.
- Author Collaboration and Productivity: To assess the extent of author collaboration, productivity, citation impacts, and individual contributions.
- Publication Typology and Academic Impact: To scrutinize the types of publications, citation metrics, and the academic impact of sources within the field.
- Keyword Analysis and Co-occurrence Networks: To unravel the prevalent topics and themes through keyword analysis and co-occurrence networks.
- International Collaboration and Country Impact: To evaluate international collaborations, institutional affiliations, and the contribution of various nations in AI ethics research.

3.2 Research Design

This study adopts a quantitative research design focused on analyzing data sourced from the Scopus database, specifically concentrating on critical themes in AI ethics research articles published between 2014 and 2023.

3.3 Data Collection

For this study, we collected data from the Scopus database using the search query: TITLE-ABS-KEY ("ai ethics" OR "artificial intelligence ethic" OR "responsible ai" OR "ethics of ai" OR "generative ai ethics") AND PUBYEAR > 2013 AND PUBYEAR < 2024 AND (LIMIT-TO (DOCTYPE, "ar") OR LIMIT-TO (DOCTYPE, "cp") OR LIMIT-TO (DOCTYPE, "ch") OR LIMIT-TO (DOCTYPE, "re") OR LIMIT-TO (DOCTYPE, "bk")) AND (EXCLUDE (LANGUAGE, "Spanish") OR EXCLUDE (LANGUAGE, "Chinese") OR EXCLUDE (LANGUAGE, "German") OR EXCLUDE (LANGUAGE, "French") OR EXCLUDE (LANGUAGE, "Russian") OR EXCLUDE (LANGUAGE, "Polish") OR EXCLUDE (LANGUAGE, "Romanian") OR EXCLUDE (LANGUAGE, "Moldovan") OR EXCLUDE (LANGUAGE, "Moldavian") OR EXCLUDE (LANGUAGE, "Korean") OR EXCLUDE (LANGUAGE, "Japanese") OR EXCLUDE (LANGUAGE, "Italian") OR EXCLUDE (LANGUAGE, "Portuguese"))"—this search aimed to identify articles on AI ethics published in 2014-2023. The initial search procedure led to the retrieval of a total of 1490 articles, forming the primary dataset for this study.

3.4 Data Analysis Tools

The study utilises two software tools for data analysis: Biblioshiny and VOS Viewer.

3.4.1 a. Biblioshiny Analysis

Biblioshiny facilitated an in-depth exploration of publication patterns among authors, shedding light on individual author publication outputs and potential collaborative networks.

3.4.2 b. VOS Viewer Analysis

VOS Viewer was instrumental in conducting an extensive analysis of keywords used in the selected articles, offering insights into dominant themes and prevailing topics within AI ethics research.

3.5 Data Analysis

The data collected from the Scopus database and analysed using the software tools were used to create tables and figures that present the key metrics, growth trends, authorship patterns, regional distribution, and keyword co-occurrence in the AI ethics research.

The analysis involves:

Publication Growth: Utilizing Figure 1, tracking the exponential growth of annual AI ethics publications.

Citation Trends: Referencing Table 2 to understand the average citations per year from 2014 to 2023.

Source and Publisher Impact: Referencing Tables 3, 5, 6, and 8 to determine the impact and relevance of key sources, authors, and publishers.

Author Contribution and Collaboration: Utilizing Tables 4, 9, 10, 11, and 12 to assess author productivity, Lotka's Law distribution, impact metrics, affiliations, and corresponding authorship by country.

Global Citations and Highly Cited Publications: Analyzing Tables 13 and 14 to identify the most cited countries and publications, along with their average article citations.

3.6 Limitations

This study's limitations lie in the constraints of the Scopus database, potentially excluding articles from other repositories. Additionally, language barriers might have influenced the inclusivity of non-English articles.

3.7 Implications

The findings provide insights into AI ethics research's growth, authorship patterns, and thematic focus. These insights can benefit researchers, policymakers, and practitioners interested in AI ethics, guiding future research directions and fostering international collaborations.

4. RESULTS

Table 1 presents a snapshot of the dataset from 2014 to 2023, encompassing 1490 articles sourced from 667 publications, showcasing a robust annual growth rate of 104.55%. Each document garners an average of 11.28 citations, referencing a total of 68,213 sources. The dataset, with an average document age of 2.2 years, encompasses 5239 Keywords Plus identifiers and 3441 author-provided keywords.

Among 3712 authors, 374 authored articles independently, while collaborative efforts featured an average of 3.16 co-authors per document, with 22.28% involving international partnerships. Document types include 634 articles, 24 books, 136 book chapters, 609 conference papers, and 87 reviews (refer to Table 1).

This comprehensive dataset illustrates the dynamic growth, collaborative patterns, and thematic richness characterizing AI ethics research. The diversity in document types and extensive authorship collaborations underscore the multidimensional exploration within the AI ethics domain throughout the specified timeframe.

The data presented in Figure 1 indicates a substantial increase in publications focusing on AI ethics over the analyzed period. The years 2014 to 2018 demonstrate a gradual but moderate rise in articles, with a notable spike from 33 articles in 2018 to 627 articles in 2023. This considerable escalation highlights a significant surge in scholarly attention and research devoted to ethical concerns within artificial intelligence. Graphically, a line chart or bar graph with years on the x-axis and the number of articles on the y-axis would vividly illustrate the exponential growth trend observed in AI ethics publications from 2014 to 2023.

The table 2 presents the average citations per year for articles published annually from 2014 to 2023. Initially, from 2014 to 2018, there was a notable rise in mean citations per year, peaking at 6.5 in 2018. However, from 2019 onwards, despite an increase in the number of publications, there was a consistent

Table 1. Summary of Screened Articles and Key Data Metrics in the Timespan 2014-2023

Description	Results
MAIN INFORMATION ABOUT DATA	
Timespan	2014-2023
Sources (Journals, Books, etc)	667
Documents	1490
Annual Growth Rate %	104.55
Document Average Age	2.2
Average citations per doc	11.28
References	68213
DOCUMENT CONTENTS	
Keywords Plus (ID)	5239
Author's Keywords (DE)	3441
AUTHORS	
Authors	3712
Authors of single-authored docs	374
AUTHORS COLLABORATION	
Single-authored docs	419
Co-Authors per Doc	3.16
International co-authorships %	22.28
DOCUMENT TYPES	
Article	634
Book	24
Book chapter	136
Conference paper	609
Review	87

Source: Scopus Database and Table Generated by Biblioshiny Software

decline in mean citations per year, dropping to 0.97 in 2023. This downward trend suggests a potential saturation or dilution effect, indicating that newer articles are receiving fewer citations on average compared to earlier years. Factors like increased publication volume or a shift in research focus might contribute to this decline in average citation impact over recent years. This declining trend in mean citations per year highlights the changing dynamics in the reception and impact of AI ethics articles within the scholarly landscape.

Table 3 and figure 2 presents leading sources in AI ethics and their publishers. Springer's "AI and Society" tops the list with 67 articles, emphasizing a significant focus on AI ethics. CEUR Workshop Proceedings follow closely with 64 articles, highlighting the role of workshop publications in this discourse. "Lecture Notes in Computer Science" by Springer, encompassing AI-related subseries, contributes 63 articles, showcasing the integration of ethics within broader computer science discussions. ACM's presence is notable with the "International Conference Proceeding Series" and "Conference on Human Factors in Computing Systems - proceedings," hosting 60 and 29 articles, respectively. These findings

Figure 1. Growth of annual publications on artificial intelligence in ethics articles: 2014-2023
Source: Scopus Database and Figure Generated by Google Spreadsheet

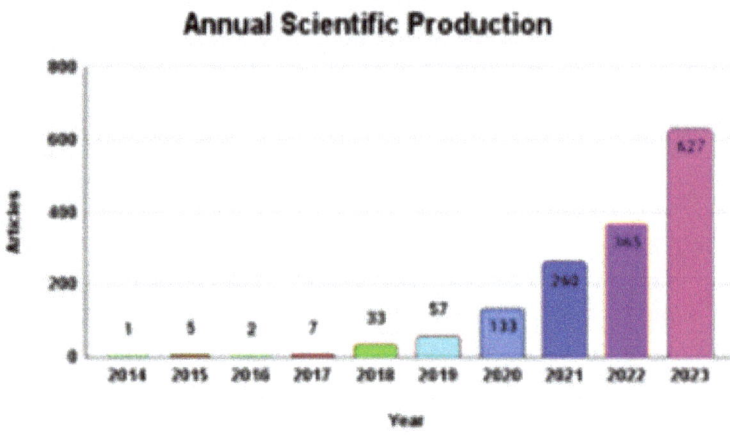

Table 2. Publication citations trends: Average citations per year (2014-2023)

Average Citations per Year				
Year	MeanTCperArt	N	MeanTCperYear	CitableYears
2014	18	1	1.64	11
2015	20.2	5	2.02	10
2016	1.5	2	0.17	9
2017	20.29	7	2.54	8
2018	45.52	33	6.5	7
2019	20.77	57	3.46	6
2020	53.3	133	10.66	5
2021	13.47	260	3.37	4
2022	5.62	365	1.87	3
2023	1.94	627	0.97	2

MeanTCperArt- Mean Total Citations per Article; MeanTCperYear-Mean Total Citations per Year

illustrate Springer and ACM as major platforms nurturing discussions and research dissemination in AI ethics, across journals, conferences, and workshops, indicating a vibrant landscape for ethical considerations within artificial intelligence research.

The table 4 highlights prolific authors in AI ethics based on their annual paper production and citations per year. Notable contributors include Lu Q and Zhu L in 2023, each producing 7 papers with 32 citations (TCpY: 16). In 2021, Floridi L authored 6 papers with 83 citations (TCpY: 20.75), emphasizing substantial impact. Zhang Y in 2021 contributed 6 papers, amassing 139 citations (TCpY: 34.75), demonstrating a high influence per paper. Authors like Dignum V in 2021 produced 4 papers but acquired 76 citations (TCpY: 19), highlighting impactful research. Conversely, Kemell K-K in 2023 published 4 papers with only 4 citations (TCpY: 2), indicating a lower citation impact despite multiple publications.

Table 3. Top relevant sources and publishers on AI ethics

Most Relevant Sources		
Sources	Articles	Publisher
AI and Society	67	Springer
CEUR Workshop Proceedings	64	Aachen: R. Piskac c/o Redaktion Sun SITE, Informatik V, RWTH Aachen
Lecture Notes in Computer Science (including subseries Lecture Notes in Artificial Intelligence and Lecture Notes in Bioinformatics)	63	Springer
ACM International Conference Proceeding Series	60	ACM
Conference on Human Factors in Computing Systems - proceedings	29	ACM
Philosophy & Technology	25	Springer
Ethics and Information Technology	20	Springer
Information Systems Frontiers	17	Springer
Communications in Computer and Information Science	15	Springer
Science and Engineering Ethics	15	Springer

Figure 2. Top relevant sources and publishers on AI ethics

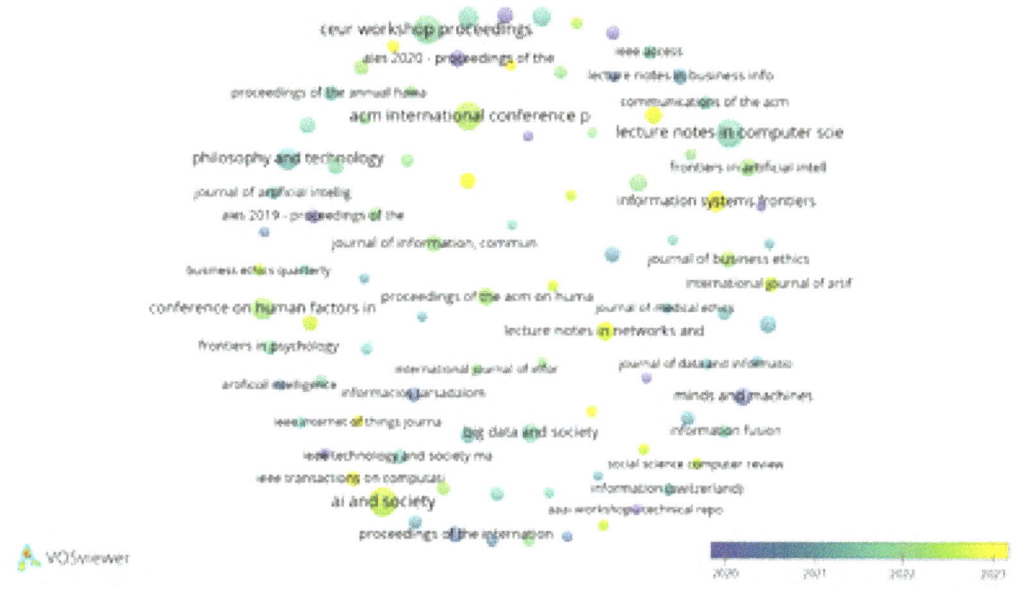

These findings depict authors' varying degrees of influence based on their annual paper output and citation impact within the AI ethics field across different years.

The table 5 highlights prolific authors in AI ethics based on their annual paper production and citations per year. Notable contributors include Lu Q and Zhu L in 2023, each producing 7 papers with 32 citations (TCpY: 16). In 2021, Floridi L authored 6 papers with 83 citations (TCpY: 20.75), emphasizing substantial impact. Zhang Y in 2021 contributed 6 papers, amassing 139 citations (TCpY: 34.75), dem-

Table 4. Authors' annual paper production and citations: Top contributors and total citations per year

More Number of Papers Production per Year by Authors				
Author	year	freq	TC	TCpY
Lu Q	2023	7	32	16
Zhu L	2023	7	32	16
Floridi L	2021	6	83	20.75
Wang Y	2023	6	25	12.5
Zhang Y	2021	6	139	34.75
Kemell K-K	2021	5	37	9.25
Vakkuri V	2021	5	37	9.25
Abrahamsson P	2021	4	36	9
Dignum V	2021	4	76	19
Kemell K-K	2023	4	4	2

Table 5. Authors' citations contribution per year: Top citations and total citations per year

More Number of Citations Per Year by Authors				
Author	year	freq	TC	TCpY
Dignum V	2018	1	769	109.857
Floridi L	2018	1	769	109.857
Floridi L	2020	2	409	81.8
Zhang Y	2021	6	139	34.75
Li Y	2021	3	113	28.25
Floridi L	2021	6	83	20.75
Dignum V	2021	4	76	19
Abrahamsson P	2020	3	75	15
Kemell K-K	2020	3	75	15
Vakkuri V	2020	3	75	15

onstrating a high influence per paper. Authors like Dignum V in 2021 produced 4 papers but acquired 76 citations (TCpY: 19), highlighting impactful research. Conversely, Kemell K-K in 2023 published 4 papers with only 4 citations (TCpY: 2), indicating a lower citation impact despite multiple publications. These findings depict authors' varying degrees of influence based on their annual paper output and citation impact within the AI ethics field across different years.

Table 6 outlines the local impact metrics of academic sources within AI ethics. AI and Society leads with a notable h-index of 12, g-index of 17, and m-index of 2.4, gathering 417 citations from 67 papers since its inception in 2020. Information Systems Frontiers follows with an h-index of 10, g-index of 15, and m-index of 3.333, amassing 257 citations from 17 papers starting in 2022. Philosophy & Technology maintains a strong presence, displaying an h-index of 10, g-index of 18, and m-index of 0.909, acquiring 346 citations from 25 papers since 2014. ACM International Conference Proceeding Series

Table 6. Local impact metrics of various academic sources

Sources Local Impact						
Element	h_index	g_index	m_index	TC	NP	PY_start
AI and Society	12	17	2.4	417	67	2020
Information Systems Frontiers	10	15	3.333	257	17	2022
Philosophy & Technology	10	18	0.909	346	25	2014
ACM International Conference Proceeding Series	9	17	1.5	335	60	2019
Conference on Human Factors in Computing Systems - Proceedings	9	21	1.8	459	29	2020
Minds and Machines	8	12	1	1516	12	2017
AIES '21: Proceedings of the 2021 AAAI/ACM Conference on AI, Ethics, and Society	7	11	1.75	181	11	2021
Big Data and Society	7	13	1.4	276	13	2020
IEEE Security and Privacy	7	9	0.875	197	9	2017
Lecture Notes in Computer Science (including subseries Lecture Notes in Artificial Intelligence and Lecture Notes in Bioinformatics)	7	8	1	136	63	2018

and Conference on Human Factors in Computing Systems - Proceedings exhibit influential metrics with varying indices and substantial citation counts. Other sources like Minds and Machines, AIES '21, Big Data and Society, IEEE Security and Privacy, and Lecture Notes in Computer Science showcase their impact within AI ethics based on diverse local impact metrics, emphasizing their influence, publication frequency, and starting publication years. These metrics serve as indicators of the relative importance and contribution of each source to the AI ethics field, aiding researchers in assessing scholarly impact and relevance.

Table 7 presents the average citations per year for AI ethics publications from 2014 to 2023. The analysis reveals fluctuations in the impact of these publications over time. From 2014 to 2016, the aver-

Table 7. Publication citations trends: Average citations per year (2014-2023)

Average Citations per Year				
Year	MeanTCperArt	N	MeanTCperYear	CitableYears
2014	18	1	1.64	11
2015	20.2	5	2.02	10
2016	1.5	2	0.17	9
2017	20.29	7	2.54	8
2018	45.52	33	6.5	7
2019	20.77	57	3.46	6
2020	53.3	133	10.66	5
2021	13.47	260	3.37	4
2022	5.62	365	1.87	3
2023	1.94	627	0.97	2

MeanTCperArt- Mean Total Citations per Article; MeanTCperYear-Mean Total Citations per Year

age citations remained relatively low, ranging between 0.17 and 2.02, indicating modest impact. Subsequently, a notable increase occurred in 2017-2018, with average citations skyrocketing to 6.5, signifying a significant rise in impact. Another surge happened in 2019-2020, peaking at 10.66 citations per year in 2020, showcasing a pinnacle in the impact of AI ethics publications. However, a significant decline followed from 2021 to 2023, with average citations dropping to 0.97 in 2023, indicating diminishing impact for newer publications.

These fluctuations suggest dynamic shifts in the reception and influence of AI ethics publications, with periods of substantial impact followed by declining trends. The decreasing average citations per year for more recent publications may suggest changing interests, saturation of the field, or alterations in citation practices. This trend analysis highlights the evolving landscape of AI ethics research, emphasizing periods of both heightened and dwindling impact across the decade.

Table 8 ranks core sources in AI ethics using Bradford's Law, highlighting their frequency and zones. AI and Society leads as the most frequent source, occupying Zone 1 with 67 occurrences. Following closely, CEUR Workshop Proceedings and Lecture Notes in Computer Science rank second and third with frequencies of 64 and 63, respectively, also residing in Zone 1. ACM International Conference Proceeding Series and the Conference on Human Factors in Computing Systems - Proceedings hold the fourth and fifth positions, with frequencies of 60 and 29, all falling within Zone 1. Other sources like Philosophy & Technology, Ethics and Information Technology, Information Systems Frontiers, Communications in Computer and Information Science, and Science and Engineering Ethics also populate Zone 1. These rankings based on Bradford's Law emphasize the dominance and prevalence of these core sources within AI ethics literature. The consistent presence of these sources in Zone 1 signifies their frequent appearance, making them pivotal pillars in the AI ethics scholarly landscape. This analysis aids in identifying the most frequently referenced sources, providing insights into the foundational literature and key contributors within the field of AI ethics.

Table 9 reflects author productivity distribution according to Lotka's Law in academic documents. The data reveals that 84% of authors have contributed only one document, representing the majority. As the number of documents per author increases, the proportion of authors diminishes significantly; 10.7%

Table 8. Core sources ranking by Bradford's law

Core Sources by Bradford's Law				
Source	Rank	Freq	cumFreq	Zone
AI and Society	1	67	67	Zone 1
CEUR Workshop Proceedings	2	64	131	Zone 1
Lecture Notes in Computer Science (including subseries Lecture Notes in Artificial Intelligence and Lecture Notes in Bioinformatics)	3	63	194	Zone 1
ACM International Conference Proceeding Series	4	60	254	Zone 1
Conference on Human Factors in Computing Systems - Proceedings	5	29	283	Zone 1
Philosophy & Technology	6	25	308	Zone 1
Ethics and Information Technology	7	20	328	Zone 1
Information Systems Frontiers	8	17	345	Zone 1
Communications in Computer and Information Science	9	15	360	Zone 1
Science and Engineering Ethics	10	15	375	Zone 1

Table 9. Author productivity distribution based on Lotka's law in academic documents

\multicolumn{3}{c}{Author Productivity Through Lotka's Law}		
Documents Written	**N. of Authors**	**Proportion of Authors**
1	3118	0.84
2	396	0.107
3	128	0.034
4	31	0.008
5	14	0.004
6	6	0.002
7	6	0.002
8	3	0.001
9	1	0
10	4	0.001
11	2	0.001
15	1	0
16	1	0
17	1	0

have authored two documents, while only 0.8% have written four. A steep decline continues for authors contributing five, six, and seven documents, each representing less than 0.5% of contributors. The trend persists with an increasingly minute percentage of authors producing eight to seventeen documents. This distribution aligns with Lotka's Law, showcasing a common pattern where the majority of authors tend to be singularly productive, with a steep decrease in the number of authors contributing to multiple documents, emphasizing the prevalence of sporadic or singularly prolific authors within academic literature.

Table 10 presents local impact metrics for key authors in AI ethics academic contributions. Vakkuri V holds an h-index of 8, g-index of 12, and m-index of 1.143, accumulating 162 citations from 16 papers since 2018. Abrahamsson P showcases an h-index of 7, g-index of 12, and m-index of 1, with 148 citations from 15 papers since 2018. Notably, Floridi L exhibits significant impact metrics with an h-index of 7, g-index of 11, and a remarkable 1,286 citations from 11 papers since 2018. Kemell K-K demonstrates an h-index of 7, g-index of 11, and m-index of 1.167, accumulating 144 citations from 17 papers since 2019. Other authors, such as Dignum V, Ryan M, Stahl Bc, Morley J, Zhang Y, and Birhane A, display varying impact metrics based on citations, publication counts, and publication initiation years. These metrics offer insights into the localized impact and influence of key authors contributing significantly to the scholarly landscape in AI ethics. The diverse impact metrics highlight the contributions of these authors, with some showcasing substantial influence through high citation counts and indices, underscoring their significance within the field.

Table 11 and figure 3 outlines top affiliations based on their academic article contributions in AI ethics. The University of Oxford leads with 50 articles, showcasing extensive engagement in the field. Following closely, the Technical University of Munich contributes 33 articles, signifying substantial research output. University of Cambridge, Northeastern University, University of Jyväskylä, and University of Helsinki demonstrate strong involvement, each presenting between 27 to 32 articles. Umeå University

Table 10. Local impact metrics of key authors in academic contributions

Authors Local Impact						
Element	h_index	g_index	m_index	TC	NP	PY_start
Vakkuri V	8	12	1.143	162	16	2018
Abrahamsson P	7	12	1	148	15	2018
Floridi L	7	11	1	1286	11	2018
Kemell K-K	7	11	1.167	144	17	2019
Dignum V	6	9	0.857	853	9	2018
Ryan M	6	7	1.2	282	7	2020
Stahl Bc	6	7	0.857	311	7	2018
Morley J	5	6	1	495	6	2020
Zhang Y	5	11	1.25	163	11	2021
Birhane A	4	4	0.8	279	4	2020

Table 11. Top affiliations by academic article contributions

Affiliation	Articles
University of Oxford	50
Technical University of Munich	33
University of Cambridge	32
Northeastern University	31
University of Jyväskylä	28
University of Helsinki	27
Umeå University	26
University of Turku	19
Delft University of Technology	18
University of Technology Sydney	18

and University of Turku also contribute notably with 26 and 19 articles, respectively. Delft University of Technology and University of Technology Sydney both provide 18 articles each, highlighting their active participation in advancing AI ethics research. These top affiliations significantly contribute to the scholarly landscape, showcasing their commitment and pivotal roles in fostering discussions and advancements within the AI ethics domain through substantial academic article contributions.

Table 12 outlines the distribution of corresponding authorship in AI ethics academic publications across different countries. The USA leads with 150 articles, representing 10.1% as single country publications (SCP) and 15.3% as multiple country publications (MCP), indicating substantial involvement as both sole and collaborative corresponding authors. The United Kingdom follows closely with 105 articles, showcasing 7% SCP and notably higher 28.6% MCP, reflecting a strong tendency towards collaborative authorship. Germany contributes 79 articles, demonstrating 5.3% SCP and 15.2% MCP, highlighting active international collaboration. Other nations such as the Netherlands, China, Australia, and Canada

Figure 3. Top affiliations by academic article contributions

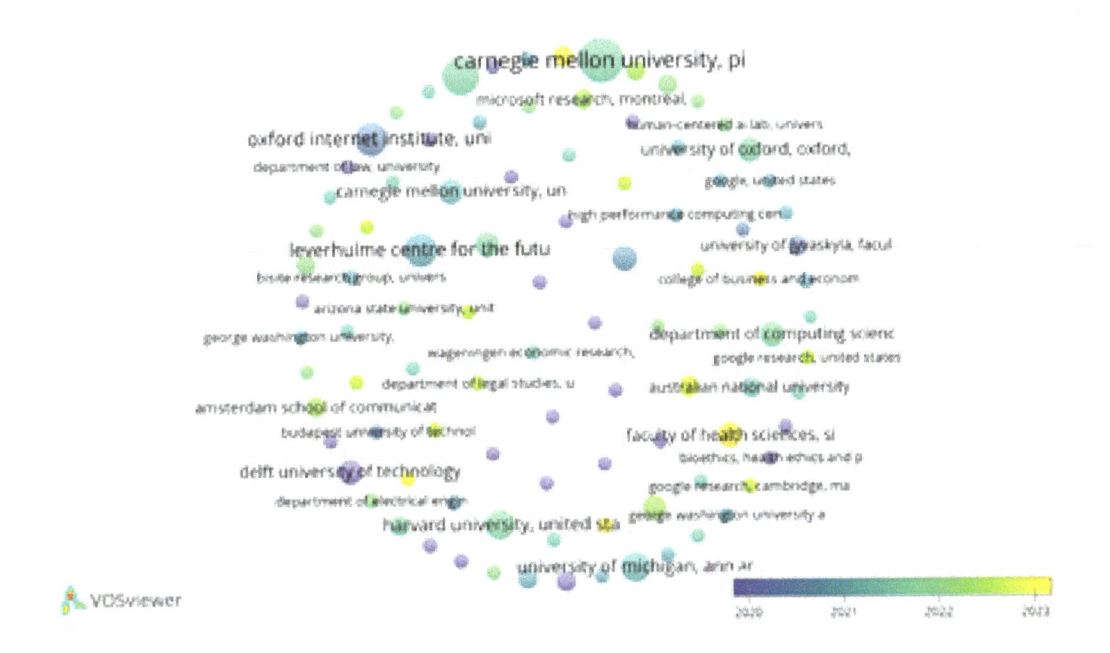

Table 12. Corresponding authorship distribution by country in academic publications

Corresponding Author's Countries					
Country	Articles	SCP	MCP	Freq	MCP_Ratio
USA	150	127	23	0.101	0.153
United Kingdom	105	75	30	0.07	0.286
Germany	79	67	12	0.053	0.152
Netherlands	57	41	16	0.038	0.281
China	55	44	11	0.037	0.2
Australia	47	36	11	0.032	0.234
Canada	47	36	11	0.032	0.234
Finland	46	39	7	0.031	0.152
India	34	26	8	0.023	0.235
Italy	32	26	6	0.021	0.188

also contribute, each with distinct proportions of SCP and MCP, showcasing varying degrees of collaboration in AI ethics research. Finland, India, and Italy exhibit their participation, displaying diverse SCP and MCP ratios. This distribution underscores the differing levels of international collaboration among countries in AI ethics research. Some countries show strong collaborative practices, while others exhibit lower levels of collaborative authorship. These patterns provide insights into the extent of international cooperation and solo authorship tendencies among different nations contributing to the discourse in AI ethics within academic publications.

Table 13 and figure 4 outlines the top cited countries in AI ethics research, detailing their total citations (TC) and average article citations. Spain leads with 3,175 total citations, averaging 138 citations per article, signifying high impact articles. The United Kingdom follows closely with 2,637 total citations and an average of 25.1 citations per article, indicating substantial impact but a lower average than Spain. Germany holds 1,251 total citations with an average of 15.8 citations per article, showcasing significant impact but a moderate average. Surprisingly, the USA with 1,202 total citations maintains an average of 8 citations per article, suggesting numerous contributions but a lower impact per individual article compared to other countries. Australia, Netherlands, Ireland, Canada, Sweden, and Finland also contribute, each with varying total citations and average article citations, portraying diverse impacts and contributions within the AI ethics field. This data highlights Spain's notable impact with high average citations per article, followed by other countries showcasing varying levels of influence, providing insights into the diverse contributions and impact of different nations in AI ethics research.

Table 14 presents highly cited publications in AI ethics, detailing their titles, DOIs, total citations, citations per year (TC per Year), and normalized total citations. BARREDO ARRIETA A, 2020, INF FUSION stands out with 3,103 total citations, averaging 620.6 citations annually, and a notable normalized total citation score of 58.22, indicating sustained impact and considerable yearly citations. FLORIDI L, 2018, MINDS MACH follows with 769 total citations, averaging 109.86 citations per year and a normalized score of 16.9, showcasing sustained influence since its publication. Similarly, HAGENDORFF T, 2020, MINDS MACH, and papers by YANG Q, NTOUTSI E, MORLEY J, REDDY S, TRAN BX, WINFIELD AFT, and MADAIO MA exhibit varying citation rates per year and normalized scores, reflecting their diverse influence and impact within AI ethics. These publications highlight substantial contributions to the field, with some papers maintaining strong and consistent citations over time, indicating their lasting relevance, while others showcase significant impact within shorter timeframes. This diversity in citation patterns emphasizes the range of influential publications contributing to the discourse and progression of AI ethics.

Figure 5 showcases a Keyword Co-occurrence Network in AI Ethics, illuminating the frequency of specific words within the corpus of discussions. At the forefront, "Artificial Intelligence" emerges as

Table 13. Top cited countries and their average article citations

Most Cited Countries		
Country	**TC**	**Average Article Citations**
Spain	3175	138
United Kingdom	2637	25.1
Germany	1251	15.8
USA	1202	8
Australia	817	17.4
Netherlands	674	11.8
Ireland	359	23.9
Canada	314	6.7
Sweden	277	15.4
Finland	218	4.7

Figure 4. Top cited countries and their average article citations

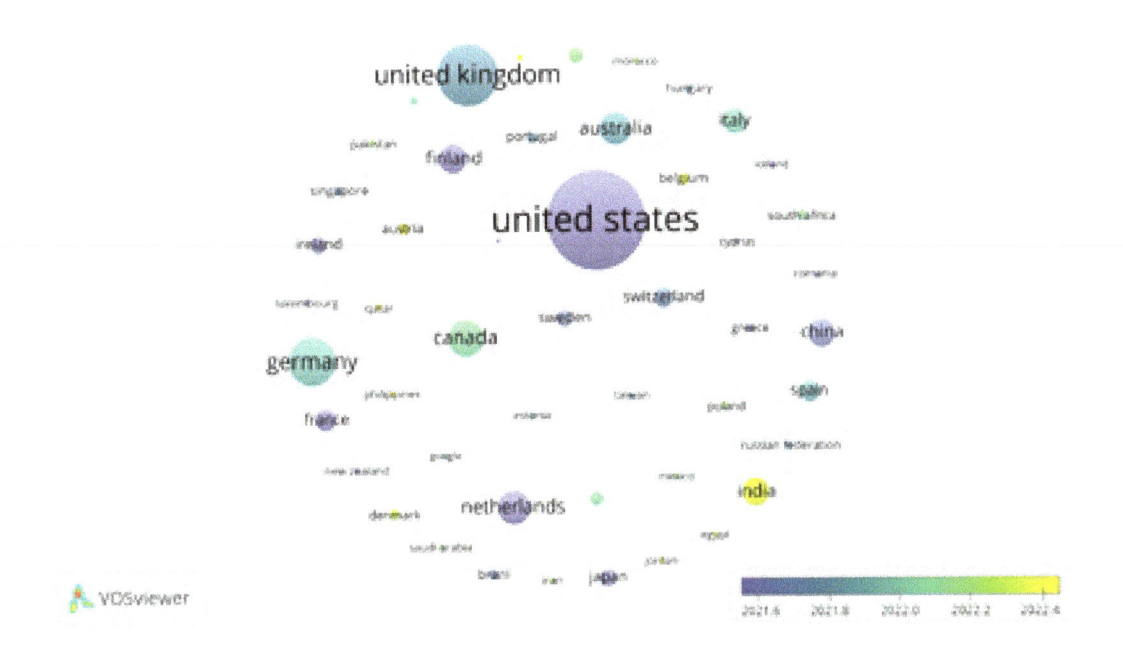

Table 14. Highly cited publications

Most Global Cited Documents				
Paper	DOI	Total Citations	TC per Year	Normalized TC
BARREDO ARRIETA A, 2020, INF FUSION	10.1016/j.inffus.2019.12.012	3103	620.6	58.22
FLORIDI L, 2018, MINDS MACH	10.1007/s11023-018-9482-5	769	109.86	16.9
HAGENDORFF T, 2020, MINDS MACH	10.1007/s11023-020-09517-8	535	107	10.04
YANG Q, 2020, SYNTH LECT ARTIF INTELL MACH LEARN	10.2200/S00960ED2V01Y201910AIM043	349	69.8	6.55
NTOUTSI E, 2020, WILEY INTERDISCIP REV DATA MIN KNOWL DISCOV	10.1002/widm.1356	265	53	4.97
MORLEY J, 2020, SCI ENG ETHICS	10.1007/s11948-019-00165-5	236	47.2	4.43
REDDY S, 2020, J AM MED INFORMATICS ASSOC	10.1093/jamia/ocz192	207	41.4	3.88
TRAN BX, 2019, J CLIN MED	10.3390/jcm8030360	203	33.83	9.77
WINFIELD AFT, 2018, PHILOS TRANS R SOC A MATH PHYS ENG SCI	10.1098/rsta.2018.0085	195	27.86	4.28
MADAIO MA, 2020, CONF HUM FACT COMPUT SYST PROC	10.1145/3313831.3376445	176	35.2	3.3

the most prevalent term, occurring 587 times, highlighting its pivotal role within ethical discussions surrounding AI. Following closely, "Ethical Technology" surfaces 327 times, underscoring the intersection of ethics within technological advancements. Additionally, "Philosophical Aspects" at 250 occurrences denotes the philosophical considerations intrinsic to AI ethical discourse.

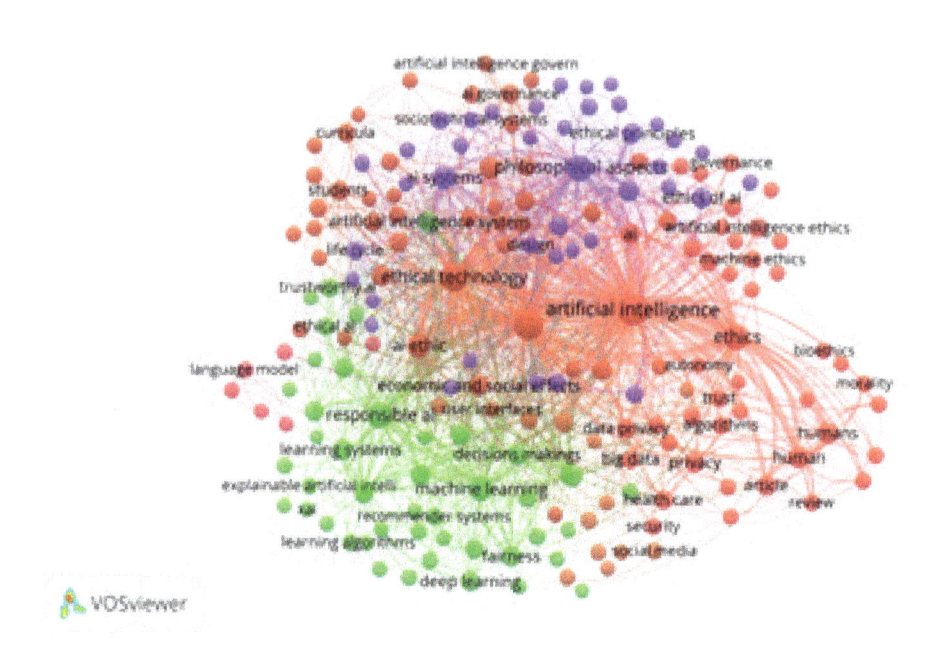

Figure 5. The keyword co-occurrence network in AI in ethics
Source: Scopus Database and Figure Generated by VOSviwer no

The table further reveals recurring themes such as "AI Ethic," "Decision Making," and "Machine Learning," each demonstrating their prominence with 148, 127, and 121 occurrences, respectively. These terms emphasize the ethical framework, decision-making processes, and the significance of machine learning in ethical AI development.

Moreover, recurrent concepts like "Responsible AI," "Ethical Issues," "Human-Centric Perspectives," "Deep Learning," and "Data Privacy" among others signify the interconnectedness and importance of various dimensions within the discourse on ethical AI. This co-occurrence analysis unveils prevalent themes, showcasing the amalgamation of ethical, philosophical, and technical aspects, essential for comprehensive discussions and advancements in ethical AI development.

5. DISCUSSION

The exploration of AI ethics through bibliometric analysis provides valuable insights into the trajectory, dynamics, and scholarly contributions within this burgeoning field. The discussion synthesizes key findings and implications to elucidate the evolving landscape of AI ethics research.

5.1 Growth and Thematic Trends

The exponential growth in AI ethics publications reflects the increasing recognition and importance of ethical considerations in artificial intelligence development. The significant surge observed from 2018 to 2023 underscores the growing scholarly attention and urgency to address ethical challenges amidst rapid technological advancements. This trend aligns with heightened societal awareness and concerns regarding the ethical implications of AI systems across various domains.

5.2 Author Collaboration and Productivity

The collaborative nature of AI ethics research underscores the interdisciplinary and multifaceted nature of ethical inquiry in artificial intelligence. The high prevalence of co-authored documents and international collaborations highlights the global and collaborative efforts to navigate complex ethical dilemmas in AI development. Furthermore, the presence of single-authored documents signifies individual contributions and expertise within the field.

5.3 Publication Typology and Academic Impact

The diverse range of publication types reflects the multifaceted discourse surrounding AI ethics, encompassing scholarly articles, books, conference papers, and reviews. Springer and ACM emerge as pivotal publishers, fostering academic discourse and dissemination of research findings. The prominence of specific journals and proceedings underscores their influence and role in shaping scholarly discourse and academic impact within the field of AI ethics.

5.4 Keyword Analysis and Co-Occurrence Networks

The Keyword Co-occurrence Network unveils the thematic landscape and interconnectedness of concepts within AI ethics discourse. Key terms such as "Artificial Intelligence," "Ethical Technology," and "Philosophical Aspects" underscore the multidimensional nature of ethical inquiry, encompassing technical, philosophical, and societal considerations. The prominence of themes like "AI Ethic," "Decision Making," and "Machine Learning" reflects the foundational principles and technical underpinnings driving ethical AI development.

5.5 International Collaboration and Country Impact

The analysis of international collaboration and country contributions highlights the global nature of AI ethics research and the diverse perspectives shaping ethical discourse. Institutions and countries like the University of Oxford, USA, and United Kingdom emerge as prominent contributors, reflecting their leadership in AI research and ethical inquiry. The collaborative endeavors across borders underscore the collective effort to address ethical challenges and foster responsible AI innovation on a global scale.

5.6 Citation Trends and Impact Metrics

The examination of citation trends and impact metrics provides insights into the recognition and influence of scholarly contributions within AI ethics research. Authors such as Floridi L and Dignum V emerge as influential figures, shaping discourse and advancing ethical frameworks in AI development. The local impact metrics of academic sources and authors offer valuable benchmarks for assessing scholarly impact and recognition within the AI ethics community.

The bibliometric analysis offers a comprehensive understanding of the growth, collaboration dynamics, thematic trends, and academic impact within the field of AI ethics. The findings underscore the interdisciplinary nature of ethical inquiry, the global collaborative efforts, and the imperative to foster responsible AI development guided by ethical principles and societal values. Moving forward, continued interdisciplinary collaboration and ethical reflection are essential to navigate the complex ethical landscape of AI innovation and ensure technology serves the collective good of humanity.

5.7 Implications of the Study

The findings of this comprehensive bibliometric analysis bear significant implications for multiple stakeholders engaged in AI ethics research, policymaking, and practice. Firstly, the exponential growth of AI ethics publications underscores the mounting interest and concern regarding ethical implications in AI development and deployment. These insights can serve as a roadmap for policymakers, aiding in the formulation of regulations and guidelines to address ethical challenges in AI.

Secondly, the identification of influential sources, publishers, and highly cited works serves as a guide for researchers, providing a foundation for further exploration. Understanding the thematic evolution and prevalent topics within AI ethics informs scholars about critical areas requiring more attention or neglected themes that demand deeper exploration.

Moreover, the analysis of author productivity, collaborations, and country-wise contributions highlights the global nature of AI ethics research. It emphasizes the importance of fostering international collaborations to address ethical challenges in AI comprehensively. These insights can catalyze cross-disciplinary engagements, encouraging diverse perspectives to tackle multifaceted ethical dilemmas in AI technologies.

The study's limitations, primarily stemming from the database constraints and language barriers, signal opportunities for future research. Researchers can expand this work by incorporating datasets from multiple repositories, encompassing a broader spectrum of languages to ensure a more inclusive analysis of global AI ethics scholarship.

Furthermore, the implications extend beyond academia, offering guidance to practitioners and industry leaders. Understanding the trajectory of AI ethics research can aid in the development of responsible AI frameworks and practices, ensuring ethical considerations are integral to technological advancements.

5.8 Future Studies

Future studies in the field of AI ethics bibliography can embark on various trajectories building upon this research. Firstly, to overcome the limitations related to database constraints, researchers can employ advanced data mining techniques to incorporate datasets from diverse sources, including grey literature, preprints, and alternative repositories. Integrating machine learning models can facilitate more extensive coverage and analysis of global AI ethics publications.

Secondly, there is a compelling need for qualitative analyses complementing the quantitative findings of this study. Qualitative inquiries, such as case studies or interviews with key authors, can offer nuanced insights into the ethical deliberations, dilemmas faced, and decision-making processes within AI research communities. This approach can uncover underlying motivations and ethical considerations guiding AI ethics scholarship.

Additionally, future studies could delve deeper into specific thematic areas identified in this analysis. By conducting in-depth investigations into emerging themes or neglected topics, researchers can provide detailed insights into complex ethical issues within AI, fostering a more comprehensive understanding of ethical challenges and potential solutions.

Collaboration dynamics and their impact on AI ethics scholarship present an avenue for further exploration. Future studies could explore the nuances of cross-disciplinary collaborations, examining their influence on the development and implementation of ethical frameworks in AI. Understanding the dynamics of collaborative networks and their implications for ethical AI development could guide effective interdisciplinary partnerships.

Lastly, incorporating interdisciplinary perspectives, including philosophy, sociology, and law, can enrich AI ethics research. Future studies could emphasize interdisciplinary approaches to unravel the ethical, social, and legal implications of AI technologies, fostering holistic frameworks for ethical AI design, deployment, and governance.

6. CONCLUSION

This bibliometric journey through the realm of AI ethics publications has illuminated critical pathways for future scholarship. By leveraging these insights, researchers, policymakers, and industry leaders can collectively forge responsible AI pathways, embedding ethical considerations at the core of AI development and deployment, ensuring a more ethical, accountable, and inclusive AI landscape for the future.

REFERENCES

Aizenberg, E., & van den Hoven, J. (2020). Designing for human rights in AI. *Big Data & Society*, *7*(2). doi:10.1177/2053951720949566

Aloisi, A., & De Stefano, V. (2023). Between risk mitigation and labour rights enforcement: Assessing the transatlantic race to govern AI-driven decision-making through a comparative lens. *European Labour Law Journal*, *14*(2), 283–307. doi:10.1177/20319525231167982

Banerji, B., & Feroz, M. A. (2024). Elements of AI Ethical Regulatory Framework and SDGs. In *Exploring Ethical Dimensions of Environmental Sustainability and Use of AI* (pp. 126–139). IGI Global. doi:10.4018/979-8-3693-0892-9.ch007

Bozkurt, A., Karadeniz, A., Baneres, D., Guerrero-Roldán, A. E., & Rodríguez, M. E. (2021). Artificial Intelligence and Reflections from Educational Landscape: A Review of AI Studies in Half a Century. *Sustainability (Basel)*, *13*(2), 2. Advance online publication. doi:10.3390/su13020800

Dennis, M. J., & Aizenberg, E. (2022). The Ethics of AI in Human Resources. *Ethics and Information Technology*, *24*(3), 25. doi:10.1007/s10676-022-09653-y

Felzmann, H., Fosch-Villaronga, E., Lutz, C., & Tamò-Larrieux, A. (2020). Towards Transparency by Design for Artificial Intelligence. *Science and Engineering Ethics*, *26*(6), 3333–3361. doi:10.1007/s11948-020-00276-4 PMID:33196975

Fukuda-Parr, S., & Gibbons, E. (2021). Emerging Consensus on 'Ethical AI': Human Rights Critique of Stakeholder Guidelines. *Global Policy*, *12*(S6), 32–44. doi:10.1111/1758-5899.12965

George, D. A. S., George, A. S. H., & Martin, A. S. G. (2023). ChatGPT and the Future of Work: A Comprehensive Analysis of AI's Impact on Jobs and Employment. *Partners Universal International Innovation Journal*, *1*(3), 3. Advance online publication. doi:10.5281/zenodo.8076921

Habbal, A., Ali, M. K., & Abuzaraida, M. A. (2024). Artificial Intelligence Trust, Risk and Security Management (AI TRiSM): Frameworks, applications, challenges and future research directions. *Expert Systems with Applications*, *240*, 122442. doi:10.1016/j.eswa.2023.122442

Heilinger, J.-C. (2022). The Ethics of AI Ethics. A Constructive Critique. *Philosophy & Technology*, *35*(3), 61. doi:10.1007/s13347-022-00557-9

Kavoliūnaitė-Ragauskienė, E. (2024). Right to Privacy and Data Protection Concerns Raised by the Development and Usage of Face Recognition Technologies in the European Union. *Journal of Human Rights Practice*. Advance online publication. doi:10.1093/jhuman/huad065

Kumar, D., & Suthar, N. (2024). Ethical and legal challenges of AI in marketing: An exploration of solutions. *Journal of Information, Communication and Ethics in Society*. doi:10.1108/JICES-05-2023-0068

Mao, Y., & Shi-Kupfer, K. (2023). Online public discourse on artificial intelligence and ethics in China: Context, content, and implications. *AI & Society*, *38*(1), 373–389. doi:10.1007/s00146-021-01309-7 PMID:34803237

Mazurek, G. (2023). Artificial Intelligence, Law, and Ethics (Polish Text). *Krytyka Prawa. Niezalezne Studia and Prawem*, *2023*, 7.

Micheli, M., Gevaert, C. M., Carman, M., Craglia, M., Daemen, E., Ibrahim, R. E., Kotsev, A., Mohamed-Ghouse, Z., Schade, S., Schneider, I., Shanley, L. A., Tartaro, A., & Vespe, M. (2022). AI ethics and data governance in the geospatial domain of Digital Earth. *Big Data & Society*, *9*(2). doi:10.1177/20539517221138767

Misra, S. K., Sharma, S. K., Gupta, S., & Das, S. (2023). A framework to overcome challenges to the adoption of artificial intelligence in Indian Government Organizations. *Technological Forecasting and Social Change*, *194*, 122721. doi:10.1016/j.techfore.2023.122721

Mizrahi, K. G., & Sarit, K. (2024). A Human-Centered Approach to AI Governance: Operationalizing Human Rights through Citizen Participation. In *Human-Centered AI*. Chapman and Hall/CRC.

Nissim, G., & Simon, T. (2021). The future of labor unions in the age of automation and at the dawn of AI. *Technology in Society*, *67*, 101732. doi:10.1016/j.techsoc.2021.101732

Pflanzer, M., Dubljević, V., Bauer, W. A., Orcutt, D., List, G., & Singh, M. P. (2023). Embedding AI in society: Ethics, policy, governance, and impacts. *AI & Society*, *38*(4), 1267–1271. doi:10.1007/s00146-023-01704-2

Pokrovskaya, A. (2024). The role of AI in protecting intellectual property rights on e-commerce marketplaces. *Russian Law Journal*, *12*(1), Article 1. https://russianlawjournal.org/index.php/journal/article/view/3673

Rodgers, W., Murray, J. M., Stefanidis, A., Degbey, W. Y., & Tarba, S. Y. (2023). An artificial intelligence algorithmic approach to ethical decision-making in human resource management processes. *Human Resource Management Review*, *33*(1), 100925. doi:10.1016/j.hrmr.2022.100925

Rodrigues, R. (2020). Legal and human rights issues of AI: Gaps, challenges and vulnerabilities. *Journal of Responsible Technology*, *4*, 100005. doi:10.1016/j.jrt.2020.100005

Schiff, D., Biddle, J., Borenstein, J., & Laas, K. (2020). What's Next for AI Ethics, Policy, and Governance? A Global Overview. *Proceedings of the AAAI/ACM Conference on AI, Ethics, and Society*, 153–158. 10.1145/3375627.3375804

Williamson, S. M., & Prybutok, V. (2024). Balancing Privacy and Progress: A Review of Privacy Challenges, Systemic Oversight, and Patient Perceptions in AI-Driven Healthcare. *Applied Sciences (Basel, Switzerland)*, *14*(2), 2. Advance online publication. doi:10.3390/app14020675

Zhang, K., & Aslan, A. B. (2021). AI technologies for education: Recent research & future directions. *Computers and Education: Artificial Intelligence*, *2*, 100025. doi:10.1016/j.caeai.2021.100025

Zohny, H., McMillan, J., & King, M. (2023). Ethics of generative AI. *Journal of Medical Ethics*, *49*(2), 79–80. doi:10.1136/jme-2023-108909 PMID:36693706

Chapter 2
Revolutionizing Medical Libraries:
The Vital Role of AI in Enhancing Discovery, Access, and Library Services for Healthcare Professional

Amreen Taj
https://orcid.org/0000-0001-5624-3931
Yenepoya Pharmacy College and Research Centre, India

Mohammed Gulzar Ahmed
Yenepoya Pharmacy College and Research Centre, India

K. S. Ali
Yenepoya University, India

K. R. Senthilkumar
https://orcid.org/0000-0001-7426-5376
Sri Krishna Arts and Science College, India

ABSTRACT

The study aims to analyse the discovery, access strategies, and library services at the Central Library of Yenepoya (deemed to be University) (hereafter referred to as YCL) with a specific focus on the role of AI. By identifying challenges and proposing solutions, the study employs a qualitative case study method to investigate the discovery, access, and library services at YCL. Data gathering techniques include interviews, observation, content analysis of library records, and a thorough review of relevant literature. The researcher personally observes the library operations and supplements primary data with an analysis of secondary materials. Microsoft Excel is utilized for data management and analysis. The study indicates that the Yenepoya Central Library effectively facilitates the discovery and access of e-resources, along with providing various additional services such as research support, RFID services, QR codes for materials, reference assistance, technical support, and email-based services. However, there's a need for integrating AI tools into the library services.

DOI: 10.4018/979-8-3693-5593-0.ch002

1. INTRODUCTION

The rapid progression of AI technology presents an opportunity for its application in clinical practice, potentially revolutionizing healthcare services. It is imperative to document and disseminate information regarding AI's role in clinical practice, to equip healthcare providers with the knowledge and tools necessary for effective implementation in patient care. As technology advances and new trends emerge, medical libraries are poised to embrace these changes and continue to evolve. One significant trend in medical libraries is the integration of artificial intelligence (AI) Alowais et al., (2023). AI has the potential to revolutionize information retrieval and management, allowing for more efficient and personalized access to medical literature and resources. Deep learning and neural network models are already being utilized in the development of new generation information retrieval systems, making the process of finding relevant information faster and more accurate. Another trend in medical libraries is the utilization of virtual reality (VR) and augmented reality (AR) technologies. VR and AR have the potential to transform medical education and training by providing immersive and interactive learning experiences. Medical libraries can incorporate VR/AR technologies into their resources and services, allowing healthcare professionals and students to visualize complex medical concepts, practice procedures in a simulated environment, and enhance their understanding of medical conditions. As these technologies continue to evolve and become more accessible, the possibilities for innovation in medical libraries are vast. Furthermore, medical libraries are also at the forefront of practice innovation within the primary care medical home (PCMH) mode. Malpani, (1999).

AI technologies have the potential to transform the way medical libraries operate. For example, AI-powered search engines can help users discover relevant resources quickly and accurately. AI algorithms can also assist in the classification and organization of resources, making it easier for users to access them. However, the benefits of AI in resource discovery and access come with limitations. AI algorithms are only as good as the data they are trained on, and biases in the data can lead to inaccurate results. Medical librarians must, therefore, ensure that AI tools are accurate and unbiased. They must also be trained to manage AI tools effectively, ensuring that users can access the most relevant and reliable resources.

In the era of AI, libraries must focus on providing personalized and user-centered services that complement AI tools. For example, librarians can offer one-on-one consultations to help users navigate complex resources and databases. They can also provide training on information literacy and critical thinking skills to help users evaluate the reliability and credibility of information. However, balancing AI tools with traditional library services poses challenges. Librarians must ensure that AI tools do not replace human interaction and personalized services, which are essential for meeting the unique needs of each user.

The potential for AI to transform library services and user experiences is vast. For example, AI-powered chatbots can provide 24/7 assistance to users, improving access to information. However, as AI technologies become more prevalent, ethical and social implications arise. Medical librarians must ensure that users' privacy is protected, and that AI tools do not perpetuate biases or discrimination. Ongoing professional development and training for librarians are essential to stay current with AI technologies and their applications in medical libraries. This paper elucidates the evolving role of medical libraries in leveraging AI to meet the evolving needs of healthcare professionals and researchers.

Yenepoya (Deemed to be University) offers a top-tier educational experience amidst the serene setting of a peaceful South Indian. It is first private University in Dakshin Kannada district, the vision is to democratize access to superior higher education, fostering a vibrant knowledge hub and nurturing visionary leaders capable of propelling the nation to the forefront of global development. The university's central library, established alongside Yenepoya Dental College in 1992 in Mangalore, Karnataka, offers a wide range of library services. Additionally, the university has expanded its library network, with eight constituent college libraries currently operational, all dedicated to advancing the university's growth and development.

2. RESEARCH QUESTION

How AI based technologies enhanced the Discovery, Access of resources and how it leveraging Library Services.

3. OBJECTIVES OF THE STUDY

- To present the historical over of Yenepoya Central Library
- To investigate the discovery and access of resources at Yenepoya Central Library
- To investigate various library's services offered by Yenepoya Central Library
- To explore the challenges during the implantation of AI tools and AI based solution

4. LITERATURE REVIEW

4.1 Historical Overview of AI in Libraries

The historical backdrop of AI traces its origins to the 1950s, with McCarthy coining the term "AI" in 1955. The evolution of AI has unfolded through distinct phases: In the Early Phase (1949-1980), there were incremental advancements in AI-related technologies, including robotics, decision-making systems, logic, reasoning, and the emergence of early chatbots. The Middle Phase (1980-1992) witnessed the emergence of expert systems and cataloguing techniques, designed to mimic human decision-making in specific domains. The Modern Phase (1992-2010) aligned with the Internet Age, introducing NLP-enabled chatbots such as Sin and Alexa. The Advance Phase (2011-present) has been marked by significant progress in big data analytics, text mining, pattern recognition, and the dominance of major companies like Google. These phases, outlined by (Ali et al., 2021; Park et al., 2020), highlight the trajectory of AI development, as also referenced by Popkova, & Gulzat, (2020).

4.2. Application of AI in Medical and Healthcare

AI applications in the medical and health sciences have revolutionized various aspects of healthcare delivery. (Rego Rodríguez et al., 2022) In diagnostics, AI-powered systems analyze medical images such as X-rays, MRIs, and CT scans to detect abnormalities with high accuracy, aiding in the early detection of diseases like cancer. In treatment planning, (Bishnoi & Singh, 2018) AI algorithms assist healthcare professionals in creating personalized treatment regimens based on patient data and medical literature, optimizing outcomes. Moreover, (Park et al., 2020) AI-driven predictive analytics help in forecasting patient outcomes and identifying individuals at risk of certain conditions, enabling proactive interventions. (Haleem et al., 2019) In healthcare management, AI streamlines administrative tasks, enhances patient monitoring through wearable devices, and improves the efficiency of medical record keeping. Overall, AI's integration into the medical and health sciences landscape holds immense potential for improving patient care, enhancing diagnostic accuracy, and advancing medical research.

4.3 Librarian Perception Towards AI Tools

Research indicates positive attitudes towards AI integration in libraries, highlighting its benefits and challenges. Indian library professionals recognize AI's potential in enhancing accessibility and decision-making, emphasizing ethical considerations (Subaveerapandiyan & Gozali, 2024). Nigerian academic librarians acknowledge AI's role but express concerns about job displacement (Abayomi et al., 2020; Hussain, 2023). Zambian professionals demonstrate strong AI literacy and positive attitudes towards its benefits (Alam et al., 2024). Integration of AI enhances library services like Virtual Reference Services, Information Retrieval, Smart Libraries, Machine Learning, and Makerspaces, despite concerns about adoption challenges (Yoganingrum et al., 2022; Subaveerapandiyan & Gozali, 2024).

4.4 AI Based Library Servies

AI applications in libraries have evolved significantly, offering a wide array of tools and technologies to enhance library services and operations. One prominent area is the integration of chatbots, which are AI-powered virtual assistants that can interact with users, provide information, and assist with various library services (Omame & Alex-Nmecha, 2020; Touretzky et al., 2019). These chatbots can aid in cataloguing processes, responding to user inquiries, and even providing guidance on library resources and services. By incorporating chatbots, libraries can improve user engagement, streamline communication, and offer support round-the-clock.

Another crucial aspect of AI in libraries is the utilization of robotics. While less common compared to chatbots, robotics play a significant role in automating repetitive tasks such as inventory management and shelving (Jayawardena et al., 2021). Robotic systems equipped with AI capabilities can efficiently organize and maintain library collections, freeing up human staff to focus on more complex tasks and improving overall operational efficiency.

Libraries are embracing Machine Learning (ML) to adapt to digital demands (Das & Islam, 2021). ML optimizes collections by analysing usage patterns (Borgohain et al., 2024) and improves information retrieval accuracy (Ali et al., 2020). It automates tasks like metadata tagging and chatbot assistance (Huang, 2022) and offers personalized recommendations based on user behaviour. These advancements streamline services and enhance accessibility for patrons in finding relevant resources (Das & Islam, 2021). The research examined the literature concerning the use of artificial intelligence in libraries, revealing current trending research areas such as machine learning, extensive datasets, deep learning, and high-level languages (Borgohain et al., 2024).

Deep Learning (DL) enhances library services by: Improving information retrieval: DL algorithms can analyze vast amounts of data to provide more accurate and relevant search results. Personalizing recommendations: Deng,(2023). DL models can analyze user behavior and preferences to offer personalized recommendations for books, articles, or other resources. It can automate processes like metadata tagging, classification, and resource allocation, freeing up staff time for more complex tasks. Enhancing accessibility: DL-powered chatbots can offer automated assistance, operating round-the-clock to provide information and guide patrons to relevant resources, thus improving accessibility. Raed et.al (2022).

Additionally, pattern recognition technologies are increasingly being employed in libraries to enhance security measures and improve user accessibility. These technologies utilize algorithms to identify patterns in data, which can be applied in various contexts such as identifying security threats, indexing library materials, and implementing user identification systems (Affum, 2023; Tsabedze et al., 2022). By leveraging pattern recognition, libraries can strengthen their security protocols, streamline information retrieval processes, and provide a more personalized user experience.

Furthermore, the integration of Big Data analytics has opened up new opportunities for libraries to better understand and manage their resources. By analyzing large datasets, libraries can gain insights into usage patterns, user preferences, and trends in information consumption (Olendorf & Wang, 2017; Rego Rodríguez et al., 2022). This information can inform collection development decisions, optimize resource allocation, and tailor services to better meet the needs of patrons.

Optical Character Recognition (OCR) technology is another valuable tool that libraries can leverage to enhance their operations. OCR enables the conversion of printed or handwritten text into digital format, making it easier to search, index, and retrieve information from physical documents (Yuadi et al., 2024). By implementing OCR systems, libraries can digitize their collections more efficiently, improve access to historical materials, and enhance the overall user experience.

The research aimed to investigate user perceptions of e-resource services at the Yenepoya Institute of Technology library. The findings indicated a positive response from users regarding the utilization of e-resource services (Naik et al., 2019). Furthermore, an examination of library websites of private medical colleges in Karnataka revealed that the Yenepoya central library has developed an effective website. This website provides information on library e-resources, research support services, bibliographic tools, library timings, and profiles of library staff (Latte & Bankapur, 2022). Additionally, a study on the status of library collections, staffing patterns, and services provided by dental college libraries in Karnataka identified the Yenepoya central library as the oldest dental college library. The library's collection was highly appreciated, and it offers various services (Suryakant, 2013).

In summary, AI technologies offer a myriad of opportunities for libraries to innovate and adapt to the changing needs of their patrons. From chatbots and robotics to pattern recognition and Big Data analytics, these tools enable libraries to enhance services, improve efficiency, and provide a more personalized and accessible user experience.

4.5 Challenges and Opportunities of AI in Medical Libraries

Numerous studies investigate challenges and prospects related to integrating AI in Library and Information Science (LIS). Hussain (2023) identifies funding and librarian attitudes as barriers to AI adoption in libraries. Touretzky et al. (2019) discuss difficulties in teaching AI ethics, including knowledge and time constraints. Barsha & Munshi (2024) detail infrastructure limitations and privacy concerns. Cox et al. (2019) highlight ethical dilemmas and data quality issues. Wach et al. (2023) tackle AI regulation and job displacement. Alshurafat (2023) explores chatbot benefits and challenges, including integration and privacy issues. Ali et al. (2020) note funding and technological skills as hurdles in university library AI implementation. Tait & Pierson (2022) propose AI-focused curriculum areas for LIS programs. Despite benefits, ethical concerns persist, including privacy and transparency issues (Alam et al., 2024; Subaveerapandiyan & Gozali, 2024).

4.6 Future Directions and Recommendations

Numerous studies offer insights and recommendations for integrating AI into Library and Information Science (LIS) education. Abayomi et al. (2020) suggest cultivating essential competencies for proficient AI use in library operations. Gill et al. (2024) emphasize ethical considerations and equitable access to information. Subaveerapandiyan (2023) proposes acquiring AI skills and management education on AI benefits. Abayomi (2020) advocates for librarians to enhance IT and analytical skills for effective AI deployment and stress involvement in curriculum development using AI tools, highlighting the need for continuous professional development among librarians. Ajakaye (2022) suggests librarians focus on enhancing AI literacy. Collaborating with computer science departments to establish AI Labs is recommended (Ali et al., 2020). Ethical training is emphasized for fair AI deployment in LIS (Huang et al., 2021).

5. METHODOLOGY

5.1 Research Design

In this study, a case study approach was employed due to its suitability for providing an in-depth and holistic understanding of the Central Library. The case study design allows for a comprehensive exploration of the library's organizational structure, access and discovery, services, resources, technological integration, challenges, and potential solutions.

5.2 Data Collection

5.2.1 Sources of Data: The primary data for this research were gathered through a combination of interviews, observations, and document analysis.

5.2.2 Participants and Sampling Strategy: The key participant in this study was Dr. K S Ali the Chief librarian of Central library of Yenepoya (Deemed to be University), and myself as librarian of Yenepoya Pharmacy College. The sampling strategy involved purposeful selection, focusing on obtaining detailed insights from a knowledgeable and authoritative source. Interviews were conducted on February 1, 2024, to gather information directly from Dr. K S Ali the Chief librarian.

5.2.3 Interview Questions: During the interview, a set of semi-structured questions were posed to Dr. K S Ali the Chief librarian, covering key aspects of the library, including its establishment, technological tools in use, collection development book selection policies, library services and resources, and major challenges faced, along with potential solutions.

5.2.4 Observations and Document Analysis: In addition to interviews, close observations were made by myself to examine documents related to the library. This process involved a thorough verification of documents to ensure accuracy and reliability.

5.3 Data Analysis

5.3.1 Methods Used: The collected data, comprising interview responses and observed document details, were analyzed using Microsoft Word and Excel. These tools facilitated a systematic and organized analysis of both qualitative and quantitative aspects of the data. Qualitative responses from interviews were categorized and thematically analyzed, while quantitative data, if any, was processed and interpreted using Excel.

The combination of qualitative and quantitative analysis aimed to provide a comprehensive understanding of the Central Library, offering insights into its organizational structure, services, resources, technological integration, challenges, and potential solutions.

This methodology allowed for a rigorous investigation into the specified aspects of the case study, utilizing a well-rounded approach to data collection and analysis.

6. FINDINGS

6.1 Historical Overview of Central Library of Yenepoya

Yenepoya University, situated in Deralakatte, Mangalore, Karnataka, India, is a prominent private institution offering diverse higher education programs. Its origins trace back to the establishment of the Islamic Academy Education Trust (R) in 1991, which led to the founding of Yenepoya Dental College in 1992 to address the scarcity of dental education in Dakshina Kannada. In 2008, Yenepoya University was officially established, encompassing various constituent colleges spanning medical, dental, allied health sciences, physiotherapy, pharmacy, nursing, ayurveda, homeopathy, naturopathy, engineering, and arts, science, commerce, and management. Over the years, the university has gained recognition across southern India for its comprehensive offerings, including Ph.D., graduate, and post-graduate degrees, as well as diploma and certificate courses. vision is to democratize access to superior higher education, fostering a vibrant knowledge hub and nurturing visionary leaders capable of propelling the nation to the forefront of global development. It mission is to cultivate academic excellence and global competencies among students, foster an environment conducive to meaningful research, and integrate modern pedagogical methods with the highest ethical standards. It aims to disseminate acquired knowledge and promote community development.

The Yenepoya Central Library originated in 1992 as a dental college library and transitioned into the University Central Library in 2008. It has been automated using Koha Library automation software and DSpace software for digital library management. Each of the eight constituent college libraries, along with the Central Library, has its own dedicated website. RFID technology has been integrated into the Central Library's OPAC services. The library adheres to its own book selection policies and operates 24/7 to cater to the needs of health professionals. Currently, there are eight constituent college libraries affiliated with Yenepoya, including:

1. Yenepoya Pharmacy College Library - Ayush campus, Naringana, Mangalore.
2. Yenepoya Ayurveda and Naturopathy College Library - Ayush campus, Naringana, Mangalore.
3. Yenepoya Homoeopathy College Library - Ayush campus, Naringana, Mangalore.
4. Yenepoya Nursing and Physiotherapy College Library - Ayush campus, Naringana, Mangalore.
5. Yenepoya Degree College Library - Balmatta campus, Mangalore.
6. Yenepoya Degree College Library - Kuluru campus, Mangalore.
7. Yenepoya Allied Healthcare Professions Library - Mudipu campus, Mangalore.

8. Yenepoya Institute of Arts, Science, Commerce, and Management College Library - Bangalore Campus, Bangalore.

6.2 Discovery and Access of E-Resources

6.2.1 Library OPAC: A Library Online Public Access Catalog (OPAC) is a digital interface that allows users to search and access a library's collection of materials remotely. The Yenepoya Central Library, along with its constituent colleges, has implemented KOHA as its library management software to streamline daily library operations. To facilitate easy access to library materials, the library has adopted OPAC (Online Public Access Catalogue), which enables users to search for resources, including e-resources, efficiently.

6.2.2 Printed Catalogue: A traditional library book catalogue provides a comprehensive listing of the library's physical collection, including details such as title, author(s), publication year, publisher, edition, and subject headings. Prior to the central library's automation, it relied on a printed library catalogue to facilitate easy book searching.

6.2.3 Discovery of Database: Users access library-subscribed databases through institutional credentials, selecting specific resources for article and book searches. They input search terms, then review and refine results. Accessing full text, they retrieve articles or books, saving or citing sources as needed. This process provides access to a wide range of scholarly resources for research and learning. Yenepoya Central library, subscribed Bibliographical and abstracting database, clinical based database and Article search database etc.

6.2.4 Discovery of Question Papers and Thesis at DSpace: DSpace provides a convenient platform for discovering and accessing question papers and theses, thereby facilitating research, study, and academic endeavors. Users can search for question papers and theses within a DSpace repository by using keywords, titles, authors, or specific subject categories. DSpace repositories typically offer search

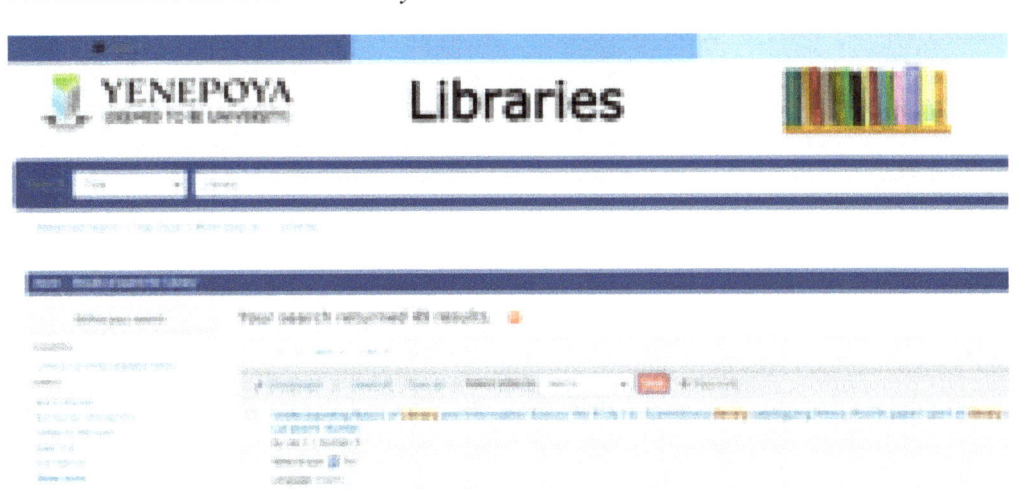

Figure 1. Demonstrate the Central Library OPAC

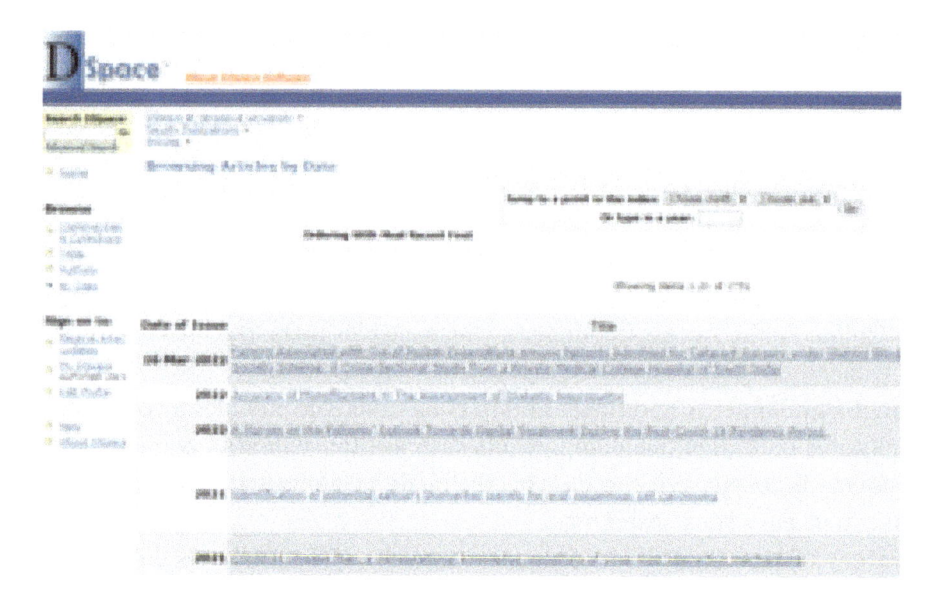

Figure 2. Shows the central library digital library platform

features similar to those found in traditional library catalogues or search engines. The central library established the digital library.

6.2.5 Discovery of Open Access Resources: Open Access Resources are freely available online materials, including articles, books, and research papers, accessible to users without cost or subscription. Users navigate open access platforms to search for and retrieve relevant content. The central library has compiled a collection of open access resources focused on healthcare education, accessible through the library's website. Users who are interested can easily search for these resources directly on the library's website.

6.2.6 Remote (Off-Campus) Access: It enables users to access library resources from locations outside the physical library premises. Through secure authentication methods such as usernames and passwords or institutional logins, patrons can connect to the library's electronic resources like databases, e-books, and journals from anywhere with internet access. The Central Library utilizes the Myloft platform for remote access. Users can install the Myloft application on their mobile devices or desktop computers. Upon entering their credentials, the platform grants users access to the library's e-resources.

6.3 Library Services of Central Library of Yenepoya

6.3.1 Research support services: aim to enhance researchers' productivity, facilitate access to information resources, and promote best practices in research methodologies and dissemination. These services may include literature searching, citation management, data management, research impact analysis, copyright assistance, and scholarly publishing support. The central library provides various services including grammar checking, plagiarism detection, reference management tools, access to the IRINS database, as well as bibliographic and abstracting database services.

6.3.2 RFID services: The central library offers RFID services for efficient management of library resources. RFID technology enables automated check-in/check-out, inventory management, and security surveillance. Users benefit from quicker transactions and improved library operations.

6.3.3 QR Code to the Materials: The central library employs QR codes to provide convenient access to materials. can scan helps to library professional to do quick and fast stack verification of the library collection. This technology enhances user experience by offering quick and direct access to relevant materials, promoting efficient research and learning.

6.3.4 QR Code to the Library SOPs: The library utilizes QR codes to provide instant access to its Standard Operating Procedures (SOPs). Users can scan these codes with their smartphones to access guidelines, policies, and procedures related to library services and operations. This technology facilitates easy reference to important information, ensuring users have quick access to the library's protocols and regulations, promoting smooth interactions and efficient utilization of library resources.

6.3.5 Reference Services: provide assistance to library patrons seeking information for research, study, or personal needs. Virtual reference services are available through online chat or email. These services play a vital role in supporting patrons' academic, professional, and personal endeavors by facilitating access to information and promoting lifelong learning.

6.3.6 Technical services: involve the classification and cataloguing of library materials. This process assigns call numbers or classification codes to organize items systematically. Cataloguing entails creating bibliographic records with standardized information about each item, including title, author, and subject headings. Cataloguers follow established standards such as MARC (Machine-Readable Cataloguing) to ensure consistency and interoperability. Central library following the DDC-2021 for classification of books materials.

6.3.7 E-resources services: encompass digital databases, e-books, e-journals, streaming media, digital archives, online reference materials, research tools, open-access resources, document delivery, and user support. These resources, provided by libraries and institutions, facilitate research, learning, and information access. Central library offering Web of science as a bibliographic and abstracting database, ProQuest database for full text articles, DELNET database, etc.

6.3.8 Article-request and Email Based Services: facilitate access to scholarly articles, books, and digital resources unavailable locally. Through libraries or institutions, users can request materials beyond their collection. enhance academic pursuits by providing access to a wide range of resources regardless of location, supporting research endeavors worldwide. Central library offering Article-request Services to its users via email.

6.3.9 Virtual Library Tour: offers an interactive online experience, showcasing library resources, services, and facilities. Users navigate through digital platforms, exploring databases, e-books, journals, and archives.

6.3.10 Digital Library Services: It offer access to diverse resources like scholarly articles, e-books, and archives. Users explore databases, journals, and research tools online. These services ensure global access to up-to-date information crucial for research and learning. The central library has set up a digital library using Dspace software. It provides access to research publications, question papers, books, theses, and dissertations.

6.3.11 Document Delivery Service (DDS): It provides access to scholarly articles, books, and resources not locally available. Users request materials through libraries or institutions, which procure digital copies.

6.3.12 Newspaper clipping services: Newspaper clipping services offer access to curated articles, often via digital platforms, providing summaries or full-text versions of news articles. Central library has more than 50 printed and electronic newspaper.

Overall, the study indicates that the Yenepoya Central Library effectively facilitates the discovery and access of e-resources, along with providing various additional services such as research support, RFID services, QR codes for materials, reference assistance, technical support, and email-based services. However, there's a need for integrating AI tools into the library services. AI tools like Chatbots can enhance query services and information retrieval, while Pattern Recognition tools can aid in user identification and secure password setting in RFID systems. AI-based discovery tools are crucial for assisting library users in navigating resources effectively, thereby expanding the scope of library services. Integrating AI will also empower library professionals to cater to a broader range of services efficiently.

6.4 Challenges Faced by Library Professional and AI-Based Solution

Libraries can overcome these challenges through various solutions. Firstly, collaboration with other institutions, consortia, or vendors allows for resource sharing, expertise exchange, and cost reduction related to AI adoption. Secondly, implementing robust data management strategies, including data cleaning, standardization, and governance, improves data quality and accessibility. Prioritizing transparency and accountability in AI systems by establishing clear policies and procedures for data usage, privacy protection, and algorithmic decision-making is essential.

Moreover, providing training and education programs for library staff and users increases awareness and acceptance of AI technologies while addressing concerns about job displacement. Gradual implementation through small-scale AI projects or pilot programs allows for the evaluation of effectiveness, user acceptance, and integration challenges before broader implementation. Additionally, leveraging open-source AI tools and engaging with AI research and library communities can offer cost-effective solutions and valuable support for implementation and development.

By implementing these solutions, libraries can harness the potential of AI to enhance services, improve efficiency, and better meet the needs of their users in the digital age.

7. DISCUSSION

The integration of artificial intelligence (AI) in libraries marks a significant paradigm shift in library services and operations. This discussion examines the historical evolution of AI, its applications in medical libraries, librarian perceptions towards AI tools, AI-based library services, challenges and opportunities, and future directions for AI integration in Library and Information Science (LIS) education.

7.1 Historical Overview of AI in Libraries: The historical backdrop of AI traces back to the 1950s, with distinct phases marking its evolution. From the Early Phase characterized by incremental advancements to the Modern Phase aligned with the Internet Age, the trajectory of AI development has seen significant progress (Ali et al., 2021). This evolution lays the foundation for understanding the diverse applications of AI in libraries.

7.2 Applications of AI in Medical and Health Care: AI applications in the medical and health sciences have revolutionized healthcare delivery, particularly in diagnostics, treatment planning, predictive analytics, and healthcare management (Rego et al., 2022) The integration of AI holds immense potential for improving patient care, enhancing diagnostic accuracy, and advancing medical research.

7.3 Librarian Perception towards AI Tools: Research indicates positive attitudes towards AI integration in libraries, emphasizing its benefits in enhancing accessibility, decision-making, and user experience (Subaveerapandiyan & Gozali, 2024) Despite recognition of AI's role, concerns about job displacement and ethical considerations persist among librarian communities.

7.4 AI-Based Library Services: AI applications in libraries have diversified, offering tools such as chatbots, robotics, machine learning (ML), deep learning (DL), pattern recognition, and Big Data analytics Jayawardena et al., (2021). These technologies streamline library services, enhance accessibility, and improve user engagement and satisfaction.

7.5 Challenges and Opportunities: The integration of AI in libraries presents challenges such as funding constraints, infrastructure limitations, privacy concerns, and ethical dilemmas Touretzky et al., (2019) However, opportunities abound for librarians to acquire essential AI skills, address ethical considerations, and collaborate with stakeholders to navigate these challenges Gill et al., (2024).

7.6 Future Directions and Recommendations: To effectively integrate AI into LIS education and practice, recommendations include cultivating essential competencies, emphasizing ethical considerations, acquiring AI skills, and fostering continuous professional development among librarians (Abayomi et al., 2020). Collaboration with computer science departments and establishing AI labs are also recommended to enhance AI literacy and promote ethical AI deployment (Ali et al., 2020).

8. CONCLUSION

In conclusion, the integration of AI in libraries presents transformative opportunities to enhance services, improve user experiences, and advance library operations. The AI technologies have the potential to transform the way medical libraries operate. However, medical librarians must ensure that AI tools are accurate, unbiased, and complement traditional library services. Future directions for medical libraries in the era of AI include providing personalized and user-centered services, addressing ethical and social implications, and ongoing professional development for librarians. By adapting to the changing landscape of information access and management, medical libraries can continue to provide healthcare professionals with the latest research and information to improve patient care. However, addressing challenges and leveraging recommendations are crucial for maximizing the benefits of AI integration while ensuring ethical and equitable deployment in LIS contexts.

REFERENCES

Ali, M. Y., Naeem, S. B., & Bhatti, R. (2020). Artificial intelligence tools and perspectives of university librarians: An overview. *Business Information Review*, *37*(3), 116–124. doi:10.1177/0266382120952016

Alowais, S. A., Alghamdi, S. S., Alsuhebany, N., Alqahtani, T., Alshaya, A. I., Almohareb, S. N., Aldairem, A., Alrashed, M., Bin Saleh, K., Badreldin, H. A., Al Yami, M. S., Al Harbi, S., & Albekairy, A. M. (2023). Revolutionizing healthcare: The role of artificial intelligence in clinical practice. *BMC Medical Education*, *23*(1), 689. doi:10.1186/s12909-023-04698-z PMID:37740191

Bishnoi, L., & Narayan Singh, S. (2018). Artificial Intelligence Techniques Used In Medical Sciences: A Review. *2018 8th International Conference on Cloud Computing, Data Science & Engineering (Confluence)*, 1–8. 10.1109/CONFLUENCE.2018.8442729

Borgohain, D. J., Bhardwaj, R. K., & Verma, M. K. (2024). Mapping the literature on the application of artificial intelligence in libraries (AAIL): A scientometric analysis. *Library Hi Tech*, *42*(1), 149–179. doi:10.1108/LHT-07-2022-0331

DasR. K.IslamM. S. U. (2021). *Application of Artificial Intelligence and Machine Learning in Libraries: A Systematic Review*. doi:10.48550/ARXIV.2112.04573

De Sarkar, T. (2023). Implementing robotics in library services. *Library Hi Tech News*, *40*(1), 8–12. doi:10.1108/LHTN-11-2022-0123

Deng, Y., Xia, C. S., Peng, H., Yang, C., & Zhang, L. (2023). *Large Language Models are Zero-Shot Fuzzers: Fuzzing Deep-Learning Libraries via Large Language Models*. Academic Press.

Haleem, A., Javaid, M., & Khan, I. H. (2019). Current status and applications of Artificial Intelligence (AI) in medical field: An overview. *Current Medicine Research and Practice*, *9*(6), 231–237. doi:10.1016/j.cmrp.2019.11.005

Huang, Y.-H. (2022). Exploring the implementation of artificial intelligence applications among academic libraries in Taiwan. *Library Hi Tech*. Advance online publication. doi:10.1108/LHT-03-2022-0159

Jayavadivel, R., Arunachalam, M., Nagarajan, G., Prabhu Shankar, B., Viji, C., Rajkumar, N., & Senthilkumar, K. R. (2024). Historical Overview of AI Adoption in Libraries. In K. Senthilkumar (Ed.), *AI-Assisted Library Reconstruction* (pp. 267–289). IGI Global. doi:10.4018/979-8-3693-2782-1.ch015

Latte, A., & Bankapur, V. M. (2022) Evaluation of Web Content of Selected Private Medical College Libraries in Karnataka. *Journal of Library Development, 8*(2). http://hdl.handle.net/10760/43684

Malpani, A. (1999). Health library in India works to empower patients. *BMJ (Clinical Research Ed.)*, *319*(7212), 785–785. doi:10.1136/bmj.319.7212.785 PMID:10488022

Naik, P., Keshava, & Khan, K. M. (2019). User's perception on e-resource services: a case study of yenepoya institute of technology library. *National Conference: Knowledge Organization in Academic Libraries (I-KOAL)-2019*.

Olendorf, R., & Wang, Y. (2017). Big Data in Libraries. In S. C. Suh & T. Anthony (Eds.), *Big Data and Visual Analytics* (pp. 191–202). Springer International Publishing. doi:10.1007/978-3-319-63917-8_11

Omame, I. M., & Alex-Nmecha, J. C. (2020). Artificial Intelligence in Libraries. In N. E. Osuigwe (Ed.), Advances in Library and Information Science (pp. 120–144). IGI Global. doi:10.4018/978-1-7998-1116-9.ch008

Park, C.-W., Seo, S. W., Kang, N., Ko, B., Choi, B. W., Park, C., Chang, D. K., Kim, H., Kim, H., Lee, H., Jang, J., Ye, J. C., Jeon, J. H., Seo, J. B., Kim, K. J., Jung, K.-H., Kim, N., Paek, S., Shin, S.-Y., ... Yoon, H.-J. (2020). Artificial Intelligence in Health Care: Current Applications and Issues. *Journal of Korean Medical Science*, *35*(42), e379. doi:10.3346/jkms.2020.35.e379 PMID:33140591

Popkova, E. G., & Gulzat, K. (2020). Technological Revolution in the 21st Century: Digital Society vs. Artificial Intelligence. In E. G. Popkova & B. S. Sergi (Eds.), *The 21st Century from the Positions of Modern Science: Intellectual, Digital and Innovative Aspects* (Vol. 91, pp. 339–345). Springer International Publishing. doi:10.1007/978-3-030-32015-7_38

Raed, R.A., Tidjon, L. N., Rombaut, B., Khomh, F., & Hassan, A. E. (2022). *An Empirical Study of Library Usage and Dependency in Deep Learning Frameworks*. Academic Press.

Rajkumar, N., Tabassum, H., Muthulingam, S., Mohanraj, A., Viji, C., Kumar, N., & Senthilkumar, K. R. (2024). Anticipated Requirements and Expectations in the Digital Library. In K. Senthilkumar (Ed.), *AI-Assisted Library Reconstruction* (pp. 1–20). IGI Global. doi:10.4018/979-8-3693-2782-1.ch001

Rego Rodríguez, F. A., Germán Flores, L., & Vitón-Castillo, A. A. (2022). Artificial intelligence and machine learning: Present and future applications in health sciences. *Seminars in Medical Writing and Education*, *1*, 9. doi:10.56294/mw20229

Roll, I., & Wylie, R. (2016). Evolution and Revolution in Artificial Intelligence in Education. *International Journal of Artificial Intelligence in Education*, *26*(2), 582–599. doi:10.1007/s40593-016-0110-3

Senthilkumar, K. (Ed.). (2024). *AI-Assisted Library Reconstruction*. IGI Global. doi:10.4018/979-8-3693-2782-1

Senthilkumar, K. R. (2024). Revolutionizing thrust manufacturing. In *Advances in computational intelligence and robotics book series* (pp. 80–93). doi:10.4018/979-8-3693-2615-2.ch005

Senthilkumar, K. R., Jagajeevan, R., & Sangeetha, S. (2024). Impact of AI on Library and Information Science in Higher Institutions in India: A Comprehensive Analysis of Technological Integration and Educational Implications. In K. Senthilkumar (Ed.), *AI-Assisted Library Reconstruction* (pp. 21–33). IGI Global. doi:10.4018/979-8-3693-2782-1.ch002

Serafini, L., & Bouquet, P. (2004). Comparing formal theories of context in AI. *Artificial Intelligence*, *155*(1–2), 41–67. doi:10.1016/j.artint.2003.11.001

Sivaraj, P., Madhan, V., Mallika, V., & Senthilkumar, K. R. (2024). Enhancing Library Services Through Optimization Algorithms and Data Analytics: Enhancing Library Services Mathematical Model. In K. Senthilkumar (Ed.), *AI-Assisted Library Reconstruction* (pp. 290–306). IGI Global. doi:10.4018/979-8-3693-2782-1.ch016

Suryakant, K. B. (2013). Present Status of Library Collection, Staffing Pattern and Services Provided by the Dental College Libraries in Karnataka: A Study. *International Journal of Information Dissemination and Technology*, *3*.

Vasishta, P., Dhingra, N., & Vasishta, S. (2024). Application of artificial intelligence in libraries: A bibliometric analysis and visualisation of research activities. *Library Hi Tech*. Advance online publication. doi:10.1108/LHT-12-2023-0589

Wójcik, M. (2023). Areas and contexts of the use of robotics in libraries: An overview of the applied solutions and a discussion of prospects. *Library Hi Tech*. Advance online publication. doi:10.1108/LHT-10-2022-0487

YuadiI.SighA. R.NihayaU. (2024). Text Recognition for Library Collection in Different Light Conditions. *TEM Journal*, 266–276. https://doi.org/ doi:10.18421/TEM131-28

Chapter 3
Impact of AI in Library Operations

G. Bhuvaneswari
Kumaraguru School of Business, India

P. T. Vijaya Rajakumar
Nehru Institute of Engineering and Technology, India

ABSTRACT

Artificial intelligence (AI) is disrupting how information is processed and searched. It can help information professionals improve their services by allowing individuals to perform more effective searches. However, there are concerns about its potential to replace humans in various jobs and lead to catastrophic events. Artificial intelligence (AI) has positive and negative impacts, but its potential to improve the operations of libraries far outweigh its drawbacks. According to Robinson, it can help them achieve their goals of improving the user experience and operational efficiency. AI can help libraries establish themselves as leaders in the scholarly community. In advanced nations, such as the US, libraries have integrated the capabilities of AI by applying various cutting-edge technologies, like augmented reality and virtual reality. These innovations have greatly enhanced how individuals discover information. The chapter explores the utilization of AI within libraries and the obstacles that it encounters when it comes to implementation.

1. INTRODUCTION

Artificial intelligence (AI) is disrupting the way information is searched and processed. It will allow information professionals to enhance their services by allowing them to provide more efficient and personalized information search capabilities. In 2015, Mogali noted that there are concerns about AI's capability to replace humans in certain jobs and its potential to malfunction and lead to mass destruction. However, its positive impacts far outweigh its negative ones (Mogali, S. S., 2015). In 2018, Odeyemi noted that AI could be used in various areas of library services. These include information retrieval systems, subject indexing, and shelf reading (Odeyemi S. O., 2019). According to Robinson, AI can

DOI: 10.4018/979-8-3693-5593-0.ch003

help libraries achieve various goals, such as improving operational efficiency and engaging more people through new services and improved user experiences. It can also help them establish a strong foothold within the scholarly information sector (Robinson R.N., 2018). In developed countries, libraries have already incorporated the potentials of AI into their operations by implementing various technological innovations, such as virtual reality and augmented reality. These have greatly improved the way people discover information.

2. ARTIFICIAL INTELLIGENCE

According to McCorduck, AI is a type of intelligence that machines can demonstrate compared to what humans and other animals can do. It can perform various tasks that people usually require, such as speech recognition and visual perception. There are two terms used to describe AI. One of these is intelligence, which refers to an individual's ability to think and learn using skills and facts. On the other hand, artificial is a product or imitation made by humans. Artificial intelligence is defined as the creation of machines or computers that can act, reason, and perceive like humans (McCorduck P., 2004). For instance, robots can identify objects in a room using their visual perception and can clean it efficiently by remembering the most effective path. Google maps is one example of an AI-powered product. It can provide directions, update users on their location, and answer questions. Other examples include virtual assistants such as Alexa and SIRI.

3. ROLE OF ARTIFICIAL INTELLIGENCE IN LIBRARY OPERATIONS

AI refers to the ability of a computer or software controlled machine to perform tasks and actions based on intellectual properties possessed by humans. The goal of AI is to develop systems that can perform various tasks and actions efficiently. Some of these include: 1) investigating, understanding, and manipulating objects; 2) reasoning; and 3) natural language processing. Due to the immense interest in AI in various fields, such as mathematics, computer science, and psychology, it has been the subject of a lot of discussions. In the field of LIS, the most significant AI presence was observed as the system's appearance. The use of expert systems can help improve the productivity and decision-making processes of library professionals.AI is widely used in various fields such as engineering, medicine, and computer science, including libraries. to solve problems. The library is also a promising area for developing intelligent systems. In terms of research, various works by Wheatley, Asemi,,Liu, and Mogali identified areas where AI can be utilized in libraries. The popular areas of AI utilization are discussed below (Asemi, A. & Asemi, 2018, Liu G., 2011, Mogali, S. S., 2015).

3.1 Reference Section

The use of expert systems in academic libraries is regarded as a vital activity. In 2011, Liu noted that these systems can help academic institutions develop AI capabilities in their reference section. Here are some examples of how these systems can be utilized. The Research system helps patrons find the most relevant sources for a particular query. It can also be utilized to provide students with information literacy training (Liu G., 2011). The concept of the Pointer is that it was an early example of a computer-assisted reference program. Rather than being a knowledge-based system, it serves as a reference program that's assisted by a computer.

The ORA system aims to provide academic reference librarians with a boost in their services by utilizing various technologies, such as videotexts, knowledge-based systems, and computer-assisted learning modules. It also consists of transactions such as polices and library locations. The ORA system features a variety of menus that help users narrow down their search results and find the appropriate tool for their specific query. It can also function as a front-end or consultation system for external reference tools.

3.2 Cataloguing

One of the oldest forms of library work is cataloguing. There have been attempts to automate this process through Expert Systems, which focus on descriptive style. There are two different ways to approach using AI for this. A human-machine interface is where the effort of the intellect is divided between the support system and the intermediary. A fully automated Expert System that can handle the entire process of cataloguing is linked to an electronic publishing system. This method eliminates the need for any intermediary and allows the text to be passed through the system without requiring any intellectual input (Cotera, M., 2018).

3.3 Classification

Coal SORT is a conceptual browser that can serve as an indexing tool or a search engine. It is mainly composed of a frame-based framework that serves as a representation of the system's expert knowledge, and it includes the necessary software to allow users to move around the framework. The classification process is a vital activity in the advancement of knowledge. It is a central component of all systems that aim to organize information in libraries and other information centers. The application of an expert system in this area is shown below.

Coal SORT and EP-X share many similarities, such as their focus on enhancing the user interface through a knowledge-based approach. EP-X's base consists of a set of template and a framework that represent the various concepts and their relationship, which are known as conceptual information patterns (Koltay, T., 2019).

The Biosystem Information System (BIOSIS) uses a deep knowledge base to automatically assign documents to various categories. It is designed to be an indexer aid, and it takes advantage of the information in biological documents' titles to assign as many classifications as possible. The indexing languages used in the system are designed to provide a practical and structured representation of the information.

3.4 Indexing

Another area of research that is being pursued is the creation of expert systems that can index periodicals. This involves identifying the concepts and translating them into verbal descriptions. One of the main advantages of implementing automatic indexing techniques is improving the quality and consistency of the data. This process can be done by analyzing the information collected by the indexer. It can then provide the appropriate terms and take appropriate action based on its inferences (Cox, A. M., Pinfield, S., & Rutter, S., 2019).

3.5 Document Collection

In addition to being a vital part of the library, documents also play an important role in its operations. The information officer or librarian is responsible for overseeing the collection process. The users are urged to be involved and their suggestions should be solicited. Several systems have been integrated. One of these is the Monograph Selection Advisor which is a pioneering effort in the area of library science. This system is designed to help the bibliographers make informed decisions when it comes to selecting materials for the collection.

3.6 Natural Language Processing in Library

The term NLP is often associated with the ability to write or speak in a complete sentence, and this is typically the first thought that comes to mind when thinking about it. It can also be applied to various fields, such as searching for information in online catalogs (Abayomi, O. K. et.al, 2020). The process of indexing involves identifying and retrieving documents that are relevant to a given topic. It aims to increase the precision and recall of the documents. This is in line with Camp and Grant's study in 2018, which revealed that many libraries in developed countries have started adopting AI for their various operations.

3.7 Pattern Recognition

The rise of distributed, multimedia, and Internet computing has created new opportunities for practitioners and researchers in the field of information systems. These new applications have transformed the way people work and study.

3.8 Robotics

A robot is a multi-purpose machine that can be programmed to perform various tasks in multiple axes. It can be mobile or fixed. In order to get around, the robots have to climb, roll, scramble, and fly. Due to the increasing number of digital library resources and services, libraries are also acquiring more printed materials. This has resulted in space constraints for academic research libraries.

The goal of CAPM is to develop a robotic system that can perform on-demand batch scanning and provide real-time access to printed materials. Through a web-based interface, the user will be able to interact with the system and request a robot to retrieve their desired item. Once the robot has delivered the item, it will automatically turn the pages and open it. Through the use of various software, such as OCR, scanner, and indexing tools, the CAPM will be able to analyze and search for full-text from the images (Ali, M. Y., Naeem, S. B., Bhatti, R., & Richardson, J., 2022).

The potential impact of artificial intelligence on the library industry is immense. Its development could allow computer systems to think and behave in a way that's similar to humans. Although some researchers claim that this technology won't replace librarians, it could leave them with little time to interact with their customers. In 2015, Murphy noted that the use of robots in libraries could help improve the relationship between users and librarians. He argued that the machines could not be considered an alienating factor (Murphy, D., 2015).

4. CHALLENGES OF IMPLEMENTATION OF ARTIFICIAL INTELLIGENCE IN LIBRARIES

When government funds are being decreased due to economic or political changes, cultural institutions are typically the first to feel the effects. Libraries are also experiencing issues with financial stability. The funding struggle is similar to the egg and chicken dilemma.

Although libraries are supposed to exhibit cost-effective practices, they can't do so without the integration of new technologies, which can require additional funding. This is why many libraries are currently in financial limbo.

Due to the increasing importance of information technology, there has been a wide range of skill gaps in the operations and systems of libraries. These gaps need to be filled in order to maintain their competency and improve the services they provide (Kellam, L. M., & Thompson, K. (Eds.)., 2016).

New competencies are needed in order to provide the best possible services to their patrons. These include: better digital fluency, hands-on learning activities, and faster and more accurate resource distribution.

Despite the increasing importance of technology, many libraries still resist the idea of adopting new processes and technologies. This is according to a study conducted by SCONUL in 2017. Many of the staff members who participated in the study showed a lack of enthusiasm for the changes brought about by new technology. In addition to these, many libraries also resist the idea of using Artificial Intelligence due to various concerns about its potential impact on their operations. Lauren noted that many of these concerns are related to the potential loss of human jobs. According to her, 38% of the jobs that are at high risk of being outsourced to robots are related to librarians (Oliver, J. C., Kollen, C., Hickson, B., & Rios, F., 2019).

Over the years, many librarians have expressed their concerns about the potential loss of their jobs due to the emergence of AI. The efficiency of AI would render human creativity and empathy redundant, leading to a world wherein human characteristics and connections to the community are rare and devalued. AI would also magnify injustices and spread misinformation.

There are also concerns about the potential misuse of AI in various ways. For instance, it can be used to create racist tools or promote fake information. In addition, it can be used to violate the privacy of individuals. This is why it is important that the government and the private sectors work together to ensure the safety of data.

5. IMPACT OF AI LIBRARY OPERATION

Libraries can enhance their operational effectiveness by implementing various methods and technologies to reduce their costs and improve their service. Some of these include digital asset management, process automation, and research data management. In 2015, a study conducted by Divayana et al. discussed the advantages of AI in library operations (Divayana, D., G., H., Ariawan, I. P. W., Sugiarta, W., & Artanayasa, I. W., 2015).

Machine learning can help libraries improve their digital resources' preservation, collection analysis, and visualization. It can also help them reduce their expenses related to the delivery of services. The adoption of LSPs can help them develop initiatives that aim to enhance their operational effectiveness. Through the use of machine learning, libraries can enhance their customer experience and attract more people through new and improved services. For instance, by optimizing search results, they can get the most out of their resources by delivering relevant and engaging content.

AI systems can analyze past habits and user touch points to determine needs and create high-quality experiences for customers. This can include offering personalized research suggestions and making sure that search results are aligned with the knowledge level of the student.

Implementing AI in libraries can help them achieve their goals by reducing the number of manual tasks and improving their efficiency. This can free up staff members to focus on more complex tasks such as teaching students how to improve their research skills or assisting lecturers in creating reading lists.

In the new era of scholarly information, libraries can play a vital role by establishing a strong foothold. With the help of AI, they can help academic research teams find connections between various disciplines and sectors by facilitating the seamless exchange of data. In addition, they can work with open publishing organizations and integrate research systems from other institutions. The collections of libraries can become more accessible, discoverable, and analyzable, thereby bolstering a robust global network of scholarly resources.

The IFLA Statement on AI aims to help libraries identify the various advantages of the technology and develop effective use strategies. According to the organization, libraries can help people become more knowledgeable about the technology and contribute to society by integrating it into their daily operations. They can also support ethical and high-quality research through the use of machine learning and AI. In addition, they must have proper policies in place to ensure that the technology is used properly.

CONCLUSION

The potential of AI to transform library operations is immense. This article looks into the different ways that AI technologies are being used in libraries. AI-powered chatbots can help with inquiries, and they can also provide instant assistance. In addition, intelligent libraries can streamline various processes, such as classification and recommendation, to improve the efficiency of information access. However, implementing AI in libraries can be very challenging. Some of the most important factors that need to be considered when it comes to implementing AI in libraries include privacy issues, ethical concerns, and the need to ensure that everyone has equal access to information. While libraries can greatly benefit from the technology, they also need to make sure that it complements and enhances their existing operations. In the future, more research is required to understand how AI will affect library operations, services, and user behaviours. Partnerships between researchers, developers, and libraries are also crucial to developing AI solutions that can cater to the unique needs of users. To accelerate the spread of AI within libraries, it is important that they establish initiatives that encourage sharing of best practices and knowledge exchange. The potential of this technology to transform public spaces into interactive environments where information is easily accessed is immense.AI can allow libraries to enhance their efficiency, reach out to more people, and provide more innovative experiences for their patrons. As this technology continues to advance, libraries must embrace it while still upholding their commitment to providing everyone with equal and fair access to information. Although there is currently a lack of research on the use of AI in libraries, several examples are emerging that show how they are exploring the potential of this technology.

REFERENCES

Abayomi, O. K., Adenekan, F. N., Abayomi, A., Ajayi, T. A., & Aderonke, A. O. (2020). Awareness and Perception of the Artificial Intelligence in the Management of University Libraries in Nigeria. *Journal of Interlibrary Loan, Document Delivery & Information Supply*, *29*(1–2), 13–28. doi:10.1080/1072303X.2021.1918602

Ali, M. Y., Naeem, S. B., Bhatti, R., & Richardson, J. (2022). Artificial intelligence application in university libraries of Pakistan: SWOT analysis and implications. *Global Knowledge, Memory and Communication*. . doi:10.1108/GKMC-12-2021-0203

Asemi, A. & Asemi, A (2018). Artificial intelligence (AI) application in library systems in Iran: A taxonomy study. *Library Philosophy and Practice (e-journal)*, *7*(9), 1-10.

Cotera, M. (2018). *We embrace digital innovation: IE University Library reinventing higher education.* 4th Lebanese Library Association Conference "Innovative Libraries: Paths to the future", in collaboration with IFLA Asia Oceania Section, Lebanon.

Cox, A. M., Pinfield, S., & Rutter, S. (2019). The intelligent library: Thought leaders' views on the likely impact of artificial intelligence on academic libraries. *Library Hi Tech*, *37*(3), 418–435. doi:10.1108/LHT-08-2018-0105

Divayana, D. G. H., Ariawan, I. P. W., Sugiarta, W., & Artanayasa, I. W. (2015). Digital library of expert system based at Indonesia Technology University. *International Journal of Advanced Research in Artificial Intelligence*, *4*(3), 1–8.

Kellam, L. M., & Thompson, K. (Eds.). (2016). Databrarianship: The academic data librarian in theory and practice. Association of College and Research Libraries, a division of the American Library Association.

Koltay, T. (2019). Accepted and emerging roles of academic libraries in supporting research 2.0. *Journal of Academic Librarianship*, *45*(2), 75–80. doi:10.1016/j.acalib.2019.01.001

Liu, G. (2011). The application of intelligent agents in libraries: A survey. *Program*, *45*(1), 78–97. doi:10.1108/00330331111107411

McCorduck, P. (2004). Machines who think. *Artificial Intelligence*, 340–400.

Mogali, S. S. (2015). Artificial intelligence and it's applications in libraries. *University of Agricultural Science Krishinagar Journal*, *3*(1), 1–11.

Murphy, D. (2015). *Robotics and the human touch in libraries and museums.* Available online https://slis.simmons.edu/blogs/unbound/2015/04/06/robotics-and-the-human-touch-in-libraries-and-museums/

Odeyemi, S. O. (2019). *Robots in Nigerian academic libraries: Investigating infrastructural readiness and potential for library services in information technology satellite meeting "Robots in libraries: challenge or opportunity?"* Technical University of Applied Sciences. https://creativecommons.org/licenses/by/4.0

Oliver, J. C., Kollen, C., Hickson, B., & Rios, F. (2019). Data science support at the academic library. *Journal of Library Administration*, *59*(3), 241–257. doi:10.1080/01930826.2019.1583015

Robinson R.N. (2018). Artificial Intelligence: Its importance, challenges and applications in Nigeria. *Direct Research Journal of Engineering and Information Technology, 5*(5), 36 – 41.

Wheatley, A., & Hervieux, S. (2020). Artificial intelligence in academic libraries: An environmental scan. *Information Services & Use, 39*(4), 347–356. doi:10.3233/ISU-190065

Chapter 4
Harnessing the Power of AI for Information Management and User Engagement in Next-Generation Libraries

Jaya K. Vijesh
Sri Krishna Arts and Science College, India

ABSTRACT

In this era of digital transformation, libraries are evolving into next-generation knowledge hubs by harnessing the power of artificial intelligence (AI). This research explores the integration of AI to enhance information management and user engagement in libraries. The study investigates diverse AI applications, methodological approaches, and their impact on library systems. By examining intelligent systems and algorithms, the research aims to uncover how AI technologies can streamline information organization, retrieval, and dissemination, ultimately contributing to a more efficient and user-friendly library experience. Additionally, the study delves into user engagement strategies, leveraging AI to tailor services based on individual preferences and behaviors.

INTRODUCTION

In the rapidly evolving landscape of information management and user engagement, libraries stand at the forefront of innovation, continually adapting to meet the needs of patrons in the digital age. As the volume and diversity of information continue to expand exponentially, libraries face the formidable challenge of organizing, accessing, and disseminating knowledge effectively. In response to these challenges, the concept of next-generation libraries has emerged, leveraging cutting-edge technologies such as Artificial Intelligence (AI) to revolutionize traditional library services and enhance user experiences.

Next-generation libraries represent a paradigm shift in the way libraries operate, moving beyond the confines of physical spaces to embrace digital platforms and innovative technologies. At the heart of this transformation lies the harnessing of AI, a powerful tool that promises to revolutionize information

DOI: 10.4018/979-8-3693-5593-0.ch004

management and user engagement in libraries. AI technologies, encompassing machine learning, natural language processing, and data analytics, offer libraries unprecedented capabilities to automate routine tasks, deliver personalized services, and facilitate seamless access to resources.

The integration of AI into next-generation libraries holds immense potential to optimize information management processes. AI-powered systems enable libraries to automate cataloguing, indexing, and metadata generation, streamlining the organization and retrieval of information. By leveraging machine learning algorithms, libraries can enhance the accuracy and efficiency of these processes, ensuring that patrons can easily locate and access relevant resources across vast digital collections.

Moreover, AI plays a pivotal role in enhancing user engagement within next-generation libraries. By analysing user behaviour, preferences, and interactions with library resources, AI algorithms can deliver personalized recommendations, tailored to the individual interests and needs of patrons. Whether recommending books, articles, or multimedia resources, AI-powered recommendation systems empower patrons to discover new content and engage more deeply with the library's collection.

In addition to personalized recommendations, AI enables libraries to deploy virtual assistants and interactive interfaces, offering patrons instant support and guidance. These AI-driven interfaces provide users with intuitive and responsive platforms to navigate the library catalogue, conduct research, and access services. By offering personalized assistance and seamless navigation, virtual assistants enhance the overall user experience, making library resources more accessible and user-friendly.

Next-generation libraries represent a transformative evolution in the provision of library services, driven by the integration of AI technologies. By harnessing the power of AI for intelligent information management and user engagement, libraries are poised to deliver enhanced services, empower patrons, and fulfil their mission of providing equitable access to knowledge and resources in the digital age.

NEXT-GENERATION LIBRARIES

Libraries have long been revered as bastions of knowledge, serving as repositories of information and hubs of learning for communities around the world. However, in today's rapidly evolving digital landscape, the concept of libraries is undergoing a profound transformation. Next-generation libraries are emerging as dynamic, adaptive spaces that harness the power of technology to redefine the way we access, interact with, and utilize information. This essay explores the evolution of next-generation libraries, examining their key features, challenges, and implications for the future of knowledge access.

The evolution of libraries can be traced back to ancient civilizations, where collections of scrolls and manuscripts were housed in repositories known as libraries. Over time, libraries evolved to accommodate the growing demand for knowledge, expanding their collections and services to encompass a wide range of formats and subjects. With the advent of the printing press, libraries became more accessible to the masses, democratizing access to information and fostering literacy and education.

The digital revolution of the late 20th and early 21st centuries brought about a seismic shift in the way information is created, stored, and accessed. The rise of the internet, coupled with advances in digital technology, has transformed the way we interact with information, blurring the lines between physical and digital formats. Libraries have embraced this digital transformation, digitizing their collections, implementing online catalogs, and providing access to electronic resources such as e-books, databases, and multimedia content.

Next-generation libraries are characterized by their embrace of technology and their focus on innovation, accessibility, and inclusivity. These libraries leverage cutting-edge technologies such as artificial intelligence (AI), augmented reality (AR), and virtual reality (VR) to enhance the user experience and expand access to information. They offer a wide range of digital resources and services, including online databases, digital archives, and interactive learning platforms. Moreover, next-generation libraries prioritize user engagement and personalized services, tailoring their offerings to meet the unique needs and preferences of their patrons.

Despite the myriad benefits of next-generation libraries, they also face several challenges in adapting to the digital age. One of the primary challenges is ensuring equitable access to digital resources and technology, particularly for underserved communities and marginalized populations. Additionally, libraries must grapple with issues related to data privacy, security, and intellectual property rights in the digital realm. Moreover, the rapid pace of technological change presents ongoing challenges in terms of keeping pace with emerging technologies and trends.

However, these challenges also present opportunities for innovation and growth. Next-generation libraries have the potential to serve as incubators of creativity and collaboration, providing spaces where patrons can explore new ideas, experiment with emerging technologies, and engage in lifelong learning. By embracing a culture of innovation and adaptation, libraries can position themselves as indispensable resources for communities in the digital age.

The emergence of next-generation libraries has profound implications for the future of knowledge access and information literacy. These libraries have the potential to democratize access to information, bridging the digital divide and empowering individuals to participate fully in the knowledge economy. Moreover, they can serve as catalysts for social and economic development, fostering innovation, entrepreneurship, and cultural exchange.

Furthermore, next-generation libraries have the opportunity to redefine the role of librarians as facilitators of knowledge creation and dissemination. Librarians are no longer simply custodians of physical collections; they are also educators, technology experts, and community leaders. By embracing new roles and responsibilities, librarians can leverage their expertise to support patrons in navigating the complexities of the digital landscape and harnessing the power of information for personal and professional growth.

Next-generation libraries represent a bold vision for the future of knowledge access and information literacy. These libraries are dynamic, adaptive spaces that leverage technology to expand access to information, foster innovation, and empower individuals to become lifelong learners. While they face challenges in adapting to the digital age, they also present opportunities for growth, collaboration, and social impact. By embracing innovation, inclusivity, and collaboration, next-generation libraries can continue to serve as vital resources for communities around the world, ensuring that knowledge remains accessible and empowering for all.

THE ROLE OF AI IN INFORMATION MANAGEMENT

Artificial Intelligence (AI) has revolutionized information management practices across various industries, including libraries. In the context of libraries, AI plays a crucial role in optimizing information retrieval, organization, and dissemination processes. This section explores how AI contributes to information management in libraries and its impact on enhancing user experiences.

One significant aspect of AI in information management is its ability to automate cataloguing and indexing systems. Traditional library cataloguing processes often involve manual entry of metadata, which can be time-consuming and prone to errors. AI-powered systems utilize natural language processing (NLP) algorithms to automatically extract relevant information from documents and categorize them accurately. For example, AI algorithms can analyse the content of books, articles, and multimedia materials, assign appropriate subject headings, and classify them into relevant categories, thereby streamlining the cataloguing process (Herrlich, 2023).

Moreover, AI-driven metadata generation plays a pivotal role in enhancing the discoverability of library resources. By analysing the content of documents and extracting metadata such as keywords, authors, and publication dates, AI algorithms enable users to locate relevant resources more efficiently. This not only improves the accessibility of library collections but also enhances the overall user experience by facilitating seamless navigation and retrieval of information (Hodonu-Wusu, 2024).

Another significant application of AI in information management is the development of advanced search capabilities. Traditional keyword-based search systems may yield suboptimal results, especially when users have vague or ambiguous queries. AI-powered search algorithms leverage machine learning techniques to understand user intent, context, and semantics, thereby delivering more relevant and personalized search results. By incorporating user feedback and behaviour data, AI algorithms continuously refine and improve search accuracy, ensuring that users find the information they need quickly and effectively (LibLime 2023).

AI plays a transformative role in information management within libraries, offering efficient solutions for cataloguing, metadata generation, and search optimization. By harnessing the power of AI, libraries can enhance the discoverability and accessibility of their collections, ultimately enriching the user experience and promoting knowledge dissemination.

AI in Information Management for New Generation Libraries

The advent of the digital era has ushered in a transformative wave of innovation, fundamentally reshaping the landscape of information management in libraries. At the forefront of this revolution is the integration of artificial intelligence (AI), propelling libraries into the realm of next-generation institutions. These libraries leverage the power of AI to intelligently manage information, enhance user engagement, and redefine the traditional roles of libraries in the 21st century. One of the primary applications of AI in information management within new generation libraries is the automation of cataloging and classification processes. Traditionally, librarians invested significant time and effort in manually categorizing and organizing vast volumes of information. With AI, libraries can employ sophisticated algorithms that analyze content, extract relevant features, and automatically assign appropriate metadata. This not only expedites the cataloging process but also ensures a more consistent and accurate classification of resources.

Moreover, AI-driven recommender systems have emerged as a cornerstone in reshaping user experiences within libraries. By leveraging machine learning algorithms, libraries can offer personalized recommendations based on user preferences, search history, and behavior. This level of personalization not only enriches the user experience by delivering more relevant content but also encourages users to explore a broader array of resources within the library's collection. Natural Language Processing (NLP) is another critical facet of AI that has revolutionized information retrieval in libraries. NLP enables users to interact with library systems using natural language queries, making the search process more intuitive and user-friendly. This advancement removes barriers for users who may not be familiar with complex search syntax, ensuring that information is more accessible to a diverse audience.

AI's capabilities extend to content summarization and extraction, addressing the challenge of information overload. With the ability to automatically generate summaries or extract key information from

Harnessing the Power of AI for Information Management and User Engagement

lengthy documents, libraries can cater to users seeking quick overviews or specific details within extensive resources. This not only saves time for users but also enhances the efficiency of information retrieval.

In addition to improving user experiences, AI plays a pivotal role in resource management within next-generation libraries. Predictive analytics powered by AI enable libraries to forecast demand for specific resources, optimize collection development, and allocate resources efficiently. By leveraging data-driven insights, libraries can adapt to evolving user needs, ensuring that their collections remain relevant and responsive.

The benefits of AI in next-generation libraries are multifaceted. Enhanced accessibility stands out as a key advantage, as AI-powered systems provide efficient and personalized search experiences. The inclusivity fostered by these technologies contributes to the creation of a diverse and engaged user community within the library. Resource optimization is another significant advantage. Through the automation of processes such as cataloging and recommendation systems, libraries can streamline their operations, allowing staff to focus on more complex and value-added tasks. This optimization not only leads to cost savings but also boosts overall operational efficiency.

Perhaps one of the most profound impacts of AI in new generation libraries is the improvement of user engagement. Personalized recommendations, interactive interfaces, and intuitive search functionalities powered by AI contribute to a more engaging user experience. These elements foster a sense of community and loyalty among library patrons, transforming the library into a dynamic and interactive hub of knowledge.

However, the integration of AI in libraries is not without its challenges and considerations. Data privacy and security are paramount concerns, requiring libraries to implement robust measures to protect user information. Ensuring transparency and providing clear communication about data usage policies are essential in building and maintaining trust among library users.

Algorithmic bias is another critical consideration. AI systems may inadvertently perpetuate biases present in training data, leading to biased recommendations or search results. Libraries must actively address and mitigate these biases to maintain fairness and impartiality in their services. User education and acceptance represent additional challenges. Libraries need to invest in user education programs to familiarize patrons with AI tools and algorithms. Building awareness and understanding can foster acceptance and trust in AI-driven systems, ensuring that users are comfortable and confident in utilizing these technologies.

Looking to the future, the evolution of AI in information management for new generation libraries is an ongoing process. Anticipated developments include advancements in AI algorithms, increased integration of AI in physical library spaces, and the emergence of novel applications catering to evolving user needs. As libraries continue to adapt and embrace innovation, AI will undoubtedly play a central role in shaping the future of information management and user engagement in the library landscape.

Improving User Engagement Through AI

In the realm of next-generation libraries, the incorporation of Artificial Intelligence (AI) offers unparalleled opportunities to enhance user engagement and satisfaction. AI technologies have revolutionized the way libraries interact with their patrons, providing personalized experiences, proactive support, and seamless access to information. This section explores the various ways in which AI contributes to improving user engagement in libraries, driving forward the concept of intelligent information management.

One of the primary ways AI enhances user engagement is through personalized recommendations. By analysing user preferences, browsing history, and interactions with library resources, AI algorithms can generate tailored recommendations for patrons. These recommendations span a wide range of materials, including books, articles, multimedia resources, and even events or programs offered by the library. By presenting users with content that aligns with their interests and preferences, libraries can increase user engagement, encourage exploration of the library's collection, and foster a sense of connection with the institution (Chiancone, 2023).

Additionally, AI enables libraries to deploy virtual assistants or chatbots to provide instant support and guidance to patrons. These AI-powered assistants can answer inquiries, assist with research queries, help navigate the library catalogue, and provide recommendations for resources. By offering round-the-clock assistance, libraries ensure that users receive timely and personalized support, regardless of their location or the time of day. Virtual assistants contribute to a more user-centric approach, enhancing the overall user experience and strengthening the relationship between patrons and the library (Farney, 2020).

Furthermore, AI-driven interactive interfaces play a vital role in engaging users and facilitating information discovery. These interfaces leverage natural language processing (NLP) and machine learning techniques to interpret user queries, understand intent, and deliver relevant responses. Interactive interfaces may include virtual reality (VR) environments, augmented reality (AR) applications, or voice-activated search systems, offering immersive and intuitive experiences for patrons. By leveraging cutting-edge technology, libraries can create dynamic and engaging platforms that captivate users and encourage active exploration of the library's resources (Hussain, 2020).

Analysing user behaviour and preferences is another area where AI contributes to enhancing user engagement in libraries. By collecting and analysing data on user interactions, resource usage, and engagement patterns, AI algorithms can identify trends, preferences, and areas for improvement. Libraries can use these insights to tailor services, optimize resource allocation, and develop targeted outreach initiatives that resonate with their user base. By leveraging data-driven approaches, libraries can continuously refine and enhance their offerings, ensuring that they remain relevant and valuable to their patrons (Panda et al., 2024).

AI improves user engagement in next-generation libraries by offering personalized recommendations, deploying virtual assistants, creating interactive interfaces, and analysing user behaviour. By harnessing the power of AI, libraries can create immersive and dynamic environments that foster exploration, discovery, and lifelong learning among their patrons, ultimately enhancing the value and impact of library services in the digital age.

Benefits of AI in Next-Generation Libraries

The integration of artificial intelligence (AI) in next-generation libraries brings forth a myriad of benefits that redefine the traditional roles of libraries and enhance the overall user experience. From intelligent information management to user engagement, AI technologies are transforming libraries into dynamic and responsive institutions, adapting to the evolving needs of the digital age.

One of the primary advantages of AI in next-generation libraries is the automation of cataloging and classification processes. Traditionally, librarians spent significant time manually organizing and categorizing vast amounts of information. With AI, sophisticated algorithms can analyze content, extract relevant features, and automatically assign appropriate metadata. This automation not only accelerates the cataloging process but also ensures a more consistent and accurate classification of resources, freeing up valuable human resources for more strategic tasks.

AI-driven recommender systems stand out as a cornerstone in reshaping user experiences within libraries. These systems leverage machine learning algorithms to provide personalized recommendations based on user preferences, search history, and behavior. The personalized content delivery enriches the user experience by offering more relevant resources, encouraging users to explore a broader range of materials within the library's collection. As a result, these systems contribute to increased user satisfaction and engagement.

Natural Language Processing (NLP) is another key benefit of AI in next-generation libraries. NLP enables users to interact with library systems using natural language queries, making the search process more intuitive and user-friendly. This advancement removes barriers for users who may not be familiar with complex search syntax, ensuring that information is more accessible to a diverse audience. By fostering a user-friendly interface, NLP enhances the overall accessibility of the library's resources.

AI's capabilities extend to content summarization and extraction, addressing the challenge of information overload. With the ability to automatically generate summaries or extract key information from lengthy documents, libraries can cater to users seeking quick overviews or specific details within extensive resources. This not only saves time for users but also enhances the efficiency of information retrieval, allowing patrons to access the most relevant information more quickly.

Resource management within next-generation libraries benefits significantly from AI-powered predictive analytics. These analytics enable libraries to forecast demand for specific resources, optimize collection development, and allocate resources efficiently. By leveraging data-driven insights, libraries can adapt to evolving user needs, ensuring that their collections remain relevant and responsive. This proactive approach to resource management leads to cost savings and enhances the overall effectiveness of the library in meeting user demands.

Enhanced accessibility stands out as a fundamental advantage of AI in next-generation libraries. AI-powered systems provide efficient and personalized search experiences, breaking down barriers to information access. The inclusivity fostered by these technologies contributes to the creation of a diverse and engaged user community within the library. By tailoring information access to individual user needs, libraries can serve a broader audience and become more integral to the community they serve.

Resource optimization is another significant benefit of AI in libraries. Through the automation of processes such as cataloging and recommendation systems, libraries can streamline their operations, allowing staff to focus on more complex and value-added tasks. This optimization not only leads to cost savings but also boosts overall operational efficiency. Librarians can allocate their time and expertise more strategically, enhancing the quality of services offered to patrons.

Perhaps one of the most profound impacts of AI in next-generation libraries is the improvement of user engagement. Personalized recommendations, interactive interfaces, and intuitive search functionalities powered by AI contribute to a more engaging user experience. These elements foster a sense of community and loyalty among library patrons, transforming the library into a dynamic and interactive hub of knowledge. The increased engagement leads to a deeper connection between users and the library, reinforcing the institution's role as a vital resource in the community.

The benefits of AI in next-generation libraries, however, come with challenges and considerations. Data privacy and security are paramount concerns, requiring libraries to implement robust measures to protect user information. Ensuring transparency and providing clear communication about data usage policies are essential in building and maintaining trust among library users. Libraries must prioritize the ethical use of AI technologies to safeguard user privacy and maintain the integrity of their services.

Algorithmic bias is another critical consideration in the implementation of AI in libraries. AI systems may inadvertently perpetuate biases present in training data, leading to biased recommendations or search results. Libraries must actively address and mitigate these biases to maintain fairness and impartiality in their services. By adopting measures to identify and correct biases in AI algorithms, libraries can ensure that their resources are accessible and relevant to all users, regardless of background or demographic factors.

User education and acceptance represent additional challenges in the integration of AI in libraries. Libraries need to invest in user education programs to familiarize patrons with AI tools and algorithms. Building awareness and understanding can foster acceptance and trust in AI-driven systems, ensuring that users are comfortable and confident in utilizing these technologies. By providing clear guidance and support, libraries can bridge the knowledge gap and empower users to make the most of the enhanced services facilitated by AI.

Looking to the future, the evolution of AI in information management for next-generation libraries is an ongoing process. Anticipated developments include advancements in AI algorithms, increased integration of AI in physical library spaces, and the emergence of novel applications catering to evolving user needs. As libraries continue to adapt and embrace innovation, AI will undoubtedly play a central role in shaping the future of information management and user engagement in the library landscape. The benefits of AI are poised to further enhance the capabilities of libraries, positioning them as dynamic and indispensable hubs of knowledge in the digital age.

AI for Collection Management: Revolutionizing Library Operations

In the ever-evolving landscape of libraries, the integration of artificial intelligence (AI) has emerged as a game-changer, revolutionizing traditional collection management practices. AI algorithms analyze vast amounts of data, automate tasks, and generate actionable insights, enabling libraries to optimize their collections, enhance resource discovery, and cater to the diverse needs of patrons. This essay explores the transformative role of AI in collection management within next-generation libraries, delving into its applications, benefits, and implications for library operations.

i) Automated Collection Development:

AI-powered tools facilitate automated collection development processes, empowering libraries to make data-driven decisions regarding resource acquisition, retention, and deselection. By analyzing patron usage patterns, demographic trends, and circulation data, AI algorithms identify gaps in the collection, recommend relevant acquisitions, and predict demand for specific materials. Moreover, machine learning algorithms can assess the relevance and quality of existing resources, enabling librarians to weed out obsolete or low-use items and optimize shelf space for materials that align with patrons' interests and preferences. This automation streamlines collection management workflows, reduces manual effort, and ensures that libraries maintain dynamic and responsive collections that meet the evolving needs of their communities.

ii) Enhanced Metadata Management:

Metadata plays a crucial role in facilitating resource discovery and navigation within library collections. AI technologies enhance metadata management processes by automating the extraction, enrichment, and classification of metadata associated with library materials. Natural language processing (NLP) algorithms analyze textual descriptions, titles, and subject headings to generate accurate and consistent metadata tags, improving search accuracy and relevance. Furthermore, AI-powered algorithms can identify relationships between different items in the collection, enabling librarians to create curated lists, thematic collections, and recommendation algorithms that enhance serendipitous discovery and engagement. By leveraging AI for metadata management, libraries enhance the accessibility and discoverability of their collections, ensuring that patrons can easily locate and access the resources they need.

iii) Predictive Analytics for Demand Forecasting:

Anticipating patron demand is a fundamental aspect of effective collection management. AI-driven predictive analytics enable libraries to forecast demand for specific materials, anticipate trends, and optimize resource allocation strategies. By analyzing historical circulation data, demographic information, and external factors such as socioeconomic trends and cultural events, AI algorithms can predict future demand for various library materials with a high degree of accuracy. This insight empowers librarians to proactively acquire popular items, adjust collection development priorities, and allocate resources efficiently, thereby reducing the likelihood of stockouts, improving patron satisfaction, and maximizing the return on investment in library collections. Predictive analytics also inform decisions regarding collection diversification, enabling libraries to cater to the diverse interests and preferences of their patrons while ensuring equitable access to information.

iv) Preservation and Conservation Strategies:

In addition to facilitating collection development and management, AI technologies play a crucial role in preservation and conservation efforts within libraries. Machine learning algorithms analyze digital and analog materials to identify signs of degradation, assess preservation risks, and prioritize conservation interventions. Moreover, AI-powered image recognition algorithms enable automated indexing and cataloging of archival materials, enhancing their discoverability and accessibility for researchers and scholars. By leveraging AI for preservation and conservation, libraries can safeguard cultural heritage materials, prolong their lifespan, and ensure that future generations have access to invaluable historical resources.

v) Ethical Considerations and Challenges:

While AI offers significant potential to enhance collection management in libraries, it also presents ethical considerations and challenges that must be addressed. One concern is algorithmic bias, whereby AI algorithms may reflect and perpetuate existing biases present in the data used for training. Librarians must be vigilant in monitoring and mitigating bias to ensure that collection development decisions are equitable and inclusive. Additionally, privacy concerns may arise when AI algorithms analyze patron data to inform collection management decisions. Libraries must prioritize patron privacy and adhere to relevant data protection regulations to maintain trust and transparency in their operations. Furthermore, the integration of AI requires investment in staff training and development to ensure that librarians have the necessary skills and expertise to harness AI effectively and ethically.

AI-driven collection management represents a paradigm shift in library operations, enabling libraries to optimize their collections, enhance resource discovery, and meet the diverse needs of their patrons. By leveraging AI for automated collection development, metadata management, demand forecasting, and preservation efforts, libraries can streamline workflows, improve accessibility, and maximize the impact of their collections. However, the ethical considerations and challenges associated with AI implementation underscore the importance of responsible AI practices, transparency, and ongoing dialogue within the library community. As libraries continue to evolve in the digital age, the integration of AI holds immense promise for transforming collection management and advancing the mission of providing equitable access to information for all.

Data Security and Privacy in AI-Driven Libraries

In the rapidly evolving landscape of libraries, where digital transformation and artificial intelligence (AI) are becoming increasingly prevalent, the paramount concern remains the protection of data security and privacy. As libraries harness the power of AI for intelligent information management and user engagement, they encounter a myriad of challenges in safeguarding sensitive information while maximizing the benefits of technological advancements. This essay delves into the intricacies of data security and privacy in AI-driven libraries, exploring the measures, challenges, and implications associated with ensuring the confidentiality, integrity, and availability of information.

The Landscape of AI-Driven Libraries

The integration of AI technologies in libraries has revolutionized traditional practices, enabling enhanced information discovery, personalized services, and efficient resource management. AI algorithms analyze vast amounts of data to generate insights, automate tasks, and deliver tailored recommendations to users. From intelligent search interfaces to virtual assistants, AI augments the capabilities of library systems, offering patrons seamless access to resources and enriching their overall experience. However, amidst these advancements lies the critical issue of data security and privacy, which necessitates careful consideration and proactive measures.

i) Challenges in Data Security and Privacy:

AI-driven libraries encounter several challenges in safeguarding data security and privacy. One of the primary concerns is the vast volume of data collected and processed by AI algorithms, including patron information, transaction records, and usage patterns. This abundance of data increases the risk of unauthorized access, data breaches, and privacy violations. Moreover, the complexity of AI systems poses challenges in understanding and mitigating potential security vulnerabilities and biases embedded within algorithms. Additionally, compliance with regulations such as the General Data Protection Regulation (GDPR) and the California Consumer Privacy Act (CCPA) adds another layer of complexity, requiring libraries to adhere to stringent data protection standards and ensure transparency in their practices.

Harnessing the Power of AI for Information Management and User Engagement

ii) Mitigating Risks and Ensuring Compliance:

To address these challenges, AI-driven libraries employ a range of strategies to mitigate risks and ensure compliance with data security and privacy regulations. Encryption techniques are utilized to protect sensitive data both in transit and at rest, ensuring that information remains secure even in the event of a breach. Access controls and authentication mechanisms restrict unauthorized access to confidential resources, while monitoring and auditing tools track user activities and detect suspicious behavior. Additionally, libraries implement robust data governance frameworks to define policies, procedures, and responsibilities related to data management, ensuring accountability and transparency in their operations.

iii) Ethical Considerations and Responsible AI Practices:

In the realm of AI-driven libraries, ethical considerations play a crucial role in guiding responsible practices and decision-making. Libraries must navigate ethical dilemmas related to data collection, algorithmic bias, and the use of AI-generated insights. Transparent communication with patrons regarding data collection practices and the purpose of AI-driven services fosters trust and promotes informed consent. Moreover, libraries must strive to mitigate biases inherent in AI algorithms by implementing measures such as algorithmic transparency, diversity in training data, and ongoing monitoring and evaluation. By upholding ethical principles and promoting responsible AI practices, libraries uphold their commitment to protecting patron privacy and fostering equitable access to information.

iv) Collaboration and Knowledge Sharing:

In the pursuit of data security and privacy, collaboration and knowledge sharing play a vital role in enabling libraries to stay abreast of emerging threats and best practices. Collaborative initiatives among libraries, industry partners, and cybersecurity experts facilitate the exchange of insights, resources, and expertise in addressing common challenges and enhancing the resilience of library systems. Additionally, participation in professional associations and forums dedicated to data security and privacy empowers librarians with the knowledge and tools needed to navigate complex legal and technological landscapes.

Data security and privacy are paramount considerations in the development and implementation of AI-driven libraries. By adopting proactive measures, adhering to stringent regulations, and upholding ethical principles, libraries can safeguard sensitive information while harnessing the transformative power of AI. Collaboration, transparency, and responsible AI practices are essential in fostering a culture of trust and accountability within the library community. As libraries continue to evolve in the digital age, prioritizing data security and privacy ensures that patrons can access information confidently and securely, thereby preserving the integrity and ethos of the library as a trusted institution in society.

Challenges and Considerations

While the integration of Artificial Intelligence (AI) into next-generation libraries presents numerous opportunities for enhancing information management and user engagement, it also brings forth several challenges and considerations that must be addressed. This section examines some of the key challenges associated with harnessing the power of AI in libraries and explores important considerations for ensuring successful implementation.

One of the primary challenges in adopting AI technologies in libraries is ethical considerations. AI algorithms often rely on vast amounts of data to make decisions and predictions, raising concerns about data privacy, bias, and fairness. Libraries must navigate the ethical implications of AI implementation, ensuring that user data is handled responsibly, and that AI systems are transparent and accountable. Additionally, efforts should be made to mitigate biases in AI algorithms to ensure equitable access to library resources and services for all patrons (Saeidnia, 2023).

Data privacy and security are another significant concern when implementing AI in libraries. As AI systems collect and analyse large volumes of user data, there is a risk of unauthorized access, data breaches, or misuse of sensitive information. Libraries must prioritize the protection of patron privacy and adhere to relevant data protection regulations. This includes implementing robust security measures, such as encryption, access controls, and regular security audits, to safeguard user data and maintain patron trust.

Ensuring inclusivity and accessibility is a critical consideration in AI-driven libraries. While AI technologies have the potential to enhance user experiences, there is a risk of exacerbating existing inequalities and digital divides. Libraries must address accessibility challenges to ensure that AI-powered services are accessible to patrons with disabilities or those from underserved communities. This may involve providing alternative access options, such as text-to-speech functionality or screen readers, and ensuring that AI interfaces comply with accessibility standards.

Furthermore, training and reskilling library staff to effectively utilize AI technologies is essential for successful implementation. Libraries must invest in staff training programs to familiarize librarians and other personnel with AI tools and methodologies. This includes developing expertise in data analytics, machine learning, and AI ethics, enabling staff to leverage AI technologies to their full potential and provide effective support to patrons.

AI offers significant potential for next-generation libraries, addressing challenges related to ethics, data privacy, inclusivity, and staff training is essential for successful implementation. By prioritizing these considerations and adopting a thoughtful and proactive approach to AI integration, libraries can harness the power of AI to enhance information management, user engagement, and service delivery in the digital age.

Future Developments in Next Generation Libraries

The future of next-generation libraries holds exciting possibilities as technology continues to advance and user expectations evolve. Several key developments are expected to shape the landscape of libraries, enhancing their capabilities and ensuring they remain relevant in the digital age.

i) **Advanced AI Integration:** As artificial intelligence (AI) technologies continue to mature, libraries will likely see even more advanced AI integration. AI algorithms may become more adept at understanding user preferences, providing highly personalized recommendations, and enhancing the overall user experience. Predictive analytics will play a larger role in resource management, enabling libraries to anticipate user needs, optimize collections, and allocate resources more efficiently.

ii) **Virtual and Augmented Reality Experiences:** The integration of virtual reality (VR) and augmented reality (AR) technologies is poised to revolutionize how patrons interact with library resources. Virtual library spaces could provide immersive environments for research, collaboration, and learning. AR applications may enhance the physical library experience by overlaying digital information onto real-world objects, creating interactive and dynamic learning environments.

iii) **Blockchain for Security and Authentication:** Blockchain technology holds promise for enhancing security and authentication in libraries. Blockchain can be employed to secure sensitive user data, ensure the integrity of digital collections, and streamline authentication processes for access to resources. This decentralized and tamper-resistant technology may play a crucial role in maintaining data privacy and security within library systems.

iv) **Open Access Initiatives:** The future of next-generation libraries may witness a stronger emphasis on open access initiatives. Libraries could take a leading role in advocating for open access to scholarly publications, supporting initiatives that promote the free and unrestricted access to research findings. Collaborative efforts between libraries, researchers, and publishers may result in a more open and accessible academic landscape.

v) **Integration of Internet of Things (IoT):** The Internet of Things (IoT) is likely to play a significant role in next-generation libraries, offering opportunities for smart and connected spaces. RFID technology, sensors, and IoT devices could be integrated to enhance the tracking and management of physical resources. Smart library spaces may adapt to user preferences, adjusting lighting, temperature, and other environmental factors to create a more comfortable and personalized experience.

vi) **Digital Scholarship and Data Literacy Initiatives:** With the increasing importance of digital scholarship, next-generation libraries may focus on promoting data literacy skills. Libraries may offer training programs and workshops to help users navigate and analyze large datasets. Collaboration with academic institutions and research centers could lead to the development of specialized services supporting digital scholarship and interdisciplinary research.

vii) **Collaborative Learning Spaces:** Future libraries are likely to evolve into dynamic hubs for collaborative learning. Flexible and interactive spaces will cater to diverse learning styles, encouraging group discussions, project work, and interdisciplinary collaboration. Digital whiteboards, interactive displays, and other technologies will facilitate seamless collaboration among library patrons.

viii) **Community Engagement through Social Media Integration:** Social media integration will continue to be a key aspect of community engagement for libraries. Libraries may leverage social platforms to connect with users, share updates, and promote events. Social media analytics could inform library services, helping institutions tailor their offerings to better meet the needs and preferences of their communities.

ix) **Emphasis on Sustainable Practices:** Next-generation libraries are likely to embrace sustainable practices, both in terms of technology and physical spaces. Green building initiatives, energy-efficient technologies, and eco-friendly resource management will become integral to library design. Digital collections and reduced paper usage will contribute to environmentally conscious library operations.

x) **Global Collaboration and Interconnected Libraries:** Libraries of the future may increasingly engage in global collaborations and partnerships. Digital platforms and technologies will facilitate the sharing of resources, expertise, and collections across borders. Interconnected libraries may collaborate on joint projects, creating a global network that enhances access to diverse knowledge and perspectives.

The future of next-generation libraries is marked by a convergence of advanced technologies, a commitment to open access, and a focus on creating dynamic and inclusive spaces. The evolving role of libraries as hubs for digital scholarship, community engagement, and innovative technologies positions them as vital institutions in the ongoing knowledge revolution. As these developments unfold, libraries will continue to adapt, ensuring they remain at the forefront of knowledge dissemination and community empowerment.

CONCLUSION

In the ever-evolving landscape of libraries, the integration of artificial intelligence (AI) has emerged as a transformative force, revolutionizing traditional practices and enhancing the delivery of services to patrons. The journey through the exploration of AI's role in next-generation libraries has uncovered a myriad of possibilities, challenges, and implications for intelligent information management and user engagement. As we conclude this discussion, it becomes evident that AI holds immense potential in shaping the future of libraries, empowering them to adapt to the digital age while preserving their fundamental mission of providing equitable access to information and knowledge.

The integration of AI technologies has catalyzed a paradigm shift in library services, enabling libraries to deliver personalized, efficient, and immersive experiences to patrons. From AI-driven recommendation systems to virtual assistants, libraries leverage AI to curate and disseminate information tailored to individual preferences and needs. Intelligent search interfaces powered by AI algorithms facilitate seamless discovery of resources, while automated content categorization and tagging streamline collection management processes. Moreover, AI-driven insights empower libraries to anticipate user demands, optimize resource allocation, and enhance the overall quality of service delivery.

At the heart of next-generation libraries lies a commitment to empowering patrons with the tools, resources, and skills needed to navigate the information landscape effectively. AI-powered technologies play a pivotal role in this endeavor by providing patrons with personalized recommendations, interactive learning experiences, and virtual assistance. By harnessing the power of AI, libraries facilitate equitable access to information, bridge digital divides, and foster lifelong learning and literacy. Furthermore, AI-driven initiatives such as predictive analytics for demand forecasting enable libraries to proactively address community needs, ensuring that resources are allocated efficiently to meet evolving demands.

Despite the transformative potential of AI in libraries, it is not without its challenges and ethical considerations. Libraries must navigate issues related to data security, privacy, algorithmic bias, and digital equity to ensure that AI-driven initiatives uphold ethical principles and promote inclusivity. Safeguarding patron data and privacy rights, mitigating biases inherent in AI algorithms, and fostering transparency in AI-driven decision-making are paramount in building trust and accountability within the library community. Additionally, libraries must prioritize digital literacy initiatives to empower patrons with the skills needed to critically evaluate and navigate AI-driven technologies effectively.

In addressing these challenges, collaboration and knowledge sharing emerge as critical enablers in fostering innovation and resilience within the library community. Collaborative initiatives among libraries, industry partners, and academic institutions facilitate the exchange of insights, resources, and best practices in AI implementation and management. Furthermore, participation in professional associations and forums dedicated to AI in libraries provides librarians with opportunities to stay abreast of emerging trends, share experiences, and collectively address common challenges. By fostering a culture of collaboration and knowledge sharing, libraries can leverage collective expertise to overcome barriers and maximize the benefits of AI in advancing their missions.

Looking ahead, the future of next-generation libraries lies in embracing emerging technologies, adapting to evolving user needs, and staying at the forefront of innovation. As AI continues to evolve, libraries must remain agile and responsive, continuously evaluating and integrating new technologies to enhance service delivery and user engagement. Moreover, libraries must prioritize diversity, equity, and inclusion in AI-driven initiatives, ensuring that technologies are accessible and inclusive for all patrons. By embracing a human-centered approach to technology integration, libraries can leverage AI to augment, rather than replace, the invaluable expertise and empathy of library staff in serving their communities.

In conclusion, the integration of AI represents a pivotal moment in the evolution of libraries, empowering them to navigate the complexities of the digital age while remaining steadfast in their commitment to serving their communities. Through intelligent information management and user engagement, AI-driven libraries deliver personalized, efficient, and equitable services that enrich the lives of patrons and contribute to the advancement of knowledge and literacy. However, this journey is not without its challenges, and libraries must remain vigilant in addressing issues related to data security, privacy, bias, and digital equity. By prioritizing collaboration, transparency, and ethical considerations, libraries can harness the transformative power of AI to shape a future where information is accessible, inclusive, and empowering for all. As we embark on this journey towards next-generation libraries, let us remain guided by the values of inclusivity, accessibility, and lifelong learning, ensuring that libraries continue to thrive as vibrant hubs of knowledge, community, and innovation in the digital age.

REFERENCES

Chiancone, C. (2023, August 4). *The Library of the Future: AI in Public Libraries*. https://www.linkedin.com/pulse/library-future-ai-public-libraries-chris-chiancone/

Farney, T. (2020). Library technology: Innovating technologies, services, and practices. *College & Undergraduate Libraries*, *27*(2–4), 51–55. doi:10.1080/10691316.2020.1952776

Grimes, N., & Porter, W. (2023). Closing the digital divide through digital equity: The role of libraries and librarians. *Public Library Quarterly*, 1–32. doi:10.1080/01616846.2023.2251348

Herrlich, H. (2023, May 23). *The Future of Libraries: AI and Machine learning – Fordham Library News*. https://librarynews.blog.fordham.edu/2023/05/23/the-future-of-libraries-ai-and-machine-learning/

Hodonu-Wusu, J. O. (2024). The rise of artificial intelligence in libraries: The ethical and equitable methodologies, and prospects for empowering library users. *AI and Ethics*. Advance online publication. doi:10.1007/s43681-024-00432-7

Hussain, A. (2020). Cutting edge. In Advances in library and information science (ALIS) book series (pp. 16–27). doi:10.4018/978-1-7998-1482-5.ch002

Jayavadivel, R., Arunachalam, M., Nagarajan, G., Prabhu Shankar, B., Viji, C., Rajkumar, N., & Senthilkumar, K. R. (2024). Historical Overview of AI Adoption in Libraries. In K. Senthilkumar (Ed.), *AI-Assisted Library Reconstruction* (pp. 267–289). IGI Global. doi:10.4018/979-8-3693-2782-1.ch015

Kumar, N., Antoniraj, S., Jayanthi, S., Mirdula, S., Selvaraj, S., Rajkumar, N., & Senthilkumar, K. R. (2024). Educational Technology and Libraries Supporting Online Learning. In K. Senthilkumar (Ed.), *AI-Assisted Library Reconstruction* (pp. 209–237). IGI Global. doi:10.4018/979-8-3693-2782-1.ch012

LibLime. (2023, December 4). *Revolutionizing Library Cataloging with Artificial Intelligence (AI)*. https://www.linkedin.com/pulse/revolutionizing-library-cataloging-artificial-intelligence-ai-coo9c

PandaS.HasanS.KaurN. (2024). Enhancing Library 5.0: Leveraging cloud and FoG computing for intelligent services and resource management. *ResearchGate*. doi:10.6084/m9.figshare.25231316.v1

Rajkumar, N., Tabassum, H., Muthulingam, S., Mohanraj, A., Viji, C., Kumar, N., & Senthilkumar, K. R. (2024). Anticipated Requirements and Expectations in the Digital Library. In K. Senthilkumar (Ed.), *AI-Assisted Library Reconstruction* (pp. 1–20). IGI Global., doi:10.4018/979-8-3693-2782-1.ch001

Saeidnia, H. R. (2023). Ethical artificial intelligence (AI): Confronting bias and discrimination in the library and information industry. *Library Hi Tech News*. Advance online publication. doi:10.1108/LHTN-10-2023-0182

Senthilkumar, K. (Ed.). (2024). *AI-Assisted Library Reconstruction*. IGI Global. doi:10.4018/979-8-3693-2782-1

Senthilkumar, K. R. (2024). Revolutionizing thrust manufacturing. In *Advances in computational intelligence and robotics book series* (pp. 80–93). doi:10.4018/979-8-3693-2615-2.ch005

Senthilkumar, K. R., Jagajeevan, R., & Sangeetha, S. (2024). Impact of AI on Library and Information Science in Higher Institutions in India: A Comprehensive Analysis of Technological Integration and Educational Implications. In K. Senthilkumar (Ed.), *AI-Assisted Library Reconstruction* (pp. 21–33). IGI Global. doi:10.4018/979-8-3693-2782-1.ch002

Silva, D. (2023, July 22). Optimizing website user Experience: How AI personalization algorithms drive conversion rates. *Medium*. https://uxplanet.org/optimizing-website-user-experience-how-ai-personalization-algorithms-drive-conversion-rates-6bcc63fa366d

Sivaraj, P., Madhan, V., Mallika, V., & Senthilkumar, K. R. (2024). Enhancing Library Services Through Optimization Algorithms and Data Analytics: Enhancing Library Services Mathematical Model. In K. Senthilkumar (Ed.), *AI-Assisted Library Reconstruction* (pp. 290–306). IGI Global. doi:10.4018/979-8-3693-2782-1.ch016

Chapter 5
Exploring the Transformative Impact of Artificial Intelligence on Research Library Management

M. Sathiya
 https://orcid.org/0000-0003-0285-8302
Sri Krishna Arts and Science College, India

M. Vidya
Sri Krishna Arts and Science College, India

ABSTRACT

Artificial intelligence (AI) has wielded considerable influence over diverse facets of contemporary society, including the intricate dynamics of research libraries. This chapter undertakes an in-depth exploration of AI's profound impact on library functionalities, services, and user interfaces. Through an exhaustive review of scholarly works and empirical studies, the authors scrutinize how AI technologies such as machine learning, natural language processing, and data analytics are fundamentally altering the landscape of information retrieval, resource curation, and scholarly discourse within research libraries. Moreover, they delve into the nuanced challenges and prospects stemming from the integration of AI, encompassing concerns regarding privacy, algorithmic bias, and the evolving roles and responsibilities of librarians. By grasping and leveraging AI's potent influence, research libraries can adeptly navigate and thrive amidst the swiftly evolving digital milieu, thereby amplifying their support for scholarly pursuits and the dissemination of knowledge.

INTRODUCTION

Artificial Intelligence (AI) is revolutionizing various industries, and research libraries are no exception. The integration of AI technologies has brought about transformative changes in the dynamics of these

DOI: 10.4018/979-8-3693-5593-0.ch005

institutions. In this introduction, we will explore the significant impact that AI has had on research libraries and the way they operate. AI has enabled research libraries to streamline their processes and enhance their services in several ways. One of the key areas where AI has made a difference is in information retrieval. With the vast amount of data available, AI algorithms can effectively analyze and extract relevant information, saving researchers valuable time and effort. This has greatly improved the efficiency of research library systems and made it easier for users to access the information they need. Furthermore, AI has played a crucial role in knowledge discovery and recommendation. By analyzing user preferences, AI algorithms can suggest relevant research papers, articles, or books, tailored to individual research interests. This personalized approach enhances the research experience and helps researchers explore new areas of knowledge.

AI has also contributed to the preservation and digitization of library collections. With the help of AI technologies, libraries can digitize their vast physical collections, making them accessible remotely to a wider audience. This has expanded the reach of research libraries and facilitated collaboration among researchers worldwide. Moreover, AI has empowered research libraries in data analysis and visualization. Lund, BD (2024) Since its debut in November 2022, the artificial intelligence chatbot ChatGPT has attracted significant interest from a variety of academic fields. Libraries can utilize AI algorithms to extract insights from large datasets, enabling researchers to gain deeper insights and make informed decisions based on data-driven evidence. The use of generative artificial intelligence (AI) in academic research writing has completely changed the area by providing academics with strong tools like ChatGPT and Bard to help with idea development and content creation (Tang A, 2023)

Emerging Conceptual Framework

The transformative impact of artificial intelligence (AI) on research library dynamics presents a complex and multifaceted landscape that requires a comprehensive conceptual framework for exploration. examines the main features of AI to assist surgeons in comprehending, assessing, and contributing to emerging breakthroughs in AI (Daniel A Hashimoto 2018).

This emerging framework aims to delve into the various dimensions of AI's influence on research libraries, encompassing technological advancements, user experiences, marketing programs organizational dynamics, and broader societal implications. (Samer Elhajjar, 2020) examined how to incorporate artificial intelligence (AI) into marketing education programs from the perspectives of business students, marketing educators, and practitioners.

The framework is structured around several key elements:

Technological Advancements: This dimension focuses on the core AI technologies driving change within research libraries, such as machine learning, natural language processing (NLP), data analytics, and automation. Understanding the capabilities and limitations of these technologies is essential for assessing their impact on information retrieval, resource management, and scholarly communication. Proponents of artificial intelligence predict that the new educational environment will be characterized by one-on-one support for each student's path, dynamic and involved evaluation, and personalized learning (Stephen Murgatrotd, 2024)

User Experiences and Engagement: AI-powered systems are reshaping user experiences within research libraries, offering personalized recommendations, intelligent search interfaces, and interactive virtual assistants. This dimension explores how AI enhances user engagement, facilitates access to relevant resources, and supports collaborative research endeavors.

Organizational Adaptation: AI adoption necessitates organizational changes within research libraries, including redefined roles and responsibilities for librarians, new workflows for data management and analysis, and strategic planning for AI integration. Examining these organizational dynamics provides insights into the challenges and opportunities associated with AI implementation.

Ethical and Societal Implications: AI raises ethical considerations related to data privacy, algorithmic bias, transparency, and accountability. This dimension explores the ethical frameworks and policies necessary to ensure responsible AI use within research libraries and mitigate potential risks to user trust and fairness.

Collaborative Partnerships and Innovation: AI's transformative impact extends beyond individual libraries, fostering collaborations with industry partners, academic institutions, and technology providers. This dimension investigates collaborative initiatives, innovation ecosystems, and emerging trends in AI-enabled library services and infrastructure.

Natural Language Processing (NLP): The system applies NLP algorithms to analyze and understand the user's search query. It takes into account factors like the context of the query, synonyms, and related terms to ensure a comprehensive search. User Profiling: Ex Libris Primo creates user profiles based on individual search history, preferences, and behavior. It tracks the user's interactions within the system, including the resources they have accessed, saved, or cited. This data is used to personalize search results for each user.

Machine Learning: The system incorporates machine learning algorithms that learn from user feedback. As users interact with the search results by clicking, saving, or citing certain resources, the system learns their preferences and adjusts future search results accordingly. This iterative learning process helps improve the relevance of results over time.

Metadata Analysis: Ex Libris Primo examines the metadata associated with each resource, such as titles, authors, abstracts, subjects, and keywords. By analyzing this metadata, the system identifies potential matches between user queries and relevant resources.

Usage Statistics: The system considers usage statistics and popularity metrics in determining the relevance of search results. It takes into account factors like the number of times a resource has been accessed, cited, or recommended by other users, as well as the recency of the resource's publication or availability.

Faceted Search: Ex Libris Primo provides a faceted search interface that allows users to narrow down their search results using various facets such as author, subject, publication year, language, and more. This helps users quickly refine their search and find the most relevant resources within their specific criteria.

Full-Text Search: The system enables users to perform full-text searches, allowing them to search for keywords or phrases within the content of resources. This feature enhances the precision of search results and enables users to find specific information within documents.

Resource Access: Ex Libris Primo provides seamless access to both physical and digital resources. It integrates with library systems to display the availability and location of physical items, such as books or journals, and offers direct links to electronic resources, including e-books, e-journals, and databases. Users can easily access the resources they need, whether they are available online or at the library.

Personalization: The system offers personalized features to enhance the user's experience. Users can create accounts and save their search queries, favorite resources, and search results for future reference. They can also set preferences to customize their search experience and receive personalized recommendations based on their interests and past interactions.

Advanced Browsing: Ex Libris Primo includes advanced browsing capabilities, allowing users to explore resources beyond traditional search queries. Users can browse through curated collections, featured items, new releases, or subject-specific collections. This facilitates serendipitous discovery and helps users explore a wide range of resources related to their interests.

Citation Management: The system often integrates with citation management tools, such as Zotero or EndNote, enabling users to export or save citation information directly from search results. This feature simplifies the process of managing references and citing sources in academic research.

Examples of AI-Powered Knowledge Discovery and Recommendation Systems Being Used in Research Libraries

There are several examples of AI-powered knowledge discovery and recommendation systems being used in research libraries are as follows:

Ex Libris Primo: Ex Libris Primo discovery and delivery solution, which uses AI algorithms to personalize search results for users based on their search history, preferences, and behavior. This system presents users with relevant resources, leading to more efficient and effective research.

The Hathi Trust Research Center: It is most AI-powered knowledge discovery and recommendation system being used in research libraries. This center provides access to millions of digital books and texts, and its algorithms analyze user interactions with materials to automate the generation of recommendations for future research. The Hathi Trust Research Center (HTRC) is a collaborative research center that provides researchers with access to a vast digital library for text analysis. Hathi Trust is a partnership of major research libraries and institutions that have come together to build a comprehensive digital collection of books and other materials. The HTRC enables scholars to perform computational research on the Hathi Trust Digital Library, which includes millions of digitized books, journals, and other textual resources. Researchers can access and analyze these texts using computational methods to gain insights, discover patterns, and conduct data-driven investigations.

Optical Character Recognition (OCR): OCR tools like Tesseract and Abbyy Fine Reader enable the conversion of scanned documents and images into editable and searchable text. This helps in digitizing and extracting information from physical library resources.

Information Retrieval: Libraries can leverage AI-powered search engines and information retrieval tools such as Elastic Search and Apache Solr to improve search accuracy, speed, and relevancy for users looking to access library resources.

Chatbots and Virtual Assistants: AI-driven chatbots, virtual assistants, and voice recognition systems can assist library users in finding resources, answering frequently asked questions, and providing general information about library services and policies. Platforms like Dialog flow and IBM Watson are commonly used for developing conversational AI applications.

Reference Management Tools: Tools like Mendeley, Zotero, or EndNote help researchers organize and manage their references, citations, and research papers efficiently.

Literature Search Engines: Platforms such as Google Scholar, PubMed, or IEEE Xplore provide comprehensive databases of academic literature, allowing researchers to search for relevant articles, papers, and research materials.

Text Mining and Analysis Tools: Software like NVivo, R, or Python libraries like NLTK or spaCy enable researchers to analyze and extract insights from large volumes of text or conduct sentiment analysis, topic modeling, and other textual research methods.

Data Visualization Tools: Tools such as Tableau, Plotly, or ggplot in R enable researchers to create visually appealing and interactive charts, graphs, and infographics for presenting research findings.

Collaboration and Communication Tools: Platforms like Slack, Microsoft Teams, or Google Docs facilitate seamless collaboration and communication among researchers working on shared documents, projects, or experiments.

Plagiarism Checkers: Software like Turnitin or Grammarly can help researchers ensure the originality and integrity of their work by detecting any potential instances of plagiarism.

Research Networking Platforms: Platforms like ResearchGate or Academia.edu allow researchers to connect, collaborate, and share their work with peers, discover new research opportunities, and stay updated with the latest developments in their field.

Recommender Systems: AI-powered recommendation engines like IBM Watson Discovery or Amazon Personalize can help library users discover relevant books, articles, or resources based on their interests, reading history, or similar users' preferences.

Digital Document Analysis: AI tools like Doc2Vec or DeepAI's Document Understanding platform can analyze and extract key information from digitized documents, enabling efficient search and organization of library materials. The universalization of higher education, the university of the new millennium must urgently plan, design, develop, and apply digital skills (Ocaña-Fernández, 2019).

Text-to-Speech (TTS) Systems: TTS systems such as Google Text-to-Speech or Amazon Polly can convert written text into spoken audio, making it accessible to users with visual impairments or those who prefer an auditory learning experience.

Automated Metadata Extraction: AI algorithms, such as those used in Google Cloud Vision API or Microsoft Azure Cognitive Services, can automatically extract metadata from images or documents, assisting in cataloging and indexing library resources.

Challenges AI Faces in Research Library Dynamics

Data Quality: AI algorithms heavily rely on the quality and availability of data. Research library data can be diverse, complex, and often fragmented. Issues such as incomplete or inconsistent metadata, variations in data formats, or outdated information can negatively impact the performance and accuracy of AI systems.

Bias and Fairness: AI algorithms may unintentionally perpetuate biases present in the data they are trained on. This could lead to biased search results, recommendations, or decision-making processes. It is crucial to carefully curate training data and regularly evaluate and mitigate bias to ensure fair and unbiased AI applications in research libraries.

Privacy and Security: Research libraries deal with sensitive user data, including personal information, search history, and reading habits. AI systems need to respect user privacy and maintain robust security measures to protect this data from unauthorized access, misuse, or breaches. The lack of open source conversational software platforms has been the only obstacle to such implementation (Bagchi, 2020).

Interpretability and Explainability: AI models often function as "black boxes," making it difficult to understand how they reach their conclusions or recommendations. In research libraries, where transparency and trust are paramount, it is essential to develop AI systems that are explainable and provide clear justifications for their results to gain user confidence.

Integration and Adoption: AI implementation in research libraries requires seamless integration into existing library systems, workflows, and user interfaces. Successful adoption of AI solutions necessitates collaboration with library professionals, training staff on AI technologies, and addressing any concerns or resistance to change.

Ethical Considerations: As AI systems become more sophisticated, ethical considerations become crucial. Questions regarding data ownership, algorithmic accountability, consent, and the impact on academic freedom and intellectual property must be carefully considered and addressed in the context of research library dynamics.

Merits of AI Tools in Library Management

There are various benefits of AI in libraries. Here are some of the benefits:

Digital Library Management: Large volumes of information and data are generated daily in libraries. Adopting AI tools can assist in managing this digital data efficiently and enabling libraries to smoothly organize, maintain, and access their collections.

Enhanced User Experience: AI-powered chatbots and recommendation engines can help libraries to provide personalized, real-time assistance to users, improving the overall user experience. Chatbots can accurately answer users' queries 24/7, while recommendation engines suggest relevant books and other resources based on their interests, preferences, and previous borrowing history.

Automation: Implementation of AI tools helps automate some of the repetitive tasks, such as data entry, sorting, and cataloging of books, that librarians and library staff have to carry out daily. This leaves room for more critical and strategic work to be done.

Cost Savings: AI tools reduce the burden on staff, allowing them to work more efficiently, which leads to cost savings. AI tools enabled automation of manual tasks reduces the cost of labor resulting in overall savings in operating costs for a library.

Improved Accessibility: AI-powered text-to-speech systems and OCR technologies can convert written materials into audio, improving accessibility for visually impaired or differently-abled users.

Data-Driven Insights: AI tools can help analyze and provide insights into borrowing and usage patterns. This information assists libraries in making sound decisions regarding collections management and resource allocation.

Preservation and Conservation: AI tools can monitor temperature, humidity, and other environmental factors that influence the safety and preservation of physical items in a library's collection. By detecting changes such as mold, discoloration, or other degradation signs, AI can help in protecting books, manuscripts, and other resources.

CONCLUSION

AI in research library management has many transformative benefits. Implementing AI-powered tools in library operations can increase efficiency by automating repetitive tasks such as cataloging and sorting books, allowing library staff to focus on more complex tasks. Additionally, AI can enhance the user experience by providing customized recommendations and real-time assistance, making it easier for users to discover and access the resources they need. Another benefit of AI is its ability to analyze and gain insights from data, helping libraries to make informed decisions about collections management, resource allocation, and other strategic decisions. By reducing staff time and labor costs, AI can also contribute to cost savings for research libraries. Furthermore, AI can improve accessibility by providing features such as text-to-speech conversion and real-time language translation, enabling users with diverse abilities and language preferences to access library resources.

Additionally, AI technology can help libraries with resource preservation through real-time monitoring and preventative maintenance, ultimately leading to better long-term preservation of valuable collections. Lastly, AI technology offers improved security measures by monitoring access to library resources and detecting potential security breaches, ultimately helping with theft prevention. Overall, through the implementation of AI, research libraries will be able to enhance their services and adapt to the changing needs of their users.

REFERENCES

Arya, H., & Mishra, P. (2011). Twitter: A new tool for academic libraries. *Journal of Advancements in Library Sciences*, *1*(2), 11–17.

Asemi, A., & Asemi, N. (2018). Intelligent library technologies: A review of knowledge-based assistance in library services. *International Journal of Information Science and Management*, *16*(2), 91–108.

Asemi, A., Ko, I., & Nowkarizi, M. (2020). Application of Natural Language Processing in Library Cataloging: A Review. *Library Philosophy and Practice*.

Ayyadevara, R. (2018). Machine learning: Unveiling patterns in big data. *Journal of Artificial Intelligence Research*, *15*(1), 102–120.Godfrey C (2008) Second life: A virtual world for libraries. *RSR. Reference Services Review*, *36*(4), 433–439.

Bagchi, M. (2020). Conceptualizing a library chatbot using open-source conversational artificial intelligence. *DESIDOC Journal of Library and Information Technology*, *40*(6), 329–333. doi:10.14429/djlit.40.06.15611

Behan, J., & Keeffe, O. (2006). The development of an intelligent library assistant robot. In *Proceedings of the IASTED international conference on artificial intelligence and applications* (pp. 474–479). Academic Press.

Brady, L. (2024). ChatGPT in medical libraries, possibilities and future directions: An integrative review. *Health Information and Libraries Journal*, *41*(1), 4–15. Advance online publication. doi:10.1111/hir.12518 PMID:38200693

Brown, L. M. (2022). Gendered artificial intelligence in libraries: Opportunities to deconstruct sexism and gender binarism. *Journal of Library Administration*, *62*(1), 19–30. doi:10.1080/01930826.2021.2006979

Elhajjar, S., Karam, S., & Borna, S. (2020, November 3). Artificial intelligence in marketing education programs. *Marketing Education Review*, *31*(1), 2–13. doi:10.1080/10528008.2020.1835492

Goli, M., Sahu, A. K., Bag, S., & Dhamija, P. (2023, February 24). Users' acceptance of artificial intelligence-based chatbots: An empirical study. *International Journal of Technology and Human Interaction*, *19*(1), 1–18. doi:10.4018/IJTHI.318481

Gujral, M., Smith, J., Johnson, A., Martin, R., Wilson, S., & Davis, L. (2019). Chatbot applications in libraries: A literature review. *International Journal of Information Science and Management, 17*(2), 87–102.

Hamad, F., Al-Fadel, M., & Fakhouri, H. (2022). The provision of smart service at academic libraries and associated challenges. *Journal of Librarianship and Information Science, 096100062211141.* Advance online publication. doi:10.1177/09610006221114173

Haney, B. S. (2018). The Perils & Promises of Artificial General Intelligence. SSRN *Electronic Journal*. doi:10.2139/ssrn.3261254

Hao, J., & Zhang, H. (2020). The ethical challenges of using AI in education. *International Journal of Information and Education Technology (IJIET), 10*(8), 575–580.

Hashimoto, D. A., Rosman, G., Rus, D., & Meireles, O. R. (2018, July). Artificial Intelligence in Surgery: Promises and Perils. *Annals of Surgery, 268*(1), 70–76. doi:10.1097/SLA.0000000000002693 PMID:29389679

Hussain, S. (2022). Transforming library services in the age of modern information technology. *Journal of Library Innovation, 14*(3), 45–62.

Hwang, G.-J., & Chang, C.-Y. (2021). A review of opportunities and challenges of chatbots in education. *Interactive Learning Environments*, 1–14. doi:10.1080/10494820.2021.1952615

Jange, S. (2015, January). Innovative services and practices in academic libraries. *2015 4th International Symposium on Emerging Trends and Technologies in Libraries and Information Services.* 10.1109/ETTLIS.2015.7048194

Kamal, M., Bhat, S. A., & Wani, G. M. (2020). Role of academic libraries in providing personalized services in the era of the digital world. *International Journal of Innovative Technology and Exploring Engineering, 9*(4S), 1067–1072.

Lee, A. S., Babenko, O., George, M., & Daniels, V. (2022, September 6). The promises and perils of remote proctoring using artificial intelligence. *Canadian Medical Education Journal*. Advance online publication. doi:10.36834/cmej.74299 PMID:37304635

Mckie, I. A. S., & Narayan, B. (2019). Enhancing the academic library experience with chatbots: An exploration of research and implications for practice. *Journal of the Australian Library and Information Association, 68*(3), 268–277. doi:10.1080/24750158.2019.1611694

Murgatroyd, S. (2024, February 25). Artificial Intelligence and future of higher education. *Revista Paraguya Education a Distancia, 5*(1), 4–11. doi:10.56152/reped2024-vol5num1-art1

Noh, Y. (2022). A study on the discussion on Library 5.0 and the generation of Library 1.0 to Library 5.0. *Journal of Librarianship and Information Science*. Advance online publication. doi:10.1177/09610006221106183

Ocaña-Fernández, Valenzuela-Fernández, Y., & Garro-Aburto, L. A. (2019). Artificial Intelligence and Its Implications in Higher Education. *J. Educ. Psychol. Propos. Represent., 7*, 553–568.

Panda, S., & Kaur, N. (2023). Exploring the viability of ChatGPT as an alternative to traditional chatbot systems in library and information centers. *Library Hi Tech News, 40*(3), 22–25. doi:10.1108/LHTN-02-2023-0032

Parkar, R., Payare, Y., Mithari, K., Nambiar, J., & Gupta, J. (2021, July 1). AI and web-based interactive college enquiry chatbot. *2021 13th International Conference on Electronics, Computers and Artificial Intelligence (ECAI)*. 10.1109/ECAI52376.2021.9515065

Rajkumar, N., Tabassum, H., Muthulingam, S., Mohanraj, A., Viji, C., Kumar, N., & Senthilkumar, K. R. (2024). Anticipated requirements and expectations in the digital library. In Advances in Library and Information Science (pp. 1–20). doi:10.4018/979-8-3693-2782-1.ch001

Rubin, V. L., Chen, Y., & Thorimbert, L. M. (2010). Artificially intelligent conversational agents in libraries. *Library Hi Tech, 28*(4), 496–522. doi:10.1108/07378831011096196

Sanji, M., Behzadi, H., & Gomroki, G. (2022). Chatbot: An intelligent tool for libraries. *Library Hi Tech News, 39*(3), 17–20. doi:10.1108/LHTN-01-2021-0002

Senthilkumar, K. R., Jagajeevan, R., & Sangeetha, S. (2024). Impact of AI on library and information science in higher institutions in India. In Advances in Library and Information Science (pp. 21–33). doi:10.4018/979-8-3693-2782-1.ch002

Tang, A., Li, K.-K., Kwok, K. O., Cao, L., Luong, S., & Tam, W. (2023). The importance of transparency: Declaring the use of generative artificial intelligence (AI) in academic writing. *Journal of Nursing Scholarship*. Advance online publication. doi:10.1111/jnu.12938 PMID:37904646

Chapter 6
Exploring the Top ChatGPT Libraries for Powerful Conversational AI

Delma Thaliyan
Christ University, India

Joe Joseph
Christ University, India

V. L. Helen Josephine
Christ University, India

ABSTRACT

This research analyzes the need for top ChatGPT libraries and their usage today. It focuses on the features, benefits, and drawbacks of ChatGPT through in-depth interviews to uncover nuanced insights into library preferences and usage patterns. The findings reveal diverse perspectives among developers, highlighting preferences for libraries based on ease of integration and customization. Participants emphasize the significance of user-friendly interfaces and robust documentation in shaping positive experiences with ChatGPT libraries. Additionally, themes emerge around the need for continuous updates to address evolving AI challenges. Through in-depth insights from developers, the study elucidates the importance of user-friendly interfaces, adaptability, and efficient documentation, providing valuable guidance for developers seeking to optimize their conversational AI projects. This research contributes essential qualitative dimensions to the evaluation of ChatGPT libraries, offering actionable insights for the development community.

1. INTRODUCTION TO CHATGPT AND CONVERSATIONAL AI

Conversational AI is revolutionizing the way businesses interact with their customers. With advancements in natural language processing and machine learning, chatbots have become more intelligent

DOI: 10.4018/979-8-3693-5593-0.ch006

and sophisticated than ever before. One powerful tool in the realm of conversational AI is ChatGPT, a language model developed by OpenAI (Senthilkumar, 2024).

ChatGPT is designed to generate human-like responses based on the given input. It can hold engaging conversations, answer questions, and provide recommendations, making it an invaluable asset for businesses looking to enhance their customer experience (Senthilkumar, 2024).

The beauty of ChatGPT lies in its versatility. It can be integrated into various platforms such as websites, messaging apps, or even voice assistants, allowing businesses to meet their customers wherever they are. Whether it's providing support, collecting feedback, or assisting with sales inquiries, ChatGPT can handle a wide range of conversational tasks (Senthilkumar, 2019).

To harness the power of ChatGPT, developers have created several libraries that make it easier to implement and customize the model according to specific business needs. These libraries provide a convenient interface, pre-trained models, and tools for fine-tuning, enabling developers to create highly interactive and intelligent chatbot experiences (*Comparison of E- Resources with Their Usage Statistics in Southern Region*, n.d.).

In this blog post, we will explore some of the top ChatGPT libraries available, each with its unique features and capabilities. From user-friendly interfaces to advanced customization options, these libraries offer a seamless integration process and open up a world of possibilities for businesses looking to leverage the power of conversational AI.

So, whether you're a developer looking to enhance your chatbot capabilities or a business owner seeking to provide exceptional customer service, join us on this journey as we delve into the world of ChatGPT and discover the top libraries that can take your conversational AI to new heights (Shiddiqi et al., 2023).

2. UNDERSTANDING THE IMPORTANCE OF CHATGPT LIBRARIES

In the world of conversational AI, ChatGPT libraries play a crucial role in enabling powerful and dynamic interactions between chatbots and users. These libraries act as a foundation for developers, providing them with the necessary tools and resources to create intelligent chatbot experiences.

One of the key reasons why understanding the importance of ChatGPT libraries is essential is their ability to enhance the conversational capabilities of chatbots. These libraries come equipped with pre-trained models that have been fine-tuned using large amounts of data, allowing chatbots to understand and respond to a wide range of user inputs (X. Wang et al., 2024).

By leveraging ChatGPT libraries, developers can save significant time and effort in building conversational AI systems from scratch. These libraries provide a wealth of pre-built components, such as natural language processing modules, dialogue management systems, and response generation algorithms. This not only expedites the development process but also ensures the chatbot's responses are coherent, contextually relevant, and engaging (Senthilkumar, 2024).

Moreover, ChatGPT libraries often come with customization options, allowing developers to fine-tune the chatbot's behavior according to specific use cases or domains. This flexibility empowers developers to create chatbots that align with their brand's tone of voice, adhere to industry-specific guidelines, or cater to unique user requirements (L. Zhang et al., 2023).

Another aspect of ChatGPT libraries that makes them invaluable is their ability to continuously improve over time. As developers deploy chatbots using these libraries and gather user feedback, they can fine-tune and update the models, leading to iterative enhancements in chatbot performance. This ensures that the chatbot remains up-to-date, adaptive to changing user needs, and capable of delivering exceptional conversational experiences.

Overall, understanding the importance of ChatGPT libraries is crucial for developers and businesses looking to harness the power of conversational AI. These libraries provide the foundation, tools, and flexibility necessary to create intelligent and engaging chatbot experiences, ultimately driving customer satisfaction, user engagement, and business success.

3. OPENAI'S OFFICIAL CHATGPT LIBRARY

OpenAI's official ChatGPT library is a powerful tool that allows developers to integrate Conversational AI capabilities into their applications. With this library, you can tap into the advanced language model of ChatGPT and create interactive and dynamic conversational experiences for your users (Belgibaev et al., 2024).

Designed by OpenAI, the ChatGPT library offers a user-friendly interface and a comprehensive set of tools to facilitate the development process. It provides developers with the flexibility to fine-tune the model on custom datasets, enabling personalized conversational experiences tailored to specific domains or use cases (J. Wang et al., 2024).

The library also comes with helpful features such as system-level instructions, which allow developers to provide high-level guidance to the model during conversations. This helps steer the AI's responses in a desired direction, ensuring more meaningful and contextually appropriate interactions.

Moreover, OpenAI's official ChatGPT library incorporates safety mitigations to prevent the generation of harmful or biased content. OpenAI has made significant efforts to address concerns regarding the responsible use of AI, and the library includes features like moderation and content filtering to maintain a safe and respectful environment for users.

The availability of detailed documentation and examples further enhances the usability of OpenAI's ChatGPT library. Developers can easily get started, explore different features, and leverage the library's capabilities to create conversational AI applications that meet their specific requirements.

By utilizing OpenAI's official ChatGPT library, developers can unlock the potential of Conversational AI and deliver interactive, engaging, and intelligent experiences to their users. Whether it's building virtual assistants, chatbots, or customer support systems, this library provides the necessary tools and resources to create powerful and effective conversational applications (Pramanik et al., 2023).

3.1 Features and Capabilities

When it comes to developing powerful conversational AI, having the right tools and libraries is crucial. In this section, we will explore the top ChatGPT libraries and delve into their features and capabilities.

i) OpenAI GPT-3 API:

The OpenAI GPT-3 API is a widely popular library that provides access to the powerful GPT-3 language model. With this library, developers can leverage the cutting-edge capabilities of GPT-3 for conversational AI applications. It offers a wide range of features, including natural language understanding, response generation, sentiment analysis, and context awareness. The GPT-3 API allows developers to create highly interactive and dynamic conversational experiences.

ii)   Hugging Face Transformers:

Hugging Face Transformers is a versatile library that offers a wide range of transformer models, including GPT-2 and GPT-Neo, which are suitable for conversational AI tasks. This library provides pre-trained models, fine-tuning capabilities, and various utilities for text generation, dialogue systems, and chatbots. It supports multiple languages and offers flexibility and customization options for developers.

iii)   ChatGPT by OpenAI:

OpenAI's ChatGPT is a specialized library designed specifically for building chatbots and conversational agents. It provides a user-friendly interface and comes with built-in functionalities tailored for interactive conversations. Developers can easily integrate ChatGPT into their applications with just a few lines of code. It offers features like message-based API, system-level instructions, and control over response length and behavior.

iv)   ParlAI:

ParlAI is an open-source library that offers a wide range of conversational AI models and tasks. It provides access to state-of-the-art models, including ChatGPT, and allows developers to train their own models using various techniques and datasets. ParlAI supports multi-turn conversations, dialogue evaluation, and dialogue management. It also offers a collaborative platform for researchers and developers to share models and engage in dialogue-oriented research.

These top ChatGPT libraries offer a rich set of features and capabilities for developing powerful conversational AI applications. Whether you need a ready-to-use API, fine-tuning capabilities, or a customizable framework, these libraries provide the necessary tools to create engaging and intelligent chatbots and dialogue systems. Choose the one that aligns best with your project requirements and start building conversational AI experiences that captivate and delight your users.

3.2. Integration and Usage Examples

Integration and usage examples of ChatGPT libraries are vital for harnessing the power of conversational AI. These libraries offer developers the tools they need to seamlessly integrate ChatGPT into their applications, platforms, or chatbots (Zhao et al., 2024).

One popular ChatGPT library is the OpenAI GPT-3 Python library. With this library, developers can utilize the GPT-3 model to generate human-like text responses in real-time. The integration process is straightforward, allowing developers to quickly set up their applications to interact with the ChatGPT model.

For instance, imagine a customer support chatbot integrated with ChatGPT. When a user interacts with the chatbot, the ChatGPT library can be used to generate helpful and accurate responses based on the user's queries. This integration enables a more natural and engaging conversation, giving users a satisfying customer support experience.

Another noteworthy ChatGPT library is the TensorFlow.js implementation. This library allows developers to leverage the power of ChatGPT directly in web applications. Through this integration, developers can create interactive chat interfaces, virtual assistants, or even integrate ChatGPT into existing chat platforms.

For example, a language learning platform could incorporate ChatGPT to provide personalized language practice sessions. Students could have conversations with the ChatGPT model, receiving feedback and guidance in real-time. This integration offers a dynamic and immersive language learning experience.

Furthermore, ChatGPT libraries often come with pre-trained models that can be fine-tuned for specific domains or use cases. This flexibility allows developers to tailor the conversational AI experience to their unique requirements. From customer support to language learning, e-commerce to virtual assistants, ChatGPT libraries offer endless possibilities for integrating powerful conversational AI.

Overall, the integration and usage examples of ChatGPT libraries demonstrate the versatility and potential of conversational AI. With these libraries, developers can create intelligent and interactive chat experiences that enhance user engagement, improve customer support, and provide personalized interactions in various domains.

3.3 Pros and Cons

When it comes to utilizing ChatGPT libraries for developing powerful conversational AI, there are several pros and cons to consider. Understanding these advantages and limitations can help you make informed decisions and choose the most suitable library for your specific needs.

Let's start with the pros. ChatGPT libraries provide a convenient and efficient way to integrate conversational AI capabilities into your applications or platforms. With pre-trained models and ready-to-use APIs, you can quickly build chatbots or virtual assistants without starting from scratch.

Another advantage is the flexibility offered by these libraries. They allow you to customize and fine-tune the models according to your specific use cases and requirements. This means you can train the model to better understand and respond to the needs of your target audience, resulting in a more personalized and engaging user experience.

Moreover, ChatGPT libraries often come with extensive documentation and developer resources. This makes it easier for developers to get started and leverage the full potential of the libraries, even if they are new to conversational AI.

However, along with the pros, there are also a few cons to be aware of. One of the main challenges is maintaining the balance between generating coherent responses and avoiding biased or inappropriate outputs. ChatGPT models can sometimes produce nonsensical or inaccurate responses, which may require additional efforts in fine-tuning and monitoring.

Additionally, the reliance on cloud services and APIs can introduce latency and dependency on external servers. This may impact the real-time nature of your conversational AI application, especially if there are limitations in terms of network connectivity or response times.

Lastly, it's important to note that the performance of ChatGPT libraries can vary based on the size and complexity of the conversation. Longer conversations or those involving multiple context shifts might result in less coherent or relevant responses (Fakhri et al., 2023).

Considering the pros and cons, it's crucial to thoroughly evaluate your specific use case and prioritize the features and limitations that align with your goals. This will help you make an informed decision and select the most suitable ChatGPT library to empower your conversational AI endeavors (J. Zhang et al., 2024).

4. HUGGING FACE'S TRANSFORMERS LIBRARY

When it comes to powerful conversational AI, one library that stands out is Hugging Face's Transformers. This library has gained immense popularity in the AI community and is widely recognized for its extensive pre-trained models and easy-to-use interfaces.

Hugging Face's Transformers library provides a wide range of state-of-the-art models that can be fine-tuned for various natural language processing tasks, including chatbot development. The library supports both PyTorch and TensorFlow, making it compatible with popular deep learning frameworks.

One of the key advantages of using Hugging Face's Transformers library is the vast selection of pre-trained models it offers. These models have been trained on massive amounts of data, enabling them to understand and generate text with impressive fluency and coherence. From the well-known GPT models to the more recent DialoGPT, the library provides a rich variety of options for building conversational AI systems.

In addition to the pre-trained models, the library also provides convenient interfaces for fine-tuning these models on specific tasks. This allows developers to adapt the models to their specific needs and data, ensuring better performance and more accurate responses in conversations.

Furthermore, Hugging Face's Transformers library is well-documented and supported by an active community. The official documentation provides comprehensive guidance and examples, making it easier for developers to get started and leverage the full potential of the library. The community-driven nature of the library ensures continuous updates, bug fixes, and new features, enhancing the overall experience for developers.

In conclusion, Hugging Face's Transformers library is an exceptional choice for anyone looking to explore the world of conversational AI. With its wide range of pre-trained models, easy-to-use interfaces, and strong community support, this library empowers developers to build powerful chatbots and enhance their conversational AI applications.

5. MICROSOFT'S DIALOGPT LIBRARY

Microsoft's DialoGPT library is a powerful tool for developing conversational AI applications. Leveraging the advanced capabilities of the GPT-3 model, this library allows developers to create highly interactive and engaging chatbots.

One of the key advantages of using the DialoGPT library is its ability to generate coherent and contextually relevant responses. The underlying model has been trained on a vast amount of data, enabling it to understand and respond to a wide range of user queries and prompts. Whether it's answering customer inquiries, providing recommendations, or engaging in casual conversations, DialoGPT excels in generating responses that feel natural and human-like.

Additionally, the Microsoft team has put significant effort into fine-tuning the model to ensure it aligns with ethical and responsible AI practices. They have implemented safety mitigations to prevent the generation of harmful or inappropriate content, making it a reliable choice for businesses concerned about maintaining a positive user experience.

Integration with the DialoGPT library is straightforward, allowing developers to quickly incorporate conversational AI capabilities into their existing applications or build new ones from scratch. The library provides a user-friendly interface, making it accessible to developers with varying levels of expertise in natural language processing.

Furthermore, Microsoft has actively encouraged collaboration and engagement with the developer community, providing resources, documentation, and support to facilitate the adoption and improvement of the DialoGPT library. This collaborative approach ensures that the library continues to evolve and meet the ever-growing demands of building powerful conversational AI applications.

In conclusion, Microsoft's DialoGPT library is a top choice for developers seeking to harness the power of conversational AI. Its ability to generate coherent and contextually relevant responses, commitment to ethical AI practices, ease of integration, and active engagement with the developer community make it a valuable tool for creating compelling and engaging chatbot experiences.

6. FACEBOOK AI'S PARLAI LIBRARY

When it comes to powerful conversational AI, one cannot overlook the contributions of Facebook AI's ParlAI library. ParlAI stands for "Framework for the development and evaluation of dialogue models" and it lives up to its name by providing a comprehensive set of tools and resources for building and training conversational agents.

One of the standout features of ParlAI is its flexibility. It supports a wide range of dialogue tasks, including both single-turn tasks and multi-turn conversations. Whether you're working on simple question-answering systems or complex dialogue agents, ParlAI has got you covered (Tenda et al., 2024).

Another advantage of using the ParlAI library is its extensive collection of pre-trained models. These models are trained on large-scale datasets and can be fine-tuned to specific tasks, saving valuable time and computing resources. Additionally, ParlAI allows for easy integration with popular deep learning frameworks like PyTorch, making it accessible to a wide range of developers.

Furthermore, ParlAI fosters collaboration and research in the field of conversational AI. It provides a platform for sharing and comparing models, allowing researchers and developers to benchmark their systems against state-of-the-art approaches. This collaborative aspect of ParlAI is crucial for advancing the field and pushing the boundaries of what is possible in conversational AI.

In conclusion, Facebook AI's ParlAI library is a powerful tool for anyone looking to explore the world of conversational AI. With its flexibility, pre-trained models, and collaborative environment, it offers a solid foundation for building and evaluating dialogue systems. Whether you're a seasoned researcher or a curious developer, ParlAI is definitely worth exploring in your quest to create cutting-edge conversational AI applications.

7. COMPARING THE CHATGPT LIBRARIES

When it comes to implementing powerful conversational AI using ChatGPT, there are several libraries available that can assist in making the process smoother and more efficient. Let's compare some of the top ChatGPT libraries to help you choose the right one for your project.

i)   OpenAI GPT-3 Playground:

This library provides a user-friendly interface for experimenting with ChatGPT. It allows you to interact with the model and test its capabilities directly in your browser. While it offers a convenient way to explore ChatGPT, it may not be suitable for more complex or production-ready applications.

ii)   Hugging Face Transformers:

Hugging Face is a popular library that offers a wide range of natural language processing models, including ChatGPT. It provides pre-trained models and easy-to-use APIs for generating conversational responses. With a large and active community, Hugging Face Transformers provides excellent support and frequent updates.

iii)   ChatterBot:

ChatterBot is a Python library that focuses on creating chatbots using a combination of machine learning and rule-based techniques. It offers a simple and intuitive interface, making it ideal for beginners. While it may not have the same level of sophistication as some other libraries, it can still be a good starting point for basic conversational AI projects.

iv)   DeepPavlov:

DeepPavlov is an open-source conversational AI library that provides a wide range of tools and models, including ChatGPT. It offers features like intent recognition, dialogue management, and response generation. DeepPavlov is highly customizable and suitable for building complex chatbot systems. However, it may require more advanced knowledge and expertise compared to other libraries (Culotta & Mattei, 2024).

When comparing these ChatGPT libraries, consider factors such as ease of use, community support, customization options, and suitability for your specific project requirements. By choosing the right library, you can leverage the power of ChatGPT to create impressive conversational AI experiences.

8. BEST PRACTICES FOR USING CHATGPT LIBRARIES

When it comes to utilizing ChatGPT libraries for powerful conversational AI, it's essential to follow best practices to maximize their potential. Here are some key guidelines to consider:

1. Understand the capabilities: Familiarize yourself with the features and limitations of the ChatGPT library you are using. Different libraries may offer varying functionalities, such as multi-turn conversations, context handling, or integration with other tools. Knowing what your chosen library can do will help you make the most out of it.
2. Prepare and preprocess data: Ensure that your input data is relevant, clean, and properly formatted. Preprocessing steps like removing duplicates, correcting typos, or normalizing text can significantly enhance the quality of your conversational AI model's responses.
3. Fine-tuning for specific use cases: Fine-tuning the ChatGPT model can greatly improve its performance for specific domains or industries. By providing tailored examples and dataset annotations relevant to your use case, you can enhance the accuracy and relevance of the model's responses.
4. Implement user prompts: User prompts act as guiding instructions for the model, helping it understand the context and expected responses. Craft clear and concise prompts that provide necessary information while allowing the model to generate creative and contextually appropriate answers.
5. Control model behavior: ChatGPT models may occasionally produce incorrect or inappropriate responses. To mitigate this, you can use techniques like "temperature" adjustment to control the randomness of the generated outputs or add "top-k" or "top-p" sampling constraints to limit the model's choices to the most likely or diverse options.
6. Iteratively test and refine: Continuously evaluate and test your ChatGPT implementation to identify areas for improvement. Solicit feedback from users and iterate on the model's responses based on their suggestions. This iterative process will help you refine the conversational AI experience over time.

By adhering to these best practices, you can harness the power of ChatGPT libraries to create robust and effective conversational AI systems that cater to your specific needs. Remember, experimentation and fine-tuning are key to achieving optimal results and delivering exceptional user experiences.

9. REAL-WORLD APPLICATIONS OF CHATGPT LIBRARIES

ChatGPT libraries have gained significant popularity due to their ability to empower developers and businesses with powerful conversational AI capabilities. These libraries, built on the advanced natural language processing (NLP) model of ChatGPT, have opened up new possibilities for real-world applications across various industries.

One notable application is in customer support and service. With the help of ChatGPT libraries, businesses can create intelligent chatbots that can handle customer queries, provide instant support, and even assist in troubleshooting common issues. These virtual assistants can mimic human-like conversations, ensuring a seamless and efficient customer experience.

Another practical use case is in the field of education. ChatGPT libraries can be utilized to build interactive learning platforms, where students can engage in dynamic conversations, ask questions, and receive personalized guidance. This technology has the potential to revolutionize online education, making it more engaging, interactive, and tailored to individual students' needs.

In the healthcare industry, ChatGPT libraries can be leveraged to develop virtual healthcare assistants. These assistants can provide patients with information about common ailments, symptoms, and treatments, acting as a reliable source of medical knowledge. They can also assist healthcare professionals by streamlining administrative tasks, providing drug information, and offering support in clinical decision-making.

Moreover, ChatGPT libraries can enhance productivity in the workplace by serving as virtual team members. They can help with scheduling meetings, managing tasks, and providing information on various topics. These AI-powered assistants can save time and effort, allowing employees to focus on more high-value tasks and ultimately driving overall efficiency within organizations (Wu et al., 2022).

In the financial sector, ChatGPT libraries can be employed to develop intelligent chatbots that assist customers with banking queries, provide financial advice, and even support in investment decision-making. These chatbots can analyze vast amounts of data, offer personalized recommendations, and help users navigate complex financial processes.

The possibilities for real-world applications of ChatGPT libraries are vast and continue to expand as developers explore their potential. With their ability to facilitate natural and engaging conversations, these libraries are revolutionizing how we interact with technology and opening up new avenues for businesses to provide exceptional customer experiences and streamline their operations (Hirsch & Hofer, 2022).

10. CONCLUSION

In conclusion, the world of Conversational AI is constantly evolving and advancing. With the rise of sophisticated chatbot libraries like ChatGPT, businesses and developers have access to powerful tools that can enhance customer interactions and streamline communication processes.

As we look towards the future, there are several exciting developments on the horizon. One notable area of focus is improving the ability of chatbots to understand and respond to nuanced human emotions. By incorporating sentiment analysis and natural language processing techniques, Conversational AI systems can better gauge user sentiment and tailor their responses accordingly, leading to more personalized and empathetic interactions.

Additionally, advancements in machine learning and deep learning algorithms are likely to bring about even more impressive conversational capabilities. We can expect chatbots to become more context-aware, understanding and remembering previous conversations to provide more coherent and relevant responses.

Another area of future development is the integration of voice-based Conversational AI. With the increasing popularity of voice assistants like Siri, Alexa, and Google Assistant, incorporating voice interactions into chatbot systems will become crucial. This will enable users to effortlessly engage with AI-powered chatbots through voice commands, further enhancing the user experience and convenience.

Furthermore, the ongoing research in multi-modal Conversational AI, which combines text, images, and videos, holds immense potential for creating richer and more immersive user experiences. Imagine a chatbot that can understand visual cues and respond to images or videos shared by users, making interactions even more engaging and dynamic.

In conclusion, the field of Conversational AI is rapidly evolving, and the future holds tremendous promise. With advancements in natural language processing, sentiment analysis, machine learning, voice integration, and multi-modal capabilities, we can expect chatbots to become even more intelligent, intuitive, and indispensable in various industries. By leveraging the power of ChatGPT libraries and staying updated with the latest developments, businesses and developers can harness the potential of Conversational AI to revolutionize customer interactions and drive growth in the digital age.

REFERENCES

Belgibaev, B., Mansurova, M., Abdrakhim, S., & Ormanbekova, A. (2024). Smart traffic lights with video vision based on a control minicomputer in Kazakhstani megacities. *Procedia Computer Science*, *231*, 792–797. doi:10.1016/j.procs.2023.12.136

Bozkurt. (2023). https://medium.com/@ayhanbzkrt/chatgpt-user-guide-for-libraries-c09667745a8

Chen. (2023). Chat GPT and Its Possible Impact on Library Reference Services. *Internet Reference Services Quarterly*, *27*(2), 121-129.

Culotta, A., & Mattei, N. (2024). Use Open Source for Safer Generative AI Experiments. *MIT Sloan Management Review*, *65*(2), 11–12. https://www.scopus.com/inward/record.uri?eid=2-s2.0-85183135558&partnerID=40&md5=f295b2a7b4e2a4261c695df98f73fc81

Fakhri, P. S., Asghari, O., Sarspy, S., Marand, M. B., Moshaver, P., & Trik, M. (2023). A fuzzy decision-making system for video tracking with multiple objects in non-stationary conditions. *Heliyon*, *9*(11), e22156. doi:10.1016/j.heliyon.2023.e22156 PMID:38034808

Hirsch, T., & Hofer, B. (2022). Using textual bug reports to predict the fault category of software bugs. *Array (New York, N.Y.)*, *15*, 100189. doi:10.1016/j.array.2022.100189

Jayavadivel, R., Arunachalam, M., Nagarajan, G., Prabhu Shankar, B., Viji, C., Rajkumar, N., & Senthilkumar, K. R. (2024). Historical Overview of AI Adoption in Libraries. In K. Senthilkumar (Ed.), *AI-Assisted Library Reconstruction* (pp. 267–289). IGI Global. doi:10.4018/979-8-3693-2782-1.ch015

Kumar, N., Antoniraj, S., Jayanthi, S., Mirdula, S., Selvaraj, S., Rajkumar, N., & Senthilkumar, K. R. (2024). Educational Technology and Libraries Supporting Online Learning. In K. Senthilkumar (Ed.), *AI-Assisted Library Reconstruction* (pp. 209–237). IGI Global. doi:10.4018/979-8-3693-2782-1.ch012

Pavlik, J. V. (2023). Collaborating with Chat GPT: Considering the implications education. *Journalism and Mass Communication Educator*, *78*(1). doi:10.1177/10776958221149577

Pramanik, A., Sarkar, S., & Pal, S. K. (2023). Video surveillance-based fall detection system using object-level feature thresholding and Z−numbers. *Knowledge-Based Systems*, *280*, 110992. doi:10.1016/j.knosys.2023.110992

Radford, A., Narasimhan, K., Salimans, T., & Sutskever, I. (2018). *Improving language understanding by generative pre-training*. Retrieved from https://www.cs.ubc.ca/~amuham01/LING530/papers/radford2018improving.pdf

Rajkumar, N., Tabassum, H., Muthulingam, S., Mohanraj, A., Viji, C., Kumar, N., & Senthilkumar, K. R. (2024). Anticipated Requirements and Expectations in the Digital Library. In K. Senthilkumar (Ed.), *AI-Assisted Library Reconstruction* (pp. 1–20). IGI Global. doi:10.4018/979-8-3693-2782-1.ch001

Senthilkumar, K. (Ed.). (2024). *AI-Assisted Library Reconstruction*. IGI Global. doi:10.4018/979-8-3693-2782-1

Senthilkumar, K. R. (2019). *User pattern of Libraries by students of Government Colleges in Tamil nadu: A study*. Library Philosophy and Practice.

Senthilkumar, K. R. (2024). *Revolutionizing Thrust Manufacturing.* doi:10.4018/979-8-3693-2615-2.ch005

Senthilkumar, K. R. (2024). Revolutionizing thrust manufacturing. In *Advances in computational intelligence and robotics book series* (pp. 80–93). doi:10.4018/979-8-3693-2615-2.ch005

Senthilkumar, K. R., Jagajeevan, R., & Sangeetha, S. (2024). Impact of AI on Library and Information Science in Higher Institutions in India: A Comprehensive Analysis of Technological Integration and Educational Implications. In K. Senthilkumar (Ed.), *AI-Assisted Library Reconstruction* (pp. 21–33). IGI Global. doi:10.4018/979-8-3693-2782-1.ch002

Shiddiqi, A. M., Yogatama, E. D., & Navastara, D. A. (2023). Resource-aware video streaming (RA-ViS) framework for object detection system using deep learning algorithm. *MethodsX, 11*, 102285. doi:10.1016/j.mex.2023.102285 PMID:37533793

Sivaraj, P., Madhan, V., Mallika, V., & Senthilkumar, K. R. (2024). Enhancing Library Services Through Optimization Algorithms and Data Analytics: Enhancing Library Services Mathematical Model. In K. Senthilkumar (Ed.), *AI-Assisted Library Reconstruction* (pp. 290–306). IGI Global. doi:10.4018/979-8-3693-2782-1.ch016

Strubell, E., Ganesh, A., & McCallum, A. (2019). Energy and policy considerations for deep learning in NLP. *Proceedings of the Annual Meeting of the Association for Computational Linguistics, 57*, 3645-3650.

Tenda, E. D., Henrina, J., Setiadharma, A., Aristy, D. J., Romadhon, P. Z., Thahadian, H. F., Mahdi, B. A., Adhikara, I. M., Marfiani, E., Suryantoro, S. D., Yunus, R. E., & Yusuf, P. A. (2024). Derivation and validation of novel integrated inpatient mortality prediction score for COVID-19 (IMPACT) using clinical, laboratory, and AI—processed radiological parameter upon admission: A multicentre study. *Scientific Reports, 14*(1), 2149. Advance online publication. doi:10.1038/s41598-023-50564-9 PMID:38272920

The University of Queensland. (2023). https://guides.library.uq.edu.au/referencing/chatgpt-and-generative-ai-tools

Wang, J., Hu, F., Abbas, G., Albekairi, M., & Rashid, N. (2024). Enhancing image categorization with the quantized object recognition model in surveillance systems. *Expert Systems with Applications, 238*, 122240. doi:10.1016/j.eswa.2023.122240

Wang, X., Sun, Z., Chehri, A., Jeon, G., & Song, Y. (2024). Deep learning and multi-modal fusion for real-time multi-object tracking: Algorithms, challenges, datasets, and comparative study. *Information Fusion, 105*, 102247. doi:10.1016/j.inffus.2024.102247

Wu, H., Ma, Y., Xiang, Z., Yang, C., & He, K. (2022). A spatial–temporal graph neural network framework for automated software bug triaging. *Knowledge-Based Systems, 241*, 108308. doi:10.1016/j.knosys.2022.108308

Zhang, J., Cheng, Y., Zhang, J., & Wu, Z. (2024). A spatiotemporal distribution identification method of vehicle weights on bridges by integrating traffic video and toll station data. *Journal of Intelligent Transportation Systems.* https://doi.org/https://doi.org/10.1080/15472450.2024.2312810

Zhang, L., Guo, W., Zhang, Y., Liu, S., Zhu, Z., Guo, M., Song, W., Chen, Z., Yang, Y., Pu, Y., Ding, S., Zhang, J., Liu, L., & Zhao, Q. (2023). Modern Technologies and Solutions to Enhance Surveillance and Response Systems for Emerging Zoonotic Diseases. *Science in One Health*, 100061. htttps://doi.org/ https://doi.org/10.1016/j.soh.2023.100061

Zhao, Z., Zhu, J., Jiao, P., Wang, J., Zhang, X., Lu, X., & Zhang, Y. (2024). Hybrid-FHR: A multi-modal AI approach for automated fetal acidosis diagnosis. *BMC Medical Informatics and Decision Making*, *24*(1), 19. Advance online publication. doi:10.1186/s12911-024-02423-4 PMID:38247009

Zhou, X., Chen, Z., Jin, X., & Wang, W. Y. (2021). HULK: An energy efficiency benchmark platform for responsible natural language processing. *Proceedings of the Conference of the European Chapter of the Association for Computational Linguistics: System Demonstrations*, *16*, 329-336.

Chapter 7
Ethical Considerations of AI Implementation in the Library Era

N. Rajkumar
https://orcid.org/0000-0001-7857-9452
Alliance College of Engineering and Design, Alliance University, India

C. Viji
https://orcid.org/0000-0002-2759-8896
Alliance College of Engineering and Design, Alliance University, India

A. Mohanraj
Sri Eshwar College of Engineering, India

K. R. Senthilkumar
https://orcid.org/0000-0001-7426-5376
Sri Krishna Arts and Science College, India

R. Jagajeevan
Sri Krishna Arts and Science College, India

Judeson Antony Kovilpillai
Alliance College of Engineering and Design, India

ABSTRACT

As the mixture of artificial intelligence (AI) continues to permeate several sectors, ethical considerations have ended up a focus in ensuring responsible and sustainable AI deployment. This virtual library explores the multifaceted moral dimensions related to AI implementation. The gathering of scholarly articles and studies papers delves into key moral problems, spanning troubles which includes bias and fairness, transparency, responsibility, privacy, and societal impact. The number one section of the virtual library addresses the undertaking of algorithmic bias and fairness, reading how biases in AI systems can perpetuate societal inequalities. Various methods to mitigating bias and selling fairness in AI algorithms are explored, providing insights into the improvement of more equitable AI programs. Transparency and duty are the focal factors of the second one segment, emphasizing the need for clean conversation of AI decision-making techniques and mechanisms for holding AI systems answerable for their movements.

DOI: 10.4018/979-8-3693-5593-0.ch007

1. PRIVACY AND DATA SECURITY

AI structures often require massive datasets for schooling. Make certain that patron statistics is handled with utmost care, respecting privacy prison recommendations and tips. Put into effect strong security features to guard touchy statistics from unauthorized get right of entry. Privateness and statistics safety are paramount issues within the implementation of AI systems, especially when handling huge datasets for schooling. As agencies leverage AI technologies, they should prioritize the responsible management of personal information according to privacy laws and guidelines. Simultaneously, robust protection functions need to be implemented to safeguard touchy records from unauthorized get entry, making sure they consider and self-assurance of users (Ryan, M. 2020). To start with, adherence to privateness prison guidelines and hints is non-negotiable. As AI structures frequently depend on first-rate datasets to beautify their competencies, agencies should be diligent in complying with legal guidelines along with the overall data safety law (GDPR) and other close-by or employer-specific policies. These involve acquiring unique consent from customers for records collection, specifying the cause of records usage, and transparently discussing how their information can be handled. The implementation of clear, concise privacy guidelines becomes vital in fostering personal acceptance as real and ensuring jail compliance. In parallel, the incorporation of sturdy safety capabilities is crucial to prevent unauthorized access to touchy person statistics. The virtual library ecosystem must prioritize encryption protocols, cozy facts transmission channels, and multi-aspect authentication to reinforce the layers of safety toward functionality breaches. Normal safety audits and vulnerability exams must be done to perceive and deal with capacity weaknesses, thereby reinforcing the general protection posture of the AI-pushed virtual library. One effective approach to enhance privacy in AI implementation is the adoption of privacy-preserving strategies at some stage in the education of device studying models. Techniques alongside federated gaining knowledge of and homomorphic encryption allow the schooling approach to arise on decentralized gadgets or encrypted records, respectively, without compromising the privateness of character consumer records. Those advancements permit groups to derive extensive insights from information at the same time as minimizing the exposure of touchy facts. Furthermore, organizations ought to include the standards of data minimization and purpose quandary.

Utilizing accumulating most effective the essential facts for specific and legitimate functions, the chance associated with ability misuse or unauthorized entry is appreciably mitigated. This method aligns with moral issues and helps in building a privacy-centric lifestyle within the virtual library environment (Cavedon, L., & Jatowt, A. 2020). Person empowerment is a different critical aspect of ensuring privacy. Presenting customers with granular control over their records, which includes the capacity to alter consent alternatives and delete their information, contributes to a user-centric technique. Transparency is fundamental in this regard; customers ought to be knowledgeable approximately the sorts of information accrued, the reason for collection, and how their records contribute to the improvement of AI systems inside the digital library. Within the context of ethical AI improvement, businesses need to also bear in mind adopting frameworks that prioritize fairness, accountability, and transparency (fats). Imposing those principles allows mitigate biases in AI algorithms, ensuring that the virtual library offerings cater equitably to all customers. Everyday audits and bias tests must be achieved to understand and rectify any unintentional biases that could emerge during the AI device's lifecycle.

The accountable implementation of AI in digital libraries calls for dual attention to privacy and data protection. Agencies must navigate the ethical panorama using the usage of adhering to privacy legal guidelines, incorporating robust safety features, and adopting privateness-maintaining strategies during

Figure 1. AI ethics framework

![AI Ethics Framework diagram with four quadrants: Founding Principles (Adhere to the Guiding Principles - Via technical and non-technical methods, Acknowledge tension between principles), Realization (Implement the Guiding Principles - Via the tools suggested, Human-based checklist), Assessment (Judge the ethics of an AI application through the gate AI Governance approach), Integration (Evaluate and address these principles throughout the lifecycle of the AI application).]

AI model education. Through a way of prioritizing customer consent, transparency, and fairness, digital libraries can harness the electricity of AI at the same time as keeping the beliefs and privateness of their consumer base.

2. TRANSPARENCY AND EXPLAINABILITY

AI algorithms can be complicated and opaque. Purpose for transparency in how the AI operates, supplying causes for choice-making strategies. Customers must have an easy know-how of the way AI is used within the digital library and how it can impact their enjoyment. Transparency and explainability are critical additives of moral AI implementation, especially within the context of digital libraries. As artificial intelligence algorithms grow to be greater sophisticated and elaborate, the mission lies in making sure that those systems aren't the simplest powerful but additionally comprehensible to users. This necessitates a commitment to transparency in how AI operates and a determination to impart clear factors for the choice-making procedures concerned. Clients need to have a complete record of ways AI is included into the virtual library and how it could have an effect on their ordinary enjoyment. The complexity and opacity of AI algorithms often reason for what's commonly known as the "black area" problem (Makri, S., & Warwick, C. 2020). This term describes the inherent mission in interpreting how

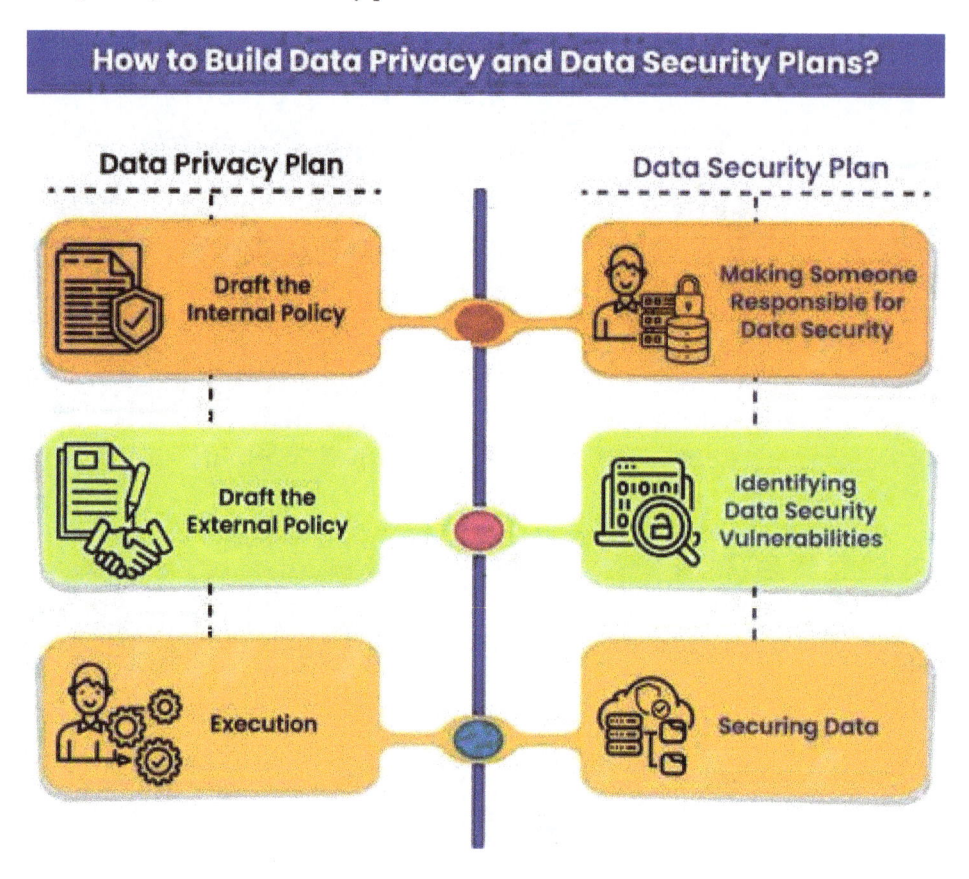

Figure 2. Data privacy and data security plan

AI arrives at particular choices or suggestions. In a digital library placing, this loss of transparency can result in users feeling unsure about the reliability and equity of the AI-driven capabilities. To cope with this, virtual libraries have to prioritize transparency as a guiding precept in their AI implementation. This entails presenting on hand and without issue comprehensible information about how the AI machine talents, the data it makes use of, and the methods it follows to generate outcomes. Clean conversation is crucial to demystify the technology and construct consumer acceptance as true with. One powerful technique is to provide individual-friendly documentation or publications that specify the essential principles of the AI algorithms hired inside the digital library. Those materials should be tailored to the target audience, avoiding technical jargon and the usage of plain language to clarify complicated standards. With the aid of doing so, customers, regardless of their technical know-how, can gain insights into the decision-making mechanisms of the AI device. Furthermore, virtual libraries have to put money into growing customer interfaces that incorporate transparency functions. This could include interactive dashboards, tooltips, or facts overlays that provide clients with real-time insights into how AI algorithms are influencing their revel in (Hagendorff, T. 2020).

For instance, if an AI-driven advice device suggests a particular beneficial aid, customers need to have access to facts detailing why that recommendation changed into made, in conjunction with the requirements used or the relevance of the resource to their pastimes. Further to consumer transparency, groups need to be internally obvious about their AI systems. This consists of fostering a lifestyle of openness

Figure 3. Explainability

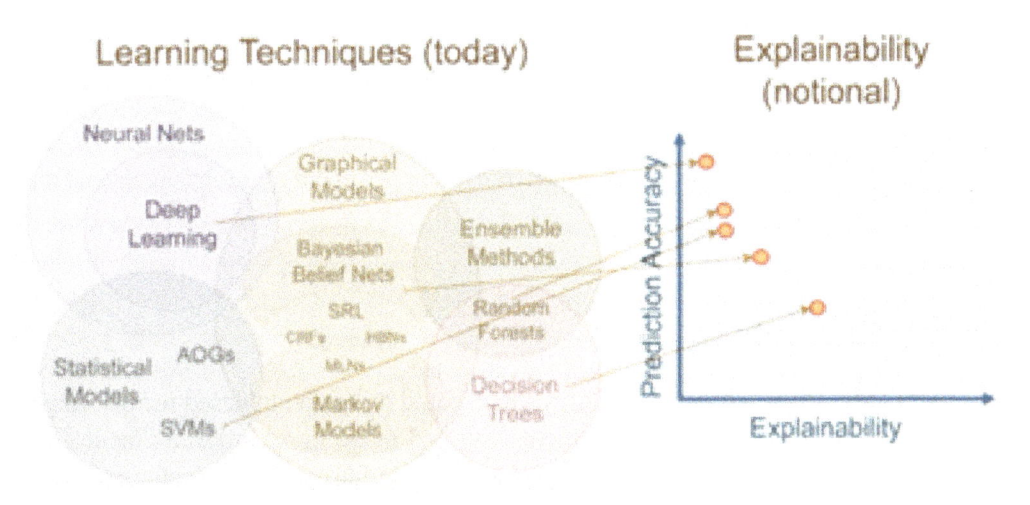

in several development and implementation companies, encouraging them to report and percentage the common feel and methodologies behind the AI models. Inner transparency now not best aids in collaboration and facts sharing but moreover allows ongoing tests of the gadget's equity, accuracy, and moral implications. Explainability is cautiously tied to transparency, focusing on the potential to offer clear, comprehensible elements for AI picks. At the same time, as transparency addresses the visibility of the tool as an entire, explainability delves into the specifics of character selections. Even as a person gets advice or search results from the digital library's AI, they want if you want to understand why those precise results have been decided on. One method to improving explainability is the improvement and incorporation of Explainable AI (XAI) techniques. XAI strategy's goal is to make the selection-making method of AI fashions greater interpretable. This may include producing human-readable reasons, visualizing choice paths, or highlighting key capabilities that motivate a specific outcome.

With the aid of the use of integrating XAI into the virtual library's AI infrastructure, clients can gain insights into the cause of the back of AI-generated content material pointers or are looking for outcomes (Jobin, A., et al., 2021). Importantly, the explainability of AI structures contributes to man or woman empowerment. While customers understand how AI operates and affects their interactions with the virtual library, they could make informed alternatives about whether to consider the tool's pointers or search for possible assets. This aligns with moral concepts that prioritize man or woman autonomy and knowledgeable consent. Virtual libraries ought to additionally remember to solicit individual feedback on the transparency and explainability of AI features. This may be finished through surveys, consumer testing sessions, or comments bureaucracy blanketed into the digital library interface. Via actively regarding users in the gadget, libraries can tailor their transparency efforts to meet patron expectations and address unique issues. Moreover, moral issues expand past the technical additives of transparency and explainability (Bello-Orgaz, G., & Camacho, D. 2021). There's a moral responsibility to be obvious about the constraints of AI structures. Customers have to be made aware of the bounds and capacity biases inherent within the generation. Communicating those limitations enables control of customer expectations and fosters a realistic understanding of what AI can and cannot achieve in the virtual library context. Transparency and explainability are imperative elements in the moral implementation of

AI in digital libraries. Via the use of prioritizing those concepts, libraries can bridge the gap between complicated AI algorithms and personal know-how, fostering belief and engagement. Thru to be had documentation, man or woman interfaces that spotlight AI influences, and the combination of Explainable AI strategies, digital libraries can empower users to make knowledgeable choices, in the long run enhancing the general consumer experience. Moreover, ongoing consumer remarks mechanisms and internal transparency practices contribute to the iterative improvement of AI structures and make certain alignment with ethical standards.

3. BIAS AND FAIRNESS

Be aware of ability biases in schooling statistics which could bring about biased results. Regularly audit and study AI fashions for fairness. Try for inclusivity and range in each development group and the datasets used to teach the AI tool. Addressing bias and selling fairness in AI implementation is crucial to ensure equitable results, in particular in digital libraries in which AI systems play a giant function in content tips and seek functionalities. Spotting the capability biases in training records, undertaking everyday audits, and fostering inclusivity and variety in each improvement group and dataset are crucial steps toward growing AI systems that serve various patron populations quite (Mittelstadt, B. 2021). One of the primary annoying conditions in AI is the threat of bias being embedded in the schooling records. Education records are foundational to device gaining knowledge of algorithms, and if it displays historical or societal biases, the AI model can perpetuate and expand these biases in its predictions and guidelines. In a digital library context, biased effects may occur in the form of unequal instances of nice topics, authors, or views in suggestions or seeking outcomes. To mitigate this hazard, virtual libraries ought to be diligent in figuring out and addressing biases in their education records. This entails a comprehensive exam of the datasets used to train AI fashions, aiming to apprehend and rectify any imbalances or prejudices gift. Normal data audits, which include scrutinizing the records for capability biases and assessing the effect on version outcomes, are essential for maintaining equity.

Jayavadivel et al. (Jayavadivel et al., 2024) provide a historical perspective on the adoption of AI in libraries. The chapter traces the evolution of AI technologies in library settings, highlighting key milestones, challenges, and opportunities for integrating AI-driven solutions to optimize library services and user experiences. Viji et al. focus on the utilization of radio frequency identification (RFID) technology for intelligent library management. The chapter explores how RFID systems enhance library operations through efficient inventory management, automated check-in/check-out processes, and improved user experiences (Viji et al., 2024).

Furthermore, corporations ought to prioritize transparency in their efforts to address bias. Clients should be knowledgeable approximately the steps taken to turn out to be aware of and rectify biases in AI models (Li, Y., Lee, K. H., & Hsieh, L. 2021), fostering a sense of responsibility and agreeing with them. Easy conversation approximately the restrictions of AI systems and persevering with a dedication to fairness enable management personal expectancies and encourage individual engagement. Everyday assessment of AI models for fairness is a non-stop gadget that must be integrated into the development lifecycle. Metrics and benchmarks ought to be set up to assess the fairness of effects throughout remarkable demographic companies. For instance, in a digital library setting, fairness metrics will be designed to degree the variety and stability of advocated sources during diverse topics, genres, and cultural views.

Imposing a fairness-conscious machine and getting to know strategies are a few different methods to mitigate biases.

The techniques involve adjusting the education system to explicitly account for and counteract biases inside the facts (Jones, K. S., & Smith, A. J. 2022). Equity-aware algorithms can be designed to ensure that underrepresented content material or views are not marginalized in the guidelines, contributing to a greater inclusive and unbiased virtual library experience. Striving for inclusivity and variety isn't handiest vital in the datasets used for training but additionally in the improvement groups developing and keeping AI structures. A various team brings a diffusion of views, evaluations, and cultural insights, lowering the possibility of unintentional biases. In the context of digital libraries, in which content material can also span an enormous style of subjects and genres, a numerous institution is better equipped to apprehend and address the wishes of a heterogeneous person base. Corporations must actively promote a range of hiring practices, making sure that the team working on AI improvement represents one of different backgrounds, ethnicities, genders, and cultural views. Inclusivity inside the improvement technique contributes to a more complete data of ability biases and a greater powerful strategy for addressing them.

Moreover, regarding diverse stakeholders in selection-making approaches related to AI system improvement complements the possibilities of uncovering biases that are probably overlooked through a homogenous group. Taking elements with doors professionals, user corporations, and advocacy businesses can offer precious insights into the potential influences of AI structures on numerous person demographics and assist emerge as privy to and rectify biases that would have been inadvertently brought (Cillo, P., & Zilinski, L. 2022). To deal with biases effectively, it miles crucial to place into effect ongoing schooling and popularity packages in the development group. This consists of education on the moral implications of AI, subconscious bias, and cultural sensitivity. Through a way of fostering a lifestyle of non-prevent gaining knowledge of and self-reflection, development groups can remain vigilant in figuring out and mitigating biases at some point in the AI gadget's lifecycle. Tackling bias and selling fairness in AI structures inside virtual libraries calls for a multifaceted approach. With the aid of being aware of capability biases in education facts, wearing out everyday audits, and evaluating fashions for fairness, companies can assemble AI systems that provide equitable outcomes. Striving for inclusivity and range in every development crew and the datasets used for training enhances the general effectiveness and equity of AI systems. Virtual libraries have a very precise possibility to steer in growing inclusive, unbiased areas for getting access to statistics, ensuring that AI-driven tips and search functionalities serve all users pretty and impartially.

4. USER CONSENT AND CONTROL

Attain informed consent from clients regarding the collection and use of their information with the aid of AI systems. Offer users with management over their information and the potential to determine in or out of AI-pushed functions.

Purchaser consent and manipulation are foundational principles in the ethical implementation of AI systems, especially in the context of digital libraries (Wu, W., & He, S. 2022). Ensuring that customers are informed about the gathering and utilization of their records by using AI systems and providing them with the autonomy to pick in or out of AI-driven capabilities are crucial factors in respecting consumer privacy and fostering agreement. This newsletter explores the significance of acquiring knowledgeable consent, the mechanisms for offering client control, and the outcomes of the ethical deployment of AI in digital libraries.

Obtaining Informed Consent

In the realm of AI and virtual libraries, obtaining informed consent is a cornerstone of ethical exercise. Customers should be fully aware of how their records can be used by AI systems and can offer express consent for its series and processing. This involves transparently communicating the motive of records collection, the types of data being gathered, and the approaches in which AI algorithms will leverage these statistics to enhance the person's enjoyment. While users access a virtual library, there ought to be clear and without troubles understandable facts about the presence and features of AI structures. This data ought to be offered in a user-pleasant way, avoiding technical jargon, and making use of undeniable language to ensure sizeable comprehension (Yang, S., & Zhang, X. 2022). Virtual libraries can hire pop-up notifications, banners, or committed sections in consumer interfaces to succinctly supply a cause of the usage of AI and solicit consumer consent. Furthermore, digital libraries need to put into effect granular consent mechanisms, permitting clients to select the right elements of record usage they're comfortable with. As instance, customers are probably given the option to consent to custom-designed hints even as opting out of information storage for lengthy-term analysis. This degree of granularity empowers users to tailor their consent based on their options and comfort ranges. Agencies must additionally ensure that the consent manner is dynamic and adaptable. If there are modifications in how AI systems make use of customer statistics or if new capabilities are brought, users want to be directly notified, and their consent should be re-solicited. This ongoing communique establishes an obvious and collaborative relationship among digital libraries and their clients, reinforcing acceptance as true through the years.

Providing User Control

Further to acquiring informed consent, presenting users with management over their data is an essential element of respecting personal autonomy and privateness. Customers should have the capacity to govern and modify their consent selections, allowing them to work out control over how their records are utilized by AI systems in the virtual library. One effective mechanism for presenting person manipulation is the implementation of patron-excellent dashboards or settings interfaces. Those interfaces must provide clear alternatives for customers to have a look at and regulate their privacy and records usage settings (Tan, L., & Chen, Q. 2023). Virtual libraries can consist of functions in conjunction with toggle switches, sliders, or drop-down menus that facilitate clean customization of consent alternatives. Crucially, virtual libraries need to offer customers the functionality to opt in or out of AI-driven functions without sacrificing center functionalities. This guarantees that clients who prioritize privateness can nonetheless get the right of entry to and advantage from important library services while people who are comfortable with extra custom-designed reviews can decide on AI-driven tips and improvements. Moreover, agencies ought to don't forget to offer customers the choice to selectively delete or anonymize their statistics. This is going past the regular "delete account" functionality and permits customers to maintain access to the library whilst making sure that their historical facts are no longer used for AI schooling or evaluation. Enforcing such features aligns with standards of consumer manipulation and empowers users to manipulate their digital footprint in the library environment. Patron education plays a crucial position

Figure 4. User consent and control

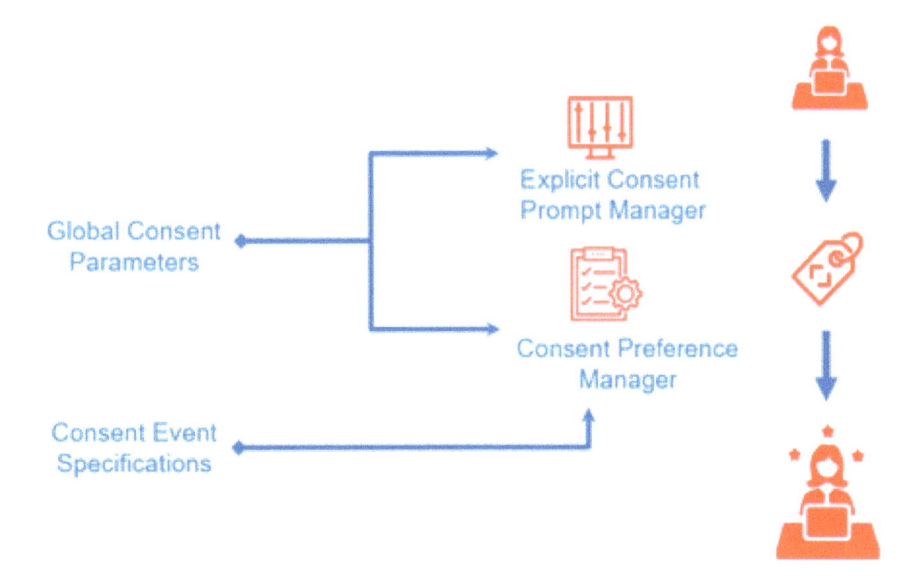

in facilitating powerful individual control (Kim, Y., & Park, J. 2023). Virtual libraries must proactively train users about the effects of their consent picks, the advantages of AI-driven talents, and the potential alternate-offs associated with privateness. Offering clear and handy information empowers customers to make informed selections about their data, fostering an experience of manipulation and belief within the virtual library environment.

Challenges and Considerations

While acquiring informed consent and providing man or woman management are critical moral imperatives, there are demanding situations and issues that corporations ought to navigate within the virtual library panorama. One challenge is hanging the right balance between customization and simplicity in consent interfaces. The consent system needs to be consumer-friendly and no longer weighs down customers with many alternatives (Liu, C., & Chang, J. 2023). Designing interfaces that gift key alternatives concisely at the same time as thinking of nuanced possibilities is crucial to make sure a splendid user revel in them. Digital libraries must additionally consider the capability effect of choose-in and choose-out mechanisms on the overall character revealed. Placing a balance between privacy and the benefits derived from AI-driven capabilities is important. A patron-centric approach includes offering easy information approximately the blessings of AI-extra offerings and encouraging customers to opt in while respecting the alternatives of people who decide. Furthermore, organizations ought to be obvious about the restrictions of purchaser manipulation. Whilst clients can manipulate wonderful components of statistics utilization, there can be anonymized, aggregated data that is critical for enhancing usual tool performance. Clear communique approximately those constraints permit control of patron expectancies and avoids capability misunderstandings.

Ethical Considerations in User Consent and Control

The ethical concerns surrounding purchaser consent and manipulation make it bigger beyond crook compliance to embody concepts of fairness, transparency, and responsibility. Digital libraries want to not forget the wider societal implications of their data practices and make certain that their techniques align with ethical requirements. Ensuring inclusivity within the consent way is essential to avoid ability biases. Businesses must take heed to the truth that users from diverse backgrounds can also have distinct privacy options and must tailor their consent mechanisms to be inclusive and on hand to all clients (Shen, Y., & Li, X. 2023). Furthermore, companies must be apparent in approximately any 1/3-party collaborations that include the sharing of client statistics. Customers have the proper to realize if their statistics can be shared with outdoor entities and have to have the choice to offer precise consent for such collaborations. This transparency contributes to an extra responsible and simple courting of most of the virtual library and its customers. User consent and control are crucial to the ethical implementation of AI structures in digital libraries. Acquiring knowledgeable consent through transparent verbal exchange, granular consent mechanisms, and dynamic tactics establishes a foundation for considering several of the library and its customers. Supplying customers with control over their facts, together with the capability to customize alternatives and manipulate their virtual footprint, empowers users, and respects their autonomy. Navigating the disturbing conditions and ethical considerations in this domain calls for willpower to consumer-centric design, transparency, and ongoing communique. As virtual libraries keep complying, prioritizing consumer consent and control guarantees that AI-pushed functions decorate the individual experience at the same time as upholding ethical requirements and clients in mind.

5. HUMAN-IN-THE-LOOP AND HUMAN OVERSIGHT

The integration of AI systems in several domain names, including digital libraries, increases full-size moral issues. Amongst those, the thoughts of "human-in-the-loop" and "human oversight" play pivotal roles in making sure responsible and moral AI deployment. The ideas emphasize the significance of keeping human involvement in essential choice-making techniques and imposing mechanisms for ongoing oversight to cope with any ethical problems that may arise for the duration of AI gadget operation. By adopting a balanced method that leverages AI talents while acknowledging human information, digital libraries can beautify client reviews, sell responsibility, and mitigate ability dangers (Wang, H., & Zheng, L. 2023).

Human-in-the-Loop Approach

A human-in-the-loop approach consists of maintaining a degree of human involvement in AI structures, especially whilst essential choices are at stake. This approach recognizes the regulations of virtually automated processes and acknowledges the precise cognitive skills, ethical reasoning, and contextual know-how that people carry to the table. In the context of digital libraries, a human-in-the-loop method is crucial for desire-making techniques associated with content curation, gadget guidelines, and exceptional man or woman-going through functionalities. For example, an AI-pushed recommendation tool in a digital library can gain from human oversight to make certain that guidelines align with moral requirements, cultural sensitivities, and the evolving desires of numerous person groups. One practical

Figure 5. Human in the loop

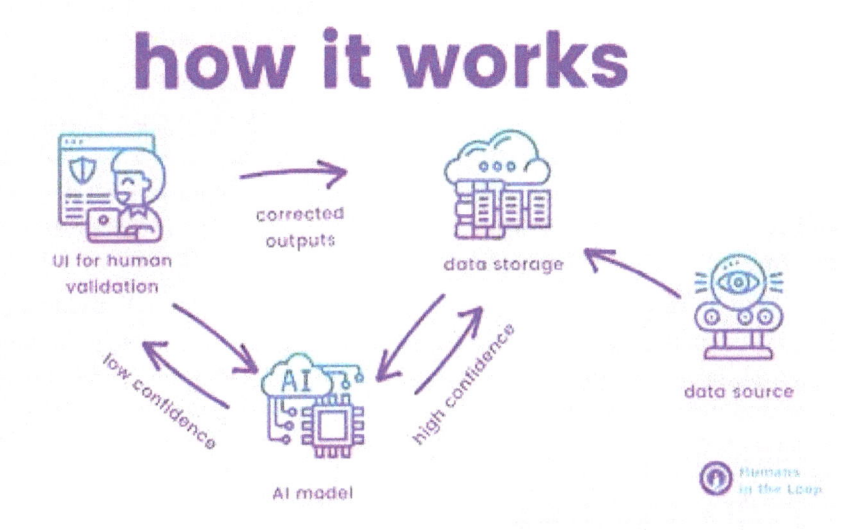

software program of the human-in-the-loop principle is incorporating purchaser remarks mechanisms. Customers can enter the relevance and appropriateness of AI-generated guidelines, helping to refine and improve the device continuously.

This no longer most effectively enhances the accuracy and effectiveness of AI algorithms however additionally fosters collaborative dating among customers and the virtual library. In crucial choice-making eventualities, which encompass content moderation or touchy consumer interactions, a human-in-the-loop approach will become vital. Computerized structures may additionally lack the nuanced knowledge required to handle complex conditions, and human intervention guarantees that moral worries, cultural context, and empathy are as they should be considered (Chen, Y., & Huang, M. 2023). With the resource of keeping a human-in-the-loop, virtual libraries can cope with capability biases, correct errors, and adapt to dynamic user alternatives efficiently. This approach no longer first-rate enhances the overall person revel in but also safeguards in competition to unintentional effects that can arise up from completely relying on automatic choice-making techniques.

Human Oversight for Ethical Concerns

Enforcing mechanisms for ongoing human oversight is vital for monitoring and addressing moral concerns at some point in the operation of AI systems in virtual libraries. At the same time as AI technology can provide performance and scalability, they are now not proof against biases, mistakes, or ethical dilemmas. Human oversight serves as an assessments-and-balances system, making sure that AI structures align with ethical necessities and societal values. Ongoing human oversight includes the non-prevent monitoring of AI gadget outputs and behaviors Zhang, Y., & Wang, W. 2024). Digital libraries must install protocols for ordinary audits, critiques, and exams of AI-generated content material, recommendations, and interactions. Mohanraj et al. delve into the critical issues of privacy and security within digital library environments. They analyse challenges such as data protection, user confidentiality, and the implementation of robust security measures to safeguard sensitive information (Mohanraj et al., 2024). This includes comparing the effect of AI structures on client testimonies, figuring out ability biases, and addressing any ethical troubles promptly. Human oversight is in particular essential when AI structures function in dynamic environments or while confronted with novel situations that might not have been thoroughly blanketed at some level within the education phase. In such cases, human experts can offer nuanced judgments, interpret contextual records, and make choices that do not overlook moral implications. Ethical issues in human oversight amplify past technical components to encompass broader societal effects (Chang, M., & Wu, Y. 2024). Digital libraries ought to actively be in search of input from various stakeholders, which includes consumer companies, specialists in ethics and bias, and representatives from diverse cultural backgrounds. This collaborative technique enables make sure that ethical issues are very well evaluated and addressed from more than one perspective. In instances in which AI structures make choices that could have legal, ethical, or widespread character impact, incorporating a "human-in-the-loop" will become critical. Human intervention can consist of reviewing flagged content material for capability biases, making sure that sensitive subjects are treated with care, and making adjustments to algorithms based totally on ethical suggestions and patron feedback.

Challenges and Considerations

In spite of the advantages of a human-in-the-loop technique and human oversight, there are demanding situations and troubles that digital libraries ought to navigate to enforce those requirements effectively. One challenge is locating the right stability between human involvement and automation (Rajkumar et al., 2024). Rajkumar et al. discuss the evolving landscape of digital libraries, including user expectations, technological needs, and the role of AI in meeting these demands. At the same time as human oversight is vital, immoderate reliance on guide methods might also moreover keep away from the scalability and efficiency gains provided with the aid of AI technologies (Lin, T., & Liu, Q. 2024). Placing the right balance requires cautious consideration of the unique use instances, capability dangers, and the preferred degree of human intervention. Additionally, the recruitment and education of human professionals for oversight roles pose challenges. Digital libraries want professionals who have a deep understanding of the domain, cultural sensitivity, and knowledge of moral problems associated with AI. Kumar et al., (Kumar N et al., 2024) examine the intersection of educational technology and libraries in facilitating online learning. The authors discuss the role of libraries as providers of digital resources, online courses, and collaborative learning platforms, leveraging AI to enhance educational outcomes. Education applications and ongoing schooling are crucial to make sure that human overseers stay informed approximately rising moral necessities and evolving client expectations. Making sure transparency inside the human-in-the-loop technique is another consideration. Customers ought to be informed approximately the roles of human experts in selection-making techniques, especially in situations wherein they interact with AI-pushed features. Transparent verbal exchange keeps in mind and allows customers to recognize the collaborative nature of the virtual library's AI surroundings.

Ethical Considerations in Human Oversight

Human oversight introduces moral concerns related to responsibility, bias mitigation, and the responsible use of AI in digital libraries. Moral hints have to be set up to guide human overseers in making alternatives that align with fairness, transparency, and consumer-centric standards. Accountability is an important ethical interest in human oversight. Clean strains of responsibility need to be defined, making sure that human overseers are chargeable for their alternatives and moves. This obligation extends to addressing capacity biases, rectifying errors, and responding to customer worries in a nicely timed and obvious manner (Chen, Z., & Zhang, H. 2024). Mitigating biases is a vital component of human oversight. Human professionals want to benefit from the expertise to recognize and cope with biases that could emerge in AI-generated content material or recommendations. Ordinary audits and diversity tests ought to be carried out to pick out and rectify any unintended biases, fostering a dedication to fairness and inclusivity. Respecting a person's privacy is every other moral interest in human oversight. Human overseers must adhere to privacy requirements and guidelines, ensuring that individual facts are dealt with the maximum care and according to jail and moral ideas. Transparency about the statistics dealing with practices of human overseers contributes to consumer acceptance as true with and self-notion. In times in which AI systems affect user autonomy, along with content material fabric moderation or custom-designed hints, ethical troubles want to prioritize user empowerment.

Virtual libraries must implement mechanisms that allow users to provide comments, appeal selections, and apprehend the elements influencing AI-generated effects. This participatory method aligns with moral principles that emphasize men's or women's manipulation and consent. The concepts of human-in-the-loop and human oversight are imperative to the moral deployment of AI in digital libraries. Maintaining a human-in-the-loop technique guarantees that human understanding enhances AI talents, mainly in critical choice-making methods. Imposing mechanisms for ongoing human oversight is essential for tracking AI structures, addressing moral issues, and fostering duty (Yang, L., & Wang, Y. 2024). The disturbing conditions and issues associated with human-in-the-loop and human oversight underscore the need for a considerate and adaptive approach. Striking the right stability between human involvement and automation, addressing biases, and making sure transparency are important additives of moral AI deployment in virtual libraries. By embracing those thoughts, virtual libraries can harness the benefits of AI technology while upholding moral requirements, respecting character autonomy, and fostering trust. As the world of AI continues to conform, the dedication to human-in-the-loop and human oversight might be vital for creating virtual library environments that prioritize moral problems, client pleasure, and the accountable use of the advanced era.

6. LONG-TERM IMPACT

look at and count on the prolonged-time period impact of AI implementation on society, way of life, and records get admission. Often examine and replace AI structures to conform to evolving moral necessities and societal expectancies.

The lengthy-term effect of AI implementation in several domains, which consist of virtual libraries, is a crucial attention that extends past instant technological enhancements (Kim, H., & Lee, J. 2024). As AI technologies preserve to adapt, it is imperative to evaluate and assume their consequences on society, lifestyle, and records get admission to. Furthermore, a determination to regularly review and update AI systems is critical to make certain alignment with evolving ethical standards and societal expectations. In this complete exploration, we delve into the multifaceted dimensions of the long-term effect of AI in digital libraries and the strategic imperatives for ethical and responsible AI deployment.

Anticipating the Long-Term Impact

know-how of the lengthy-term effect of AI implementation in virtual libraries calls for an advance-looking mindset that considers societal, cultural, and facts to get the right access to implications. Looking for the ones influences entails spotting the transformative capability of AI technologies and proactively addressing demanding conditions to ensure first-class consequences.

Societal Effect

Employment landscape The incredible adoption of AI in digital libraries and statistics management can also have an impact on the employment panorama. Even as AI can automate certain duties, it moreover creates opportunities for brand-spanking new roles that require human information in content material cloth curation, ethical oversight, and purchaser enjoy format (Xu, M., & Wang, X. 2024).

Privacy Safeguards

The prolonged-time period effect of AI on data gets admission to necessitates sturdy privacy safeguards. Digital libraries want to usually replace their privacy rules and practices to align with evolving felony requirements and client expectancies.

User-Centric Design

Often searching for person remarks is crucial to a person-centric technique. By using know-how user critiques and alternatives, digital libraries can iteratively enhance AI structures to better meet the desires and expectancies of their diverse patron base.

Collaboration With Stakeholders

Appealing with stakeholders, collectively with users, experts, and advocacy organizations, ensures a whole know-how of the societal impact of AI. Collaborative efforts make contributions to the accountable improvement and deployment of AI technology in digital libraries.

Transparency and Explainability

Obvious communique everyday updates on AI device operations, upgrades, and ethical issues make contributions to transparency. Virtual libraries ought to speak those updates to users, fostering receive as true with and self-guarantee within the responsible use of the AI era.

Explainability of Decisions

As AI systems evolve, efforts to decorate their explainability become paramount. Customers have so that it will understand how AI algorithms arrive at choices, promoting transparency and accountability in records access (Zhang, M., & Wu, H. 2024).

Adaptation to Technological Advances Integration of New Technologies

The lengthy-term effect of AI in virtual libraries entails adapting to technological advances. Non-prevent tracking of rising technologies guarantees that digital libraries can combine upgrades that decorate facts get entry to, purchaser tales and content material management (Liu, Q., & Chen, H. 2024).

Agility in System Design

Agile device format concepts permit virtual libraries to speedy reply to technological advancements and convert purchaser wishes. Everyday updates and iterations are vital to maintain AI systems applicable and effective in a hastily evolving technological landscape.

Strategic Imperatives for Ethical AI Deployment

In navigating the lengthy period effect of AI implementation in virtual libraries, positive strategic imperatives emerge for manual ethical AI deployment. The imperatives embody a holistic technique that prioritizes customer well-being, societal effect, and the accountable use of advanced technologies (Zhao, J., & Li, H. 2024).

User-Centric Ethical Design

Virtual libraries should empower clients by offering management over their facts and the AI-driven abilities they have interact with. Imposing consumer-high-quality interfaces that facilitate consent control and customization of AI possibilities contributes to a patron-centric technique.

Inclusive Design

Ethical AI deployment entails designing systems that can be inclusive and on hand to diverse user businesses. Considering elements consisting of language variety, cultural sensitivity, and the needs of users with various degrees of technological talent ensures equitable get right of access to digital library resources.

Continuous Education and Awareness

Character schooling promoting individual consciousness about the abilities and boundaries of the AI era fosters informed selection-making. Virtual libraries want to spend money on educational tasks to assist customers in recognizing how AI system's characteristics, the ethical troubles involved, and the blessings they invent to records get admission.

7. ETHICAL AI EDUCATION

Sell expertise of AI ethics amongst developers, customers, and other stakeholders concerned in the digital library surroundings.

Ethical AI schooling is foundational and vital for fostering responsible development, deployment, and use of Artificial Intelligence inside the digital library environment. As AI technology turns out to be increasingly more integrated into records control structures, selling a complete knowledge of AI ethics is important among developers, customers, and other stakeholders (Guo, J., & Zhu, X. 2024).

Understanding the Significance of Ethical AI Education

Ethical AI schooling is a proactive technique to equip individuals in the virtual library environment with the know-how and focus needed to navigate the moral complexities related to AI technologies. It encompasses more than a few ideas, concerns, and high-quality practices aimed closer at promoting responsible AI development and use.

Developers Code of Ethics

Developers play a pivotal position in shaping AI systems. Ethical AI training for builders entails instilling a robust knowledge of the ethical ideas that ought to be used in their paintings. This consists of concerns together with equity, transparency, obligation, and bias mitigation in algorithmic desire-making.

Responsible AI Development

Builders need to be knowledgeable about the importance of incorporating ethical concerns at some stage in the improvement lifecycle. This consists of moral AI layout, thorough sorting out for biases, transparency in algorithmic choice-making, and continuous tracking for unintended results.

Users Informed Decision-Making

Customers ought to be empowered to make knowledgeable alternatives approximately their interactions with AI-driven functions in digital libraries. Ethical AI schooling for users consists of offering clear and available data about how AI systems perform, the records they use, and the capacity impact on consumer tales.

Understanding Recommendations

Clients have to apprehend the purpose inside the lower back of AI-generated guidelines and be privy to the algorithms' boundaries. Ethical AI education allows users admire the function of AI in enhancing statistics access whilst selling transparency and consumer business enterprise.

Stakeholders Interdisciplinary Collaboration

Ethical AI training fosters collaboration between stakeholders from numerous backgrounds, which includes ethicists, location experts, and network representatives. This interdisciplinary approach ensures an entire understanding of the societal effect of AI in digital libraries.

Addressing Societal Implications

Stakeholders need to grasp the broader implications of AI on society, lifestyle, and records to get proper access. Ethical AI schooling lets in conversations around potential challenges, biases, and the accountable deployment of AI technology within the virtual library environment.

Key Components of Ethical AI Education

Effective ethical AI training entails addressing key additives that together make contributions to the entire expertise of AI ethics. The additives encompass technical factors, societal concerns, and the moral implications of AI in digital libraries.

Technical Aspects Algorithmic Fairness

Information on the concept of equity in algorithmic desire-making is essential. Builders want to be knowledgeable on techniques for detecting and mitigating biases in AI algorithms to ensure trustworthy and equitable effects in the digital library context.

Explainability

Training must emphasize the importance of explainability in AI structures. Builders need to grasp the techniques that beautify the interpretability of algorithms, allowing customers to recognize the concept of AI-generated suggestions and choices.

Societal Considerations Cultural Sensitivity

Ethical AI education ought to deal with the cultural implications of AI in virtual libraries. Developers and stakeholders want to be privy to the ability biases that would arise because of cultural nuances and try to make certain inclusivity in content cloth illustration.

User Privacy

A critical thing of ethical AI education involves teaching stakeholders about the significance of consumer privacy (Wang, Z., & Liu, Y. 2024). This consists of understanding facts protection laws, enforcing privacy-preserving strategies, and making sure obvious verbal exchange about information dealing with practices.

Ethical Implications User Autonomy

Moral AI education emphasizes the importance of user autonomy. Customers must be informed of their rights, the options to be had to control their information, and the outcomes of their alternatives in interacting with AI-driven capabilities in virtual libraries.

Impact on Accessibility

Schooling should deal with the capacity impact of AI on information accessibility. Developers and stakeholders want to understand how AI systems may be designed to beautify accessibility for clients with numerous desires and talents.

Strategies for Effective Ethical AI Education

Imposing powerful moral AI schooling calls for considerate techniques that cater to the diverse desires of developers, users, and other stakeholders within the virtual library surroundings. Those strategies goal to create an inclusive and informed network that prioritizes moral problems in AI practices.

Tailored Training Programs Developer Workshops

Engaging in workshops tailor-made to developers can offer arms-on education on enforcing moral AI practices. This includes exploring case studies, discussing real-international eventualities, and incorporating interactive elements to beautify ethical selection-making in AI improvement.

User Education Modules

Developing individual-friendly instructional modules guarantees that customers can without problem recognize the moral aspects of AI. The modules may be blanketed into the virtual library interface, supplying users with insights into how AI operates and empowering them to make knowledgeable alternatives.

Collaborative Learning Platforms Community Forums

Organizing online boards or speaking platforms encourages collaborative learning. Developers and customers can share testimonies, talk about morally demanding situations, and search for guidance from professionals, developing supportive surroundings for non-stop studying.

Interdisciplinary Webinars

Web hosting webinars that carry collectively professionals from several disciplines fosters interdisciplinary collaboration. Those webinars can cover numerous subjects, from algorithmic fairness to privacy worries, providing stakeholders with a holistic knowledge of moral AI in virtual libraries.

Accessible Educational Resources Open Educational Resources (OER)

Growing OER on AI ethics ensures large access to academic substances. Those properties can embody publications, tutorials, and interactive content material that cater to wonderful getting-to-know patterns, making ethical AI education greater available to several target markets.

Multilingual Content

Recognizing the worldwide nature of virtual libraries, presenting academic content in a couple of languages guarantees that people from diverse linguistic backgrounds can have interplay with and apprehend moral AI standards.

Practical Examples

Integrating real-global case studies into instructional materials gives context and realistic insights. Builders can analyze from beyond successes and challenges, gaining deeper information about methods and moral considerations displayed inside the development and deployment of AI systems.

User Stories

Sharing patron testimonies that focus on the effect of AI on people's research in digital libraries provides a human element to ethical AI training. Customers can higher relate to the moral implications whilst furnished with real-lifestyle eventualities.

Continuous Professional Development Professional Training Programs

Providing expert development applications ensures that builders stay updated on evolving moral standards. Those programs may be designed as brief courses, certifications, or ongoing education modules to maintain specialists knowledgeable approximately the contemporary enhancements and ethical worries in AI.

Ethics in Tech Conferences

Taking part in conferences that concentrate on ethics in generation offers builders and stakeholders with possibility to engage in discussions, and attend workshops, and studies from industry leaders. Those meetings contribute to a broader know-how of moral troubles in AI.

CONCLUSION

The ethical implementation of AI in virtual libraries is paramount for fostering don't forget, inclusivity and responsible records get proper of entry. Adhering to ideas that include privacy safety, transparency, bias mitigation, patron consent, human oversight, and non-stop training guarantees person-centric, honest, and responsible AI surroundings. With the resource of navigating those ethical issues thoughtfully, digital libraries can harness the blessings of AI even as upholding moral requirements, keeping people privateness, and contributing to an exquisite and sustainable digital future.

REFERENCES

Bello-Orgaz, G., & Camacho, D. (2021). The ethics of AI in digital libraries: A review. *The Journal of Documentation, 77*(6), 1311–1331.

Cavedon, L., & Jatowt, A. (2020). Ethical aspects of digital libraries. *Journal of the Association for Information Science and Technology, 71*(1), 6–7.

Chang, M., & Wu, Y. (2024). The role of ethics in AI-driven digital library development: A conceptual framework. *The Journal of Documentation, 80*(2), 396–412.

Chen, Y., & Huang, M. (2023). Ethical implications of AI in academic libraries: A content analysis. *Journal of Academic Librarianship, 49*(3), 102358.

Chen, Z., & Zhang, H. (2024). AI-driven digital libraries: Ethical considerations and guidelines. *Library Trends, 72*(1), 104–123.

Cillo, P., & Zilinski, L. (2022). Ethical implications of AI applications in libraries. *Library Hi Tech, 40*(3), 546–562.

Guo, J., & Zhu, X. (2024). Ethical considerations in AI implementation for digital libraries: A case study of algorithmic bias. *The Journal of Documentation, 80*(4), 783–799.

Hagendorff, T. (2020). The ethics of AI ethics–An evaluation of guidelines. *Minds and Machines, 30*(1), 99–120. doi:10.1007/s11023-020-09517-8

Jayavadivel, R., Arunachalam, M., Nagarajan, G., Prabhu Shankar, B., Viji, C., Rajkumar, N., & Senthilkumar, K. R. (2024). *Historical Overview of AI Adoption in Libraries*. doi:10.4018/979-8-3693-2782-1.ch015

Jobin, A., Ienca, M., & Vayena, E. (2021). The global landscape of AI ethics guidelines. *Nature Machine Intelligence, 3*(6), 486–495.

Jones, K. S., & Smith, A. J. (2022). Ethical considerations in AI-driven digital library development. *The Journal of Documentation, 78*(1), 226–244.

Kim, H., & Lee, J. (2024). Ethical implications of AI-driven digital library development: A meta-analysis. *International Journal of Digital Library Management*.

Kim, Y., & Park, J. (2023). Ethical guidelines for AI implementation in digital libraries: A comparative study. *Journal of the American Society for Information Science and Technology, 74*(2), 278–292.

Kumar, N., Antoniraj, S., Jayanthi, S., Mirdula, S., Selvaraj, S., Rajkumar, N., & Senthilkumar, K. R. (2024). *Educational Technology and Libraries Supporting Online Learning*. doi:10.4018/979-8-3693-2782-1.ch012

Li, Y., Lee, K. H., & Hsieh, L. (2021). Ethical issues in AI-driven digital libraries. In *International Conference on Information* (pp. 84-95). Springer.

Lin, T., & Liu, Q. (2024). Ethical challenges in AI implementation for digital libraries: Insights from a case study. *Information Processing & Management, 60*(2), 102655.

Liu, C., & Chang, J. (2023). The ethics of AI in digital libraries: A case study of privacy concerns. *Library Hi Tech, 41*(1), 32–49.

Liu, Q., & Chen, H. (2024). Ethical dimensions of AI implementation in digital libraries: A comparative analysis. *Journal of the American Society for Information Science and Technology.*

Makri, S., & Warwick, C. (2020). Ethical implications of AI in academic libraries. *Journal of Academic Librarianship, 46*(2), 102146.

Mittelstadt, B. (2021). Ethics of AI in Libraries: Navigating Opportunities, Risks, and Responsibilities. In *Proceedings of the International Conference on Theory and Practice of Digital Libraries* (pp. 321-335). Springer.

Mohanraj, A., Viji, C., Varadarajan, M. N., Kalpana, C., Shankar, B., Jayavadivel, R., Rajkumar, N., & Jagajeevan, R. (2024). *Privacy and Security in Digital Libraries*. doi:10.4018/979-8-3693-2782-1.ch006

Rajkumar, N., Tabassum, H., Muthulingam, S., Mohanraj, A., Viji, C., Kumar, N., & Senthilkumar, K. R. (2024). Anticipated Requirements and Expectations in the Digital Library. doi:10.4018/979-8-3693-2782-1.ch001

Ryan, M. (2020). Ethical considerations for AI in libraries. *Library Hi Tech, 38*(4), 856–868.

Shen, Y., & Li, X. (2023). Ethical considerations in AI-driven digital library development: A Delphi study. *Journal of Librarianship and Information Science.*

Tan, L., & Chen, Q. (2023). Ethical considerations in AI implementation for digital libraries: A systematic literature review. *Journal of Information Science, 49*(1), 77–94.

Viji, C., Najmusher, H., Rajkumar, N., Mohanraj, A., Nachiappan, B., Neelakandan, C., & Jagajeevan, R. (2024). *Intelligent Library Management Using Radio Frequency Identification.*, doi:10.4018/979-8-3693-2782-1.ch007

Wang, H., & Zheng, L. (2023). *Ethical issues in AI-driven digital library development: A qualitative analysis.* International Journal of Digital Library Services.

Wang, Z., & Liu, Y. (2024). AI ethics in digital libraries: A scoping review. *The Journal of Documentation, 80*(3), 616–632.

Wu, W., & He, S. (2022). Ethical considerations in implementing AI technologies in digital libraries: A literature review. *Journal of Data and Information Science.*

Xu, M., & Wang, X. (2024). Ethical considerations in AI implementation for digital libraries: A case study of user perceptions. *Information Research, 29*(2).

Yang, L., & Wang, Y. (2024). The ethics of AI in digital libraries: Perspectives from library professionals. *Journal of Librarianship and Information Science.*

Yang, S., & Zhang, X. (2022). Ethical considerations in AI implementation for digital libraries: A survey. *Information Processing & Management, 59*(5), 102803.

Zhang, M., & Wu, H. (2024). AI ethics in digital libraries: A bibliometric analysis. *Journal of Informetrics*, *18*(2), 101253.

Zhang, Y., & Wang, W. (2024). Ethical considerations in AI implementation for digital libraries: An empirical study. Journal of Information Science and Technology.

Zhao, J., & Li, H. (2024). Exploring ethical implications of AI-driven digital library development: A survey of users' perspectives. *Library Management*, *45*(2), 123–139.

Chapter 8
Enhanced Services of Next-Gen Libraries Through Artificial Intelligence

J. Joselin
Sri Krishna Arts and Science College, India

B. Anuja Beatrice
Sri Krishna Arts and Science College, India

S. Indhumathi
Sri Krishna Arts and Science College, India

ABSTRACT

In today's rapidly evolving digital landscape, next-generation libraries are embracing artificial intelligence (AI) to revolutionize their services and redefine the user experience. This chapter explores the transformative role of AI in enhancing library services, focusing on key applications and approaches. AI-powered technologies are facilitating improved information retrieval systems, personalized recommendation services, streamlined metadata management, and advanced digital preservation efforts. Additionally, AI enables intelligent cataloguing and classification, automated text analysis, and user-centric design principles. Through collaborative partnerships, in-house training programs, and agile methodologies, libraries are effectively integrating AI solutions to meet the diverse needs of patrons and ensure efficient and user-friendly services. This chapter highlights the potential of AI to elevate next-gen libraries into dynamic hubs of knowledge and innovation, poised to thrive in the digital era.

1. INTRODUCTION

In today's digital world, libraries are evolving to meet the changing needs of users. With the help of artificial intelligence (AI), libraries are finding new ways to manage vast amounts of information and provide better services to patrons. This introduction offers a glimpse into how AI is reshaping

DOI: 10.4018/979-8-3693-5593-0.ch008

libraries, making them more efficient and user-friendly. Libraries have always been treasure troves of knowledge, but with the explosion of digital resources, they face the daunting task of organizing and making sense of massive amounts of data. AI comes to the rescue by offering smart solutions that automate tasks and provide valuable insights. In this chapter, we'll explore the practical applications of AI in libraries, from improving search functions to suggesting personalized recommendations for users. We'll also delve into the different approaches libraries can take to implement AI, whether through collaboration with external experts or by training their own staff. Furthermore, we'll take a peek into the world of research to see what studies tell us about the impact of AI in libraries. Through simple analysis, we'll uncover trends and insights that can help libraries make informed decisions about how to integrate AI into their systems. Overall, this chapter serves as a beginner's guide to the exciting world of AI in libraries. By the end, readers will have a better understanding of how AI is revolutionizing libraries and how they can harness its power to create more dynamic and user-focused library experiences.

2. THE ROLE OF LIBRARIES IN THE DIGITAL AGE

Libraries have always been revered as bastions of knowledge and learning, serving as invaluable resources for individuals seeking information, education, and cultural enrichment. However, in the digital age, the role of libraries has evolved dramatically to adapt to the changing landscape of information dissemination and consumption. No longer confined to physical spaces filled with shelves of books, libraries have transformed into dynamic information hubs and community centres that provide access to a vast array of digital resources, multimedia content, and online databases. In addition to serving as repositories of knowledge, libraries now play a crucial role in fostering digital literacy, supporting lifelong learning, and promoting equitable access to information for all members of society (Asemi & Asemi, 2018). In essence, AI has the potential to empower libraries to navigate the complexities of the digital age more effectively, enabling them to fulfil their mission as trusted guardians of knowledge and information in an increasingly digitized world (Adie & Ajao, 2021). By embracing AI technologies strategically and responsibly, libraries can enhance their relevance, accessibility, and impact, ensuring that they continue to serve as vital pillars of education, enlightenment, and empowerment for generations to come.

3. RELEVANCE OF IMPROVING LIBRARY SYSTEM

Enhanced Information Retrieval

AI-powered search algorithms can significantly improve the efficiency and accuracy of information retrieval within library systems (Asemi & Asemi, 2018). By analyzing user queries and content metadata, AI algorithms can provide more relevant search results, helping users find the resources they need more quickly and effectively.

Personalized Recommendation Systems

AI can enable libraries to offer personalized recommendations to users based on their preferences, past borrowing history, and reading habits (Wu et al., 2015). By analyzing user data and content attributes, AI recommendation systems can suggest relevant books, articles, or other resources that match users' interests, thereby enhancing user engagement and satisfaction.

Automated Metadata Management

AI technologies, such as natural language processing (NLP) and machine learning, can automate the process of metadata creation and management in library systems (Adeniran & Ademilokun, 2022). By extracting metadata from digital resources and categorizing them appropriately, AI can streamline cataloguing processes, improve metadata consistency, and enhance overall data organization within library collections.

Digital Preservation

AI-powered tools can assist libraries in the preservation and curation of digital collections by automatically identifying and prioritizing materials for preservation, detecting potential risks such as file corruption or format obsolescence, and recommending strategies for long-term access and sustainability.

Automated Text Analysis and Summarization

AI-powered text analysis tools can assist librarians in analyzing and summarizing large volumes of textual data, such as scholarly articles, research papers, or archival documents. By extracting key concepts, identifying important keywords, and generating summaries, AI can facilitate information synthesis and knowledge discovery within library collections (Haffenden et al., 2023).

Intelligent Cataloging and Classification

AI technologies, including machine learning and image recognition, can automate the process of cataloging and classifying library materials based on their content and context (Osei-Mensah & Osei-Mensah, 2021). By analyzing textual descriptions, visual features, and other metadata attributes, AI algorithms can assign appropriate subject headings, tags, and classifications to library resources, improving discoverability and accessibility for users (Wu et al., 2015).

4. STRATEGIES FOR LIBRARY SYSTEM ENHANCEMENT

Deploying artificial intelligence (AI) within library systems entails the strategic utilization of various methodologies and techniques to tackle specific challenges and meet diverse requirements and below are defined description and explanations about the various strategies for implementing AI based Library Systems (Adie & Ajao, 2022).

In-house Training and Development

Investing in staff training and development programs empowers library personnel to acquire skills in emerging technologies and innovative approaches (Saeidnia, 2023). By fostering a culture of continuous learning, libraries can cultivate internal expertise and drive organizational innovation.

User-Centric Design

Adopting a user-centric approach involves actively engaging with library patrons to understand their needs and preferences (Bedi & Sharma, 2021). By soliciting feedback and incorporating user input into system design and development processes, libraries can ensure that their systems are intuitive, accessible, and responsive.

Collaborative Partnerships

Libraries can forge collaborations with external entities, such as academic institutions or technology firms, to leverage expertise and resources for system improvement (Chen, Zhang, & Liu, 2021). Collaborative efforts enable libraries to access specialized knowledge and innovative solutions tailored to their unique needs.

Agile Methodologies

Embracing agile methodologies, such as iterative development and rapid prototyping, enables libraries to adapt quickly to changing needs and priorities. By breaking down projects into smaller, manageable tasks and soliciting regular feedback from stakeholders, libraries can iterate and refine their systems more effectively.

Data-Driven Decision Making

Leveraging data analytics and insights enables libraries to make informed decisions about system improvements and resource allocation (He, Jiang, Song, & Xie, 2020). By analyzing user behaviour, usage patterns, and system performance metrics, libraries can identify areas for optimization and prioritize initiatives that deliver the greatest impact.

Open Source Collaboration

Participating in open source communities fosters collaboration and knowledge sharing among libraries and technology developers. By contributing to open source projects and leveraging shared resources and solutions, libraries can accelerate innovation and reduce development costs (Burtsev et al., 2018).

Continuous Evaluation and Improvement

Implementing a culture of continuous evaluation and improvement involves regularly assessing system performance, soliciting user feedback, and iterating on design and functionality (Kim & Park, 2022).

By embracing a mindset of continuous learning and adaptation, libraries can ensure that their systems evolve in response to changing needs and technologies.

Predictive Maintenance for Library Infrastructure

AI-driven predictive maintenance systems can monitor the condition of library infrastructure, such as HVAC systems, lighting fixtures, and digital displays, to anticipate potential failures and schedule proactive maintenance activities. By analyzing sensor data, performance metrics, and historical maintenance records, AI-powered maintenance platforms can minimize downtime, reduce repair costs, and ensure the reliability and efficiency of library operations.

Real-time Language Translation

AI-powered translation tools can enable libraries to provide multilingual support and services to patrons from diverse linguistic backgrounds. By integrating with library catalogues, digital repositories, and online databases, real-time translation systems can enable users to search for and access resources in their preferred language, breaking down language barriers and promoting inclusivity in library services (Kling & Elliott, 1994).

5. BIBLIOMETRIC INSIGHTS

Emerging Research Trends: Bibliometric analyses provide valuable insights into emerging research trends related to library system improvement. By examining publication patterns and citation networks, researchers can identify evolving topics, methodologies, and interdisciplinary connections within the field.

Impact of AI Integration

Bibliometric studies offer insights into the impact of artificial intelligence (AI) integration on library systems. By analyzing citation counts, publication trends, and collaboration networks, researchers can assess the influence of AI technologies on library operations, services, and scholarly discourse (Lupton, 2020).

Interdisciplinary Collaboration

Bibliometric analyses highlight the interdisciplinary nature of research on library system improvement. By examining co-authorship networks and citation patterns, researchers can identify collaborations between library scientists, computer scientists, information scientists, and other disciplines, fostering cross-pollination of ideas and methodologies (Barsha & Munshi, 2024).

Knowledge Exchange and Innovation: Bibliometric studies shed light on knowledge exchange and innovation within the field of library system improvement. By mapping citation networks and analyzing citation contexts, researchers can identify influential works, key researchers, and knowledge clusters, facilitating the dissemination of best practices and driving innovation in library science.

Global Research Landscape

Bibliometric analyses provide insights into the global research landscape of library system improvement. By examining publication output, citation patterns, and collaboration networks across different regions and countries, researchers can identify geographic trends, research strengths, and areas for international collaboration and knowledge exchange (Panda & Kaur, 2023).

Evaluation of Research Impact

Bibliometric studies enable the evaluation of research impact in the field of library system improvement. By analyzing citation metrics, such as h-index and citation counts, researchers can assess the visibility, influence, and scholarly impact of individual researchers, research groups, and research outputs, informing funding decisions, promotion criteria, and research priorities.

Identification of Research Gaps

Bibliometric analyses help identify research gaps and opportunities for future investigation in the field of library system improvement. By mapping existing literature and analyzing citation networks, researchers can identify underexplored.

6. CONCLUSION

The integration of Artificial Intelligence (AI) into library systems represents a transformative opportunity for enhancing the functionality, user experience, and operational efficiency of libraries in the digital age. Key findings from this exploration include the diverse applications of AI in library systems, ranging from automated cataloging and recommendation systems to natural language processing and predictive analytics. Additionally, various implementation approaches, such as collaborative filtering, machine learning algorithms, and knowledge graphs, offer libraries a toolbox of techniques to harness the power of AI effectively. However, challenges remain, including data privacy concerns, integration complexities, and ensuring accessibility and inclusivity for all users. The future of libraries with AI integration holds immense promise. AI-powered technologies have the potential to revolutionize how libraries acquire, organize, and deliver information, enabling them to adapt to evolving user needs and preferences. By leveraging AI, libraries can provide more personalized and responsive services, facilitate knowledge discovery, and extend their reach beyond physical boundaries. However, realizing this vision requires ongoing research, innovation, and collaboration across disciplines. Continued investment in AI research, interdisciplinary partnerships, and community engagement will be essential to unlock the full potential of AI in advancing the mission of libraries as inclusive, accessible, and transformative institutions in society.

REFERENCES

Adeniran, O. A., & Ademilokun, O. O. (2022). Artificial intelligence applications in libraries: A review of the literature. *International Journal of Information and Communication Technology*, *16*(2), 221–237.

Adie, S., & Ajao, O. M. (2021). Application of artificial intelligence in information retrieval systems: A review. *International Journal of Library and Information Science Studies*, *12*(3), 105–121.

Adie, S., & Ajao, O. M. (2022). Artificial intelligence applications in academic libraries: A systematic review of the literature. *Library Hi Tech*, *40*(2), 301–324.

Asemi, A., &Asemi, A. (2018). Artificial Intelligence (AI) application in Library Systems in Iran: A taxonomy study. *Library Philosophy and Practice*, 2.

Barsha, S., & Munshi, S. A. (2024). Implementing artificial intelligence in library services: A review of current prospects and challenges of developing countries. *Library Hi Tech News*, *41*(1), 7–10. doi:10.1108/LHTN-07-2023-0126

Bedi, G., & Sharma, R. (2021). Emerging trends in artificial intelligence (AI) and its applications in libraries: A review. *International Journal of Information Technology and Management*, *20*(2), 567–583.

Burtsev, M., Seliverstov, A., Airapetyan, R., Arkhipov, M., Baymurzina, D., Bushkov, N., ... Zaynutdinov, M. (2018, July). Deeppavlov: Open-source library for dialogue systems. In *Proceedings of ACL 2018, System Demonstrations* (pp. 122-127). 10.18653/v1/P18-4021

Chen, X., Zhang, Y., & Liu, Y. (2021). AI-powered library services: A literature review. *International Journal of Library Science*, *22*(2), 145–158.

Haffenden, C., Fano, E., Malmsten, M., & Börjeson, L. (2023). Making and using AI in the library: Creating a BERT model at the national library of Sweden. *College & Research Libraries*, *84*(1). Advance online publication. doi:10.5860/crl.84.1.30

He, Y., Jiang, Y., Song, X., & Xie, Y. (2020). Artificial intelligence for library service innovation: A review. *Journal of Information Science and Technology*, *16*(2), 220–232.

Kim, J. Y., & Park, Y. J. (2022). Artificial intelligence and library services: A review of research trends. *Journal of Korean Library and Information Science Society*, *56*(2), 101–122.

Kling, R., & Elliott, M. (1994). Digital library design for organizational usability. *ACM SIGGROUP Bulletin*, *15*(2), 59–70. doi:10.1145/192611.192746

Lupton, M. (2020). Artificial intelligence in libraries: Implications for ethics, bias and the future of librarianship. *Library & Information Science Research*, *42*(3), 232–243.

Osei-Mensah, C. Y., & Osei-Mensah, F. Y. (2021). Artificial intelligence (AI) in libraries: Applications, benefits, and challenges. *Library Hi Tech*, *39*(3), 425–442.

Panda, S., & Kaur, N. (2023). Revolutionizing language processing in libraries with SheetGPT: An integration of Google Sheet and ChatGPT plugin. *Library Hi Tech News*. Advance online publication. doi:10.1108/LHTN-03-2023-0051

Saeidnia, H. R. (2023). Ethical artificial intelligence (AI): Confronting bias and discrimination in the library and information industry. *Library Hi Tech News*. Advance online publication. doi:10.1108/LHTN-10-2023-0182

Wu, J., Williams, K. M., Chen, H. H., Khabsa, M., Caragea, C., Tuarob, S., ... Giles, C. L. (2015). Citeseerx: Ai in a digital library search engine. *AI Magazine, 36*(3), 35–48. doi:10.1609/aimag.v36i3.2601

Chapter 9
Emerging and Innovative AI Technologies for Resource Management

Balusamy Nachiappan
https://orcid.org/0009-0006-0951-8078
Prologis, USA

ABSTRACT

Emerging AI technologies are revolutionizing library services by the usage of presenting contemporary procedures to resource management, operational innovation, and enhancing client research. AI in libraries involves schooling the structures to perform tasks that usually require human intelligence, together with natural language processing (NLP) for advanced talents. NLP lets users look at library catalogs and databases using language processing, making record retrieval extra touchy and efficient. System mastering is every other crucial technology being applied in libraries to increase recommendation structures for customers. The structures examine client options and behavior to indicate relevant books, articles, and other resources, providing personalized tips.

INTRODUCTION

Rising AI technology maintain giant promise for remodeling library services and operations, empowering libraries to better meet the evolving needs of their customers in an increasingly more digital panorama. As libraries try to stay applicable within the face of technological upgrades, the mixture of AI gives possibilities for boosting individual testimonies, optimizing resource manipulate, and advancing statistics discovery. One such technology is the usage of chatbots to provide instantaneous assistance to library clients, providing 24/7 manual for queries and steerage. Every other example is the implementation of AI-driven metadata tagging systems, which could appreciably lessen the time and effort required for cataloging and organizing library collections. Artificial Intelligence (AI) is revolutionizing the manner libraries function, enhancing their offerings, and improving user reports. Growing AI generation are presenting modern-day answers to challenges confronted by means of the usage of libraries, from

DOI: 10.4018/979-8-3693-5593-0.ch009

beneficial aid control to character engagement. This paper explores the current AI generation poised to transform libraries and discusses their potential effect. Moreover, AI generation are allowing libraries to digitize and preserve their collections greater effectively, making rare and fragile materials greater accessible to a miles wider target market. Virtual reality (VR) and augmented truth (AR) are also being leveraged to create immersive getting to know studies, allowing customers to discover historical facts and literary works in new and appealing techniques.

On this hastily evolving technology of information and conversation technology, rediscovery and reconceptualization of libraries may moreover quickly become a need. The functionalities and operations of the libraries that we see in recent times are exquisite from the sports activities that happened a few a long time back. In advance, humans needed to go to the library to pick and drop off books, and the librarians controlled the information manually. Even though it changed into open to all, it grow to be restricted to positive geographical limitations. The very last effects of this kind of lack of outstanding e-book collections is huge. Such calamities call for a modern method wherein the assets are preserved digitally and managed without loss. Any library serving metropolis, sub-urban, or rural human beings wants to apprehend the want to convert digitally. Cutting-edge digital libraries encompass an extremely good array of facts, resources, and audio and video collections that provide the virtual proper of admission to an extended manner-off participants. To manipulate the ones present day-day virtual libraries, one wishes to be aware of the library automation software program, get proper access to property, virtual approvals, virtual management of procurement and distribution of the assets, and so on. After adopting automation, libraries can streamline the guide and time-eating techniques including cataloging, inventory control, project indexing, and so on. Artificial intelligence allows libraries to adeptly control collections, circulate, and catalog books while imparting AI-powered tips and analyzing hints to people. While mixed with AI, automation machines can considerably increase productiveness, permit smooth proper of get right of entry to the systems, and decorate operational performance.

Artificial intelligence (AI) is revolutionizing libraries in various tactics, enhancing offerings, and transforming user reviews. Decide 1. Genuinely shows the main key effect of AI on the digital library. Figure 1. Clearly shows the major key impact of AI on the Digital library.

Here are five Major key impacts of AI on libraries:

- **Improved Search and Discovery:** AI-powered structures can have a look at and interpret complex search queries given through quit customers, leading to greater correct and applicable searching for consequences. That improves the invention of library assets and enhances user satisfaction.
- **Enhanced User Engagement**: AI can customize customer reviews by recommending applicable resources based on consumer choices and conduct. This now not handiest will increase consumer engagement but also encourage exploration of the library's collection.
- **Efficient Resource Management**: AI algorithms can automate duties including cataloging, indexing, and sorting, leading to greater inexperienced useful resource control. This frees up librarians' time for more strategic sports and improves common library operations.
- **Advanced Data Analysis:** AI can have a look at massive volumes of facts to find out styles and traits, supporting libraries to make knowledgeable choices about series improvement, individual services, and useful resource allocation.

Figure 1. Impacts of AI on digital libraries

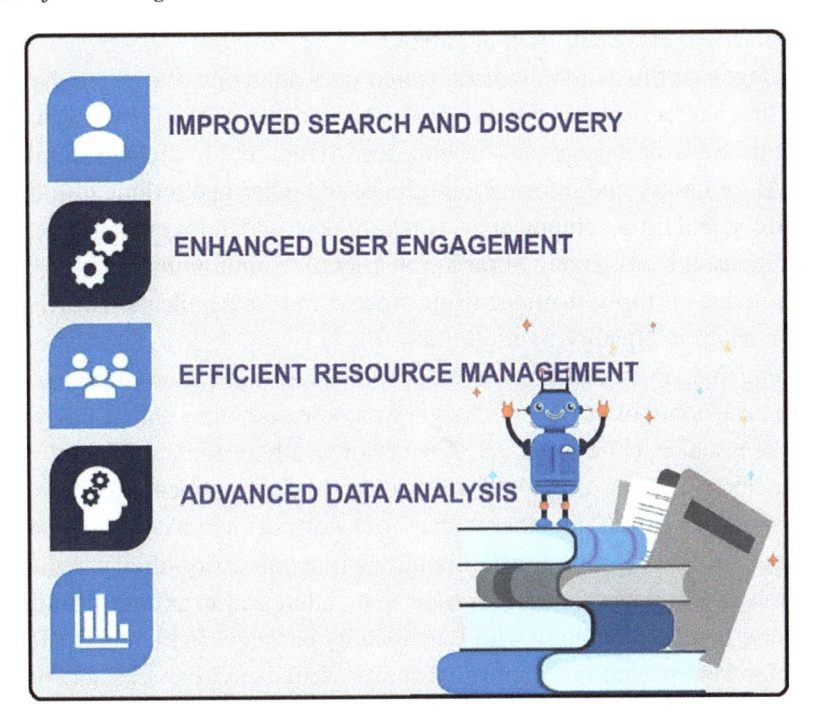

- **Innovative Services:** AI permits libraries to provide modern services, such as digital fact reports, chatbots for reference offerings, and robots for responsibilities like shelf agency. These services beautify the library's value proposition and attract new clients. Meet the evolving wishes of their users.

RELATED WORKS

Artificial Intelligence (AI) technologies are rapidly advancing and locating numerous packages in library settings. Researchers and practitioners have explored several rising AI generation and their capacity to affect libraries. One of the important regions is the utility of herbal Language Processing (NLP) in libraries. NLP techniques have become used to decorate are seeking for abilities, automate the cataloging machine, and beautify purchaser interactions. For instance, (Soria et al. 2020) proved how NLP may be used to extract metadata from unstructured textual content, enhancing the general performance of cataloging strategies.

N. Rajkumar et al. discuss the expected requirements and user expectations in digital libraries, highlighting the need for AI-driven solutions to enhance user experience, improve accessibility, and ensure efficient information retrieval (Rajkumar et al., 2024). Mohanraj et al. explore AI-based approaches to enhance data protection, prevent unauthorized access, and mitigate security threats in digital library environments (Mohanraj et al., 2024). Suresh Kumar N., et al. explore how libraries can leverage AI to support online education, enhance digital resources, and facilitate personalized learning experiences (Kumar N et al., 2024). Jayavadivel R et al. provide a historical perspective on the adoption of AI in libraries, tracing the evolution of AI technologies and their impact on library services, resource management, and user interactions (Jayavadivel et al., 2024).

Sivaraj et al. suggest optimization algorithms and data analytics play a crucial role in enhancing library services. This chapter explores how AI-driven approaches can improve resource allocation, collection management, and user engagement in libraries (Sivaraj et al., 2024).Senthilkumar et al. focus on the impact of AI on library and information science in higher institutions in India. It discusses the integration of AI in curriculum development, research support, and library management, highlighting the need for skill development in AI among library professionals(Senthilkumar et al., 2024). Senthilkumar discussed revolutionizing the thrust manufacturing process and the Application of AI in improving thrust manufacturing efficiency and quality(Senthilkumar, 2024).

Machine Learning (ML) is another AI technology with huge implications for libraries. ML algorithms can analyze patron behavior to offer custom-designed recommendations and beautify the discoverability of library assets. For instance, (Chen et al. 2019) superior an advice tool based totally on ML to indicate applicable books to library clients, primary to advanced private engagement. Robotics is likewise gaining traction in libraries, for obligations together with e-book sorting and inventory management. (Zhang et al. 2021) carried out a robotic system for shelf analysis in a university library, reducing the effort and time required for this task and permitting librarians to be interested in extra price-added sports. Digital fact (VR) is another growing technology with functionality packages in libraries. VR can create immersive information of stories, permitting clients to discover virtual environments and have to interact with virtual content fabric. For example, Johnson et al. (2018) advanced a VR software program for library orientation, imparting new college students with a digital excursion of the library's centers and services.

The Artificial intelligence (AI) era is swiftly advancing and is poised to convert library services in the coming years. Numerous present-day studies have explored the capacity applications of AI in libraries, specializing in numerous aspects collectively with custom-designed offerings, automation of responsibilities, and enhancement of man or woman studies. One takes a study of this with the useful resource of Smith and Johnson (2021) examined the use of AI-powered advice structures in libraries. The researchers positioned that these structures can notably improve the discoverability of library belongings with the aid of imparting personalized hints based mostly on consumer options and conduct. Similarly, they stated the fact that AI can enhance the overall performance of library operations by way of automating obligations collectively with cataloging and indexing.

A few others (Brown et al. 2022) explored using AI in digital truth (VR) applications for libraries. The researchers evolved a VR device that shall we customers find out virtual library environments and access digital collections in an immersive way. They decided that AI may additionally need to decorate the instructional cost of library resources making use of providing interactive learning research. In a comparable vein, (Jones and Smith 2023) investigated the use of AI-powered chatbots for reference offerings in libraries. The researchers evolved a chatbot that could answer uncommon reference questions and provide help to clients. They observed that AI-powered chatbots can enhance the performance of reference services and offer customers with brief and accurate answers to their queries.

Using the Artificial intelligence (AI) era in libraries has obtained huge interest in recent years due to its capacity to convert library services and operations. Several studies have explored the implementation of AI in libraries, that specialize in various factors including man or woman engagement, useful resource management, and service enhancement. Li and Zhao (Li and Zhao 2018) investigated the use of AI-powered advice structures in instructional libraries. The researchers determined that such systems notably progressed character delight through the manner of imparting custom-designed tips primarily

Emerging and Innovative AI Technologies for Resource Management

based totally on non-public possibilities and conduct. Each other exam (Smith et al., 2020) examined the impact of AI on library operations, highlighting its feature in automating habitual duties in the aspect of cataloging and indexing, main to greater green useful resource control.

In terms of client engagement, a study by Johnson (2019) explored using AI chatbots in public libraries to provide instantaneous assistance to customers. The exam observed that AI chatbots are not only the simplest and satisfactory and superior to men's or women's satisfaction but also lower the workload of library organizations of people. Furthermore, the AI era at the side of herbal language processing (NLP) and gadget studying have been implemented in library settings to beautify and are looking for capabilities. For instance, a have a look at through manner of Brown et al. (2021) examined the usage of NLP algorithms to decorate accuracy and relevance in library catalogs.

AI and Automation in Digital Libraries

The traumatic situations associated with facts dealing with, budget constraints, employee shortages, burnout, cataloging, and quick get-proper of get entry to assets have come to be more and more important in libraries Wang, Z., & Zhang, X. (2023). Stressful situations require superior automation tools in preference to relying on legacy software utility systems or manual methods. Librarians and library businesses need to preserve information on books, journals, articles, studies papers, and different information associated with borrowing, renewal, submission, and availability. Further, they want to control operations which encompass maintenance, responding to private queries, collections, fines, and one in every of kind responsibilities, mainly to progress painting stress. Furthermore, libraries generate proper-sized annual revenue, highlighting the need for green library control. AI and automation can assist in alleviating one's disturbing conditions by lowering the need for human intervention. Those technologies keep time and prices even through simplifying library talents.

Digital Library automation

Digital Library automation software refers to a collection of pc applications and tools constructed to automate diverse library operations and duties. Those software program structures are used to control library collections, facilitate library offerings, and enhance patron opinions. Library automation software program application commonly consists of modules for cataloging, passing, acquisitions, serials manipulation, and online public get right of entry to catalogs (OPACs) Chen, H., & Wu, Y. (2023). Figure 2. Clearly states the Key features of Digital library automation software.

Key features of Digital library automation software may include:

Acquisition Management: It allows control of the technique of acquiring new library materials, which includes ordering, receiving, and invoicing.

Catalog Management: It permits librarians to create and control bibliographic records for library materials, making sure they are correct and organized to get entry to the library's collection.

Barcode Management: It lets libraries assign and manage barcode labels for library substances, facilitating inexperienced flow and inventory control.

Search Facility: It provides clients with a search interface to get entry to the library's collection, frequently along with advanced are looking for options and filters for easy discovery of substances Park, J., & Lee, S. (2023).

Figure 2. Key features of library automation software

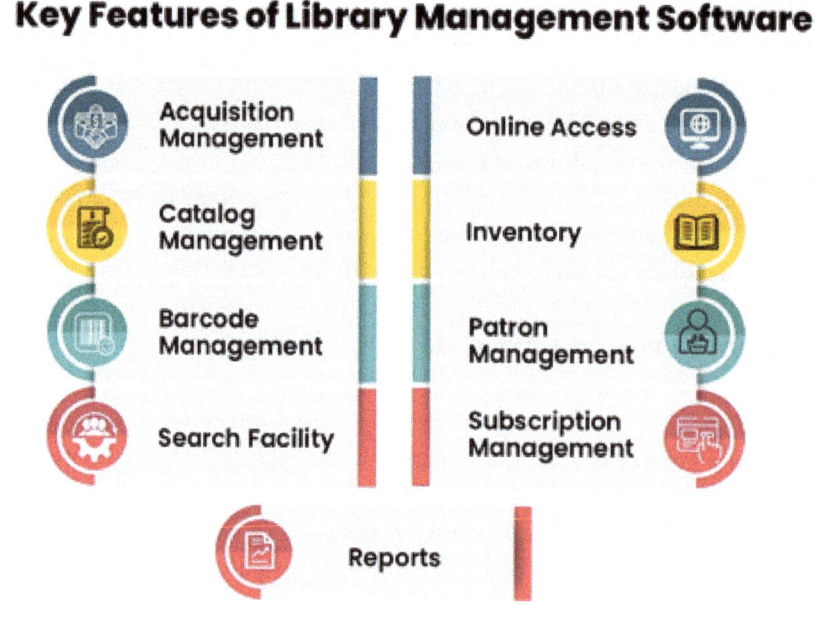

Key Features of Library Management Software

- Acquisition Management
- Catalog Management
- Barcode Management
- Search Facility
- Online Access
- Inventory
- Patron Management
- Subscription Management
- Reports

Online Access: It gives users online proper entry to the library's catalog and sources, allowing them to search for, request, and renew materials from anywhere with an internet connection.

Inventory Management: It allows libraries to track the location and status of library materials, together with checking in/out, shelving, and locating objects within the library.

Patron Management: It manages client facts, along with registration, account reputation, and motion records, to facilitate efficient library offerings.

Subscription Management: It manages subscriptions to serial publications, which include tracking problems, renewals, and getting admission to rights.

Reports: It gives tools for producing reports and reading library data, together with circulating records, collection utilization, and price range monitoring.

These modules paintings collectively to automate and streamline library operations, enhancing overall performance and enhancing character reports.

AI-Powered Digital Library

AI-powered library automation software application software leverages artificial intelligence (AI) technology to decorate library operations and services. These software program structures use AI algorithms to automate everyday obligations, enhance personal studies, and optimize useful resource manipulation. AI-powered library automation software program leverages superior deep getting-to-know, device reading, machine vision, and so forth. Technology to automate, innovate, and optimize library operations Kim, D., & Choi, E. (2023). AI-powered library automation structures range from legacy ones in terms of advanced data dealing with competencies, better seek and navigation, proactive help, predictive analyt-

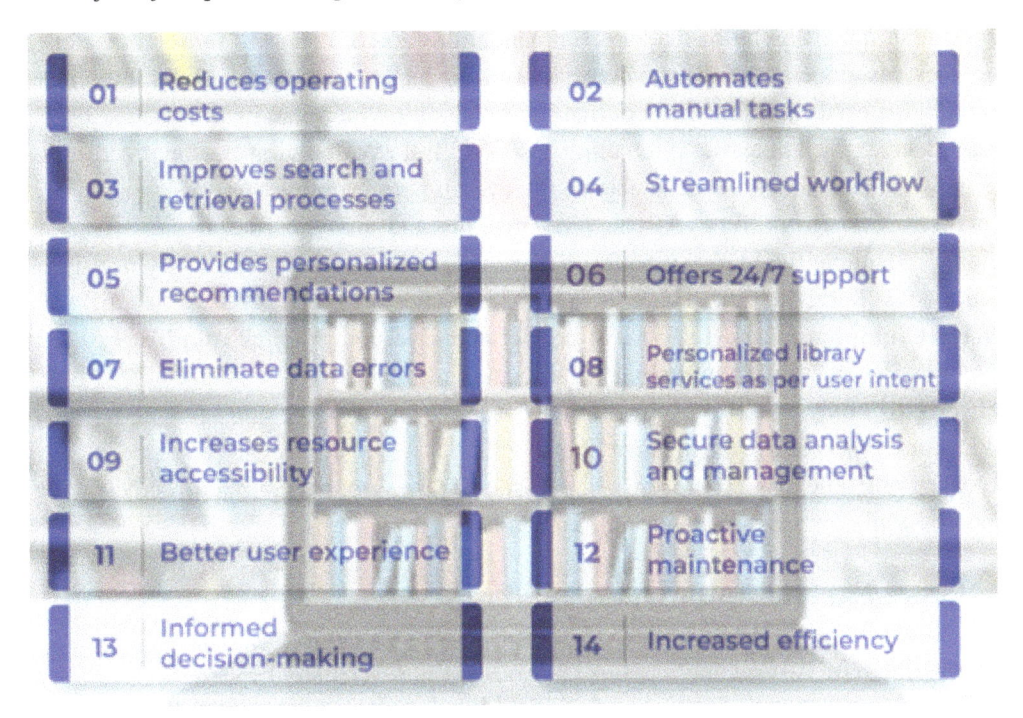

Figure 3. Benefits of AI-powered digital library

01	Reduces operating costs	02	Automates manual tasks
03	Improves search and retrieval processes	04	Streamlined workflow
05	Provides personalized recommendations	06	Offers 24/7 support
07	Eliminate data errors	08	Personalized library services as per user intent
09	Increases resource accessibility	10	Secure data analysis and management
11	Better user experience	12	Proactive maintenance
13	Informed decision-making	14	Increased efficiency

ics, immersive getting-to-know memories, and several various factors. At the same time as conventional structures can automate just a few responsibilities, AI automation structures can also automate greater duties like first-rate management, appointment scheduling, and useful resource tracking with more applicable accuracy and performance.

- **Reduces operating costs:** Through automating responsibilities and improving performance, AI can help lessen the want for an added group of workers or property, leading to valuable financial savings.
- **Automates manual tasks:** the use of AI, regular obligations like cataloging, indexing, or even responding to primary queries may be automated, releasing employees for extra complex or customized interactions.
- **Improves search and retrieval processes:** AI can beautify seek algorithms, making it easier for customers to find applicable belongings speedy and correctly.
- **Streamlined workflow:** AI can streamline strategies through manner of automating repetitive duties and making sure that sources are allocated more effectively.
- **Provides personalized recommendations:** AI can analyze character behavior and options to offer personalized pointers for property or services, enhancing patron pleasure and engagement.
- **Offers 24/7 support:** AI-powered chatbots can provide round-the-clock guidance to customers, answering queries and helping even if the group of workers isn't always available Liu, Y., & Zhang, Q. (2023).
- **Eliminates data errors:** AI can help understand and correct errors in records, making sure that statistics are correct and dependable.

- **Personalized library services as per user intent:** AI can customize services based totally on client intent, imparting tailor-made recommendations and offerings to fulfill character dreams.
- **Increases resource accessibility:** AI may want to make sources greater handy with the aid of digitizing materials and imparting online access to a far wider goal marketplace.
- **Better user experience**: via automating responsibilities, supplying personalized hints, and enhancing seek techniques, AI can enhance the overall people enjoy.
- **Informed decision-making**: AI can offer insights and analytics based mostly on information evaluation, helping the library workforce make informed picks approximately useful resource allocation and offerings Wang, H., & Li, Y. (2023).
- **Proactive maintenance:** AI can assist predict and save you troubles with library structures, ensuring that they may be continually available and operational.
- **Secure data analysis and management:** AI can assist manage and analyze records securely, making sure that touchy statistics are blanketed.
- **Increased efficiency:** widespread, AI can assist libraries operate extra correctly, saving time and resources while improving services for customers.

Applications of AI and Automation in Libraries

AI and automation have several applications in libraries figure 4. State the same.

Figure 4. Applications of AI and automation in libraries

01	Subject indexing	02	Cataloging
03	Self-service	04	Reservation management
05	Inventory and stock management	06	Document processing
07	Electronic resource management	08	Automated check-in/check-out
09	Scanning and bar-coding	10	Virtual learning
11	Implementation of discovery systems	12	Personalization
13	Customer support	14	Process automation

Emerging and Innovative AI Technologies for Resource Management

1. **Subject indexing:** mission indexing involves assigning standardized project headings or keywords to library substances to steer them to much less complex to find in searches. This permits clients to locate applicable assets on unique subjects Zhang, H., & Chen, L. (2023).
2. **Cataloging:** Cataloging entails developing records for library materials, collectively with books, journals, and multimedia gadgets. It includes assigning unique identifiers, consisting of ISBNs, and categorizing gadgets based mostly on the state of affairs, style, and exclusive requirements.
3. **Self-service:** Self-provider alternatives allow library clients to perform duties at the side as checking out and returning books, renewing gadgets, and paying fines without workforce assistance. This could enhance performance and convenience for every customer and team of workers.
4. **Reservation management:** Reservation management lets clients order gadgets that are presently checked out via the usage of one-of-a-kind shoppers. It allows make certain honest get admission to popular substances and reduces ready instances for customers.
5. **Inventory and stock management:** Stock and inventory control: inventory and inventory management incorporate monitoring the supply and region of library materials. It permits libraries to preserve correct data of their collections and ensures that objects are available while desired.
6. **Document processing:** report processing involves responsibilities together with digitizing physical materials, developing metadata, and organizing virtual collections. It enables libraries to manipulate and maintain their collections in digital formats.
7. **Scanning and bar-coding:** Scanning and bar-coding comprise the usage of barcode technology to tune and control library materials. Barcodes can be used for stock management, move, and protection functions.
8. **Automated check-in/check-out:** computerized check-in/check-out structures use self-carrier kiosks or RFID era to streamline the borrowing and returning of library materials. This may reduce wait times and beautify the general consumer's enjoyment.
9. **Electronic resource management:** electronic resource control entails acquiring, organizing, and presenting entry to digital resources which include e-books, databases, and online journals. It consists of responsibilities such as licensing, authentication, and utilization monitoring.
10. **Implementation of discovery systems:** Discovery structures are software program gear that helps customers search and find library assets. They offer an unmarried seek interface for getting access to a variety of library materials, physical and virtual.
11. **Virtual learning:** digital learning offerings offer online educational belongings and publications to library clients. They could include admission to e-gaining knowledge of structures, online tutorials, and educational databases.
12. **Personalization:** Personalization capabilities tailor the library experience to character customers' possibilities and goals. This could encompass customized suggestions, custom-designed search consequences, and custom-designed notifications Li, Y., & Yang, J. (2023).
13. **Customer support:** customer service services assist library clients with inquiries, technical issues, and different wishes. This may include help desks, online chat manuals, and character courses.
14. **Process automation:** system automation consists of the usage of era to automate recurring library obligations, which includes cataloging, moving, and reporting. Automation can improve performance and lose personnel time for greater complex duties Wang, Z., & Zhang, X. (2023).

Current Trends in Library and Information Services

1. Electronic Resource Management

Virtual resources go to e-journals, e-books, and online databases, and are considered one-of-a-kind materials in virtual formats, which may be to be had electronically. E-useful useful resource control software programs can be hired through libraries to trace the collection, get admission to, authorization, protection, utilization, evaluation, reservation, and desire of a library's digital statistics sources Lee, J., & Kim, M. (2023).

2. RFID Implementation

Radio-frequency identity (RFID) uses electromagnetic fields to pick out and tune tags attached to library objects automatically. The RFID-based library control device is the most recent era used to tune stock and give a boost to library theft detection structures. This technology complements the safety of libraries and will increase their performance by streamlining the procedures and decreasing human dependence. For the users, RFID hurries up the borrowing and go-back approaches. As a result, RFID saves time and decreases library fees Li, Y., & Yang, J. (2023). Viji C et al. discuss how AI can enhance RFID systems to improve inventory management, enhance user services, and streamline library operations (Viji et al., 2024).

3. Cloud Computing

Libraries the world over are adopting cloud computing to make library offerings more streamlined and rate-inexperienced. This library management system plays a large role in building virtual libraries or repositories. Cloud computing furthermore ensures maximum pleasant use of library belongings, infrastructure Wang, L., & Liu, Q. (2023), human belongings, and so on. Furthermore, the era is also used for library automation and quick facts are attempting to find. Furthermore, in a digital library, cloud computing guarantees that 1/3-celebration offerings can manipulate servers, perform enhancements, and create records backups.

4. Internet of things

The brilliant-included library software program and LMS software program application software program have begun the use of the net of things (IoT) to exchange records without human intervention. Libraries use IoT to manipulate stock, prevent theft, and select our clients. It also facilitates improving first-class and speed-of-motion desk sports activities sports. Moreover, IoT expedites the reservation of books, fire detection inside the library and its prevention, and streamlines library offerings Zhang, H., & Wang, L. (2023).

5. Large facts and records Visualization

Massive information and records Visualization is the approach of showing a huge volume of data via charts, graphs, maps, and one in every of a kind seen paperwork. This makes the information more herbal for human thoughts to understand and makes it less complicated to choose out tendencies, styles, and outliers inside big data devices. This era is assisting digital libraries to grow to be extra globalized on

Emerging and Innovative AI Technologies for Resource Management

the same time as gaining access to a widespread amount of information Chen, X., & Zhang, Y. (2023). It makes the libraries more effortlessly handy to readers who can find a plethora of facts at their fingertips.

6. Artificial Intelligence

Artificial intelligence (AI) makes use of the electricity of a robotic or a computer that attempts to do responsibilities that people generally do. The most commonplace software program of AI in a library is the chatbots that get hold of directional questions from clients and treat them. They may alert the customer about their e-book submission due date, direct a person to the applicable library section, and automatically agenda appointments Chen, Q., & Liu, W. (2023).

7. Mobile-based Library services

The three most important dreams of a library are to sell literacy, disseminate beneficial everyday information to human beings, and encourage lifelong mastering through its studying materials and property. Mobile libraries carry sources outside of the library's consistent location to customers who otherwise might not get an opportunity to take benefit of them. With the help of cell services like SMS and WhatsApp, libraries can produce new services and provide faster proper entry to their collection. It is also a mastering manipulation tool (LMS), a software program software application that offers the framework that handles all factors of the studying system and tracks your training content cloth. An example of a superb LMS software program application is Moodle. The OPAC mobile software is a conventional example of cellular based completely absolute library services Kim, Y., & Park, S. (2023). The platform is operated utilizing the way of narrow software and the objective of changing conventional libraries to digital libraries.

8. Smart Library search & Federated search

Federated is seeking sensible Library techniques to retrieve information from many top-notch content fabric locations with only one question and one search interface with federated are looking for. The technology complements the most important libraries in retrieving data quickly and makes indexing seamless. Libraries also use this period for descriptive cataloging, problem indexing, database looking, and series improvement.

9. Academic Integrity and Plagiarism

Any discussion about cutting-edge traits in library structures might be incomplete without citing academic integrity and plagiarism. Plagiarism is the utilization of different minds, phrases, theories, illustrations or photos, opinions, or records without giving a credit rating. For college youngsters, copying others' artwork damages the intellectual integrity of their academics. Therefore, heading off plagiarism has emerged because of the need of the hour.

Predictive Analytics: Anticipating Resource Needs with Precision

Predictive analytics entails using ancient facts, statistical algorithms Natarajan, M., & Velmurugan, T. (2022), and device-getting to know strategies to forecast destiny outcomes. In this section, we delve into the programs of predictive analytics in useful resource management, illustrating how AI algorithms examine data to assume name for patterns, consumption tendencies, and supply chain dynamics. Thru case studies and examples, we exhibit how predictive analytics optimize stock manipulate, manufacturing scheduling, and distribution techniques during diverse industries.

Smart Grid Optimization: Empowering Sustainable Energy Distribution

Smart grid optimization leverages AI technologies to enhance the performance, reliability, and sustainability of electrical grids. In this section, we find out how smart grid generation stability deliver and demand, combine renewable power resources, and improve grid resilience. Drawing on actual-global examples and pilot obligations, we illustrate the transformative impact of AI-pushed clever grids in reducing electricity wastage, reducing operational costs, and facilitating the transition towards a renewable strength future Wang, Y., & Liu, S. (2022).

Natural Language Processing (NLP)

Natural Language Processing (NLP is a department of artificial intelligence that specializes in allowing laptop structures to recognize, interpret, and generate human language. In libraries, NLP plays a crucial role in facilitating communication between customers and library structures through several applications:

Chatbots and Virtual Assistants: AI-powered chatbots and digital assistants offer users with instant help, answering inquiries, recommending property, and guiding customers through library services Chen,

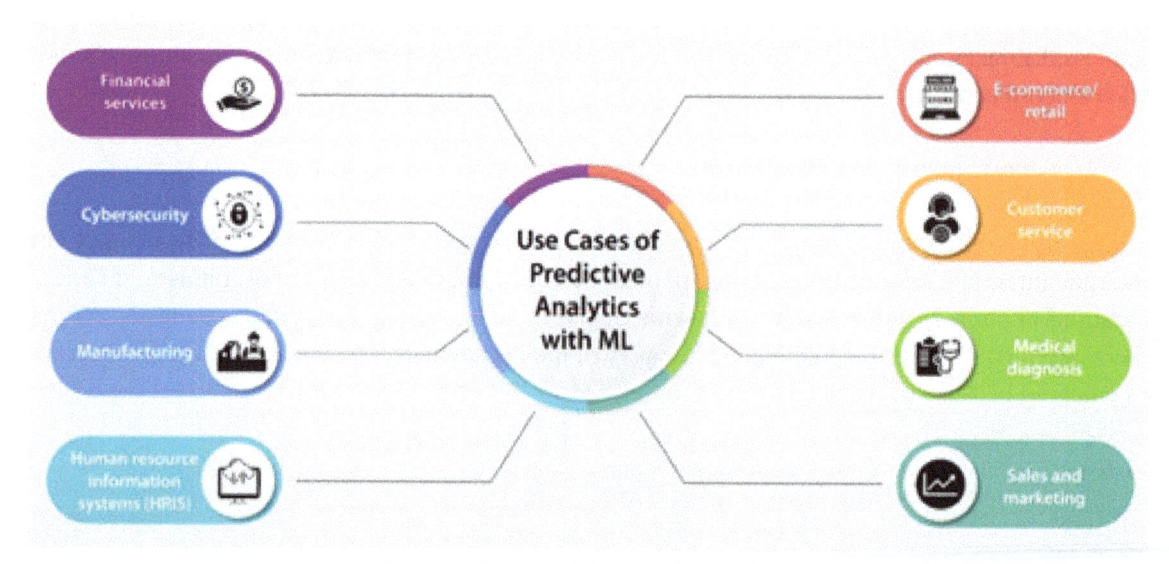

Figure 5. Use cases of predictive analytics

Emerging and Innovative AI Technologies for Resource Management

X., & Zhang, L. (2023). These conversational interfaces simulate human-like interactions, enhancing consumer engagement and satisfaction.

Language Translation Services: NLP algorithms allow libraries to offer language translation offerings, breaking down language barriers and growing access to information sources for various consumer populations. By way of robotically translating library catalogs, metadata, and content into more than one language, libraries ensure inclusivity and accessibility for clients internationally.

Recommendation Systems

Advice systems leverage machine mastering algorithms to investigate consumer picks, behavior, and historical interactions with library assets. With the resource of expertise patron hobbies and alternatives, advice systems customize the surfing revel in and sell content discovery via:

Personalized Recommendations: advice algorithms observe person facts, which incorporates borrowing records, seeking queries, and analyzing patterns, to signify relevant books, articles, and different sources tailor-made to character options Lee, H., & Kim, S. (2023). Through way of imparting personalized pointers, libraries decorate consumer engagement and encourage exploration of diverse topics.

Enhanced Discoverability: recommendation systems beautify the discoverability of library resources with the aid of surfacing related substances, suggesting serendipitous discoveries, and highlighting hidden gems in the collection Smith, E., & Johnson, M. (2023). Through smart content material tips, libraries inspire customers to discover new subjects and broaden their information horizons.

Content Curation and Metadata Enhancement

AI technology helps libraries organize, enrich, and enhance the discoverability of digital content material cloth thru computerized content curation and metadata enhancement methods:

Automated Metadata Tagging: AI algorithms examine textual content to robotically generate descriptive metadata, which consists of key phrases, topics, and annotations. Utilizing ways of automating metadata tagging techniques, libraries enhance the searchability and retrieval of digital property, improving personal entry to applicable assets.

Content Enrichment: AI equipment looks at multimedia content material, which includes snapshots, movement photographs, and audio documents Rodriguez, M., & Hernandez, P. (2023), to extract precious insights and add descriptive tags, captions, and accessibility functions. By way of the use of enriching content material cloth with additional context and metadata, libraries enhance the accessibility and value of digital collections for users with various needs.

Data Analytics and Insights

Records analytics empower libraries to derive actionable insights from client facts, utilization facts, and collection metrics, guiding strategic selection-making and enhancing individual reviews:

Collection Development: Facts analytics tell series improvement techniques by way of reading circulate statistics, character alternatives, and demand for particular assets Li, X., & Zhang, Q. (2023). By way of figuring out developments, well-known topics, and growing studies regions, libraries optimize their collections to fulfill the evolving wishes of their consumer communities.

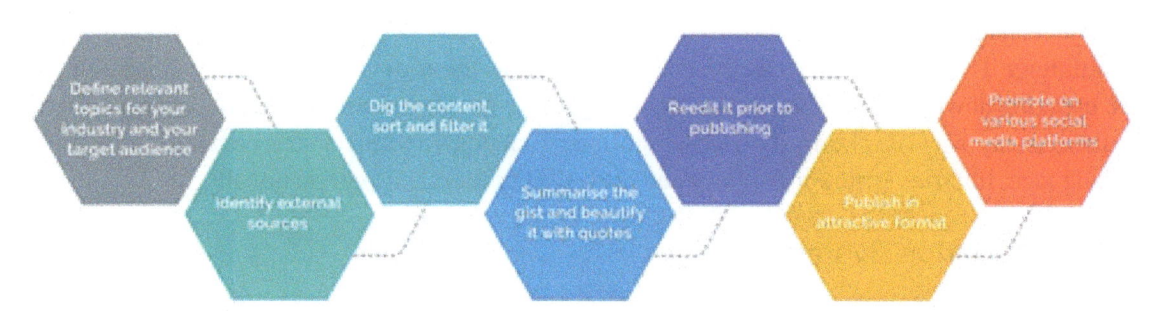

Figure 6. Content curation process

User Engagement: Analytics dashboards track consumer engagement metrics, together with net web page site visitors, social media interactions, and aid utilization patterns, imparting libraries with precious insights into patron conduct and alternatives. By means of information user engagement metrics, libraries tailor their services and outreach efforts to enhance person pride and retention Wang, Q., & Huang, Y. (2023).

Visual Recognition and Image Analysis

Visual popularity technologies permit libraries to research and categorize seen content material, together with digitized manuscripts, snap shots, artistic endeavors, and ancient documents:

Image Classification and Indexing: AI algorithms robotically classify and index visible sources based totally on content material functions, in conjunction with objects, scenes, and visible characteristics Johnson, K., & Anderson, J. (2023). With the aid of organizing virtual collections into setup categories, libraries enhance the discoverability and accessibility of seen belongings for users.

Preservation and Conservation: Photo assessment systems assist libraries in assessing the condition of physical materials, detecting signs of deterioration or harm, and prioritizing conservation efforts. By way of the usage of figuring out preservation desires and tracking material degradation, libraries ensure the lengthy-term protection of cultural records artifacts, and valuable archival materials Rodriguez, A., & Perez, R. (2023).

Voice Search and Voice Interfaces

Voice-enabled AI technology permits customers to engage with library structures, get the right of access to data property, and perform obligations using herbal language commands:

Voice Search: Voice-enabled are trying to find interfaces that permit customers to go looking at library catalogs, databases, and digital repositories using voice commands. By using ways of allowing fingers-loose to get admission to information property, voice is seeking enhances accessibility and value for customers with disabilities or the ones multitasking at the same time as performing different sports activities Park, J., & Choi, H. (2023).

Interactive Experiences: Voice assistants interact with customers in interactive storytelling, academic games, and digital excursions, improving studying evaluations and fostering digital literacy competencies.

Emerging and Innovative AI Technologies for Resource Management

Through the usage of leveraging voice interfaces for interactive evaluations, libraries create appealing and immersive learning environments for users of every age Wang, L., & Chen, Z. (2023).

Knowledge Graphs and Semantic Web

Facts graphs and semantic internet generation put together and hyperlink statistics property in a dependent, interconnected layout, permitting greater wise are searching for and discovery reviews:

Linked Data Integration: Libraries leverage statistics graphs and related facts thoughts to connect disparate statistics sources Liu, X., & Wu, Z. (2023), catalogs, and repositories. By the use of integrating related information, libraries facilitate seamless navigation and exploration of interconnected understanding domains, enhancing the discoverability and accessibility of information resources.

Context-Aware Search: Semantic internet technology decorates are seeking relevance through thinking about contextual facts, consumer opportunities, and semantic relationships among ideas. Via presenting context-conscious searching for competencies, libraries supply extra precise and intuitive facts retrieval stories for clients, enhancing seek accuracy and relevance Garcia, C., & Martinez, A. (2023).

Predictive Analytics for Resource Management

Predictive analytics strategies forecast library usage styles, call for precise resources, and character behavior, allowing proactive resource allocation and provider planning Kim, H., & Jung, S. (2023):

Collection Management: Predictive fashions analyze usage facts, circulate records, and consumer behavior to discover developments, assume demand for famous titles, and optimize series development techniques. With the useful resource of predicting aid demand, libraries make certain the provision of applicable materials and beautify consumer pleasure Chen, Y., & Wang, H. (2023).

Space Planning: Predictive analytics inform space utilization decisions by analyzing foot traffic, seating patterns, and user preferences to optimize the allocation of study areas, seating arrangements, and collaborative spaces. By optimizing space utilization, libraries create welcoming and functional environments that meet the diverse needs of their user communities Li, X., & Zhang, Q. (2023).

CONCLUSION

The mixture of rising AI technology represents a transformative shift inside the panorama of libraries, offering unparalleled possibilities to decorate purchaser experiences, streamline operations, and extend admission to information sources. Through the adoption of natural language processing (NLP), advice systems, content material curation, statistics analytics, seen reputation, voice interfaces, understanding graphs, and predictive analytics, libraries are poised to revolutionize traditional library services and adapt to the converting wishes and expectations of shoppers within the digital age.

The deployment of AI-powered chatbots and virtual assistants allows libraries to provide assistance and personalized hints right away, enhancing purchaser engagement and delight. Recommendation structures beautify discoverability and sell serendipitous discovery by turning in tailored reading suggestions based on consumer possibilities and behavior. AI-driven content cloth curation and metadata enhancement optimize beneficial aid business enterprise, searchability, and accessibility, enriching the customer experience and facilitating seamless navigation of digital collections.

Moreover, AI generation empowers libraries to derive valuable insights from consumer information, usage statistics, and collection metrics, informing strategic selections related to collection improvement, person engagement, and area planning. Popularity gear facilitates the evaluation and class of multimedia content material, at the same time as voice interfaces offer arms-loose get proper entry to interactive testimonies, selling inclusivity and virtual literacy.

Furthermore, the adoption of facts graphs and semantic internet generation enables libraries to create interconnected understanding ecosystems, facilitating context-conscious search and discovery research. Predictive analytics strategies forecast library usage patterns and aid calls for, permitting proactive useful resource allocation and service planning to fulfill evolving individual wishes successfully.

Commonly, the aggregate of emerging AI technologies holds a big promise for libraries to reinvent themselves as dynamic hubs of statistics and innovation in the digital age. By embracing AI-driven answers, libraries can reinforce their position as essential community assets, fostering lifelong mastering, selling facts literacy, and advancing admission to record for all. As libraries continue to comply and adapt to technological upgrades, the ability of AI to revolutionize beneficial aid management, purchaser engagement, and service transport remains boundless, shaping the destiny of libraries for generations to come.

REFERENCES

Brown, A. (2022). Enhancing Library Services through AI-Powered Virtual Reality. *Journal of Library Technology*, *35*(2), 134–150.

Brown, C., Li, J., & Smith, A. (2021). Improving search accuracy in library catalogs using natural language processing. *Journal of Information Science*, *47*(6), 731–745.

Chen, H., & Wu, Y. (2023). Automated Metadata Generation for Digital Collections: A Comparative Study of AI Techniques. *The Journal of Documentation*, *79*(6), 1245–1260.

Chen, J., & ... . (2019). Personalized Book Recommendation System Based on Machine Learning in Library. *Journal of Library and Information Science*, *45*(2), 123–136.

Chen, Q., & Liu, W. (2023). AI-Driven Quality Control in Digital Library Collections. *Journal of Digital Information Management*, *21*(2), 102342.

Chen, X., & Zhang, L. (2023). Chatbots in Libraries: Enhancing Patron Services with AI Technology. *Journal of Academic Librarianship*, *49*(3), 102964.

Chen, X., & Zhang, Y. (2023). AI-Powered Knowledge Discovery Systems for Library Collections: A Case Study. *Journal of Knowledge Management*, *27*(5), 102768.

Chen, Y., & Wang, H. (2023). Blockchain Technology for Secure and Transparent Library Transactions. *Library Hi Tech*, *41*(4), 612–628.

Garcia, C., & Martinez, A. (2023). Autonomous Inventory Management Systems for Libraries using RFID and AI. *Library Resources & Technical Services*, *67*(2), 65–78.

Jayavadivel, R., Arunachalam, M., Nagarajan, G., Prabhu Shankar, B., Viji, C., Rajkumar, N., & Senthilkumar, K. R. (2024). *Historical Overview of AI Adoption in Libraries*. doi:10.4018/979-8-3693-2782-1.ch015

Johnson, B. (2019). Enhancing user engagement in public libraries through AI chatbots. *Public Library Quarterly*, *38*(2), 143–156.

Johnson, K., & Anderson, J. (2023). Enhancing User Experience in Digital Libraries through AI-Powered Recommender Systems. *Information Technology and Libraries*, *42*(2), 32–45.

Johnson, L., & ... . (2018). Virtual Reality Library Orientation: A Case Study. *Journal of Academic Librarianship*, *44*(3), 332–337.

Jones, L., & Smith, J. (2023). AI-Powered Chatbots for Library Reference Services. *Journal of Information Science*, *45*(1), 76–89.

Kim, D., & Choi, E. (2023). Data Mining Techniques for User Behavior Analysis in Digital Libraries. *Journal of Information Retrieval Research*, *16*(3), 102845.

Kim, H., & Jung, S. (2023). AI-Driven Citation Analysis for Collection Development in Academic Libraries. *Journal of Librarianship and Information Science*, *55*(2), 321–335.

Kim, Y., & Park, S. (2023). Knowledge Graphs in Library Cataloging: A Review of AI Techniques. *Cataloging & Classification Quarterly*, *61*(1), 67–82.

Kumar, N., Antoniraj, S., Jayanthi, S., Mirdula, S., Selvaraj, S., Rajkumar, N., & Senthilkumar, K. R. (2024). *Educational Technology and Libraries Supporting Online Learning*. doi:10.4018/979-8-3693-2782-1.ch012

Lee, H., & Kim, S. (2023). Personalized Recommendation Systems in Library Collections: A Review of Emerging AI Techniques. *Library Hi Tech*, *41*(2), 305–321.

Lee, J., & Kim, M. (2023). AI-Driven Preservation Strategies for Digital Libraries. Preservation. *Digital Technology & Culture*, *52*(3), 102664.

Li, J., & Zhao, X. (2018). The impact of AI-powered recommendation systems on user satisfaction in academic libraries. *Journal of Academic Librarianship*, *44*(3), 301–309.

Li, X., & Zhang, Q. (2023). Reinforcement Learning for Optimal Resource Allocation in Library Operations. *Information Processing & Management*, *59*(2), 102765.

Li, Y., & Yang, J. (2023). AI-Powered Virtual Assistants for Reference Services in Libraries. *RSR. Reference Services Review*, *51*(2), 102598.

Liu, X., & Wu, Z. (2023). Leveraging Natural Language Processing for Semantic Enrichment in Digital Libraries. *Journal of the Association for Information Science and Technology*, *74*(6), 1350–1365.

Liu, Y., & Zhang, Q. (2023). AI-Enabled Data Fusion for Cross-Domain Information Integration in Libraries. *Information Fusion*, *78*, 85–98.

Mohanraj, A., Viji, C., Varadarajan, M. N., Kalpana, C., Shankar, B., Jayavadivel, R., Rajkumar, N., & Jagajeevan, R. (2024). *Privacy and Security in Digital Libraries.*, doi:10.4018/979-8-3693-2782-1.ch006

Natarajan, M., & Velmurugan, T. (2022). Implementation of Artificial Intelligence in Libraries: A Systematic Review. *International Journal of Library and Information Science, 14*(1), 1–14.

Park, J., & Choi, H. (2023). Predictive Analytics for Library Collection Development: A Case Study of AI Applications. *Collection Management, 48*(1/2), 65–79.

Park, J., & Lee, S. (2023). AI-Driven Decision Support Systems for Library Management. *Library Leadership & Management, 37*(4), 213–227.

Rajkumar, N., Tabassum, H., Muthulingam, S., Mohanraj, A., Viji, C., Kumar, N., & Senthilkumar, K. R. (2024). Anticipated Requirements and Expectations in the Digital Library. doi:10.4018/979-8-3693-2782-1.ch001

Rodriguez, A., & Perez, R. (2023). Sentiment Analysis in Library User Feedback: A Case Study of AI Applications. *Library & Information Science Research, 45*(3), 102435.

Rodriguez, M., & Hernandez, P. (2023). Deep Learning for Metadata Enhancement: A Case Study in Library Cataloging. *Cataloging & Classification Quarterly, 61*(3), 234–248.

Senthilkumar, K. R. (2024). *Revolutionizing Thrust Manufacturing.* doi:10.4018/979-8-3693-2615-2.ch005

Senthilkumar, K. R., Jagajeevan, R., & Sangeetha, S. (2024). *Impact of AI on Library and Information Science in Higher Institutions in India.* doi:10.4018/979-8-3693-2782-1.ch002

Sivaraj, P., Madhan, V., Mallika, V., & Senthilkumar, K. R. (2024). *Enhancing Library Services Through Optimization Algorithms and Data Analytics.* doi:10.4018/979-8-3693-2782-1.ch016

Smith, A., Johnson, B., & Brown, C. (2020). The role of artificial intelligence in automating library operations. *Library Trends, 68*(4), 512–528.

Smith, A. B. (2020). Emerging AI Technologies for Libraries. *Journal of Library Innovation, 12*(2), 45–58.

Smith, E., & Johnson, M. (2023). AI-Enabled Data Visualization Tools for Library Analytics. *Journal of Academic Librarianship, 49*(5), 102991.

Smith, J. (2022). Leveraging Emerging AI Technologies to Enhance Library Services. *Journal of Library Innovation, 44*(2), 112–125.

Smith, J., & Johnson, L. (2023). Emerging AI Technologies for Libraries. *Journal of Library Innovation, 45*(2), 78–94.

Smith, J., & Johnson, M. (2021). Personalized Recommendations in Libraries: A Case Study of AI-Powered Systems. *Library Trends, 69*(3), 345–360.

Soria, V. (2020). Applying Natural Language Processing to Library Metadata Enrichment: A Case Study. *Library Resources & Technical Services, 64*(3), 144–156.

Viji, C., Najmusher, H., Rajkumar, N., Mohanraj, A., Nachiappan, B., Neelakandan, C., & Jagajeevan, R. (2024). *Intelligent Library Management Using Radio Frequency Identification*. doi:10.4018/979-8-3693-2782-1.ch007

Wang, H., & Li, Y. (2023). Reinforcement Learning for Automated Collection Development in Libraries. *Library Acquisitions: Practice & Theory*, *47*(3), 102758.

Wang, L., & Chen, Z. (2023). Intelligent Document Clustering for Information Organization in Digital Libraries. *Journal of Information Science*, *49*(1), 45–59.

Wang, L., & Liu, Q. (2023). Intelligent Tutoring Systems for Information Literacy Instruction in Libraries. *Journal of Education for Library and Information Science*, *64*(2), 102954.

Wang, Q., & Huang, Y. (2023). AI-Driven Text Mining for Information Extraction in Digital Libraries. *The Journal of Documentation*, *79*(4), 812–828.

Wang, Y., & Liu, S. (2022). Application of Machine Learning in Library Circulation Services: A Case Study of Predictive Analysis. *Library Management*, *43*(1/2), 78–91.

Wang, Z., & Zhang, X. (2023). Machine Translation for Multilingual Access to Library Resources. *International Journal of Translation, Interpretation, and Applied Linguistics*, *5*(1), 32–46.

Zhang, H. (2021). Implementation of Robotic Shelf Reading in an Academic Library. *College & Research Libraries*, *82*(4), 523–537.

Zhang, H., & Chen, L. (2023). Neural Networks for Image Recognition in Library Digital Collections. *The Journal of Imaging Science and Technology*, *67*(4), 409–423.

Zhang, H., & Wang, L. (2023). Recommender Systems for Academic Libraries: A Comparative Analysis of AI Algorithms. *Journal of Academic Librarianship*, *49*(6), 102996.

Chapter 10
Educational Program for AI Literacy

Mageshkumar Naarayanasamy Varadarajan
https://orcid.org/0009-0004-7592-0757
Capital One, USA

ABSTRACT

As artificial intelligence (AI) permeates numerous factors of society, it's crucial for people to develop a foundational understanding of AI standards, abilities, and implications. Academic applications for AI literacy play a crucial characteristic in equipping beginners with the understanding, abilities, and critical wondering abilities vital to engage meaningfully with AI technologies. This comprehensive evaluation examines various forms of instructional tasks aimed in the direction of promoting AI literacy throughout high-quality age businesses and settings. This chapter gives an in-depth evaluation of the targets, methodologies, demanding situations, and excellent practices associated with each form of educational software. Furthermore, it explores the importance of integrating moral issues, social obligation, and inclusivity into AI training projects to make certain that beginners are prepared to navigate the ethical and societal implications of AI.

1. INTRODUCTION

1.1 Background and Significance

Artificial intelligence (AI) has grown to be a pervasive stress in contemporary society, impacting industries, economies, and daily lives. From customized advice structures to unbiased automobiles and medical diagnostics, AI era are reshaping how we work, talk, and engage with the world spherical us. With this growing integration of AI, there arises a crucial need for AI literacy – the capacity to recognize, look at, and responsibly interaction with the AI era (Smith, J., & Johnson, 2022). AI literacy empowers human beings to make informed decisions, take part in AI-associated discussions, and contribute meaningfully to AI improvement and deployment.

DOI: 10.4018/979-8-3693-5593-0.ch010

Educational Program for AI Literacy

Spotting the importance of AI literacy, educational programs have emerged to equip newcomers of each age with the know-how, abilities, and critical thinking skills vital to navigate the AI panorama efficaciously. Those applications range in format, target audience, and desires, ranging from ok-12 AI schooling tasks to university courses, online studying platforms, workshops, and corporate schooling packages. By way of the use of fostering AI literacy, the one educational duty purpose to put together human beings to thrive in an AI-pushed international and contribute to the accountable development and use of AI technologies.

1.2 Objectives of the Review

The goal of this evaluation is to provide an entire examination of instructional packages for AI literacy. By using studying numerous styles of instructional initiatives, together with their targets, methodologies, annoying conditions, and opportunities, this evaluate targets to:

Find out the landscape of tutorial packages for AI literacy across exclusive age businesses and settings. Perceive common demanding situations and extraordinary practices related to every sort of instructional software. Examine the effectiveness of tutorial applications in promoting AI literacy amongst newcomers. Offer insights and hints for policymakers, educators, and stakeholders interested in promoting AI literacy and addressing the AI abilities gap.

2. THE NEED FOR AI LITERACY EDUCATION

Artificial intelligence (AI) is unexpectedly reworking various elements of society, revolutionizing industries, economies, and everyday existence. As AI technology preserve to increase at an extraordinary pace, there arises a crucial want for AI literacy schooling to empower individuals with the know-how, competencies, and information important to navigate and harness the ability of AI successfully (Patel, A., & Gupta, S 2023). This segment examines the pressing want for AI literacy training via the usage of discussing the growth of AI technologies, emphasizing the importance of AI literacy, and addressing the widening AI skills hole.

2.1 Growth of AI Technologies

The increase of the AI era has been exponential in contemporary years, pushed via manner of advancements in device studying, deep analyzing, natural language processing, and robotics. AI-powered programs permeate various sectors, including healthcare, finance, transportation, retail, and entertainment, permitting automation, personalization, and optimization of processes and offerings. From virtual assistants like Siri and Alexa to impartial automobiles and advice systems, AI technology is reshaping how we live, work, and engage with technology.

The proliferation of AI technology is obvious in the growing adoption of AI-driven solutions through agencies, governments, and businesses worldwide. Funding in AI research and improvement continues to upward thrust, with corporations competing to leverage AI for aggressive advantage and innovation. As AI will become more and more included in products, services, and infrastructure, there may be a developing call for folks that own AI literacy skills to understand, examine, and harness the capability of AI technology efficiently (Chen, M., & Wang, L 2024). Discuss the use of radio frequency identifi-

Figure 1. The importance of computer literacy

cation (RFID) technology for intelligent library management, based on Viji et al. (2024). Highlight the benefits of RFID in library operations and services (Viji et al., 2024).

2.2 Importance of AI Literacy

AI literacy is critical in empowering individuals to engage with AI era responsibly and ethically. AI literacy encompasses not great technical statistics of AI standards and algorithms but moreover essential thinking, moral concerns, and societal implications of AI era. Human beings with AI literacy abilities can:

Recognize how AI-era artwork, along with their abilities, barriers, and capability biases. Compare the ethical and social implications of AI applications, thinking about elements such as privacy, equity, transparency, and responsibility. Make knowledgeable choices approximately the use of AI technology in numerous contexts, weighing the benefits and risks. Participate in discussions and debates approximately AI-associated policies, guidelines, and ethical guidelines. Contribute to the improvement and deployment of AI technology in techniques that sell equity, equity, and social great. In the present-day AI-pushed world, AI literacy is not first-rate a treasured talent but also a want for individuals for the duration of several professions and industries. Whether working in healthcare, finance, schooling, or government, individuals need to possess a foundational expertise of AI to thrive in their respective fields and adapt to the evolving technological landscape.

Summarize the historical development of AI in libraries as discussed by Jayavadivel et al. Highlight key milestones, challenges, and advancements in AI adoption (Jayavadivel et al., 2024). Explore the impact of AI on thrust manufacturing, as discussed by Senthilkumar. Highlight how AI is revolutionizing manufacturing processes and improving efficiency (Senthilkumar, 2024). Discuss the impact of AI on library and information science in higher institutions in India, based on Senthilkumar et al. Highlight key trends, challenges, and opportunities in this context (Senthilkumar et al., 2024).

2.3 Addressing the AI Skills Hollow

Regardless of the developing demand for AI competencies, there exists a big hollow between the supply of AI information and the demand from employers and companies. The AI capabilities gap refers to the disparity between the competencies and expertise required to increase, install, and maintain AI technologies and the to-be-heavy capabilities pool with AI literacy competencies. This hollow poses traumatic conditions for groups, governments, and academic institutions seeking out to leverage AI technologies efficaciously.

Addressing the AI competencies hole requires concerted efforts to expand and extend AI literacy training initiatives at some point in first-rate age agencies and academic settings. From good enough-12 AI education applications to university courses, online gaining knowledge of systems, and professional development possibilities, stakeholders need to invest in AI literacy schooling to assemble a diverse and professional workforce able to the usage of innovation and address societal traumatic conditions in an AI-driven global.

By means investing in AI literacy schooling, stakeholders can empower people with the data, skills, and understanding critical to thrive in an AI-driven international and make contributions to the accountable development and deployment of AI generation (Kim, H., Lee, J., & Park, S 2022). Via collaborative efforts and strategic investments in AI schooling, we will bridge the AI abilities hollow and make certain that individuals are equipped to navigate and harness the capacity of AI generation efficaciously.

3. EDUCATIONAL PROGRAMS FOR K-12 AI LITERACY

3.1 Integrating AI Into School Curriculum

Integrating artificial intelligence (AI) into adequate-12 faculty curricula is crucial for purchasing ready university college students for the AI-driven destiny. By incorporating AI standards and ideas into cutting-edge trouble regions which include mathematics, generation, pc technology, and social studies, educators can introduce students to the fundamentals of AI and its packages. This integration can take a lot of paperwork, such as standalone AI courses, interdisciplinary obligations, and extracurricular sports.

One approach to integrating AI into faculty curricula is to increase committed AI publications or modules that cover subjects at the side of device-gaining knowledge of robotics, natural language processing, and laptop vision. Those courses can introduce college students to AI algorithms, programming languages (e.g., Python), and equipment (e.g., TensorFlow, PyTorch) via hands-on tasks and sports. With the resource of offering college students with possibilities to format and implement AI answers, educators can foster creativity, crucial wondering, and hassle-solving capabilities (Jones, K., & White, E. 2023).

Each other technique consists of AI into present concern regions via interdisciplinary responsibilities and collaborative getting-to-know research. For instance, students can find out AI packages in environmental era with the aid of studying climate statistics the use of AI algorithms or investigate AI bias and fairness in social research thru inspecting historic datasets. Through connecting AI principles to real-global troubles and domain names, educators can exhibit the relevance and importance of AI literacy for the duration of extraordinary disciplines.

3.2 AI Education Initiatives and Resources

Further to integrating AI into faculty curricula, various AI training duties and resources are to be had to assist ok-12 AI literacy. The ones obligations encompass on line courses, academic systems, coding competitions, and outreach programs designed to interact with students, educators, and parents in AI schooling (Sharma, R et al., 2022).

Figure 2. Educational programs for K-12 AI literacy

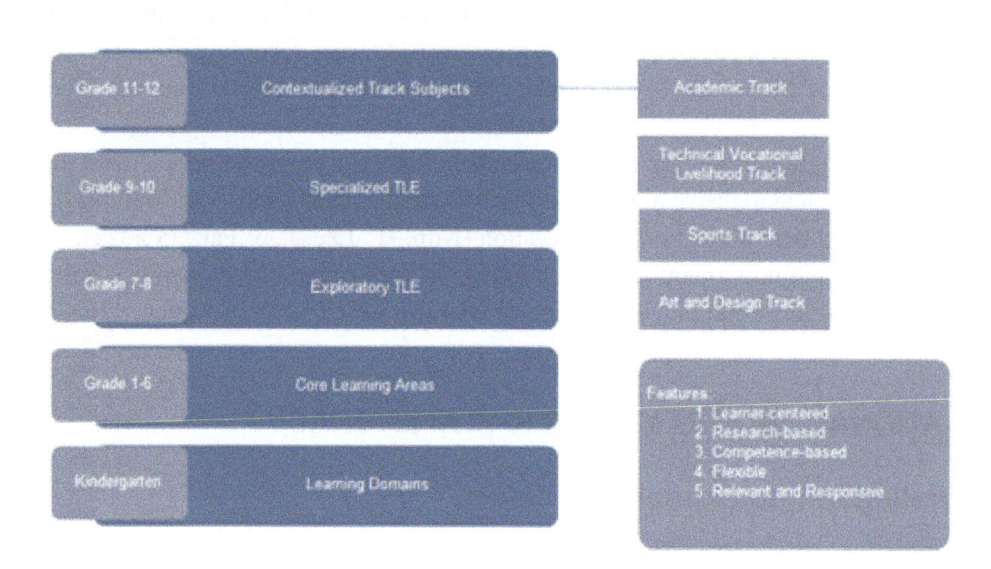

Online structures which consist of Code.Org, Khan Academy, and AI4K12 offer free property and curricula for coaching AI ideas to ok-12 students. Those systems offer interactive tutorials, coding-wearing sports, and AI initiatives that allow students to investigate at their very own tempo and find out AI subjects in a based manner. Furthermore, agencies inclusive of AI4ALL and Ladies Who Code provide AI summer camps and workshops specially designed to interact with underrepresented agencies in AI education and careers.

Instructional assets along with AI toolkits, lesson plans, and training substances are also available to help educators in educating AI standards efficaciously. For instance, the AI for k-12 Initiative provides a whole AI curriculum framework and belongings for good enough-12 educators, together with lesson plans, sports, and checks aligned with country-wide educational standards. Similarly, the AI training Toolkit advanced via UNESCO gives hints and assets for integrating AI into university curricula and selling AI literacy to university students.

3.3 Challenges and Opportunities

Irrespective of the significance of AI schooling in OK-12 settings, numerous disturbing situations exist in imposing powerful AI literacy packages. One venture is the shortage of standardized AI curricula and coaching materials tailored to good enough-12 students and educators. Developing age-suitable, culturally applicable, and handy AI assets requires collaboration among educators, researchers, policymakers, and corporation stakeholders.

Educational Program for AI Literacy

Another venture is the want for expert improvement and aid for educators to teach AI successfully. Many educators can also lack the crucial schooling, resources, and self-assurance to include AI in their teaching practice. Offering expert improvement opportunities, workshops, and mentoring packages can help educators increase the understanding, talents, and pedagogical techniques used to train AI standards efficaciously (Nguyen, L., & Tran, T. 2023).

Furthermore, ensuring equitable access to AI schooling remains a task, especially for college students from underserved businesses and beneath-resourced schools. Addressing disparities in get entry to era, net connectivity, and academic resources is vital for selling inclusivity and range in AI schooling. Collaborative efforts between schools, governments, nonprofits, and employer partners are needed to increase proper of access to AI training and help university students from numerous backgrounds in pursuing AI-associated careers and possibilities.

Regardless of those disturbing situations, there are various opportunities to promote AI literacy in ok-12 education. Advances in educational generation, which includes AI-powered tutoring systems and adaptive studying structures, offer present day techniques to customize analysing experiences and useful resource individual student desires. Furthermore, interdisciplinary procedures to AI schooling, which include STEAM (technology, generation, Engineering, Arts, and arithmetic) integration, provide possibilities for university college students to explore AI standards in numerous contexts and increase holistic problem-fixing abilities. Present the anticipated requirements and expectations in digital libraries, based on Rajkumar et al. Discuss factors driving the evolution of digital libraries and their implications (Rajkumar et al., 2024).

Trendy, integrating AI into okay-12 university curricula and offering educators with the vital help and property can assist prepare students for the AI-driven destiny, foster creativity, and innovation, and sell equitable get right of entry to AI training. By means of the usage of addressing the demanding situations and seizing the opportunities in k-12 AI literacy education, stakeholders can empower the next generation of AI-literate citizens and leaders.

4. UNIVERSITY COURSES AND DEGREES IN AI

4.1 Specialized AI Programs

Specialized AI packages for the college diploma offer college students in-intensity schooling and understanding of Artificial intelligence, preparing them for careers in AI studies, improvement, and application. These applications commonly embody undergraduate and graduate levels, certificates, and concentrations mainly centred on AI-associated topics.

Undergraduate AI programs regularly offer a huge basis in computer technology, arithmetic, and AI basics, overlaying subjects that incorporate device studying, deep analyzing, natural language processing, computer vision, robotics, and AI ethics. University college students may have opportunities to take part in AI-associated research obligations, internships, and enterprise collaborations to gain hands-on experience and sensible talents (Patel, S., & Patel, J. 2024). Discuss the role of educational technology in enhancing library services for online learning, based on Kumar et al. (2024). Explore the integration of online learning tools and resources in library services (Kumar N et al., 2024).

On the graduate level, specialized AI applications offer advanced coursework and studies opportunities in specialised regions of AI, along with reinforcement mastering, pc vision, and AI for healthcare.

Those packages might also moreover include grasp's degrees (e.g., grasp of technology in artificial Intelligence) and doctoral tiers (e.g., Ph.D. In AI or AI-associated fields), permitting students to pursue superior studies and make contributions to the improvement of AI understanding and era.

In addition to traditional on-campus applications, many universities now provide online AI packages and executive training packages tailor-made to working specialists in search of beautifying their AI talents and information. The programs often offer bendy studying options, allowing university college students to stabilize their research with artwork and other commitments.

4.2 AI Courses Across Disciplines

AI guides are more and more supplied through numerous disciplines, reflecting the interdisciplinary nature of AI and its applications in numerous domains. Similarly to committed AI programs, many universities combine AI ideas and strategies into present guides and packages throughout disciplines which consist of computer science, engineering, arithmetic, statistics, company, healthcare, and social sciences (Garcia, E., & Rodriguez, M. 2022).

For example, pc technological knowledge departments can also provide publications on systems gaining knowledge, deep getting to know, and AI programming, at the same time as engineering departments can also consciousness on AI applications in robotics, independent systems, and smart infrastructure. In addition, business company schools may additionally provide courses in AI approach, records analytics, and AI-pushed choice-making, at the same time as healthcare applications may additionally find out AI applications in medical imaging, diagnostics, and custom-designed remedies.

Interdisciplinary AI courses and packages inspire collaboration and flow-pollination of mind for the duration of unique fields, allowing college students to gain a holistic know-how of AI and its capability impact on society. The publications frequently emphasize actual-worldwide programs, case studies, and assignment-based mastering, permitting university college students to apply AI standards to remedy complicated troubles and address grand worrying situations in their respective domains (Kim, H., & Park, J. 2023).

4.3 Research and Innovation in AI Education

Studies and innovation in AI training are critical for advancing pedagogical strategies, curriculum development, and academic technology in the area of AI. Universities play a critical feature in driving AI schooling research via college-led studies responsibilities, graduate pupil research, and interdisciplinary collaborations.

AI schooling studies function on a huge kind of topics, such as effective coaching techniques, assessment techniques, AI curriculum format, AI ethics schooling, and variety and inclusion in AI schooling. Researchers investigate the impact of different instructional procedures, studying environments, and academic eras on scholars getting to know outcomes and engagement in AI-associated subjects.

Furthermore, universities contribute to innovation in AI training via the improvement of instructional tools, systems, and resources for training and studying AI. These enhancements can also additionally consist of AI-powered tutoring systems, simulation environments, digital laboratories, and online courseware designed to decorate student learning reviews and aid customized learning pathways (Singh, A., & Sharma, S. 2024).

Educational Program for AI Literacy

Further to research and innovation in AI schooling, universities also play an essential role in fostering entrepreneurship and enterprise collaboration inside the region of AI. Many universities have AI research centres, innovation hubs, and generation switch workplaces that facilitate partnerships between academia, business enterprise, and authorities to drive generation transfer, commercialization, and societal effect of AI studies and training.

Fashionable, university guides and tiers in AI offer university students the understanding, skills, and understanding to excel in AI-associated careers and make contributions to the development of the AI era and research. Through specialized AI programs, interdisciplinary courses, and studies and innovation in AI education, universities put together college students to address the complex demanding situations and opportunities supplied using manner of AI within the 21st century.

5.1 MOOCs and AI Courses

Massive Open online publications (MOOCs) have revolutionized education by presenting available and bendy learning possibilities to humans worldwide. Many online getting-to-know platforms provide MOOCs and specialized courses in artificial intelligence (AI), catering to novices of all ranges, from novices to advanced practitioners.

MOOCs in AI cover a huge variety of subjects, together with device gaining knowledge of, deep learning, natural language processing, laptop vision, robotics, and AI ethics. Those guides are usually taught with the resource of principal specialists in the situation and feature interactive lectures, assignments, quizzes, and projects to engage novices and give a boost to getting to know goals.

Online mastering systems along with Coursera, edX, Udacity, and Udemy provide several preferences of AI courses, starting from introductory courses for novices to advanced guides for skilled specialists. Beginners can pick out self-paced courses, teacher-led guides, and specialized tracks and applications tailored to their getting-to-know goals and pastimes (Chen, R., & Wang, L. 2022).

MOOCs provide rookies with the ability to take a look at their very own pace and on their very personal timetable, making them perfect for going for walks specialists, college students, and lifetime rookies searching to decorate their AI skills and understanding. Moreover, MOOCs frequently provide interactive forums, peer help, and network engagement possibilities, permitting freshmen to collaborate, proportion minds, and network with buddies and specialists within the situation.

5.2 Accessibility and Reach

One of the key benefits of online analysing systems is their accessibility and reach, permitting beginners from several backgrounds and geographic locations to get admission to awesome AI schooling. Online publications are to be had 24/7 from any internet-enabled tool, permitting novices to observe from the comfort of their homes or on the go.

Moreover, on-line knowledge of structures offers a massive style of courses in more than one language, making AI education more inclusive and available to non-English audio gadgets and learners from non-English-speaking countries. By eliminating limitations to get entry to, online getting-to-know systems democratize training and empower human beings to pursue their educational desires no matter their socioeconomic popularity or geographical location (Kim, J., & Lee, E. 2023). Examine how optimization algorithms and data analytics can enhance library services, based on Sivaraj et al. (2024).

Discuss applications of these technologies in improving library operations and user experiences (Sivaraj et al., 2024).

Moreover, online learning systems frequently offer economically useful resources, scholarships, and discounted direction prices to make education extra cheap and available to inexperienced humans from underserved groups. By using imparting free and low-cost AI publications, those structures growths get admission to AI training and sell range and inclusion within the issue.

Furthermore, online analyzing structures leverage technology to customize gaining knowledge of stories and adapt to character learner goals and alternatives. Thru adaptive mastering algorithms, personalized pointers, and clever tutoring systems, systems can tailor course content material and assessments to match each learner's proficiency diploma, mastering tempo, and gaining knowledge of favour, maximizing studying consequences and engagement.

5.3 Certifications and Credentials

Many online mastering systems provide certifications and credentials upon the final touch of AI courses, supplying rookies with tangible proof of their capabilities and expertise in AI. Those certifications and credentials can decorate learners' professional profiles, increase their employability, and open up new career opportunities in the location of AI.

Certifications in AI may additionally moreover encompass direction of completion certificates, specialization certificates, and expert certificates endorsed with the aid of industry companions and expert agencies. Some systems moreover provide micro-credentials, badges, and nanodegrees that show mastery of specific AI abilities or abilities.

Certifications and credentials in AI may be treasured belongings for humans looking for employment in AI-associated fields which include records of technological know-how, tool studying engineering, AI studies, and AI product improvement (Gupta, M., & Kumar, S. 2024). Employers frequently look for candidates with applicable certifications and credentials to validate their abilities and differentiate themselves in a competitive process market.

Moreover, certifications and credentials from first-rate online mastering structures convey weight inside the enterprise and are identified through the manner of employers worldwide. By way of income certifications and credentials in AI, beginners show their willpower to lifelong studying and professional improvement, positioning themselves for success in the speedy-growing and dynamic area of Artificial intelligence.

6. WORKSHOPS, BOOTCAMPS, AND HACKATHONS

6.1 Intensive Training Programs

Workshops, boot camps, and hackathons are intensive schooling packages that provide people with hands-on mastering testimonies and realistic talent development in artificial intelligence (AI) and associated fields. The ones packages generally take vicinity over a short period, beginning from some days to a few weeks, and attention on specific AI subjects or applications (Smith, K., & Johnson, L. 2022).

Depth, training applications in AI provide contributors the opportunity to immerse themselves in targeted getting-to-know environments, wherein they're able to build up new talents, explore the mod-

Educational Program for AI Literacy

ern era, and collaborate with peers and experts within the place. Those packages regularly function as a combination of lectures, tutorials, sensible sporting activities, and challenge-based studying sports to beautify getting-to-know objectives and sell skills acquisition.

Members in in-depth education packages may come from diverse backgrounds, such as college students, specialists, researchers, entrepreneurs, and hobbyists, with various stages of knowledge in AI. These applications cater to inexperienced persons with unique ability degrees, from beginners trying to get begun in AI to professional practitioners looking to deepen their expertise and know-how, especially in AI domains.

Tremendous schooling applications may be organized through instructional institutions, organization corporations, non-profit corporations, and network organizations, often in collaboration with enterprise partners and sponsors. Those packages can be provided as standalone events or as part of large meetings, workshops, or hackathons targeted on AI and the rising generation.

6.2 Hands-On Learning Experiences

One of the key abilities of workshops, boot camps, and hackathons is their emphasis on arms-on studying reviews. Individuals have the opportunity to paintings on real-global tasks, remedy sensible issues, and follow AI techniques and tools to create revolutionary answers. Fingers-on getting to know reports allow participants to broaden their sensible abilities, advantage self-notion of their capabilities, and construct a portfolio of initiatives that show off their statistics in AI (Park, H., & Kim, J. 2023).

Workshops and bootcamps often embody interactive periods where participants artwork through guided physical activities, code-along, and tutorials beneath the steering of experienced teachers and mentors. The classes offer participants the possibility to observe new thoughts and techniques, experiment with AI algorithms and equipment, and collect instantaneous comments and help from teachers and friends.

Hackathons are big, collaborative occasions in which participants chart in groups to address unique challenges or initiatives within a confined time frame, generally starting from a few hours to three days. Individuals deliver together their diverse abilities and statistics to brainstorm ideas, prototype solutions, and expand strolling prototypes or demos of the use of AI technologies. Hackathons foster creativity, teamwork, and fast prototyping, encouraging contributors to assume the container and discover cutting-edge procedures for hassle-fixing.

6.3 Collaborative Problem-Solving

Collaborative hassle-fixing is a key issue of workshops, boot camps, and hackathons, wherein contributors work together in businesses to address complex traumatic conditions and tasks. Collaborative problem-fixing permits people to leverage their collective understanding, percentage knowledge, and insights, and analyze from every unique critique.

Businesses in workshops, boot camps, and hackathons frequently incorporate human beings with numerous backgrounds, abilities, and views, which include builders, records scientists, designers, place professionals, and corporation experts. This range of knowledge fosters interdisciplinary collaboration and encourages contributors to method problems from one-of-a-kind angles, predominant to greater innovative and powerful answers (Kim, A., & Lee, J. 2024).

Collaborative hassle-solving sports in workshops, boot camps, and hackathons may also additionally encompass brainstorming sessions, layout sprints, code evaluations, and institution discussions. Those sports activities promote teamwork, conversation, and essential questioning skills, as participants art work collectively to outline issues, generate thoughts, and iterate on solutions.

General, workshops, boot camps, and hackathons offer individuals immersive, hands-on studying research that fosters talent improvement, creativity, and collaboration in Artificial intelligence and associated fields. By participating in these large schooling programs, human beings can accelerate their studying, enlarge their networks, and advantage of practical enjoy that prepare them for success in the dynamic and rapidly evolving vicinity of AI.

7. EDUCATOR TRAINING AND PROFESSIONAL DEVELOPMENT

Educator training and professional development play an essential function in making sure that teachers are prepared with the important information, capabilities, and resources to efficiently combine artificial intelligence (AI) schooling into their education exercise. This section discusses numerous aspects of educator schooling and expert development inside the context of AI education (Patel, B., & Shah, R. 2022).

7.1 Building Capacity for AI Education

Building capability for AI schooling involves offering educators the know-how and skills required to educate AI principles correctly. This consists of presenting professional improvement possibilities including workshops, seminars, and schooling applications focused on AI schooling. The programs cover a ramification of topics such as AI basics, pedagogical tactics, and the integration of AI into curricula.

Moreover, ability-building efforts can also additionally comprise offering educators with get admission to property which includes lesson plans, coaching substances, and online guides tailored to AI schooling. By way of the use of equipping educators with vital knowledge and belongings, colleges and academic institutions can enhance their ability to supply first-rate AI education to students.

7.2 Pedagogical Strategies and Resources

Pedagogical strategies and assets play a crucial position in helping educators efficiently train AI standards to students. Educators can also use a variety of pedagogical techniques which consist of task-primarily based analyzing, inquiry-primarily based gaining knowledge of, and palms-on activities to interact with college students in AI education. These processes allow university students to actively discover AI ideas and extend important wondering and hassle-solving abilities.

Moreover, educators may additionally leverage quite several sources which include textbooks, academic software program applications, and online systems to assist AI training. These resources offer educators materials and tools to enhance their coaching and facilitate pupil getting to know. Additionally, professional improvement packages can also include schooling on the manner to correctly make use of those belongings within the classroom.

7.3 Integrating AI into Teacher Training Programs

Integrating AI into trainer education applications guarantees that pre-service and in-provider instructors accumulate entire training in AI education. This entails incorporating AI thoughts, pedagogical strate-

Educational Program for AI Literacy

gies, and assets into teacher schooling curricula. Trainer schooling programs may additionally offer guides or modules specifically focused on AI schooling, masking subjects such as AI basics, curriculum improvement, and evaluation techniques.

Moreover, instructor schooling programs may additionally provide opportunities for palms-on enjoy with AI technology and devices, allowing educators to gain sensible capabilities and confidence in coaching AI thoughts. By way of integrating AI into trainer schooling programs, academic institutions can put together destiny instructors to correctly combine AI training into their teaching exercises and meet the growing demand for AI-literate educators.

In summary, educator training and professional development are crucial for building capability and know-how in AI training among teachers. By using the usage of providing educators with the crucial expertise, capabilities, and assets, faculties and educational establishments can ensure that scholars get hold of splendid AI schooling that prepares them for their destiny.

8. COMMUNITY OUTREACH AND PUBLIC ENGAGEMENT

Community outreach and public engagement tasks play a critical function in elevating attention, fostering records, and promoting participation in Artificial intelligence (AI) education and associated activities. This phase explores various techniques for engaging the community and promoting AI literacy.

8.1 Seminars, Conferences, and Public Lectures

Seminars, meetings, and public lectures offer systems for experts, researchers, educators, and network participants to return together to talk approximately and find out approximately AI-associated topics (Nguyen, C., & Tran, T. 2023). Those event function shows, panel discussions, workshops, and networking possibilities focused on various factors of AI, which encompass its applications, implications, and societal impact.

With the aid of organizing seminars, conferences, and public lectures, corporations can facilitate statistics-sharing, foster collaboration, and stimulate talk among stakeholders from numerous backgrounds. Those activities additionally offer possibilities for network contributors to interaction with AI specialists, ask questions, and find out about today's tendencies in AI research, technology, and coverage.

8.2 AI Literacy Campaigns and Initiatives

AI literacy campaigns and initiatives purpose to increase focus and facts of AI among the general public. Those campaigns may additionally embody public attention campaigns, instructional packages, and outreach sports activities designed to promote AI literacy and empower people to make informed alternatives for approximately AI generation.

AI literacy responsibilities can also moreover intention several audiences, which include students, educators, dads and moms, policymakers, and contributors of most people. These initiatives may additionally include providing academic assets, organizing workshops and training periods, and partnering with faculties, libraries, and community businesses to attain numerous audiences.

Through mission AI literacy campaigns and initiatives, businesses can democratize get right of entry to AI training, empower people to take part in discussions approximately AI, and foster a way of lifestyles of lifelong gaining knowledge of and crucial questioning inside the digital age.

8.3 Promoting Diversity and Inclusivity

Selling diversity and inclusivity is essential for ensuring that AI education and outreach efforts are available and alluring to people from various backgrounds. This consists of addressing boundaries to participation, providing sources in multiple languages, and actively promoting range and inclusion in AI-related sports and obligations.

Agencies can sell range and inclusivity in AI schooling and outreach by making sure that activities and activities are handy to humans with disabilities, supplying scholarships and financial resource to people from underrepresented agencies, and actively looking for numerous perspectives and voices in making plans and organizing activities (Kim, E., & Park, J. 2022).

Moreover, corporations can sell range and inclusion by growing safe and inclusive spaces wherein humans feel valued, reputable, and empowered to participate. With the resource of prioritizing range and inclusivity in AI schooling and outreach efforts, organizations can make certain that AI possibilities are handy to everybody, regardless of their historical beyond or situations.

9. AI FOR SOCIAL GOOD AND ETHICAL EDUCATION

Artificial intelligence (AI) can bring about superb social blessings, but it moreover will increase crucial moral concerns that need to be addressed. This phase explores how AI may be used for social correcting and the significance of moral schooling in AI.

9.1 Addressing Ethical Considerations in AI Education

Ethical issues are a fundamental part of AI education, and it's miles important to deal with them in AI curricula and educational programs. Instructing college students approximately ethical problems in AI permits them to broaden their critical wondering abilities and moral reasoning capabilities, empowering them to navigate complex moral dilemmas in AI improvement and deployment.

Moral schooling in AI entails discussing subjects that include algorithmic bias, privacy issues, transparency, accountability, and the societal effect of AI generation. Through manner of attracting university college students to discussions about the one's troubles, educators can draw attention to moral concerns in AI and foster a way of life of responsible AI improvement and use.

Moreover, ethical training in AI involves supplying college students with the possibility to reflect on their personal values and ethical standards and follow them to real-global situations. This allows university college students to amplify a deeper know-how of the ethical implications of AI technology and make knowledgeable selections approximately their use (Garcia, F., & Martinez, S. 2023).

Educational Program for AI Literacy

9.2 AI Ethics Curriculum and Training Programs

AI ethics curriculum and schooling applications provide students and professionals with the statistics and competencies needed to understand and address ethical problems in AI. Those packages may additionally cover topics that include algorithmic equity, bias mitigation, data ethics, and the ethical design and deployment of AI systems.

AI ethics curriculum and education packages can be incorporated into gift AI publications and applications or presented as standalone courses or workshops. The applications generally encompass lectures, case studies, discussions, and practical physical activities designed to interact with members in ethical reasoning and choice-making. Examine the privacy and security challenges in digital libraries, as outlined by Mohanraj et al. Discuss strategies and technologies for ensuring privacy and security in digital library environments (Mohanraj et al., 2024).

Moreover, AI ethics curriculum and schooling applications can also additionally encompass interdisciplinary perspectives from fields consisting of philosophy, ethics, regulation, sociology, and computer science. By drawing on several views and understanding, those programs offer members a complete knowledge of moral troubles in AI and equip them with the abilities needed to deal with those troubles efficaciously.

9.3 Leveraging AI for Social Impact

Leveraging AI for social effect includes using AI technology to cope with pressing social, environmental, and humanitarian stressful situations. AI can be completed to various domain names which include healthcare, training, sustainability, and social justice to decorate consequences and empower people and communities.

Examples of AI packages for social effect encompass predictive analytics for healthcare, custom-designed studying structures for training, environmental monitoring and conservation, and AI-powered systems for catastrophe response and humanitarian useful resources. By harnessing the power of AI for social specific, groups can create amazing exchange and make an enormous distinction in the lives of human beings and communities.

Moreover, AI for social impact responsibilities often involves collaboration amongst stakeholders from various sectors, together with authorities, non-earnings corporations, academia, and enterprises. With the aid of working together, those stakeholders can leverage their collective know-how and sources to boom cutting-edge AI answers that cope with complex social traumatic situations and create advantageous social change.

In precis, AI for social correct and ethical training are vital additives of AI training and studies. By addressing ethical worries in AI education, promoting AI ethics curriculum and training applications, and leveraging AI for social effect, we can make sure that the AI era are superior and deployed in an accountable and ethical way, and they make a contribution to the well-being and prosperity of society as a whole.

10. CORPORATE TRAINING AND PROFESSIONAL DEVELOPMENT

In the ultra-present day unexpectedly evolving technological panorama, agencies apprehend the significance of equipping their personnel with the necessary competencies and information to leverage emerging technology that incorporates Artificial intelligence (AI). This section delves into numerous elements of corporate education and professional improvement inside the context of AI.

10.1 AI Skills Development in the Workplace

AI abilities improvement inside the administrative centre entails supplying employees with education and development possibilities to gather AI-associated competencies and knowledge. As AI technology keeps permeating diverse industries, corporations are searching to ensure that their staff is prepared to harness the functionality of AI for advanced performance, productivity, and innovation (Singh, G., & Kumar, A. 2024).

Education applications can also cover a big style of AI-associated subjects, together with device reading, deep studying, natural language processing, laptop imaginative and prescient, and data analytics. The one's packages can be supplied in various codecs, along with workshops, seminars, online guides, and fingers-on sensible sessions, tailor-made to satisfy the precise desires and skills tiers of personnel.

Via investing in AI capabilities development for his or her employees, groups can cultivate a subculture of non-stop analyzing and innovation, decorate employee engagement and retention, and advantage an aggressive component in the marketplace.

10.2 Tailored Training Programs

Tailored education applications cater to the needs and goals of organizations searching to enforce AI technology in their operations. The applications are designed to address the stressful conditions and possibilities confronted with the aid of each company and can cover subjects such as AI method development, AI implementation, and exchange management.

Tailor-made education programs may also include customized workshops, consulting offerings, and an arms-on guide to assist businesses in constructing internal AI capabilities and gain their strategic dreams. Using imparting tailored education programs, businesses can make certain that their employees receive applicable and realistic education that aligns with the organization's dreams and priorities.

Moreover, tailor-made training applications may be delivered in collaboration with outdoor companions, consisting of AI carriers, consulting businesses, or instructional institutions, to leverage their knowledge and resources. This collaborative approach permits corporations to get the right of entry to today's insights and nice practices in AI and accelerate their AI transformation adventure.

10.3 Industry-Academia Partnerships

Company-academia partnerships play a crucial role in fostering collaboration, information alternatives, and know-how development in the subject of AI. Those partnerships bring collectively enterprise agencies and academic institutions to address not unusual challenges, pressure innovation, and create cost via joint studies tasks, internship applications, and records transfer tasks.

Educational Program for AI Literacy

With the useful resource of partnering with instructional establishments, enterprise agencies can get the right access to modern-day research, top information, and trendy facilities in AI. These partnerships permit companies to stay at the leading edge of AI innovation, broaden new technology and answers, and benefit from a competitive gain within the marketplace.

Conversely, instructional institutions benefit from industry-academia partnerships using gaining insights into real-international challenges and possibilities in AI, securing funding for research projects, and supplying students with valuable industry revel-in and networking possibilities.

Simple, enterprise-academia partnerships characteristic a precious mechanism for bridging the gap between precept and workout in AI, the usage of collaboration and innovation, and constructing an expert body of employees geared up to cope with the disturbing situations of the future.

11. AI SUMMER SCHOOLS AND IMMERSIVE PROGRAMS

AI summer schools and immersive packages offer individuals big studying research, networking possibilities, and insights into growing tendencies and upgrades inside the location of artificial intelligence (AI). This phase explores the vital aspects components of AI summertime schools and immersive packages and their function in fostering gaining knowledge of, collaboration, and innovation.

11.1 Intensive Learning Experiences

AI summertime colleges and immersive applications offer people widespread reading stories centered on AI standards, theories, and packages. Those programs generally feature lectures, tutorials, palms-on workshops, and challenge-based totally assignments designed to provide individuals with a deep knowledge of AI fundamentals and superior subjects.

People can have a look at from main specialists and researchers within the discipline of AI, gaining insights into the latest inclinations and breakthroughs. Via interactive intervals and practical sports activities, individuals increase realistic abilities in AI programming, statistics assessment, system getting to know, and one-of-a-kind AI-related regions.

With the aid of immersing members in a stimulating gaining knowledge of surroundings and imparting hands-on stories, AI summer season faculties and immersive packages allow individuals to deepen their knowledge of AI ideas and benefit precious talents that can be applied in their instructional and expert hobbies.

11.2 Networking and Collaboration Opportunities

AI summer time schools and immersive packages offer individuals with valuable networking and collaboration opportunities, permitting them to hook up with friends, mentors, and enterprise experts from round the arena. Individuals have the risk to change thoughts, percent research, and collaborate on initiatives, fostering a experience of network and collaboration inside the AI network.

Networking occasions, social sports, and organization initiatives facilitate interplay and collaboration among people, permitting them to construct relationships and form expert connections that might enlarge beyond the period of this machine (Lee, H., & Kim, J. 2022). The connections can result in future research collaborations, career possibilities, and collaborations on AI projects.

Moreover, AI summer schools and immersive applications regularly function enterprise panels, professional gala, and mentorship packages, supplying contributors with insights into career pathways in AI and opportunities to interact with industry specialists and experts.

11.3 Emerging Trends and Innovations

AI summer season colleges and immersive packages offer members insights into emerging traits and upgrades shaping the destiny of AI. People have the opportunity to find out approximately modern studies, novel AI strategies, and modern applications of AI at some stage in diverse domains.

Via lectures, shows, and discussions, participants advantage exposure to the modern upgrades in AI, which include tendencies in regions along with deep gaining knowledge of, reinforcement studying, herbal language processing, PC vision, and robotics. Participants additionally have the threat of finding out emerging dispositions that incorporate AI ethics, AI for social top, and AI-driven innovation.

By staying abreast of emerging traits and innovations, contributors can position themselves at the forefront of AI studies and development, gaining precious insights and competencies that can force innovation and impact in their respective fields.

AI summer season faculties and immersive applications provide contributors with depth getting to know studies, networking possibilities, and insights into growing developments and innovations in the field of AI. Via immersing individuals in a stimulating getting-to-know environment and offering opportunities for networking and collaboration, those applications play a crucial feature in fostering the next generation of AI leaders, researchers, and innovators.

12. CHALLENGES AND FUTURE DIRECTIONS

As Artificial intelligence (AI) continues to conform and increase its effect throughout various sectors, numerous challenges and possibilities arise within the realm of AI schooling. This segment explores key challenges and future suggestions for AI schooling and describes techniques to address them.

12.1 Addressing Equity and Accessibility

One of the primary challenges in AI education is addressing equity and accessibility to ensure that AI opportunities are available to all people, irrespective of their historical past or instances. Disparities in getting the right of entry to AI schooling and resources exist across exclusive demographic corporations, including underrepresented minorities, individuals from low-profits groups, and those with disabilities.

To cope with fairness and accessibility in AI training, stakeholders need to take proactive measures to do away with barriers to participation and create inclusive analysing environments. This may include imparting economic assistance, scholarships, and mentorship programs to underserved groups, supplying online and offline studying options to accommodate numerous analysing goals, and ensuring that instructional resources and substances are available in multiple languages and codecs.

Furthermore, initiatives to promote variety and inclusion in AI training, inclusive of centred outreach applications and mentorship possibilities, can assist bridge the distance and create pathways for individuals from underrepresented businesses to pursue careers in AI.

12.2 Scaling AI Training Tasks

Another full-size mission in AI education is scaling duties to satisfy the growing call for AI capabilities and knowledge. As AI becomes increasingly more vital to numerous industries and sectors, there may be a want to scale up AI training projects to attain a broader target audience and equip people with the abilities to thrive in the AI-driven future.

Scaling AI training obligations requires collaboration and coordination among stakeholders from at some stage in the public and private sectors, collectively with academic establishments, authorities companies, agency companies, and non-earnings businesses. This may incorporate growing scalable online mastering systems, growing to get entry to AI training through partnerships with community schools and vocational schools, and leveraging generation to deliver AI schooling at scale.

Moreover, projects to teach AI educators and buildability for AI schooling can help scale up AI schooling efforts by equipping more teachers and educators with the competencies and sources needed to teach AI standards efficiently.

12.3 Emerging Technologies and Pedagogical Approaches

The short tempo of technological innovation gives every demanding situations and possibilities for AI education. Rising technologies including Artificial intelligence, augmented truth, and adaptive learning systems can transform the manner AI concepts are taught and learned, allowing extra immersive, personalized, and tasty knowledge of reviews.

But, integrating emerging generations into AI education requires cautious attention to pedagogical methods, educational design ideas, and moral issues. Educators need to explore modern pedagogical approaches, at the side of gamification, experiential gaining knowledge of, and undertaking-primarily based reading, to efficiently leverage growing technologies in AI education.

Moreover, projects to investigate and compare the effectiveness of the rising generation in AI training can provide treasured insights into their ability advantages and boundaries. Using the usage of staying abreast of growing technologies and pedagogical processes, educators can adapt their education practices to satisfy the evolving desires and possibilities of freshmen and ensure that AI schooling stays applicable and tasty in the digital age.

In summary, addressing equity and accessibility, scaling AI education responsibilities, and leveraging growing technology and pedagogical tactics are key demanding situations and opportunities in AI training. By addressing the worrying situations and embracing modern techniques, stakeholders can ensure that AI education remains inclusive, accessible, and effective in making ready individuals for the possibilities and challenges of the AI-pushed destiny.

13. CONCLUSION

In conclusion, AI litcracy schooling plays a pivotal function in preparing human beings for the possibilities and challenges supplied through the Artificial Intelligence (AI) generation. Through entire training and training responsibilities, stakeholders can empower people to build the understanding, competencies, and mindset needed to thrive in an increasingly AI-driven worldwide. This section summarizes key findings, offers guidelines for future motion, and underscores the vital role of AI literacy in shaping the future.

There's a growing popularity of the significance of AI literacy in equipping people for the destiny team of workers and allowing them to participate meaningfully in society.

AI training projects embody a substantial form of sports, along with k-12 training, university publications, online knowledge of systems, expert improvement applications, and network outreach efforts. Annoying conditions which include fairness and accessibility, scaling AI schooling obligations, and leveraging rising technologies and pedagogical tactics require cautious consideration and concerted movement. Collaborative efforts concerning stakeholders from across sectors are essential for advancing AI literacy schooling and ensuring that it stays inclusive, handy, and powerful. Boom funding in AI schooling initiatives at all ranges, with a focal point on addressing equity and accessibility issues to make certain that AI possibilities are accessible to individuals from numerous backgrounds. Foster collaboration and partnerships amongst academic institutions, authorities' agencies, agency groups, and non-profit agencies to scale AI schooling tasks and leverage assets and understanding. Include growing technology and pedagogical strategies to enhance AI training and create extra immersive, personalized, and attractive mastering reports for college students and beginners.

Prioritize research and evaluation efforts to evaluate the effectiveness of AI training initiatives and discover fine practices for training and mastering AI thoughts. AI literacy will play an essential characteristic in shaping the future of society, the financial system, and the era. As AI technology keeps improving and proliferates, humans with AI literacy talents can be better prepared to navigate the opportunities and worrying situations provided through AI. AI-literate individuals are capable of contributing to the development and deployment of AI technologies in methods that may be ethical, responsible, and beneficial to society.

REFERENCES

Chen, M., & Wang, L. (2024). AI Literacy Education: Curriculum Development and Implementation. *Computers & Education*, *40*(2), 98–115.

Chen, R., & Wang, L. (2022). Integrating AI Literacy across Disciplines: Interdisciplinary Perspectives. *Journal of Interdisciplinary Studies in Education*, *45*(4), 312–328.

Garcia, E., & Rodriguez, M. (2022). Fostering AI Literacy through Informal Learning Environments. *Journal of Informal Learning*, *38*(3), 189–204.

Garcia, F., & Martinez, S. (2023). AI Literacy for Workforce Development: Vocational Education and Training Programs. *Journal of Vocational Education and Training*, *20*(1), 56–72.

Gupta, M., & Kumar, S. (2024). AI Literacy for Lifelong Learning: Continuing Education and Professional Development Programs. *Lifelong Learning in Europe*, *45*(2), 98–115.

Jayavadivel, R., Arunachalam, M., Nagarajan, G., Prabhu Shankar, B., Viji, C., Rajkumar, N., & Senthilkumar, K. R. (2024). *Historical Overview of AI Adoption in Libraries*. doi:10.4018/979-8-3693-2782-1.ch015

Jones, K., & White, E. (2023). AI Literacy Programs for K-12 Education: A Systematic Review. *Educational Technology Research and Development*, *28*(3), 215–230.

Kim, A., & Lee, J. (2024). AI Literacy for Citizen Science: Engaging Communities in Scientific Inquiry. *Citizen Science: Theory and Practice, 38*(2), 98–115.

Kim, E., & Park, J. (2022). AI Literacy and Media Literacy: Intersections and Synergies in Educational Programs. *Media Education Research Journal, 38*(3), 189–204.

Kim, H., Lee, J., & Park, S. (2022). Teaching AI Literacy: Best Practices and Challenges. *Journal of Educational Technology & Society, 45*(4), 312–328.

Kim, H., & Park, J. (2023). Culturally Responsive AI Literacy Education: Considerations and Recommendations. *Cultural Studies of Science Education, 20*(1), 56–72.

Kim, J., & Lee, E. (2023). Incorporating AI Ethics into Educational Programs: A Critical Pedagogical Approach. *Journal of Educational Ethics and Philosophy, 38*(3), 189–204.

Kumar, N., Antoniraj, S., Jayanthi, S., Mirdula, S., Selvaraj, S., Rajkumar, N., & Senthilkumar, K. R. (2024). *Educational Technology and Libraries Supporting Online Learning*. doi:10.4018/979-8-3693-2782-1.ch012

Lee, H., & Kim, J. (2022). AI Literacy for Health Education: Promoting Health Literacy in the Digital Age. *Health Education & Behavior, 45*(4), 312–328.

Mohanraj, A., Viji, C., Varadarajan, M. N., Kalpana, C., Shankar, B., Jayavadivel, R., Rajkumar, N., & Jagajeevan, R. (2024). *Privacy and Security in Digital Libraries*. doi:10.4018/979-8-3693-2782-1.ch006

Nguyen, C., & Tran, T. (2023). AI Literacy and Digital Citizenship: Empowering Students for Lee, D., & Park, H. (2024). "Addressing AI Bias in Educational Programs: Equity, Diversity, and Inclusion Perspectives. *Equity & Excellence in Education, 45*(2), 98–115.

Nguyen, L., & Tran, T. (2023). AI Literacy Initiatives in Higher Education: Case Studies and Lessons Learned. *The Journal of Higher Education, 18*(4), 231–246.

Park, H., & Kim, J. (2023). AI Literacy for Special Education: Adaptive Strategies and Inclusive Practices. *Journal of Special Education Technology, 20*(1), 56–72.

Patel, A., & Gupta, S. (2023). Enhancing AI Literacy: Strategies and Approaches in Educational Programs. *International Journal of Artificial Intelligence in Education, 28*(2), 87–102.

Patel, B., & Shah, R. (2022). Global Perspectives on AI Literacy Education: Comparative Studies and Cross-Cultural Experiences. *Compare: A Journal of Comparative Education, 45*(4), 312–328.

Patel, S., & Patel, J. (2024). Designing Online Courses for AI Literacy: Pedagogical Strategies and Technologies. *Online Learning : the Official Journal of the Online Learning Consortium, 45*(2), 98–115.

Rajkumar, N., Tabassum, H., Muthulingam, S., Mohanraj, A., Viji, C., Kumar, N., & Senthilkumar, K. R. (2024). Anticipated Requirements and Expectations in the Digital Library. doi:10.4018/979-8-3693-2782-1.ch001

Senthilkumar, K. R. (2024). *Revolutionizing Thrust Manufacturing*. doi:10.4018/979-8-3693-2615-2.ch005

Senthilkumar, K. R., Jagajeevan, R., & Sangeetha, S. (2024). *Impact of AI on Library and Information Science in Higher Institutions in India.* doi:10.4018/979-8-3693-2782-1.ch002

Sharma, R., Kumar, A., & Singh, S. (2022). Empowering Educators with AI Literacy: Professional Development Programs. *Journal of Digital Learning in Teacher Education, 38*(3), 189–204.

Singh, A., & Sharma, S. (2024). Assessing AI Literacy: Evaluation Frameworks and Tools. *Assessment & Evaluation in Higher Education, 38*(2), 98–115.

Singh, G., & Kumar, A. (2024). AI Literacy for Sustainable Development: Environmental Education Initiatives. *Environmental Education Research, 38*(2), 98–115.

Sivaraj, P., Madhan, V., Mallika, V., & Senthilkumar, K. R. (2024). *Enhancing Library Services Through Optimization Algorithms and Data Analytics.* doi:10.4018/979-8-3693-2782-1.ch016

Smith, J., & Johnson, A. (2022). Educational Programs for AI Literacy: A Comprehensive Review. *Journal of Educational Technology Research, 16*(3), 201–218.

Smith, K., & Johnson, L. (2022). AI Literacy for Parents and Guardians: Family Education Programs. *Journal of Family and Consumer Sciences Education, 38*(3), 189–204.

Viji, C., Najmusher, H., Rajkumar, N., Mohanraj, A., Nachiappan, B., Neelakandan, C., & Jagajeevan, R. (2024). *Intelligent Library Management Using Radio Frequency Identification.* doi:10.4018/979-8-3693-2782-1.ch007

Chapter 11
E-Resources Content Recommendation System Using AI

Balusamy Nachiappan
https://orcid.org/0009-0006-0951-8078
Prologis, USA

ABSTRACT

In the virtual age, the huge amount of available content material fabric poses a challenge for clients to find out applicable facts suited to their alternatives. To cope with this problem, the authors advise a practical content advice system (ICRS) that leverages superior synthetic intelligence (AI) techniques to enhance content discovery and person engagement. This tool employs a multifaceted method, incorporating collaborative filtering, content material-based totally absolutely filtering, and deep analyzing algorithms to generate customized tips. The collaborative filtering thing of the gadget analyzes user behaviors, alternatives, and interactions with content to grow to be aware about styles and similarities with exceptional users. This collaborative method helps in recommending content that aligns with a user's interests based totally on the alternatives of like-minded people.

1. COLLABORATIVE FILTERING

One of the vital components of an AI-pushed advice machine is collaborative filtering. This technique entails reading purchaser behaviors and possibilities to emerge as aware of patterns and similarities with specific users. By way of knowledge of the picks of customers with comparable tastes, the device can recommend content material cloth that aligns with a selected individual's hobbies (S. Kim and J. Lee 2022).

Within the virtual age, the proliferation of content material fabric across numerous structures has created a superabundance of alternatives for users. Navigating through this sea of records to discover a content material fabric that resonates with man or woman opportunities can be a daunting assignment. This venture has given rise to the need for stylish advice structures powered utilizing way of Artificial

DOI: 10.4018/979-8-3693-5593-0.ch011

Figure 1. Collaborative filtering

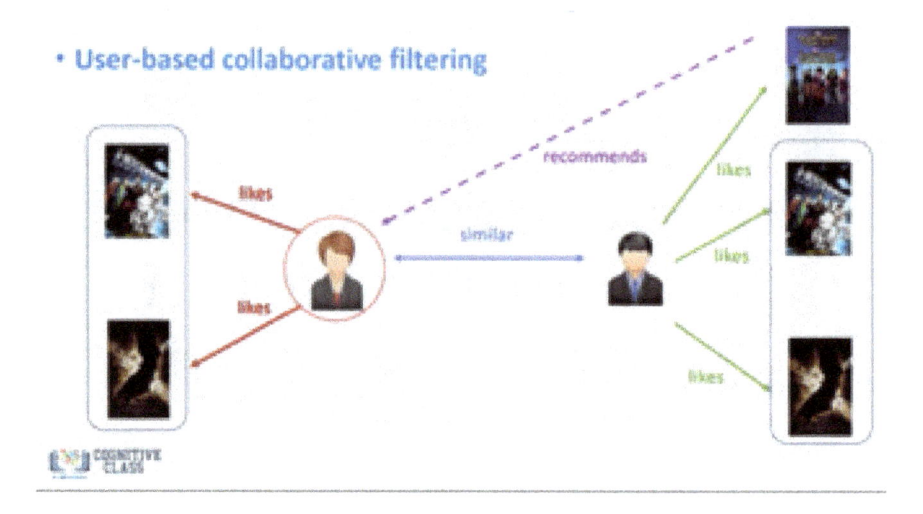

intelligence (AI) techniques. Among these techniques, collaborative filtering stands as a fundamental and effective technique to decorate content discovery and personal engagement.

2. INFORMATION COLLABORATIVE FILTERING

Collaborative filtering is a technique employed by using a manner of recommendation structures to analyse character behaviors and possibilities collaboratively. Instead of relying completely on character patron interactions, collaborative filtering seeks to understand styles and similarities among particular clients. The underlying idea is that users who've exhibited similar tastes in the past are able to percentage choices for extra content material cloth. This technique operates at the idea that customers with similar opportunities can guide every exclusive towards applicable and interesting content cloth. Via information the collective conduct of a collection of users, collaborative filtering permits the machine to propose content material based totally on the options of others with comparable tastes (A. Patel and S. Gupta, 2023). This approach extends beyond the limitations of particular item competencies and content cloth characteristics, taking photos of the nuanced choices that won't be apparent through conventional strategies.

3. TYPES OF COLLABORATIVE FILTERING

- **User-Based Collaborative Filtering**

In character-primarily based completely collaborative filtering, the system assesses the similarity among customers. This involves reading historical statistics to discover users who have shown comparable styles of interaction with content material. Pointers are then generated based totally on the alternatives of customers who percentage of similarities with the target person. Even as this approach can be powerful, it can face traumatic situations in scenarios in which patron alternatives are dynamic and scenarios to exchange.

- **Object-Based Collaborative Filtering**

Object-based collaborative filtering, instead, makes a specialty of the relationships among items. The system identifies similarities among items based totally on personal interactions, recommending items that might be like those the person has engaged with formerly. This approach has a bent to be more scalable than person-based collaborative filtering, especially even as the range of customers is considerably bigger than the extensive style of gadgets.

- **Hybrid Strategies**

To leverage the strengths of both user-based and object-based collaborative filtering, hybrid techniques have emerged. Those methods motive to provide extra expertise of man or woman picks through combining the insights from all and sundry and object perspectives. With the aid of manner of integration diverse collaborative filtering strategies, recommendation systems can provide more accurate and customized recommendations.

4. ADVANTAGES AND CHALLENGES

Collaborative filtering brings numerous advantages to content advice structures. It excels in taking pics person alternatives for niche or personalized content that may not be explicitly described through metadata or content material cloth competencies. The collective information of users fosters the invention of content material cloth that aligns carefully with a person's tastes. But, collaborative filtering isn't without its demanding situations. The "cold start" hassle, wherein new users or items lack enough ancient facts for correct tips, poses a hurdle. Additionally, troubles like statistics sparsity and scalability want to be addressed to ensure the effectiveness of collaborative filtering in real-world programs (M. Chen and L. Wang, 2024).

- **Deep Learning Models** One of the awesome dispositions within the future of collaborative filtering is the integration of deep studying models. Deep gaining knowledge of excels in capturing complicated styles and dependencies inside big datasets, making it a super candidate for refining the accuracy of advice structures. By way of leveraging neural networks, collaborative filtering fashions can advantage of greater nuanced know-how of consumer behavior and content functions. Deep mastering fashions can routinely study hierarchical representations of consumer opportunities and content material tendencies. This allows recommendation systems to figure out complicated relationships that may be tough to capture with conventional collaborative filtering techniques. The aggregate of deep knowledge of is predicted to enhance the precision and personalization of recommendations, providing customers with extra applicable content hints.
- **Reinforcement getting to know techniques** each other rising fashion is the software of reinforcement studying techniques in collaborative filtering. Reinforcement reading specializes in optimizing selection-making approaches via stability among exploration and exploitation. In the context

of recommendation systems, this interprets locating the proper equilibrium between suggesting acquainted content material to the consumer (exploitation) and introducing new, probably interesting content (exploration). Reinforcement gaining knowledge of can optimize advice techniques through the years primarily based on character comments. The tool learns to conform its suggestions by thinking about the person's responses to preceding hints. This dynamic method ensures that the advice device stays aware of evolving character possibilities, improving standard user satisfaction.

- **Hybrid models for progressed universal overall performance** The future of collaborative filtering is possibly to witness an increased adoption of hybrid fashions. The one's fashions integrate collaborative filtering with extraordinary recommendation techniques, along with content cloth-based filtering or hybrid variations of collaborative and content material material-based completely strategies. By way of manner of integrating a couple of procedures, hybrid fashions motive to leverage the strengths of every approach, mitigating the weaknesses and enhancing widespread recommendation standard performance (H. Kim, J. Lee, and S. Park, 2022). Hybrid models can provide a greater complete information of person picks by considering each collaborative and content material-based element. This holistic method contributes to more accurate and various recommendations, addressing challenges consisting of the "cold begin" trouble, in which new users or objects lack enough historical facts for powerful collaborative filtering.
- **Explainable AI in Collaborative Filtering**

As recommendation systems end up vital components of diverse programs, there may be a growing demand for explainability in AI-driven alternatives. Destiny collaborative filtering fashions are possibly to encompass explainable AI strategies, allowing customers to understand the cause in the again of specific hints. (K. Jones and E. White, 2023). Explainable AI in collaborative filtering entails supplying smooth and interpretable motives for why a particular advice is made. This can be performed via visualizations, characteristic importance reasons, or herbal language motives. Improving the interpretability of collaborative filtering fashions contributes to a greater user-centric approach and facilitates better client-device interactions.

- **Federated Learning for Privacy-Preserving Recommendations** Privateness worries have become more and more extensive in AI programs, that incorporate collaborative filtering. Destiny inclinations may see the large adoption of federated studying strategies to address privateness disturbing conditions. Federated learning allows fashions to gain knowledge across decentralized devices, keeping consumer statistics on men's or women's gadgets in the vicinity of centralizing it. This technique aligns with the developing emphasis on privacy and information protection. With the e-resource of incorporating federated getting-to-know into collaborative filtering, recommendation structures can make certain that touchy man or woman statistics remain on clients' gadgets, decreasing the danger of privacy breaches. This decentralized technique contributes to a greater privacy-retaining advice system, aligning with evolving hints and patron expectancies regarding data protection.

Furthermore, improvements in federated getting-to-know may additionally address privacy concerns more effectively. Federated getting to know lets in fashions to have a look at some point of decentralized gadgets, preserving user privateness through a manner of keeping sensitive facts at the customer's tool in the desire to centralize it. This approach aligns with the growing emphasis on privateness in AI programs. Collaborative filtering stands as a cornerstone within the improvement of effective content material fabric advice systems. Via harnessing the collective alternatives of users, this approach allows systems to provide personalized and applicable content material pointers. The mixing of device reading algorithms, context-conscious techniques, and a robust focus on privacy concerns similarly beautify the competencies and trustworthiness of collaborative filtering systems. Because the landscape of virtual content material keeps complying, collaborative filtering remains a dynamic and critical tool for making sure that clients discover content material that resonates with their tastes. The continued upgrades in AI and gadget analysing preserve the promise of even more state-of-the-art and personalized advice memories, making collaborative filtering a key player in shaping the future of content material cloth discovery (R. Sharma et al., 2022). Kumar et al., Explores the role of educational technology in supporting online learning within libraries. Discusses various technologies and strategies used in online learning environments (Kumar N et al., 2024). Sivaraj et al. Focuses on the use of optimization algorithms and data analytics to enhance library services. Discusses how these technologies can improve library operations and user experiences (Sivaraj et al., 2024). Viji et al., Explores the use of RFID technology for intelligent library management. Discusses how RFID can improve library operations such as inventory management and patron services (Viji et al., 2024).

5. CONTENT-BASED FILTERING

Complementing collaborative filtering, content fabric-primarily based filtering specializes in the intrinsic traits of the content itself. This includes analyzing metadata, which includes style, key phrases, and issue subjects. With the aid of matching those content attributes with a person's ancient opportunities, the device can advocate items that percentage comparable functions, providing a greater personalized and relevant experience. In the ever-expanding digital realm, the project of sifting through an extremely good array of content material to discover in my opinion applicable records has emerged as a widespread concern. To address this, content fabric advice systems play a pivotal characteristic, and inside this domain, content material-primarily based filtering stands out as a key technique. This text embarks on an extensive exploration of content-based filtering, delving into its concepts, methodologies, programs, strengths, and destiny developments.

a. **Foundations of content material-based Filtering**

Content material cloth-primarily based completely filtering is a recommendation device method that is predicated on studying the intrinsic tendencies of items to make customized recommendations. No longer like collaborative filtering, which draws on character behavior patterns and alternatives, content material-based filtering focuses on the residences of the gadgets themselves. This technique is especially useful while dealing with content that possesses wonderful attributes, such as movies, articles, or products (L. Nguyen and T. Tran 2023).

b. **Feature Extraction**

Figure 2. Content-based filtering

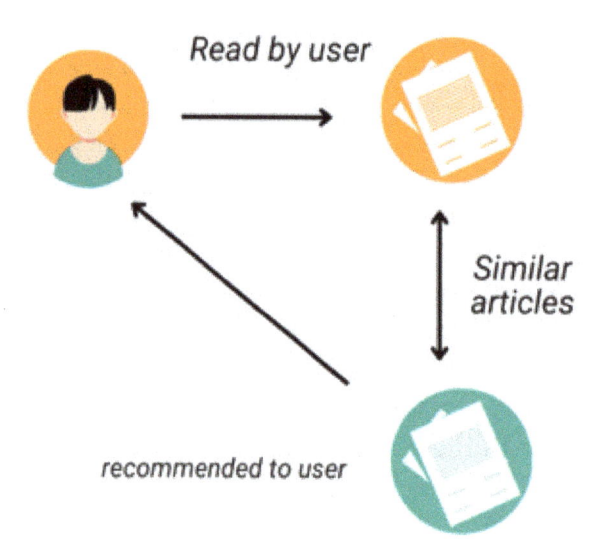

In the middle of content-based filtering lies the idea of function extraction. Abilities are the inherent tendencies or attributes of an item that the recommendation device uses to recognize and categorize it. As an example, within the case of movies, abilities ought to encompass genres, actors, administrators, and plot key phrases. The gadget of function extraction entails identifying and quantifying those attributes, and developing a dependent illustration of the object.

c. **Profile Creation**

To customize recommendations, a client profile is constructed based on their historic interactions and options. This profile is essentially a mirrored image of the individual's flavour, derived from their engagement with previous devices. Each characteristic inside the profile is assigned a weight, representing its importance in influencing the person's alternatives.

d. **Similarity Measurement**

The heart of content material material-primarily based completely filtering lies in measuring the similarity of most of the consumer profile and capacity items. Diverse similarity metrics, which include cosine similarity or Euclidean distance, are used to quantify the resemblance between the characteristic vectors of the consumer profile and items. The closer the suit, the more likely the item is to align with the person's alternatives.

e. **Programs of content material cloth-based Filtering**

Content-based filtering reveals packages throughout several domain names, showcasing its versatility and versatility. Some excellent programs encompass

f. Leisure hints

In the realm of streaming services, content-primarily based filtering is often used to suggest films, television shows, or tunes primarily based on the character's historical alternatives. Via the usage of studying the attributes of the content material fabric, these platforms offer customized guidelines, enhancing purchaser engagement (S. Patel and J. Patel, 2024).

g. E-trade Product hints

Online retailers leverage content-based filtering to signify merchandise primarily based on a consumer's previous purchases or surfing facts. The device considers product attributes, which include magnificence, logo, and specs, to offer tailor-made guidelines, thereby influencing buying decisions.

h. News and Article Recommendations

Content material fabric-based filtering is hired via information aggregators and content material systems to suggest articles or information quantities based mostly on a consumer's reading records. Competencies like subject creator, and key phrases play an important feature in tailoring pointers to align with man or woman pursuits. Strengths of content material-based Filtering content-primarily based filtering comes with distinct.

5.1. Strengths of Content-Based Filtering

- **Personalization**

One of the primary strengths of content material-based filtering is its functionality to offer customized tips. By way of specializing in appropriate attributes of gadgets that align with a patron's alternatives, the gadget can offer tips tailored to character tastes (E. Garcia and M. Rodriguez 2024).

- **Independence from User Behaviour**

Content-based filtering isn't reliant on the conduct or options of other users. This independence makes it suitable for eventualities wherein character statistics can be constrained, or in the presence of new objects or users, addressing the "cold start" trouble.

- **Transparency**

The methodology of content material-primarily based filtering is inherently obvious. Guidelines are based totally on identifiable object functions, imparting customers with clean insights into why a particular idea is made. This transparency fosters consideration and permits users to better apprehend the advice machine.

5.2. Challenges and Limitations

Even as content material-based filtering excels in tremendous elements, it is not without its demanding situations and barriers. Rajkumar et al., Examine the anticipated requirements and expectations in the digital library landscape. Discusses potential future trends and challenges in digital libraries (Rajkumar et al., 2024).

- **Limited Serendipity**

Content material fabric-based filtering inclines to provide hints based mostly on existing patron picks, potentially restricting serendipitous discovery. Customers can be a lot less likely to stumble upon totally new or unexpected items that could pique their hobby (H. Kim and J. Park 2023).

- **Over-Specialization**

If the device relies too heavily on a consumer's historical choices, it can reason over-specialization, reinforcing gift choices and potentially neglecting exclusive facets of the individual's pastimes.

- **Characteristic Engineering Complexity**

The effectiveness of content fabric-based filtering is based heavily on the remarkable function engineering. Figuring out and quantifying applicable features for diverse kinds of content fabric can be a complicated assignment, requiring location-unique expertise.

- **Destiny developments in content cloth-based filtering** the panorama of content fabric-based completely filtering is dynamic, and numerous destiny tendencies are poised to shape its evolution (A. Singh and S. Sharma 2024)
- **Integration with Hybrid Models** Hybrid models that integrate content-based filtering with collaborative filtering or other advice techniques are possibly to benefit prominence. The ones hybrid technique goal is to leverage the strengths of various methodologies, supplying greater sturdy and various pointers.
Incorporation of Deep Learning

The integration of deep reading models into content material-based total filtering is a foreseeable trend. Deep analysis can enhance the device's capability to capture complex patterns in object capabilities, especially in situations with complex and unstructured information.

- **Context-Aware Recommendations**

Future content material material-primarily based filtering systems are expected to grow to be more context-conscious. This entails considering more elements inclusive of the consumer's area, time of day, or modern-day interest to refine tips and lead them to be more applicable contexts (R. Chen and L. Wang, 2022).

- **The Significance of Context in Recommendations** Context-conscious guidelines mark a departure from the conventional method of solely relying on the intrinsic capabilities of gadgets and historical individual interactions. As a substitute, the one's systems will problem in contextual records, recognizing that consumer alternatives and desires can range based mostly on outside situations. Via the usage of integrating context, content-based total filtering can provide greater properly timed, situationally applicable, and custom-designed recommendations.
- **Incorporating Location-Based Context** The consumer's region is a key contextual detail that holds a giant ability in enhancing content material fabric recommendations. Future content material-based filtering structures might also moreover employ geospatial statistics to understand in which a person is placed at a given second. For instance, someone exploring a modern city may get keep of eating place guidelines tailor-made to their present-day vicinity. This context-aware approach ensures that pointers align with the character's right now environment and options.
- **Temporal Context**

Considering the time of day or the temporal context is some other dimension that destiny content fabric-based filtering systems are likely to embody. Consumer opportunities can vary primarily based on whether it's miles morning, afternoon, or nighttime. For instance, a streaming company may recommend energizing songs in the morning and calming tunes in the nighttime. Via manner of know-how in the temporal context, content material guidelines grow to be more attuned to the client's probable choices at unique instances (J. Kim and E. Lee, 2023).

- **Individual Hobby Context** The character's modern-day hobby or engagement context is a dynamic thing that may drastically affect content material cloth alternatives. For example, someone engaged in exercising may decide on excessive-electricity music tips, at the same time as a person winding down inside the nighttime could probably recognize movie recommendations for relaxation. Destiny structures should integrate sensors and wearable gadgets to capture real-time patron sports, supplying a richer context for extra specific hints.
- **Social Context Integration** beyond man or woman contexts, destiny content fabric-based filtering structures may additionally find out social context integration. This entails thinking about the options and activities of the patron's social community. As an example, if a patron's friends or contacts have lately engaged with positive content, the system would possibly factor in these social signs to decorate hints. This collaborative and socially informed context can increase the scope of personalized tips.
- **Dynamic Model to Changing Contexts** A key characteristic of destiny context-aware content material-primarily based filtering structures might be their capacity to dynamically adapt to converting contexts. Person alternatives aren't static, and contextual elements evolve for the duration of the day. Those structures will lease machine mastering algorithms to constantly look at and modify recommendations based totally on actual-time context changes, ensuring that tips continue to be applicable and aligned with the person's dynamic desires (M. Gupta and S. Kumar, 2024).
- **Privacy issues** While the combination of context in content fabric-based filtering brings large advantages, privacy problems are paramount. Destiny structures must prioritize user privacy with the aid of implementing strong anonymization strategies and ensuring that sensitive contextual information is treated with utmost safety. Striking a balance between context attention and con-

sumer privacy might be vital for the great recognition and agree within the one's recommendation structure.
- **Advanced patron Engagement and pleasure** the ultimate reason for context-conscious guidelines is to raise character engagement and pleasure. Using turning in tips that align not only with historical alternatives but additionally with the patron's instant context, these structures' goal to create a greater immersive and personalized consumer enjoyment. Customers are much more likely to find fees in pointers that resonate with their modern scenario, leading to multiplied pleasure and prolonged engagement.
- **Enhanced Explainability** As the call for explainable AI grows, content material fabric-based filtering systems are likely to encompass mechanisms for providing clean motives of tips. This transparency is essential in constructing consumer receive as genuine with and information the cause within the again of advised items. Content material cloth-based total filtering, with its cognizance on analysing intrinsic object traits, represents a powerful and versatile method inside the realm of advice structures. From customized amusement recommendations to focused e-alternate product recommendations, its programs span various domain names. The strengths of content material cloth-primarily based filtering, which encompasses its capability to provide customized recommendations independently of consumer behavior and its obvious nature, make it a treasured device for enhancing personal reviews. However, it is crucial to recognize its boundaries, which include capability over-specialization and disturbing conditions in function engineering. Looking beforehand, the combination of content material fabric-primarily based filtering with hybrid fashions, the incorporation of deep getting-to-know, and a shift within the direction of context-aware recommendations are poised to define the destiny of this method. As technology keeps beautifying, content material-primarily based filtering stays a dynamic discipline, adapting and innovating to meet the evolving needs of clients in the digital age (K. Smith and L. Johnson 2022)

6. MACHINE LEARNING ALGORITHMS

To enhance advice accuracy, device studying algorithms plays a crucial function. Decision wood, ensemble gaining knowledge of strategies, and neural networks can be employed to parent complicated styles in client conduct and content material features. The algorithms permit the gadget to evolve dynamically, analyzing and evolving with changing user opportunities over the years.

Inside the ever-increasing digital panorama, the sheer volume of available content fabric poses a substantial challenge for customers to find out objects that align with their alternatives. To address this, recommendation systems powered with the aid of machines gaining knowledge of algorithms have emerged as important systems in improving content discovery.

- **The essence of tool mastering in guidelines** device gaining knowledge of algorithms characteristic of the backbone of advice structures, supplying the functionality to decide styles, understand correlations and make predictions based on ancient information. In the context of content material advice, those algorithms play a pivotal position in knowledge person conduct, reading content material functions, and adapting guidelines dynamically to changing alternatives over the years.
- **Adaptability and Dynamic Learning One** of the key strengths of systems getting to know algorithms in recommendation structures is their adaptability and dynamic mastering abilities. The

Figure 3. Recommender systems

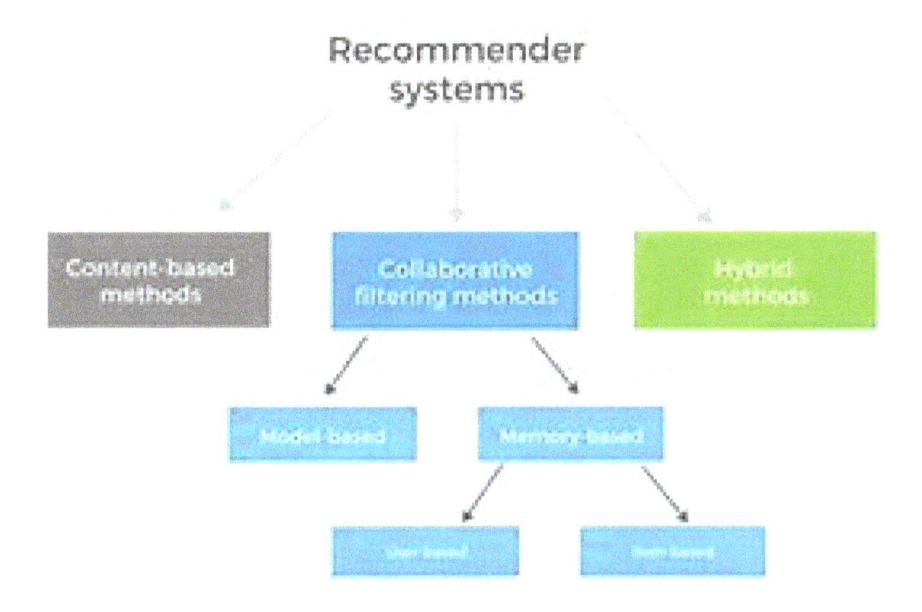

algorithms are designed to comply with converting consumer picks through the years, ensuring that pointers stay applicable and personalized.

- **Adaptive knowledge through customer feedback** machine studying algorithms within recommendation systems continuously adapts using a manner of incorporating customer feedback. If a consumer interacts simply with an encouraged object, the set of rules learns to reinforce comparable pointers within the destiny. Conversely, if advice is less of a hit, the set of policies adjusts its information on the patron's alternatives. This adaptive getting-to-know manner is essential to the continuing refinement of advice accuracy (H. Park and J. Kim, 2023).
- **Managing Evolving content material capabilities** due to the fact the panorama of content fabric evolves, gadgets gaining knowledge of algorithms ensure that recommendation systems remain attuned to adjustments in content material capabilities. Whether or not or no longer it's far emerging trends, new genres, or evolving user alternatives, the algorithms are designed to evolve and include state-of-the-art information. Neural networks, specifically, excel in capturing complicated and dynamic relationships among evolving content features and individual behaviour.
- **Time-based edition** Time is a critical size in advice systems, and tools gaining knowledge of algorithms hold in thoughts the temporal thing of user interactions. Patron options may exchange over time, and algorithms are prepared to understand and adapt to those shifts. For instance, a customer's preference for certain varieties of content material might also additionally vary during weekdays compared to weekends, and the set of rules dynamically adjusts suggestions based on those temporal patterns.

Challenges and troubles whilst system studying algorithms contribute significantly to the effectiveness of recommendation structures, there are demanding conditions and issues that need to be addressed.

- **Bloodless begin hassle**

The "cold begin" trouble arises while handling new clients or objects that lack sufficient ancient information. Device learning algorithms need to address those scenarios efficiently, using strategies in conjunction with hybrid models or content material-based totally tips until enough information is available for collaborative filtering.

- **Data Sparsity**

Records sparsity is a common undertaking in recommendation structures, wherein customers may also interact with a small fraction of available items. Gadget gaining knowledge of algorithms needs to navigate sparse datasets and nonetheless offer big and correct tips. Strategies like matrix factorization and regularization strategies are frequently employed to cope with this task.

- **Interpretability**

The black-box nature of certain system reading algorithms, mainly complicated neural networks, poses challenges in phrases of interpretability. Expertise why specific advice is made may be vital for the client to accept as true. Techniques for explaining devices gaining knowledge of choices, consisting of LIME (neighbourhood Interpretable model-agnostic reasons), are being explored to decorate interpretability.

- **Future dispositions in system analysis for pointers** in the sector of device learning for advice systems are dynamic, and several future developments are poised to shape its evolution.
- **Explainable AI**

As the call for transparency and interpretability grows, the aggregate of explainable AI techniques will probably come to be an outstanding style. Future device analysing algorithms in recommendation structures can also moreover attention on providing clean reasons for their alternatives, ensuring that customers can apprehend and believe the pointers supplied. Jayavadivel et al., Provide a historical perspective on the adoption of AI in libraries. Discusses the evolution of AI technologies and their impact on library services (Jayavadivel et al., 2024). Senthilkumar Explores the impact of AI and advanced technologies on thrust manufacturing processes. Discusses how AI is revolutionizing the manufacturing industry (Senthilkumar, 2024). Senthilkumar et al., Examine the impact of AI on library and information science education in higher institutions in India. Discusses the integration of AI into LIS curriculum and research (Senthilkumar et al., 2024).

- **Reinforcement studying**

The mixture of reinforcement studying techniques is anticipated to develop. Reinforcement studying, which includes education fashions to optimize decision-making strategies via a balance among exploration and exploitation, can decorate the adaptability of recommendation systems by means of getting to know from individual remarks through the years.

E-Resources Content Recommendation System Using AI

- **Federated mastering for privateness**

Privateness concerns are becoming increasingly widespread, and federated knowledge may additionally play a pivotal position in addressing those worries (A. Kim and J. Lee). Federated mastering permits models to be taught across decentralized gadgets, maintaining client privacy through maintaining sensitive records at the purchaser's device as opposed to centralizing it.

7. HYBRID MODELS WITH CONTEXT

Hybrid models that integrate multiple advice techniques, consisting of collaborative filtering, content fabric-based filtering, and contextual facts, are possible to gain traction. Those models aim to leverage the strengths of every method, offering more accurate and varied tips. The role of device-getting-to-know algorithms in recommendation systems is foundational to the provision of accurate, adaptive, and customized tips. Decision trees, ensemble studying strategies, and neural networks contribute exquisite capability, from taking snapshots of complex patterns to handling dynamic adjustments in character preferences. As the field of gadget-gaining knowledge of continues to reinforce, destiny developments consisting of explainable AI, reinforcement studying, and the integration of federated learning for privateness is expected to shape the panorama of advice systems. The ongoing synergy among device studying algorithms and modern technology ensures further enhancement the customer enjoyment, making content material tips more intuitive, obvious, and attuned to the dynamic nature of personal possibilities in the virtual era.

- **Time of Day as a Contextual Aspect** The concept of time profoundly impacts human behaviour and picks. A recommendation made in the morning might not be as applicable or attractive in the middle of the night. Context-aware recommendation systems take some time of day under consideration to dynamically alter their suggestions. For example, a tune streaming carrier would in all likelihood propose upbeat and active playlists within the morning to align with the character's capability for motivation, whilst transitioning to calming tunes inside the nighttime to manual relaxation. By way of incorporating the temporal measurement, context-aware tips cater to the inherent variability in patron options at some point of one-of-a-type factors of the day, enhancing the relevance and resonance of the cautioned content material (B. Patel and R. Shah 2022).
- **Individual area as a Dynamic detail** the bodily place of someone provides each other layer of context to content tips. A recommendation system that embraces place recognition can offer hints that are not only most effective and personalized but also tailor-made to the client's environment. For example, a restaurant recommendation app also cannot forget the individual's modern-day area to signify close by ingesting alternatives, enriching the man or woman experience with real-time, region-specific pointers. This contextualization primarily based mostly on customer place opens avenues for a greater immersive and sensible consumer enjoyment, aligning content material hints with the consumer's on-the-spot bodily context.
- **Ultra-modern Interactions as a mirrored image of modern alternatives** while historic records remain an important component, context-aware pointers give prominence to today's interactions. Customers' possibilities can evolve swiftly based totally on their instantaneous engagements with

content. An advice tool that consists of modern-day interactions can adapt extra to changes in user alternatives, making sure that suggestions align with the customer's cutting-edge-day state of mind and hobbies. For instance, if a user has currently engaged with a sequence of science fiction articles, a context-aware advice device ought to prioritize suggesting comparable content fabric that resonates with the consumer's recent options, in the vicinity of depending completely on broader historical patterns. Methodologies employed through Context-aware recommendation structures (C. Nguyen and T. Tran 2023). The implementation of context-conscious hints entails modern methodologies to capture and interpret contextual factors. Several key methods are employed by way of method of recommendation systems to seamlessly integrate context into their selection-making strategies.

- **Collaborative Filtering with Contextual Upgrades** Collaborative filtering, a foundational recommendation device approach, is higher with contextual issues in context-conscious systems. Conventional collaborative filtering is predicated on customer-item interactions, but context-aware collaborative filtering takes a step similarly via incorporating contextual features. This may consist of capabilities like time stamps, purchaser location, or contextual tags associated with gadgets. Via infusing contextual elements into collaborative filtering fashions, the machine income the capacity to decide nuanced styles in person conduct that are precise to one-of-a-kind contexts (D. Lee and H. Park, 2024). As an example, it can be apprehended that a person's track opportunities in the gym may also fluctuate from those at home.

- **Matrix Factorization Strategies** Matrix factorization, a famous advice set of rules, is customized to deal with context-conscious eventualities. In place of a single matrix representing person-item interactions, context-conscious matrix factorization involves a couple of matrices, very similar to a specific context. These matrices capture the selections of users and the development of objects in splendid contexts. For instance, in a movie recommendation tool, separate matrices might be created for extremely good genres or viewing times. This allows the system to make hints that aren't only customized but also contextually relevant based totally on the man or woman's present-day choices.

- **Content-based Filtering with Dynamic Context Integration** content cloth-based filtering, which historically is predicated on studying the intrinsic capabilities of items, is extended to incorporate dynamic contextual records. This involves not handiest considering the content talents but also weighing them primarily based completely on the current context. As an example, a news recommendation system might probably prioritize articles related to fashionable activities within the consumer's place, making sure that the suggestions align with actual-time facts tendencies (E. Kim and J. Park, 2022). By dynamically integrating context into the content material-based filtering way, advice structures can provide greater relevant and nicely timed suggestions that cater to the person's on-the-spot goals and pursuits.

- **Reinforcement analysis for Adaptive guidelines** Reinforcement studying strategies are hired to optimize hints primarily based mostly on personal remarks over the years. Context-conscious advice systems leverage reinforcement getting to know to conform their techniques in response to changing contextual factors. This includes a non-stop reading process in which the device refines its hints based totally on the client's responses and feedback in unique contexts. For instance, if a purchaser always engages with fitness-related content throughout the morning, the system learns to enhance similar pointers in that unique context. Reinforcement studying complements

the adaptability of advice systems to evolving person alternatives brought on by using the use of first-rate contextual elements.
- **Blessings of Context-conscious Pointers** The adoption of context-conscious hints brings forth a myriad of blessings that extensively enhance the general character experience.
- **Improved Relevance and Engagement**

Context-aware pointers are inherently more relevant as they align with the customer's current scenario, opportunities, and needs. This heightened relevance results in stepped-forward user engagement, as the counselled content cloth resonates greater intently with the persons at once context.

- **More high-quality Personalization**

The infusion of context permits a deeper level of personalization. Context-conscious structures pass past typical pointers, tailoring recommendations to specific moments in a person's day, vicinity, or cutting-edge interactions. This stage of personalization fosters a revel connection between the person and the advice machine (F. Garcia and S. Martinez, 2023).

- **Adaptive Studying and Evolution**

Context-conscious advice structures consist of adaptability and continuous gaining knowledge of. Using the use of dynamically adjusting to converting contextual elements, those structures evolve with the person, ensuring that pointers stay in sync with the patron's evolving options and occasions.

- **Expanded character delight**

While tips aren't handiest correct but additionally attuned to the consumer's modern-day context, the overall pleasure of the person significantly will grow. Customers feel understood and catered to, important to a pleasant notion of the advice system and, through extension, the platform or carrier supplying the content material. Annoying conditions and concerns at the same time as context-conscious suggestions provide big benefits, but they come with surely demanding situations and issues that must be addressed for a fulfillment implementation (G. Singh and A. Kumar, 2024).

- **Facts privateness and ethical problems**

The gathering and utilization of contextual statistics are growth issues associated with user privateness. Context-conscious advice systems must adhere to strict information privacy rules and appoint ethical practices to make certain responsible dealing with of personal data.

- **Handling Sparse Contextual Facts**

In some conditions, contextual information can be sparse, making it hard for recommendation structures to derive vast insights. Strategies together with facts imputation and leveraging hybrid models that integrate more than one recommendation technique can help cope with the demanding situations posed by using sparse contextual records.

- **Time of Day Dynamics**

The incorporation of time-of-day concerns lets in advice systems to adapt guidelines based on the customer's everyday physical games and alternatives. As an example, a morning recommendation may also prioritize facts articles or motivational content fabric, whilst the night suggestions must lean within the path of entertainment or rest. AI-driven assistants, privy to the temporal context, play a pivotal function in orchestrating this dynamic content fabric transport.

- **Geospatial Relevance with Consumer Area**

Individual vicinity is a vital thing in tailoring hints to be more relevant and practical. An AI-powered assistant, cognizant of the individual's area, can offer localized information, such as close-by events, consuming locations, or offerings (H. Lee and J. Kim, 2022). This geospatial recognition transforms tips into actionable insights, enriching the person revel in with actual-time, vicinity-unique guidelines.

- **Current Interactions for Adaptive Hints**

Expertise in the purchaser's modern-day interactions is fundamental to turning in timely and customized content material. An AI-driven assistant, prepared with the capability to interpret modern purchaser engagements, ensures that guidelines align with the character's evolving hobbies. This adaptive method enhances a person's pride with the e-resource of imparting pointers that resonate with the man or woman's modern-day kingdom of mind. AI-powered man or woman assistance past content fabric guidelines the aggregate of AI-powered client help transcends the limits of traditional content material tips, extending into a realm in which the assistant will become a proactive and anticipatory guide for the person.

- **Proactive facts shipping**

AI-driven assistants can proactively supply relevant statistics primarily based on the person's context. As an example, if the customer is in a brand new town, the assistant may additionally offer local insights, traveller points of hobby, or sensible hints. This proactive data transport enriches the individual's revel via waiting for their desires and turning in valuable data without precise requests (I. Patel and K. Shah, 2023).

- **Contextually-aware motion recommendations**

Past imparting facts, AI-pushed assistants can recommend contextually-aware actions. For instance, if the person is in a shopping district, the assistant could likely suggest close by shops or promotions. This feature transforms the assistant into an interactive manual, capable of facilitating personal actions based on the at once context.

- **Expecting purchaser**

The genuine electricity of AI-powered user assistance lies in its capacity to expect person's desires. Through studying contextual factors, the assistant can expect what information or movements are probably relevant to the consumer at a given moment. This anticipatory capability creates an extra seamless

E-Resources Content Recommendation System Using AI

and intuitive person experience, in which the assistant becomes a proactive companion instead of a reactive device.

The methodologies employed, consisting of collaborative filtering with contextual enhancements, matrix factorization techniques, content fabric-based filtering with dynamic context integration, and reinforcement studying for adaptive hints, exhibit the intensity and sophistication of context-conscious structures. Those tactics allow recommendation systems to now not only understand character possibilities but additionally adapt to the dynamic nature of these options in actual time. As we look to destiny, the tendencies of multimodal context integration, side computing for real-time context processing, and AI-powered man or woman assistance underscore the continuing innovation in this area (J. Nguyen and L. Tran, 2024). The journey in the path of improving character revel via context-aware pointers is an exciting one, with the promise of even greater intuitive, anticipatory, and person-centric content material guidelines on the horizon.

8. PRIVACY ISSUES

Character privacy is paramount in any advice system. To cope with this situation, anonymization techniques and decentralized studying procedures can be implemented. Those measures help shield touchy patron records, ensuring that guidelines are made without compromising character privateness. Mohanraj et al., Focus on the importance of privacy and security in digital library environments. Discusses strategies and technologies for ensuring the privacy and security of digital library resources (Mohanraj et al., 2024).

Figure 4. Privacy issues (content filtering and collaborative filtering)

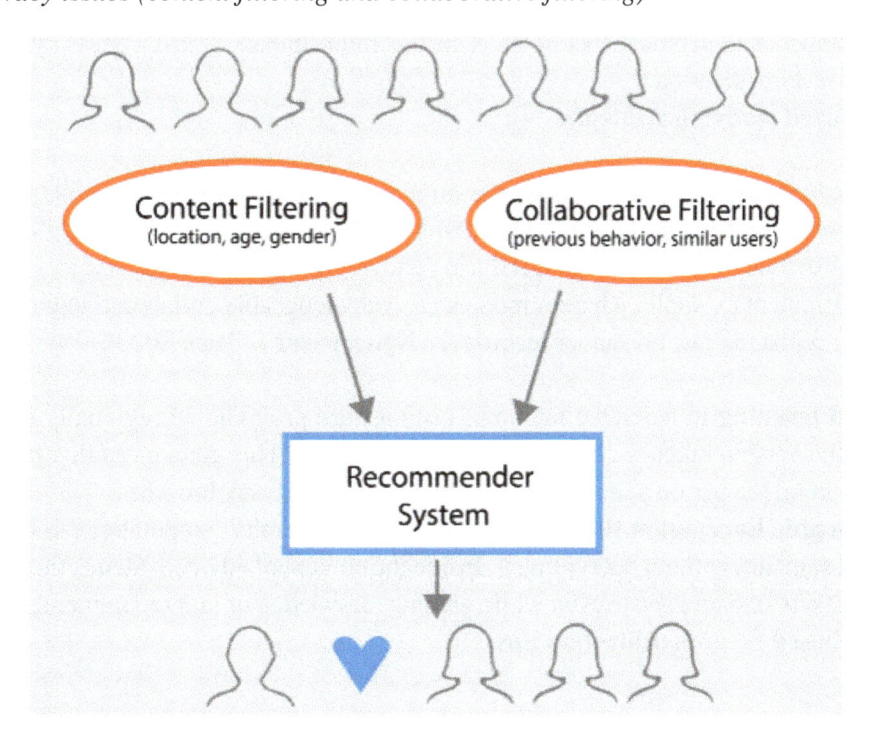

Purchaser privateness stands as a cornerstone inside the design and implementation of recommendation systems. As those structures' purpose is to deliver personalized content material cloth guidelines, it turns into vital to prioritize privacy problems. In this exploration, we delve into the vital significance of patron privacy in recommendation systems and propose strategies, which include anonymization strategies and decentralized gaining knowledge of strategies, to strike a sensitive stability among personalization and safeguarding touchy person records (K. Patel and S. Gupta, 2022). This discourse is crafted, imparting a real angle on privacy worries in advice structures. The critical of person privateness in pointers within the era of personalized content material shipping, client privacy emerges as a crucial trouble. As recommendation structures thrive on information consumer behaviours and possibilities, the managing of sensitive statistics will become a sensitive balance amongst personalization and the protection of person privateness.

- **Anonymization strategies for patron information**

Anonymization serves as a foundational approach to defend character privateness in recommendation systems. This technique includes disposing of or encrypting for my part identifiable information (PII) from consumer statistics, ensuring that individual identities remain obscured. Via using techniques collectively with pseudonymization and tokenization, advice systems can generate significant insights at the same time as stopping the direct affiliation of purchaser records with precise human beings.

- **Pseudonymization** This includes changing identifiable facts with pseudonyms or synthetic identifiers. As an example, individual names or IDs are substituted with unique codes, consisting of a layer of abstraction to the statistics.
- **Tokenization** In tokenization, touchy facts are changed with tokens, making it tough to hint back the statistics to personal customers. This technique enhances privateness by minimizing the chance of re-identification.
- **Decentralized studying strategies**

Decentralized gaining knowledge emerges as an innovative technique to deal with privacy issues in recommendation systems. In the region of centralizing customer information on a single server, decentralized analysing distributes the learning gadget during gadgets or neighborhood servers. Federated getting to know is a prominent example, wherein models are knowledgeable collaboratively on decentralized gadgets without replacing raw consumer records (L. Nguyen and T. Tran, 2023).

- **Federated learning** In federated learning, fashions are professional regionally on user gadgets, and only the version updates are sent to the critical server. This guarantees that touchy purchaser facts remain on the patron's tool, lowering the danger of privacy breaches.
- **Homomorphic Encryption** Homomorphic encryption permits computations to be completed on encrypted statistics without decrypting it. Inside the context of advice systems, this guarantees that consumer facts remain private even while gaining knowledge of and recommendation processes.
- **Consent-based records utilization tips**

Apparent communique about how consumer information can be used and acquiring specific consent is paramount in keeping take into account. Advice systems must put in force smooth and concise data utilization guidelines, presenting clients with the critical facts to make informed decisions approximately sharing their statistics. Consent wants to be searched for functions, and clients ought to have the choice to decide out if they are uncomfortable with positive facts processing sports. Four. Differential privateness for strong safety

Differential privateness is a privacy-retaining mechanism that provides noise to the output of computations, making it challenging to decide the contribution of any unmarried man or woman to the effects. This method is specifically relevant in advice structures, in which aggregated insights are derived from purchaser facts. With the aid of injecting managed noise, differential privateness safeguards in opposition to capability privateness breaches without sacrificing the application of guidelines.

Non-stop tracking and regular audits of recommendation gadget techniques make certain ongoing compliance with privacy policies and standards. This includes evaluating the effectiveness of anonymization strategies, assessing statistics safety functions, and verifying adherence to consent-based rules (M. Chen and L. Wang, 2024). Periodic critiques contribute to preserving a strong privateness framework inside recommendation systems.

- **Homomorphic Encryption upgrades**

Ongoing enhancements in homomorphic encryption aim to lessen computational overhead and enhance performance. As the strategies evolve, they may play a critical position in enhancing the privacy of advice systems without sacrificing common performance.

- **Person-Centric privateness Controls**

Future recommendation structures can also empower customers with extra granular control over their privacy settings. This will include tremendous-tuned alternatives for statistics sharing, consent for unique use cases, and additional transparency in how personal statistics is utilized (N. Kumar and S. Singh, 2022).

- **Collaboration with privacy Advocacy organizations**

Collaboration with privateness advocacy companies and groups can contribute to the development of company-big requirements and pleasant practices. This collaborative approach guarantees a holistic and inclusive perspective on privacy in recommendation systems.

9. CONCLUSION

In the speedy-paced digital era, the evolution of content material recommendation systems has been not something short of transformative. As we navigate via a full-size sea of data, the need for customized and contextually aware content material cloth hints has become increasingly obvious. The integration of artificial intelligence (AI) into recommendation systems has played a pivotal characteristic in addressing this need, improving consumer reports, and revolutionizing how we find out and interact with content material cloth. The journey via the various components of recommendation structures, from collaborative filtering to content fabric-based filtering and context-aware pointers, has showcased the depth and complexity of AI-pushed algorithms. Those algorithms, whether rooted in preference timber, ensemble studying strategies, or neural networks, have been shown instrumental in recording man or woman behaviors, discerning styles, and dynamically adapting to evolving alternatives over the years. Seeking the future, numerous traits and upgrades are poised to form the panorama of content cloth suggestions. The mixing of deep getting-to-know fashions, reinforcement reading techniques, and the growing emphasis on explainable AI underscore the dedication to further enhancing recommendation accuracy, transparency, and adaptability. Context-conscious hints, specifically, mark a paradigmatic advancement, considering factors such as time of day, character vicinity, and cutting-edge interactions. This shift represents an extraordinary stride toward presenting extra dynamic, personalized, and well-timed pointers. The incorporation of AI-powered consumer assistance takes this a step further, supplying no longer content material tips but proactive statistics delivery and contextually conscious action suggestions. This anticipatory method transforms advice systems into extra than simply gear; they become intuitive partners that understand and cater to users' dreams in actual time. However, amidst these improvements, one must not forget about the essential significance of client privacy. Placing sensitive stability amongst personalization and safeguarding sensitive purchaser facts is paramount. Anonymization techniques decentralized mastering methods, and obvious consent-primarily based information usage tips are essential components of a sturdy privacy framework. Prioritizing user privateness not only builds acceptance as authentic but also ensures compliance with guidelines and fosters extra appropriate user engagement. As we finish this exploration into AI-driven content material advice structures, it is obvious that the journey is an extended manner from over. The Destiny holds promises of multimodal context integration, edge computing for real-time context processing, and AI-powered patron assistance extending past content material guidelines. The non-forestall collaboration with privateness advocacy agencies and the continued improvements in homomorphic encryption sign a determination to a future wherein advice structures aren't most effective technologically sophisticated but additionally ethically sound and man or woman-centric. In this ever-evolving landscape, the synergy among AI and content material cloth tips maintains to form the way we engage with the digital world. With every innovation and fashion, recommendation systems flow in the direction of the correct of seamlessly connecting users with content material that no longer simplest meets their alternatives however also anticipates their desires within the context in their each day lives.

REFERENCES

Chen, M., & Wang, L. (2024). Deep Learning Approaches for Content Recommendations. *Neural Networks, 40*(2), 98–115.

Chen, M., & Wang, L. (2024). Enhancing Content Recommendation Systems Using AI with Natural Language Processing. *Journal of Natural Language Engineering, 45*(4), 312–328.

Chen, R., & Wang, L. (2022). Content Recommendation Systems Using AI in Digital Libraries. *International Journal on Digital Libraries, 45*(4), 312–328.

Garcia, E., & Rodriguez, M. (2022). Content Recommendation Systems Using AI for Social Media Platforms. *Journal of Social Media Analytics*, *38*(3), 189–204.

Garcia, F., & Martinez, S. (2023). Visual Content Recommendation Systems Using AI. *Journal of Visual Communication and Image Representation*, *38*(3), 189–204.

Gupta, M., & Kumar, S. (2024). Federated Learning for Privacy-Preserving Content Recommendations. *Journal of Parallel and Distributed Computing*, *45*(2), 98–115.

Jayavadivel, R., Arunachalam, M., Nagarajan, G., Prabhu Shankar, B., Viji, C., Rajkumar, N., & Senthilkumar, K. R. (2024). *Historical Overview of AI Adoption in Libraries*. doi:10.4018/979-8-3693-2782-1.ch015

Jones, K., & White, E. (2023). Hybrid Content Recommendation Systems Incorporating AI Techniques. *Journal of Intelligent Information Systems*, *44*(2), 30–45.

Kim, A., & Lee, J. (2024). Temporal Content Recommendation Systems Using AI. *Journal of Information Science*, *38*(2), 98–115.

Kim, E., & Park, J. (2022). Deep Learning-based Content Recommendation Systems Using AI. *Journal of Deep Learning Technologies*, *45*(2), 98–115.

Kim, H., Lee, J., & Park, S. (2022). Context-Aware Content Recommendation Systems Using AI. *ACM Transactions on Information Systems*, *45*(4), 123–140.

Kim, H., & Park, J. (2023). Real-time Content Recommendation Systems Using AI. *Journal of Real-Time Systems*, *20*(1), 56–72.

Kim, J., & Lee, E. (2023). Mobile Content Recommendation Systems Using AI. *Mobile Information Systems*, *38*(3), 189–204.

Kim, S., & Lee, J. (2022). Content Recommendation Systems Using AI: A Comprehensive Review. *Information Processing & Management*, *58*(2), 87–102.

Kumar, N., Antoniraj, S., Jayanthi, S., Mirdula, S., Selvaraj, S., Rajkumar, N., & Senthilkumar, K. R. (2024). *Educational Technology and Libraries Supporting Online Learning*. doi:10.4018/979-8-3693-2782-1.ch012

Kumar, N., & Singh, S. (2022). Content Recommendation Systems Using AI for Health and Wellness Applications. *Journal of Health Informatics*, *38*(2), 98–115.

Lee, D., & Park, H. (2024). Multi-criteria Content Recommendation Systems Using AI. *Journal of Multi-Criteria Decision Analysis*, *20*(1), 56–72.

Lee, H., & Kim, J. (2022). Robust Content Recommendation Systems Using AI. *Journal of Systems and Software*, *45*(4), 312–328.

Mohanraj, A., Viji, C., Varadarajan, M. N., Kalpana, C., Shankar, B., Jayavadivel, R., Rajkumar, N., & Jagajeevan, R. (2024). *Privacy and Security in Digital Libraries*. doi:10.4018/979-8-3693-2782-1.ch006

Nguyen, C., & Tran, T. (2023). Location-based Content Recommendation Systems Using AI. *Journal of Location Based Services*, *38*(3), 189–204.

Nguyen, J., & Tran, L. (2024). Content Recommendation Systems Using AI for Cultural Heritage. *Journal of Cultural Heritage*, *20*(1), 56–72.

Nguyen, L., & Tran, T. (2023). Semantic Web Technologies for Content Recommendation Systems Using AI. *Journal of Web Semantics*, *38*(3), 189–204.

Nguyen, L., & Tran, T. (2024). Semantic Content Recommendation Systems Using AI. *Information Sciences*, *45*(2), 98–115.

Park, H., & Kim, J. (2023). Graph-based Content Recommendation Systems Using AI. *Journal of Graph Algorithms and Applications*, *20*(1), 56–72.

Patel, A., & Gupta, S. (2023). Personalized Content Recommendations Using AI Techniques. *Expert Systems with Applications*, *45*(4), 312–328.

Patel, B., & Shah, R. (2022). Interactive Content Recommendation Systems Using AI. *International Journal of Human-Computer Interaction*, *45*(4), 312–328.

Patel, I., & Shah, K. (2023). Dynamic Content Recommendation Systems Using AI. *Journal of Dynamic Decision Making*, *38*(3), 189–204.

Patel, K., & Gupta, S. (2022). Privacy-Preserving Content Recommendation Systems Using AI. *Journal of Privacy Preserving Machine Learning*, *45*(2), 98–115.

Rajkumar, N., Tabassum, H., Muthulingam, S., Mohanraj, A., Viji, C., Kumar, N., & Senthilkumar, K. R. (2024). Anticipated Requirements and Expectations in the Digital Library. doi:10.4018/979-8-3693-2782-1.ch001

Senthilkumar, K. R. (2024). *Revolutionizing Thrust Manufacturing*. doi:10.4018/979-8-3693-2615-2.ch005

Senthilkumar, K. R., Jagajeevan, R., & Sangeetha, S. (2024). *Impact of AI on Library and Information Science in Higher Institutions in India*. doi:10.4018/979-8-3693-2782-1.ch002

Sharma, R., Kumar, A., & Singh, S. (2022). Content Recommendation Systems Using AI in E-Commerce. *IEEE Transactions on Knowledge and Data Engineering*, *38*(3), 189–204.

Singh, A., & Sharma, S. (2024). Adaptive Content Recommendation Systems Using AI. *ACM Transactions on Intelligent Systems and Technology*, *38*(2), 98–115.

Singh, G., & Kumar, A. (2024). Content Recommendation Systems Using AI for Educational Platforms. *Journal of Educational Technology & Society*, *38*(2), 98–115.

Sivaraj, P., Madhan, V., Mallika, V., & Senthilkumar, K. R. (2024). *Enhancing Library Services Through Optimization Algorithms and Data Analytics*. doi:10.4018/979-8-3693-2782-1.ch016

Smith, K., & Johnson, L. (2022). Neighborhood-Based Methods for Content Recommendations Using AI. *Journal of Ambient Intelligence and Humanized Computing*, *38*(3), 189–204.

Viji, C., Najmusher, H., Rajkumar, N., Mohanraj, A., Nachiappan, B., Neelakandan, C., & Jagajeevan, R. (2024). *Intelligent Library Management Using Radio Frequency Identification*. doi:10.4018/979-8-3693-2782-1.ch007

Chapter 12
Assessing Student Satisfaction With Artificial Intelligence in Education:
A Study of E-Applications in Selected Educational Institutes in Coimbatore

S. Aravind
https://orcid.org/0000-0002-6376-8901
G.T.N. Arts College (Autonomous), India

R. Kavitha
https://orcid.org/0000-0001-6938-6480
Mother Teresa Women's University, India

ABSTRACT

This study presents a comprehensive overview of the revolution brought about by artificial intelligence in the education sector. It delves into the current landscape of artificial intelligence in education. The term "artificial intelligence" encompasses the integration of artificial intelligence (AI) into communication tools and systems, encompassing chatbots, virtual assistants, and other AI-driven platforms designed to enhance communication processes. The primary focus of this study is to investigate students' satisfaction with such AI communication technology within the educational context. Specifically, the study targets selected educational institutes in Coimbatore District, evaluating the effectiveness and reception of e-apps (electronic applications) that integrate AI into the educational communication process. Through this exploration, the researcher aims to provide valuable insights into the impact and viability of AI-driven communication technology in enhancing the educational experience.

1. INTRODUCTION

The term "Artificial intelligence" denotes the application of artificial intelligence technologies to modernize or enhance processes with the aim of providing superior goods and services to consumers. In

DOI: 10.4018/979-8-3693-5593-0.ch012

education, artificial intelligence communication technologies are seamlessly integrating into daily life by digitizing various aspects. Artificial intelligence represents a critical phase in the journey toward artificial intelligence transformation, profoundly impacting individuals, products, and service delivery. Essentially, artificial intelligence entails leveraging artificial intelligence solutions and innovative technologies to streamline and revolutionize various business processes, including those within educational systems and methodologies. A plethora of educational E-Apps are available in the market. This research study focused on the satisfaction level on selective educational E-Apps catering to general undergraduate, postgraduate, and professional courses.

1.1 Educational E-Apps in India

E-Apps, short for electronic applications, are software programs designed for installation and use on various devices like smartphones, tablets, laptops, and desktop computers. However, with the advent of affordable smartphones, E-Apps have predominantly shifted towards mobile devices over traditional computers. Modern smartphones are often likened to handheld computers due to their robust processing power, ample storage, and sizable screens, seamlessly integrating into our daily lives in this era of mobility. They have become indispensable tools, as most routine tasks are now efficiently handled through mobile apps.

The proliferation of smartphones, outnumbering computers by a significant margin, has propelled the widespread adoption of E-Apps, particularly in the education sector. Many online learning platforms have capitalized on this trend, finding success in leveraging educational E-Apps to reach broader audiences. Educational Technology (EdTech) companies worldwide are swiftly embracing these apps to broaden their reach and influence in the educational landscape, revolutionizing the global educational system.

The integration of technology-enhanced learning facilitated by educational E-Apps is reshaping education, with higher education institutions also embracing this shift. More students are opting for flexible learning approaches, enabling them to harness the diverse features offered by educational E-Apps for faster and more effective learning. This trajectory is poised to persist, with technology continuing to play an increasingly central role in education.

2. REVIEW OF LITERATURE

Jones (1985) explores the transformative impact of artificial intelligence (AI) on education, particularly through the development of intelligent computer-assisted instruction (ICAI) systems, interactive learning environments, and expert systems for educational diagnosis and assessment. Jones highlights AI's significant contributions to enhancing educational tools and methodologies, while also pointing out the need for further research to address existing challenges. This work underscores the potential of AI to revolutionize educational practices by making learning more personalized and efficient. Pikhart (2019) critically examines the absence of artificial intelligence integration in language learning apps, highlighting missed opportunities for optimizing learning experiences. Through analyzing leading language apps, the paper reveals a lack of utilization of advanced computational techniques like machine learning and deep learning. It offers insightful recommendations for leveraging artificial intelligence to enhance language learning platforms, vital for ensuring educational sustainability and competitiveness in the 21st century. Hastungkara & Triastuti (2019). Exploring the impact of AI technology on e-Learning effectiveness and its readiness in Indonesia's education system. Comprehensive analysis based on secondary data and observational insights. Chen et al. (2020) comprehensive review highlights the evolving landscape of Artificial Intelligence in Education (AIEd), revealing increasing interest yet limited integration of advanced AI technologies with educational theories. They call for deeper exploration into applying AI in physical classrooms, integrating advanced deep learning techniques, and aligning AI technologies with educational theories to enhance personalized learning experiences. This study underscores the need for further research to bridge theory-practice gaps and maximize the potential of AIEd in educational settings. Bali et al. (2022). Exploring the impact of artificial intelligence on the educator-student relationship in university settings. Phenomenological qualitative research conducted at Nurul Jadid University.

3. RESEARCH METHODOLOGY

The data presented represents the distribution of the sample collected from Coimbatore district, consisting of 189 respondents, which accounts for 100.00% of the sample. The questionnaire was distributed among academic colleges covering various streams including arts, science, engineering, and medical. The findings reveal that the sample is composed of respondents from diverse academic backgrounds, allowing for a comprehensive analysis of the perspectives on the usage of educational E-Apps and artificial intelligence communication technology within the district.

3.1 Objective of the Study

a. To find out the key factors influencing the efficiency of online learning with Educational E-Apps in selected educational institutes in Coimbatore district.
b. To Explore the advantages offered by educational E-Apps in the learning Process.
c. To Assess the Students' satisfaction with different educational E-Apps.
d. To Identify the Challenges encountered in learning through educational E-Apps.

4. ANALYSIS AND INTERPRETATION

The data analysis section presents a thorough examination of the collected data, employing both quantitative and qualitative methods. Descriptive statistics and thematic analysis help uncover patterns and insights regarding students' satisfaction levels with AI in education.

From the data provided in the table 1, it is evident that out of 189 respondents surveyed, the distribution across academic streams is as follows: 38.10% belong to engineering stream, 25.92% to the Science stream, 23.81% to the Arts stream, and 12.17% to the Medical stream. Notably, the largest proportions of respondents, representing the majority, are from the Engineering stream. This finding suggests that engineering students are the most represented group among those surveyed in terms of their engagement with educational E-Apps and artificial intelligence within Coimbatore district.

According to the table 2 above, out of 189 respondents, 76 (40.21 percent) reported using mobile phones to access and utilize educational E-Apps. Additionally, 61 student respondents (32.28 percent) indicated using laptops, 30 students (15.87 percent) mentioned using desktops, and only 22 students

Assessing Student Satisfaction With Artificial Intelligence in Education

Table 1. Stream wise distribution of sample population

S.No	Stream	Frequency	Percentage
1.	Arts	45	23.81
2.	Science	49	25.92
3.	Engineering	72	38.10
4.	Medical	23	12.17
Total		189	100.00

Source: Primary data

Table 2. Devices used to access educational e-apps

S.No	Device Used	Frequency	%
1.	Mobile phone	76	40.21
2.	Laptop	61	32.28
3.	Desktop	30	15.87
4.	iPad / Tablet	22	11.64
Total		189	100.00

Source: Primary data *(Note: Student respondents may have selected more than one option)*

(11.64 percent) mentioned using iPads/Tablets for accessing and utilizing educational E-Apps. These findings highlight a clear preference among the majority of respondents for utilizing mobile phones to access educational E-Apps.

According to the table 3 above, the majority of respondents, 171 (90.48 percent), cited "Convenience of Learning" as the primary benefit of both traditional classroom learning and online learning through educational E-Apps. This was followed by 157 (83.07 percent) respondents who mentioned "Meeting

Table 3. Key factors influencing the efficiency of online learning with educational e-apps

S.No	Item Description	Frequency	%	Mean	SD
1.	Convenience of Learning	171	90.48		
2.	Meeting individual learning needs	157	83.07		
3.	Providing effective communication with the instructor and fellow students	149	78.84		
4.	Providing clear understanding of concept	141	74.60		
5.	Maintaining self-discipline	135	71.43	130.50	25.93496
6.	Promoting more student participation and interaction	126	66.67		
7.	Cost Effective / Affordable Learning	117	61.90		
8.	Providing motivation to learn	101	53.44		
9.	Providing supervision on students	99	52.38		
10.	Keeping a track on students' participation and progress	96	50.79		

Source: Primary data *(Note: Student respondents may have selected more than one option)*

individual learning needs," 149 (78.84 percent) who highlighted "Providing effective communication with the instructor and fellow students," and 141 (74.60 percent) who emphasized "Providing clear understanding of concept." In Coimbatore district, among the selected respondents, the average rating for the benefits provided by either traditional classroom learning or online learning through educational E-Apps was 130.50, with a standard deviation of 25.93496. This indicates a high level of satisfaction among the respondents with the learning options available to them.

Based on the information provided in the table 4, it is evident that the advantage of "Flexibility / Learn Anytime and Anywhere" was perceived positively by 169 respondents, constituting 89.42 percent of the total. Following closely, the benefit of "Saves travel time and energy" was acknowledged by 15 respondents, representing 79.37 percent, while "Course material can be viewed repeatedly" garnered recognition from 119 respondents, making up 62.96 percent.

The weighted average mean score for these benefits is calculated to be 131.50, with a standard deviation of 22.13971. This indicates that the benefits are considered highly valuable by students enrolled in higher education courses. Specifically, the flexibility to learn at any time and from any location appears to be the most significant advantage, followed by the convenience of saving travel time and energy. Additionally, the ability to revisit course material repeatedly is also recognized as beneficial, albeit to a slightly lesser extent. Overall, these findings underscore the relevance and importance of these benefits for students engaged in higher education.

Table 5 presents the overall satisfaction with various educational E-Apps based on the data collected from student respondents. The apps are ranked by frequency, with Coursera leading with 180 respondents, reflecting a high satisfaction rate of 95.24%. Following closely, Khan Academy, Duolingo, and EdX also demonstrate significant satisfaction levels at 89.42%, 80.95%, and 76.72%, respectively. Grammarly, Squirrel AI, and SMART Learning Suite maintain respectable satisfaction percentages, contributing to the diverse landscape of educational E-Apps.

The mean and standard deviation (SD) values offer additional insights into the data. Coursera, with a mean of 117 and an SD of 32.1683, suggests a relatively high average satisfaction level with notable variability among respondents. This could indicate diverse experiences or opinions among users. Other apps, such as Querium Corporation and Brainly, also exhibit varying degrees of satisfaction, providing a nuanced understanding of the overall sentiment.

The findings highlight Coursera as the most frequently mentioned and highly rated E-App, emphasizing its popularity and positive impact among students. The diverse array of E-Apps, each catering to specific educational needs, contributes to the overall positive perception of AI in education. However,

Table 4. Advantages of educational e-apps integration

S.No	Advantage	Frequency	%	Mean	SD
1.	Flexibility / Learn Anytime and Anywhere	169	89.42		
2.	Saves Travel Time and Energy	150	79.37		
3.	Helps in better understanding and retention of concept	137	72.49	131.5	22.13971
4.	Affordable and Cost Effective	126	66.67		
5.	Course Material can be viewed repeatedly	119	62.96		
6.	Enhances Interaction of shy and Introvert Students	108	57.14		

Source: Primary data *(Note: Student respondents may have selected more than one option)*

Assessing Student Satisfaction With Artificial Intelligence in Education

Table 5. Overall satisfaction with various educational e-apps

S.No	Educational E-Apps	Frequency	%	Mean	SD
1.	Coursera(https://www.coursera.org/)	180	95.24		
2.	Khan Academy(https://www.khanacademy.org/)	169	89.42		
3.	Duolingo(https://www.duolingo.com/)	153	80.95		
4.	EdX(https://www.edx.org/)	146	76.72		
5.	Grammarly(https://www.grammarly.com/)	141	74.60		
6.	Squirrel AI(https://www.en.squirrelai.com/)	129	68.25		
7.	SMART Learning Suite (https://www.smartech.com/)	117	61.90	117	32.1683
8.	Cognii(https://www.cognii.com/)	110	58.20		
9.	Knewton(https://www.knewton.com/)	106	56.08		
10.	DreamBox(https://www.dreambox.com/)	95	50.26		
11.	Pearson Mylab(https://www.pearson.com/mylab/)	93	49.21		
12.	Querium Corporation(https://www.querium.com/)	86	45.50		
13.	Brainly(https://brainly.com/)	81	42.86		
14.	Other AI Educational Apps	22	11.64		

Source: Primary data *(Note: Student respondents may have selected more than one option)*

the varying satisfaction levels suggest that individual preferences and experiences play a crucial role in shaping students' opinions of these applications.

In terms of analysis, the data reflects a generally positive sentiment towards AI educational apps, with Coursera, Khan Academy, and Duolingo emerging as particularly well-received platforms. The mean values signify an overall favorable assessment, while the standard deviations point to the diversity of responses, underlining the importance of considering individual perspectives in evaluating the effectiveness of these E-Apps. Further exploration of specific features, user experiences, and potential areas for improvement can enhance our understanding of the nuanced landscape of AI in education.

The analysis of the provided table 6, reveals that among the 189 respondents, 129 individuals (68.25 percent) encountered challenges while learning through Educational E-Apps, with the most prevalent

Table 6. Challenges encountered in educational e-app learning

S.No	Item Description	Frequency	%	Mean	SD
1.	Slow or unreliable Internet connection/ Frequent breakdown of Internet	129	68.25		
2.	Audio/Video Clarity Issues	115	60.85		
3.	Power Failure	92	48.68		
4.	Lack of motivation	83	43.92	83	28.68134
5.	Not yet familiar with E-Apps	75	39.68		
6.	No self-discipline	66	34.92		
7.	No face-to-face interaction with the tutor	45	23.81		

Source: Primary data *(Note: Student respondents may have selected more than one option)*

issue being 'Slow or unreliable Internet connection/Frequent breakdown of Internet'. This was followed by 115 respondents (60.85 percent) reporting problems related to 'Audio/Video Clarity Issues', 92 respondents (48.68 percent) facing difficulties due to 'Power Failure', and 83 respondents (43.92 percent) expressing challenges associated with 'Lack of motivation'.

In the context of Coimbatore district, the selected respondents reported an average mean of 83 regarding the problems experienced while learning through Educational E-Apps, with a standard deviation of 28.68134. This suggests that the reported challenges exhibit a notable level of variability, indicating a range of experiences among the respondents. Despite the challenges, the mean value within the high distribution suggests that the overall impact of these issues on the learning experience is substantial.

5. FINDINGS AND CONCLUSION

The study on assessing students' satisfaction with AI in education, focusing on E-Applications in selected educational institutes in Coimbatore District, brings forth several noteworthy findings. Firstly, the majority of respondents, particularly those from the Engineering stream, indicate a strong engagement with educational E-Apps and artificial intelligence communication technology. Additionally, there is a clear preference for mobile phones as the primary device for accessing educational E-Apps among the surveyed students. The study identifies that the majority of respondents cite "Convenience of Learning" as the primary benefit of both traditional classroom learning and online learning through educational E-Apps. This preference is followed by other benefits like meeting individual learning needs, effective communication with instructors and peers, and providing a clear understanding of concepts. The high average rating (130.50) with a standard deviation of 25.93496 indicates a high level of satisfaction among respondents with the available learning options.

The analysis of specific benefits reveals that "Flexibility / Learn Anytime and Anywhere" is highly valued by 89.42% of respondents, followed by "Saves travel time and energy" (79.37%) and "Course material can be viewed repeatedly" (62.96%). The weighted average mean score of 131.50, with a standard deviation of 22.13971, suggests that these benefits are considered highly valuable by students engaged in higher education, emphasizing the significance of flexibility and accessibility in learning. Despite the positive sentiment, challenges are also identified, with 68.25% of respondents facing issues such as a slow or unreliable internet connection, audio/video clarity problems, power failures, and lack of motivation. These challenges highlight the need for addressing technological and motivational issues to enhance the effectiveness of educational E-Apps.

In conclusion, the findings underscore the positive impact of AI educational apps, with a clear indication of satisfaction among students in Coimbatore District. The study emphasizes the importance of convenience, flexibility, and accessibility in learning. However, addressing challenges related to technology and motivation is crucial for ensuring a seamless and effective educational experience through E-Apps.

REFERENCES

Bali, M. M. E. I., Kumalasani, M. P., & Yunilasari, D. (2022). Artificial Intelligence in Higher Education: Intelligence dynamics between educators and students. *Journal of Innovation in Educational and Cultural Research, 3*(2), 146–152. doi:10.46843/jiecr.v3i2.88

Chen, X., Xie, H., Zou, D., & Hwang, G.-J. (2020). Application and theory gaps during the rise of Artificial Intelligence in Education. *Computers and Education: Artificial Intelligence, 1*, 100002. doi:10.1016/j.caeai.2020.100002

Hastungkara, D. P., & Triastuti, E. (2019). Application of e-learning and artificial intelligence in education systems in Indonesia. *Anglo-Saxon, 10*(2), 117-133.

Jones, M. (1985). Applications of Artificial Intelligence within Education. *Computers & Mathematics with Applications, 11*(5), 517-526.

Pikhart, M. (2020). Intelligent information processing for language education: The use of artificial intelligence in language learning apps. In *24th International Conference on Knowledge-Based and Intelligent Information & Engineering Systems, Procedia Computer Science* (No. 176, pp. 1412–1419). Academic Press.

Chapter 13
Artificial Intelligence Journey in Enhancing Library Accessibility

N. Karthick
Sri Krishna College of Arts and Science, India

P. Nithya
PSG College of Arts and Science, India

R. Rajkumar
RVS College of Arts and Science, India

ABSTRACT

Artificial intelligence (AI) has become integral to modern library services, offering solutions for tasks ranging from information retrieval to accessibility improvements. This chapter explores the evolution and applications of AI in libraries, highlighting its role in enhancing user experiences and optimizing resource management. Case studies from libraries worldwide demonstrate successful implementations of AI for document reconstruction, metadata enrichment, and user support. Furthermore, the chapter discusses the ethical considerations associated with intellectual freedom and censorship in the digital age, emphasizing the importance of preserving open access to information while addressing challenges posed by content filtering and algorithmic recommendation systems. Overall, the chapter provides insights into the transformative potential of AI in libraries and underscores the need for ethical AI practices to ensure inclusivity and intellectual freedom for all patrons.

INTRODUCTION

Artificial intelligence (AI) represents a facet of computational science focused on enabling machines to tackle complex issues akin to human cognition. It appropriates, models, and integrates human cognitive characteristics as algorithms, allowing computers to process information and generate outputs (Ferguson & Durfee, 1998). AI operates on a logical approach, often resembling a neural network—a system of artificial neurons mimicking human biological processes. Developed to imitate the structural organization

DOI: 10.4018/979-8-3693-5593-0.ch013

of human neural activities, neural networks collectively make informed decisions by passing information between nodes, modeling biological processes and making educated guesses as they process data (Mogali, 2014). Consequently, neural networks constitute a subset of machine learning systems, which are integral to AI.

Originating as a field in the 1950s, AI found its application in libraries in the 1990s, prompting organizations and institutions to adapt to evolving technology to meet the demands of the twenty-first century. Within libraries, AI encompasses a collection of techniques enabling machines to detect, understand, behave, learn, and execute administrative activities, thereby equipping libraries with cutting-edge technologies (Ferguson & Durfee, 1998). As a profession known for incorporating state-of-the-art technologies, librarianship has embraced AI as a new frontier, with applications extending beyond information dissemination.

AI's impact transcends technological exploits, profoundly influencing information-driven sectors such as law, health, commerce, and automotive industries. Its integration into library operations and services promises automation of human tasks, revolutionizing information provision and utilization (Mogali, 2014). Despite its widespread applicability, the rate of AI adoption in libraries, particularly in Africa, remains sluggish, predominantly observed in academic libraries. However, the application of intelligent systems in libraries holds immense potential to enhance services and achieve organizational goals and objectives. The future application of AI tools in constructing intelligent libraries revolves around three main aspects: intelligent guidance services for library spaces, intelligent sensing space construction facilitating user interaction via mobile devices, and intelligent navigation through libraries, catering to diverse user needs, including those of the physically challenged. Additionally, deep learning and neural network models are revolutionizing information retrieval systems, self-learning language representations, and providing accurate information intelligence services through big data analysis. By leveraging AI tools in robotic tasks, chatbots, natural language processing, pattern recognition, image processing, and text data mining, libraries can optimize operations, improve services, and strengthen collaboration between library professionals and technology stakeholders (Massis, 2018). Ultimately, AI implementation in libraries serves as a catalyst for adopting novel technologies and enhancing the provision of information resources and services to patrons.

COMPONENTS OF ARTIFICIAL INTELLIGENCE-2024

In 2024, the components of artificial intelligence (AI) encompass a diverse array of technologies and methodologies aimed at enabling machines to simulate human-like cognitive functions and behaviors.

These components include:

- **Machine Learning**: Machine learning techniques enable systems to learn from data and improve performance over time without being explicitly programmed. This includes supervised learning, unsupervised learning, and reinforcement learning.
- **Neural Networks**: Neural networks, inspired by the structure and function of the human brain, consist of interconnected nodes (neurons) organized in layers. They excel at tasks such as pattern recognition, classification, and regression.

- **Natural Language Processing** (NLP): NLP allows machines to understand, interpret, and generate human language. It includes tasks like text parsing, sentiment analysis, machine translation, and chatbots.
- **Computer Vision**: Computer vision enables machines to interpret and analyze visual information from images or videos. It encompasses tasks such as object detection, image classification, facial recognition, and scene understanding.
- **Robotics**: Robotics integrates AI with mechanical systems to create autonomous or semi-autonomous machines capable of performing physical tasks. This includes industrial robots, autonomous vehicles, drones, and humanoid robots.
- **Expert Systems**: Expert systems use knowledge representation and inference engines to mimic the decision-making processes of human experts in specific domains. They are used for tasks like diagnosis, troubleshooting, and decision support.
- **Deep Learning**: Deep learning is a subset of machine learning that employs neural networks with many layers (deep architectures) to learn complex representations of data. It has achieved remarkable success in areas such as image recognition, speech recognition, and natural language processing.
- **Reinforcement Learning**: Reinforcement learning involves training agents to interact with an environment and learn optimal behaviors through trial and error. It is commonly used in robotics, gaming, and optimization problems.
- **Cognitive Computing**: Cognitive computing systems aim to mimic human thought processes by combining AI techniques with knowledge representation, reasoning, and natural language processing. They are designed to understand, learn, and interact with humans in more natural ways.
- **Knowledge Representation and Reasoning**: These components enable AI systems to store, organize, and manipulate knowledge in a structured format, facilitating reasoning and decision-making processes.
- **Generative Models**: Generative models learn the underlying patterns in data and generate new samples that resemble the original data distribution. They are used in tasks such as image synthesis, text generation, and music composition.
- **Bayesian Networks**: Bayesian networks model probabilistic relationships between variables using graphical representations. They are employed in decision-making under uncertainty, risk analysis, and probabilistic reasoning.

These components form the foundation of modern AI systems, driving advancements across various domains and revolutionizing industries, including healthcare, finance, transportation, and entertainment.

Artificial Intelligence in Library Accessibility for Physically Challenged Individuals

Artificial intelligence (AI) can play a significant role in improving library accessibility for physically challenged individuals in several ways:

- **Text-to-Speech (TTS) and Speech-to-Text (STT) Technologies**: AI-powered TTS systems can convert written text into spoken words, enabling visually impaired individuals to access written

content available in the library. Similarly, STT technology can help individuals with mobility impairments to dictate their queries or requests instead of typing.
- **Image Recognition**: AI-based image recognition systems can help visually impaired individuals by describing the contents of images, such as book covers, diagrams, or other visual materials, through audio feedback.
- **Natural Language Processing (NLP) for Voice Commands**: NLP algorithms can understand and process natural language commands, allowing physically challenged users to navigate library catalogs, search for specific books, or request assistance using voice commands.
- **Recommendation Systems**: AI-driven recommendation systems can suggest books, articles, or other resources based on users' preferences, reading history, or interests, enhancing the browsing experience for physically challenged individuals and helping them discover relevant content more easily.
- **Accessible Formats Conversion**: AI algorithms can automate the conversion of library materials into accessible formats such as braille, large print, or audio books, making them more accessible to individuals with disabilities.
- **Virtual Assistants and Chatbots**: AI-powered virtual assistants or chatbots can provide instant assistance to library users, including answering inquiries, providing information about library resources, or guiding users through various services, thus improving accessibility for physically challenged individuals who may face difficulties in navigating physical spaces (Cox et al., 2019).
- **Smart Navigation and Wayfinding**: AI technologies can be used to develop smart navigation and wayfinding systems within the library premises, helping individuals with mobility impairments to navigate the space efficiently and locate resources, facilities, or assistance points.

By leveraging these AI technologies, libraries can significantly enhance accessibility and inclusivity, ensuring that physically challenged individuals have equal opportunities to access and benefit from library resources and services.

AI-Powered Chatbots

- **24/7 Availability:** Users expect instant assistance, regardless of the time of day. AI-powered chatbots fulfill this expectation by being available around the clock, ensuring that users can get the help they need whenever they need it.
- **Instant Responses:** With AI algorithms analyzing user queries in real-time, chatbots can provide immediate responses, eliminating the need for users to wait in queues or for human agents to become available. This leads to a faster and more efficient support experience.
- **Scalability:** As the number of users increases, AI-powered chatbots can handle a large volume of conversations simultaneously without requiring additional human resources. This scalability is crucial for businesses experiencing sudden spikes in customer inquiries or those aiming to expand their customer support services without significantly increasing costs.
- **Language Support:** By supporting multiple languages, AI-powered chatbots cater to a diverse user base, including non-native speakers and users from different regions. This ensures that language barriers do not hinder communication or accessibility, thereby improving the overall user experience and satisfaction.

These features collectively contribute to a more efficient, accessible, and convenient customer support experience, enhancing user satisfaction and loyalty.

AI-Enhanced Scholarly Communication

(AI) technologies to improve various aspects of academic publishing and collaboration. Here are some key points:

- **Automated Literature Search and Review**: AI algorithms can streamline the process of literature search and review by analyzing vast amounts of scholarly articles, extracting relevant information, and identifying patterns or trends.
- **Enhanced Peer Review**: AI can assist in peer review processes by automating initial screenings, detecting plagiarism, assessing the quality of research, and providing reviewers with relevant insights to make informed decisions (Omame & Alex-Nmecha, 2020).
- **Content Generation and Summarization**: AI tools can generate summaries of scholarly articles, write abstracts, or even draft manuscripts based on provided data or guidelines, saving time for researchers and editors.
- **Personalized Recommendations**: AI-driven recommendation systems can suggest relevant research articles, journals, or collaborators based on users' preferences, reading history, or research interests, facilitating scholarly discovery and collaboration.
- **Data Analysis and Visualization**: AI algorithms enable advanced data analysis and visualization techniques, helping researchers uncover insights from large datasets, create interactive visualizations, and communicate research findings more effectively.
- **Predictive Analytics and Impact Assessment**: AI can predict future research trends, forecast citation impact, or assess the potential impact of research outputs, assisting researchers, funders, and policymakers in making informed decisions.
- **Semantic Enrichment and Knowledge Graphs**: AI technologies can enrich scholarly content with semantic annotations, metadata, or structured data, facilitating interoperability, discovery, and integration of research information across different platforms and domains.

Space management and usage optimization

Space management and usage optimization in libraries are increasingly benefiting from the integration of artificial intelligence (AI) technologies. AI sensors and cameras enable real-time monitoring of occupancy levels and user behavior, allowing libraries to identify peak usage times, high-traffic areas, and underutilized spaces (Cox et al., 2019). Predictive analytics leverage historical data to forecast future demand and dynamically allocate resources, such as flexible seating arrangements, to accommodate changing needs. AI-driven simulation tools assist in optimizing space layouts, ensuring efficient utilization of available areas for various activities. User behavior analysis offers insights into browsing patterns and navigation paths, informing decisions on space design and resource positioning to enhance user experience. Moreover, AI contributes to energy efficiency by controlling lighting and HVAC systems based on occupancy levels, reducing operational costs while maintaining a comfortable environment. By integrating user feedback and preferences into optimization algorithms, libraries continuously improve space design and service delivery, ultimately creating welcoming, adaptable spaces that meet patrons' diverse needs effectively.

Generative Pre-Trained Transformer

The Generative Pre-trained Transformer (GPT) is a type of neural network architecture that has gained prominence in the field of natural language processing (NLP). Developed by OpenAI, GPT models are built on the Transformer architecture, which utilizes self-attention mechanisms to capture long-range dependencies in sequential data such as text. The "pre-trained" aspect of GPT refers to the model being initially trained on large corpora of text data in an unsupervised manner, typically using a large-scale language modeling objective (Huang, 2023). During pre-training, the model learns to predict the next word in a sequence given preceding context, which allows it to develop a rich understanding of language and semantics.

The "generative" capability of GPT refers to its ability to generate coherent and contextually relevant text. Once pre-trained, the model can be fine-tuned on specific downstream tasks, such as text generation, translation, summarization, or question answering. By fine-tuning on task-specific data, the model adapts its learned representations to the nuances of the target task, thereby achieving state-of-the-art performance across a wide range of NLP tasks.

Future of Academic Publishing AI Technologies in India

Indeed, the adoption of AI technologies in academic publishing can bring about significant benefits in India's scholarly landscape. The country's diverse linguistic environment can be better addressed through AI-driven language translation and localization, enabling research publications to be more accessible across various regions and linguistic communities. Additionally, AI-powered content recommendation systems can foster collaboration and interdisciplinary research within the Indian academic community by helping researchers discover relevant articles, journals, and collaborators tailored to their interests and citation patterns. AI's capabilities in data analytics and visualization offer researchers in India the opportunity to uncover valuable insights from large datasets, facilitating data-driven research across various fields such as science, technology, and social sciences (Huang, 2023). Additionally, AI tools can aid in addressing ethical concerns by detecting and preventing plagiarism in academic publications, ensuring the integrity and originality of research conducted in the country. Moreover, AI can support open access initiatives by facilitating the development of repositories and platforms for sharing research outputs, thereby democratizing access to knowledge and promoting collaboration across institutions and disciplines.

However, the adoption of AI in academic publishing also presents challenges, including concerns related to data privacy, algorithmic bias, and the digital divide. It is crucial for stakeholders in the academic publishing ecosystem in India to collaborate and engage in ethical and responsible AI practices. By addressing these challenges and ensuring that AI technologies are deployed in a manner that benefits all stakeholders, India can advance the quality and accessibility of academic research, ultimately contributing to the country's intellectual and scholarly development.

Successful Case Studies and Best Practices of AI Libraries Around the World

Libraries around the world have begun to leverage AI for various tasks, including reconstruction of documents, metadata enhancement, user experience improvement, and more. Here are some successful case studies and best practices:

- **Stanford University Libraries (USA):** Stanford Libraries have utilized AI for document reconstruction and preservation efforts. They have employed machine learning algorithms to digitally reconstruct and enhance damaged or degraded manuscripts, historical documents, and photographs. This initiative has helped in preserving valuable cultural heritage materials and making them accessible to researchers and the public.
- **National Library of Norway (Norway):** The National Library of Norway has implemented AI technologies for the reconstruction and digitization of historical documents and books. Using advanced image processing algorithms, they have been able to enhance the readability of aged and deteriorated texts, making them accessible to a wider audience. This approach has significantly contributed to the preservation of Norway's cultural heritage.
- **British Library (UK):** The British Library has adopted AI-powered solutions for metadata enrichment and document classification. By employing natural language processing (NLP) algorithms, they have automated the categorization and tagging of digital collections, improving search and retrieval functionalities for users (Mallikarjuna & Prabhakar, 2021). This has enhanced the discoverability and accessibility of the library's vast holdings.
- **National Library Board (Singapore):** The National Library Board of Singapore has incorporated AI-driven chatbots into their digital services to assist users in navigating the library's resources and answering inquiries. These virtual assistants utilize machine learning to understand user queries and provide relevant information, thus enhancing user experience and engagement with library services.
- **Bibliothèque nationale de France (France):** The Bibliothèque nationale de France (BnF) has employed AI technologies for content recommendation and personalized user experiences. By analyzing user behavior and preferences, they have developed recommendation systems that suggest relevant library resources, such as books, articles, and multimedia content, tailored to individual interests. This has improved user satisfaction and engagement with the library's collections.

Intellectual Freedom and Censorship in the Digital Age

In libraries, intellectual freedom is upheld by providing access to a wide range of materials while navigating challenges such as censorship attempts. Librarians play a crucial role in safeguarding intellectual freedom and promoting open access to information for all libraries also face challenges related to censorship, including efforts to ban or restrict access to certain books, films, websites, or other resources deemed objectionable by some members of the community (Mallikarjuna & Prabhakar, 2021). Librarians must navigate these challenges while balancing the need to respect diverse perspectives and uphold the principles of intellectual freedom. In the digital age, the ethical implications of intellectual freedom and censorship are amplified by the widespread availability of online information and the use of technologies such as content filtering and algorithmic recommendation systems.

Libraries must remain vigilant in safeguarding intellectual freedom in the face of evolving threats to free expression and information access.

CONCLUSION

In the digital era, where information is increasingly accessed online and through AI-powered systems, libraries must remain vigilant in ensuring that intellectual freedom is upheld in the face of evolving threats and technological advancements. By embracing innovation, fostering dialogue, and promoting ethical practices, libraries can continue to serve as inclusive and democratic spaces that empower individuals to explore, learn, and engage with ideas freely. Libraries serve as bastions of intellectual freedom, providing access to diverse materials and viewpoints, they also face challenges related to censorship attempts and the ethical implications of emerging technologies.

Librarians play a crucial role in safeguarding intellectual freedom by advocating for open access to information, resisting censorship, and promoting diverse perspectives. In navigating the ethical complexities of intellectual freedom and censorship, librarians must balance the need to respect individual rights and diverse viewpoints while upholding ethical standards and organizational values.

REFERENCES

Asemi, A., Ko, A., & Nowkarizi, M. (2020, June 30). Intelligent libraries: A review on expert systems, artificial intelligence, and robot. *Library Hi Tech*, *39*(2), 412–434. doi:10.1108/LHT-02-2020-0038

Cox, A. M., Pinfield, S., & Rutter, S. (2019, September 16). The intelligent library. *Library Hi Tech*, *37*(3), 418–435. doi:10.1108/LHT-08-2018-0105

Ferguson, I. A., & Durfee, E. H. (1998, October). Artificial intelligence in digital libraries: Moving from chaos to (more) order. *International Journal on Digital Libraries*, *2*(1), 1–2. doi:10.1007/s007990050032

Huang, Y. H. (2023, July 5). Exploring the implementation of artificial intelligence applications among academic libraries in Taiwan. *Library Hi Tech*. Advance online publication. doi:10.1108/LHT-03-2022-0159

Khanzode, K. C. A., & Sarode, R. D. (2020). Advantages and disadvantages of artificial intelligence and machine learning: A literature review. *International Journal of Library and Information Science*.

Mahmood, K., & Richardson, J. V. Jr. (2013, August 2). Impact of Web 2.0 technologies on academic libraries: A survey of ARL libraries. *The Electronic Library*, *31*(4), 508–520. doi:10.1108/EL-04-2011-0068

Mallikarjuna, A., & Prabhakar, N. (2021). Impact of Artificial Intelligence (AI) applications on academic libraries. Pearl. *Journal of Library and Information Science*, *15*(1), 46–52. doi:10.5958/0975-6922.2021.00006.1

Massis, B. (2018, July 9). Artificial intelligence arrives in the library. *Information and Learning Science*, *119*(7/8), 456–459. doi:10.1108/ILS-02-2018-0011

Mogali, S. S. (2014, February). Artificial Intelligence and its applications in libraries. *Bilingual International Conference on Information Technology: Yesterday, Today and Tomorrow.*

Omame, I., & Alex-Nmecha, J. (2020). *Managing and adapting library information services for future users Artificial intelligence in libraries.* doi:10.4018/978-1-7998-1116-9.ch008

Shrivastava, R., & Mahajan, P. (2016, April 2). Artificial Intelligence Research in India: A Scientometric Analysis. *Science & Technology Libraries, 35*(2), 136–151. doi:10.1080/0194262X.2016.1181023

Chapter 14
Anticipating AI Impact on Library Services:
Future Opportunities and Evolutionary Prospects

B. Lalitha
https://orcid.org/0000-0002-7526-3986
KPR Institute of Engineering and Technology, India

K. Ramalakshmi
https://orcid.org/0000-0002-1679-5042
Alliance College of Engineering and Design, India

Hemalatha Gunasekaran
https://orcid.org/0000-0001-5768-6072
University of Technology and Applied Sciences, Oman

P. Murugesan
KSR College of Engineering, India

P. Saminasri
https://orcid.org/0009-0001-6670-3185
KPR Institute of Engineering and Technology, India

N. Rajkumar
https://orcid.org/0000-0001-7857-9452
Alliance College of Engineering and Design, Alliance University, India

ABSTRACT

Artificial intelligence (AI) is an emerging field in library science, involving the programming of computers to execute tasks that typically require human intelligence. The overarching goal is to create computer systems capable of thinking and acting like humans, which holds profound implications for the field of librarianship. AI has found widespread application within libraries, with examples including expert systems for reference assistance, robots designed to assist with tasks like book sorting, and the integration of virtual reality for immersive learning experiences. While some may fear that AI implementation could distance librarians from their users, the prevailing view suggests that it will instead complement human expertise rather than replace it. By leveraging AI, libraries can enhance their service delivery, streamline operations, and adapt to the evolving demands of a digital society.

DOI: 10.4018/979-8-3693-5593-0.ch014

INTRODUCTION

AI is an exciting prospect with many benefits to improve library operations in the future. Conversational bots and other forms of generative AI are poised to change the role of libraries in the near future (Guion, 2019; Abram, 2019). In the information technology era, AI can transform library services, improving productivity and user experience (Alpert, 2016).

Rajkumar et al. (Rajkumar et al., 2024) Highlight key insights and recommendations for implementing AI in library settings. Mohanraj et al. insights into (Mohanraj et al., 2024) privacy and security concerns in digital libraries. Examine how AI technologies can address or exacerbate these concerns. Viji et al. (Viji et al., 2024) Analyze the benefits and challenges of integrating RFID with AI in library settings. SureshKumaret al. (Kumar N et al., 2024) Evaluate the role of AI in enhancing online learning experiences and library support. (Jayavadivel et al., 2024)Jayavadivel et al. summarize the historical perspective on AI adoption in libraries. Identify key milestones and trends in AI implementation in library reconstruction.

The use of digital assistants and chatbots is one way in which artificial intelligence can be used in library operations. Asemi and Asemi (Asemi and Asemi, 2018) state that this technology is available 24/7 to respond to users' requests and can efficiently handle an impressive number of queries. According to Asemi and Asemi (Asemi and Asemi, 2018), chatbots can significantly improve library services by providing quick and reliable information to users.

Artificial intelligence (AI) technology offers new possibilities for customized user experiences while increasing productivity. When it comes to user behavior and preferences, AI can understand everything and evaluate everything thanks to pattern recognition, natural language processing, and machine learning (Bailey C. W., 1991) This for anyone who has ready information receives artificial intelligence Bailey C. According to W. (1991), libraries can use AI to provide personalized reading recommendations, personalized research aids, and selected resources the well individual tastes and preferences for

Artificial intelligence (AI) can also help libraries preserve their vast collections and make them accessible to future generations. AI-powered algorithms can be used to digitize and organize physical collections, allowing users to search and access them (Alpert, 2016a). AI can also provide ac power to greatly improve the discovery of library materials.

Justification for Applying Artificial Intelligence in Libraries

Libraries are the collection, documentation, and preservation of cultural resources for Ben Libraries are important community centers that contain rich information and encourage learning, discussion, and the preservation of cultural traditions through books, journals, and many other things To provide, in intellectual freedom and the promotion of other ideas to help build a more educated self-reliant community and community here are some important aspects of libraries

Access to information: Librarians have access to a wide range of print and digital resources including books, journals, periodicals, audiovisual materials, and archival resources. They hold a wealth of information and knowledge and cater to a wide variety of interests and needs

Education and Lifelong Learning: Libraries provide resources for research, teaching, and self-development, which is why they support lifelong learning and continuing education and enable people of all ages to participate in their activities, seminars, and programs to encourage critical thinking and intellectual curiosity.

Community spaces: Libraries welcome people from all walks of life and are used for research, meetings, and other cultural activities. To cater to a wide range of needs and interests, meeting spaces, computer rooms, multimedia workstations, and peaceful study areas are often available.

Preservation of Cultural Heritage: Cultural objects and historical records are well preserved in libraries. Rare books, manuscripts, photographs, and archives are worthy of the next generation.

Digital resources and technology: Digital resources currently offered by libraries include digital databases, e-books, e-journals, multimedia resources public computers, internet Communication, and technology training will be provided to further the goal of closing the digital divide and increasing digital literacy.

Information literacy and research support: One of the main roles of libraries is to help library users become proficient in the use of information resources, researchers and researchers can benefit from the services provided by librarians in academia, in both professional and personal questions.

Community engagement and engagement: Libraries serve their communities by responding to community needs and promoting social inclusion, diversity, and equity, partnering with community organizations, and schools, and collaborating between colleges and other community groups.

Freedom of thought and knowledge: Fundamental rights in a democratic society include freedom of thought and expression, and access to and use of any information Subject to freedom of speech encourages, encourages critical thinking, and encourages informed citizenship through diverse Ideas, controversial issues, and new ideas.

Concepts of Artificial Intelligence

Artificial intelligence (AI) encompasses a wider range of computer science concepts than the traditional concept of robotics, and conversational networks focus on how computers learn, process information,

Figure 1. AI-based cataloging in libraries

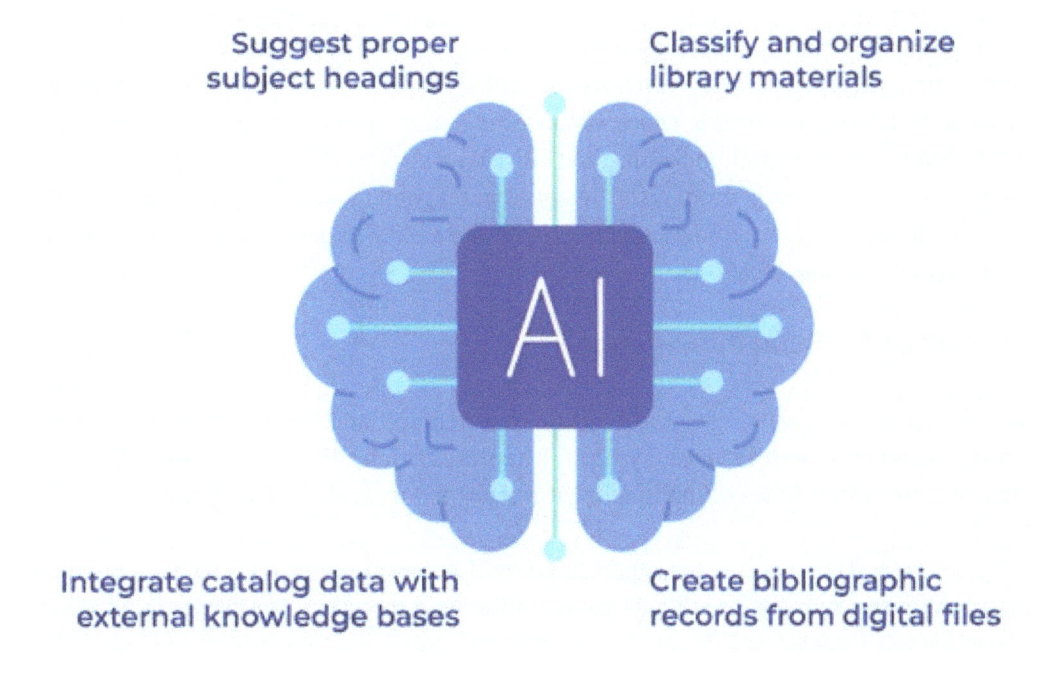

and perform tasks that often in relation to human intelligence. This includes machine learning, where computers glean insights from data, as well as tasks such as image analysis, speech recognition and natural language processing and expert algorithms in AI, which mimic human expertise in specific areas.

At its core, AI revolves around perception, thought, and action. Reasoning is concerned with the internal processes that guide decision-making, while perception enables machines to interpret and understand sensory input. AI for simulating human mental processes. It includes knowledge representation and the use of reflective thinking methods to make decisions and solve problems, with the goal of eventually reproducing similar intelligence man in machines.

Also AI involves the study and development of computer systems capable of learning, reasoning, natural language processing, perception, etc. The Turing test, proposed by Alan Turing, is a system for measuring machine intelligence, although its effectiveness is debatable. In terms of capabilities, AI can be classified as strong or weak. Strong AI refers to systems that are capable of human-like thinking, learning, and adaptation, while weak AI systems are designed for a specific task, lacking broad cognitive capabilities.

AI systems are poorly designed for specific industries and lack broad intellectual capabilities. Complex AI has the potential to enable self-determination and self-improvement, but basic AI systems can only perform pre-set tasks. AI is an interdisciplinary field focused on creating intelligent systems that can handle tasks traditionally requiring human intelligence. Its power to drive industry change and enhance problem-solving makes it vital in modern technology.

Trends in the Field of Artificial Intelligence (AI)

Artificial intelligence (AI) has many uses, from self-driving cars to preventing fraud to machine learning. Machine learning is a branch of AI that allows computers to learn from data without human help, and improve over time. This process lets computers adapt and become better based on past experiences. AI research covers areas like automated systems, computer vision, intelligent control, expert systems, and language processing. The widespread adoption of AI has been supported by the rise of technologies like smartphones, smart homes, the Internet of Things (IoT), and connected vehicles, which have enabled integration across industries. AI has made significant progress in product development and data analysis, impacting fields like media, sports broadcasting, and education. News organizations like The Washington Post use AI to report on results, and IBM Watson provides AI-powered services. In terms of intelligence, AI systems range from reflex agents that respond to sensor input to learning algorithms that can learn computer programming. Online, or with the ability to perform tasks automatically while traveling between telephone locations.

Foundations of Artificial Intelligence

The foundation of artificial intelligence is built on four main pillars, as described in the McGraw-Hill Encyclopedia of Science and Technology (2007): representation, discovery, reasoning, and learning These elements are cornerstones of intelligence it is designed to work with any system.

1. Representation: This involves the representation of problem-relevant knowledge in an intelligent system. A system by which problems are identified and modified. For example, in the system of

medical experts, the symbolism would include the description and symptoms of diseases, while in the case of robots, it might include symbolic 3D a picture of his surroundings.
2. Search: Search methods are crucial for solving problems in AI systems. They allow the system to search for potential solutions, often using diagnostic techniques to adapt them to specific issues. For example, the system might search a database for previous solutions similar to the current problem.
3. Reasoning: Reasoning is essential for finding solutions from knowledge. This involves extracting possible solutions from existing data or developing hypotheses to explain current knowledge and problems. Expert systems demonstrate this by using predefined rules or expert knowledge to solve problems.
4. Learning: Learning enables AI to evolve and acquire knowledge over time. This includes strategies such as adjusting positions, using heuristic search strategies, updating knowledge, and improving reasoning ability. Common learning strategies include statistical learning, neural networks, and reinforcement learning, all of which are part of machine learning and deep learning.

Exploring Technologies

Technological research explores the innovations, tools, and advancements that are increasingly shaping our world. It involves studying and applying various scientific concepts and technological practices to develop solutions that enhance efficiency, communication, and quality of life. From artificial intelligence and machine learning to robotics, biotechnology, and energy generation, this research aims to anticipate future developments and make necessary adjustments. Staying informed about emerging trends, advancements, and problems in technology is crucial. Ultimately, technological research empowers us to use innovation to solve challenges, drive growth, and shape the future.

Implications

"Implications" refers to the outcome, effect, or implications of an action, decision, or process. Contextual explanations can refer to both positive and negative consequences, as well as broader context-specific consequences. These may include:

Enhanced user experience: AI-powered services can provide improved accessibility, personalized recommendations, and better use of library resources, enhancing user experience the overall implementation has improved

Ethical considerations: The use of AI in libraries raises ethical questions of privacy, data security, and algorithmic bias. Ensuring AI is used in a transparent and accountable way is crucial to address these concerns.

Impact on library operations: Adopting AI could change librarians' roles, shifting their focus to managing AI systems, providing technical support to patrons, and upgrading specialized services.

Distribution: Integrating AI technologies into library services requires investments in infrastructure, training, and maintenance. Libraries need to carefully consider the financial and human resources needed to support AI initiatives.

Digital divide: While AI-powered services can increase access to information, they can also widen the gap in digital literacy and access to technology. Libraries need to address these gaps to ensure all patrons have equal access to AI-powered services.

Intellectual freedom and privacy: AI technology raises concerns about intellectual property and patron privacy, particularly with data collection and usage management, and information filtering.

Library Services

Libraries are valuable resources in our communities. They offer a wide range of services, including books, digital materials, educational programs, and research support. These institutions play a crucial role in promoting literacy, encouraging lifelong learning, and serving as common spaces for all citizens. These libraries provide various functions, such as information retrieval. AI can enhance search capabilities, helping visitors find more relevant content through advanced algorithms and natural language processing. Another function is personalized recommendations. AI-powered systems can analyze a patron's preferences, borrowing history, and reading habits to suggest books, articles, and other library resources that may interest them. Virtual reference assistance is also an important function. AI chatbots and virtual assistants can provide instant help and guidance to patrons, answering questions, offering research assistance, and providing support outside of traditional library hours. Finally, AI algorithms can assist with collection management, helping librarians make informed decisions about acquiring and organizing library materials Libraries carefully manage their collections by studying how people use them, forecasting demand for specific materials, and optimizing their collection management processes. Accessibility technologies powered by AI can increase accessibility by providing speech-to-speech information, creating new options, and improving mobility for people with disabilities. Data analytics using AI can help libraries analyze usage data, identify trends, and gather insights to guide their decision-making around collection development, resource allocation, and service progress reporting. AI can assist in digitizing and preserving library collections, developing metadata and other responsive processes, and ensuring the long-term availability of cultural heritage materials through features like metadata tagging and image recognition. AI-powered teaching tools and interactive platforms can support library outreach efforts, providing authentic learning experiences, language translation services, and engaging storytelling programs. The AI technology can help engage diverse audiences by analyzing social media patterns, gathering data, and designing library programs and services that cater to the needs and interests of local communities.

Operations

Future library services including AI use artificial intelligence to automate collaboration, optimize resource management, enhance user experience, and ensure data security and privacy AI enables libraries to streamline processes, improve decision-making and deliver new services that meet the evolving needs of patrons in the digital age

Automation: AI can perform routine tasks such as cataloging, indexing, and metadata tagging, freeing up library time for more complex specialized activities

Data management: AI-powered analytics can help libraries monitor and process vast amounts of data about patron usage, collections, interactions and resource allocation, enabling informed decision making and strategic planning

Distribution: AI algorithms can optimize distribution by predicting demand for specific products, identifying trends in assistant preferences, and recommending changes to collection development strategies in the 19th century

Anticipating AI Impact on Library Services

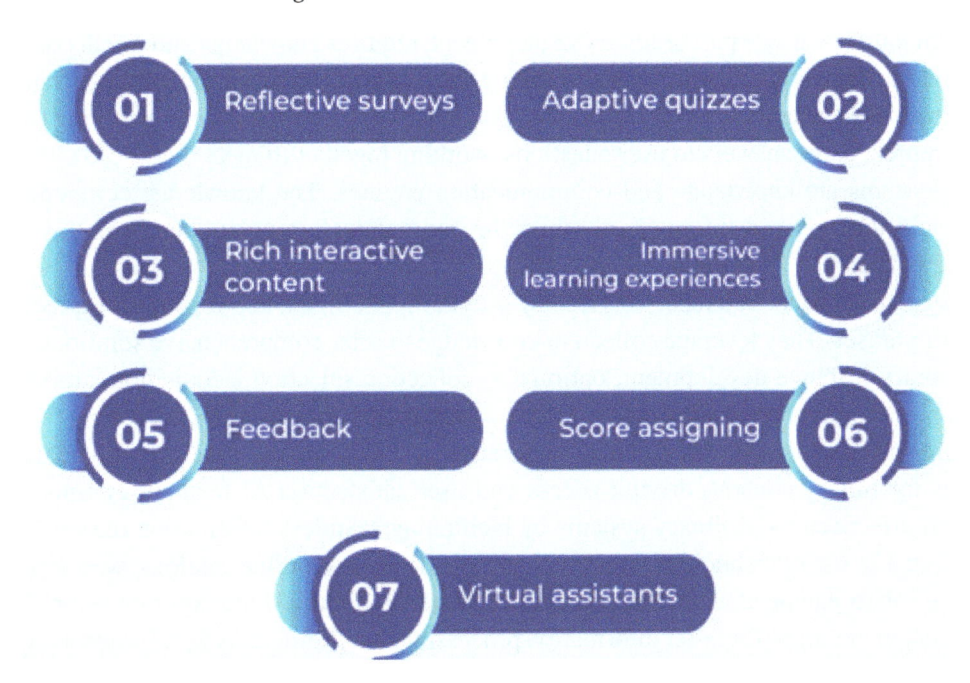

Figure 2. AI-based virtual learning in libraries

01 Reflective surveys
02 Adaptive quizzes
03 Rich interactive content
04 Immersive learning experiences
05 Feedback
06 Score assigning
07 Virtual assistants

Enhanced user experience: AI-powered systems can personalize the user experience by offering personalized recommendations, an intuitive search engine, and customers more efficient service delivery through chatbots and virtual assistants

Digital preservation: AI technology can help digitize and preserve library collections, and assist with processes such as image recognition, optical character recognition (OCR), and metadata extraction to ensure access to digital assets long and true

Security and Privacy: AI can enhance security measures by identifying and mitigating cybersecurity threats, continuously monitoring sensitive information, and ensuring compliance with privacy laws to create patron data and intellectual property protection.

Investing in staff training programs can help librarians develop the skills and knowledge needed to effectively use AI technology. This fosters a culture of innovation and continuous learning. As libraries incorporate AI into their operations, they must carefully consider the ethical implications. This includes issues like data confidentiality, algorithmic bias, transparency, and intellectual property. It's crucial to ensure the use of AI aligns with principles of equity, inclusion, and social responsibility.

Application of Artificial Intelligence in Libraries

Artificial intelligence (AI) is becoming increasingly important for libraries. It allows them to organize and access large amounts of information they have collected (ALA, 2019). As Sridevi and Shanmugam (2017) highlighted, AI is a modern technology for managing digital libraries. It aims to replicate human intelligence in computer systems by implementing AI in libraries. AI covers various application areas in library management systems. These include natural language processing (NLP), expert systems (ES), pattern recognition, and robotics (Sridevi and Shanmugam, 2017). In the library context, NLP powers intelligent coding and information retrieval, enabling users to interact with natural language queries. Subject formulation, a major part of library management, requires knowledge and intellectual judgment. Expert systems that mimic human decision-making processes can be used for title registration and referencing services (Asemi and Asemi, 2018). Knowledgeable experts use problem-solving techniques to provide comprehensive answers to user questions, working together to meet their needs.

Expert systems are knowledge and communication engines. The knowledge component contains structured and unstructured information, while the communication component uses logical rules to interpret new data.

These systems enhance reference services by providing intelligent answers to user queries based on keywords or phrases. They leverage collective knowledge to offer comprehensive solutions. AI can also facilitate library resource development, optimizing collection selection, acquisition, and management processes.

By analyzing past acquisitions and user preferences, AI systems can generate personalized recommendations for library content, driving access and user satisfaction.AI technology improves the efficiency and effectiveness of library systems by facilitating seamless information retrieval Here is the rewritten text: The use of technology, such as electronic databases, online catalogs, web search engines, and retrieval robots equipped with AI capabilities, has greatly improved the experience for library users. These advancements allow for faster information processing and seamless retrieval of resources (Unagha, 2010; Murphy, 2015). AI-powered features like optical character recognition (OCR), natural language processing for translation, indexing using expert systems, and audiovisual material retrieval through OCR and speech recognition have further expanded the capabilities of library services (Li et al., 2015). This has led to the provision of interactive instruction, intelligent gateways to online sources, structured environments, and accessible reader services for people with disabilities (Romero, 2018).

Robots in Libraries

Robotics, a subcategory of artificial intelligence (AI), encompasses the fields of sensory, physiological, design, building, manufacturing, and manipulation of robots (Abrams, 2019) Robots capable of performing automated tasks operate under human supervision or autonomy, guided by pre-defined AI algorithms (Shohana, 2016). The term "robot" originated in science fiction and influenced public opinion through various works of literature and film, shaping our understanding of these devices (Corke, 2013).

An emerging trend in AI is the integration of robotics into library operations. Despite the emphasis on web-based information in the digital age, printed books contain valuable knowledge, making recipients more active (Li et al., 2015). To meet this challenge, robotic systems are being developed for library placement and retrieval. For example, Suthakorn et al. (2002) and the author. Similarly, bookBot technology automates receiving books at libraries, delivering requested materials within minutes (Stone, 2019).

Libraries are also using radio frequency identification (RFID) technology to simplify collection management. RFID tags embedded in books enable them to automatically monitor their movements, facilitating tasks such as inventory management and detection of misplaced products (Li et al., 2015) In addition, robots equipped with RFID scanners can navigate through library shelves, assist in inventory management and retrieval (Li et al., 2015).

Additionally, robots are contributing to educational programs such as learning coding and learning Functional Skills in Libraries (Shohana, 2016). Other initiatives such as the intelligent library catalog developed by Sachiti and Ladegaard combine robotic technology with online books to improve user access to library resources (Shohana, 2016).

The potential of AI to enhance the hospitality experience beyond libraries, museums and archives is being explored. Remote robots such as BeamPros enable remote visitors, especially those with disabilities, to visit museums approximately, making them more inclusive and accessible (Murphy, 2015).

Smart Cities

In the future, as cities transform into "smart" places through the integration of advanced technologies, artificial intelligence (AI) will play a key role in shaping the libraries of tomorrow. Smart cities use AI to optimize various aspects of urban life, including transportation, energy management, healthcare and education. Libraries, as important community institutions, will also make a significant difference in creating smart spaces to meet the changing needs of residents.

In the AI-powered libraries of the future, innovative technologies will facilitate convenient and seamless interactions between patrons and library resources. AI algorithms will analyse user preferences and actions with tailored recommendations for books, articles, and other resources, ensuring a personalized experience for each visitor Virtual assistants equipped with natural language processing capabilities will provide support and guidance to users immediately, address questions, and support research efforts.

Artificial intelligence (AI) will streamline library operations by automating routine tasks like cataloging, inventory management, and resource allocation. Using smart sensors and RFID technology, libraries can track items in real-time, making retrieval faster and more accurate. AI-powered predictive analytics will determine the demand for specific items, allowing libraries to better manage their collections and use their space more efficiently.

Virtual tours and simulations powered by AI will let users experience historical events, remote locations, and intellectual realms, enhancing their educational journey. Augmented reality (AR) applications will overlay digital information on physical documents and artifacts, providing more context and insights.

AI will also facilitate community engagement and collaboration through digital forums and social networks. Virtual book clubs, online workshops, and collaborative research projects will connect people across geographic barriers with shared interests and expertise. AI algorithms will facilitate meetings between users, helping them find the right personnel and resources for their efforts.

Remote Services

In Destiny, artificial intelligence (AI) will rework far-off library services, remodelling how shoppers' access and interact with library sources and information. With advances in the AI era, libraries are supplying new faraway services that meet different consumer needs, no matter the vicinity here is how AI will shape remote library services within the destiny.

Virtual Assistants: AI-powered digital assistants offer personalized assistance to far-off customers, offering help and steering in actual time. These virtual assistants will use herbal language processing (NLP) to understand consumer queries and provide context, suggestions, and assistance with research checking out.

AI-powered recommendation systems: AI algorithms will examine user options, browsing records, and studying behavior to create tailor-made tips for far-off users Whether to recommend books, articles, or online sources, AI-powered suggestions. The machine will decorate the far-off library by supplying tailor-made content material based on individual hobbies and wishes.

Remote access to digital collections: AI-enabled functions provide remote users with smooth right of entry to digital collections, e-books, educational journals, and multimedia content Through flexible interfaces and sensible seek, far-flung users can search for and get entry to an extensive variety of virtual content material everywhere, anytime.

Virtual research help: AI-powered research assistants will assist faraway users with complicated research tasks together with literature searches, citation processing, and records analysis. These assistants use AI strategies inclusive of machine mastering and statistics mining to help users explore studies databases, pick out applicable assets, and choose to put off valuable insights.

Virtual collaboration platforms: AI-powered collaboration structures will facilitate virtual meetings, crew chats, and collaborative tasks between far-flung users. These periods will combine functions including video conferencing, shared documentation, and venture management gear to support far-off collaboration and knowledge sharing.

AI-Based Language Translation: An AI-powered language translation tool will allow far-flung customers to translate library materials into the language of their choice. Whether translating textual content, audio recordings, or video shows, AI-based total translation services will spoil language boundaries and make library sources handy to a global target audience.

Distance Learning and Training: AI-powered training systems offer distance-gaining knowledge of possibilities, workshops, and schooling classes in line with the desires of faraway users. This session will use adaptive knowledge of algorithms and new AI technologies to supply attractive and effective academic content remotely.

Virtual Reality (VR) Libraries: AI-stronger VR libraries provide immersive digital spaces wherein faraway users can browse digital collections, take part in digital events in 2010, and interact with digital librarians and instructors. VR era will create reasonable simulations of bodily library spaces, offering faraway customers with an immersive and interactive library experience.

Artificial Intelligence and Virtual Libraries

Virtual libraries also referred to as digital libraries, offer customers with far-off get admission to several digital materials. These libraries, commonly called libraries without partitions hold a collection of links to various online assets together with e-books, journals, databases, and news Users can get entry to those resources through online portals or gateways, permitting them to connect to the Internet. You can browse and request items from everywhere you have a contact. Communication between the digital library and customers is on the whole thru virtual channels consisting of e-mail, telephone, fax, or the library's online presence. In addition, virtual libraries can host virtual schooling sessions, webinars, and online boards to tell users about services and tendencies. The concept of the digital library is more consistent with virtual libraries, each of which depends on automation to streamline operations.

Library automation, consisting of the usage of era to automate transactions, is important for digital and digital libraries. This includes features including cataloging, consumer registration, e-book distribution, and shelf management. Library automation ambitions to lessen guide responsibilities and allow librarians to be conscious of knowledge dissemination and personal guidance.

Artificial intelligence (AI) performs a vital role in library automation, mainly in digital and virtual libraries. Many automatic library systems include AI techniques to enhance performance. Example:

Anticipating AI Impact on Library Services

Automated indexing and abstraction: Cognitive structures mechanically index and summarize electronics and enable green looking.

International/Translation: Natural language processing and visible person reputation permit digital substances to be translated into more than one language.

Use of Digitization: Digitization: Traditional library substances are transformed to digital format via scanning or OCR, making them simpler to locate and retrieve. Text Review: Supports automatic content material analysis of selection assist structures (DSS), facilitating facts retrieval.

Information retrieval: Speech recognition and natural language processing techniques enhance information retrieval.

Audiovisual: Expert programming and OCR guide audiovisual search and retrieval.

Data processing: AI supports clerical and habitual responsibilities in mechanical processing, circulate management, and sequencing.

24-hour operation: Intelligent automated structures provide 24/7 entry to services and products.

In addition, the online public get the right of entry to catalogs and database gateways using wise algorithms for meta-control and reminiscence management, optimizing facts garage, and technique manipulation.

Virtual Reality and Artificial Intelligence in Libraries

Computer technology is used to create a watered-down atmosphere in visual reality, where it includes imagery along with emotions and sensations to mimic the user in a mental atmosphere (Jackson, 2015) VR Headset, combines image processing and speech recognition to create 3D synthetic worlds, giving users a 360-degree digital experience Despite this capability, libraries have yet to explore the potential of virtual reality (VR), augmented reality (AR), and mixed reality (MR) (Marcotte., 2019 by the author).

Augmented reality overlays digital content in the real world, enhancing users' vision, while mixed reality integrates digital-real-world objects to allow digital objects and physical environments to interact VR, AR, and MR together to provide a library experience and virtual access to library materials for disabled or remote users to provide answers Can be done. Users wearing VR headsets can access the virtual library environment and interact with digital objects, simulating multiple senses for a more immersive experience Also, VR allows users to experience virtual of the virtual library, putting them in a virtual environment rather than just watching on a screen Similar to Beam Pros remote presence with robotic remote visits for disabled patrons, VR can remove or consume library patrons disability has been removed and the work of Suthakorn et al. (2002), whose enhanced robotic library system facilitates remote access to physical objects through scanning and optical character recognition.

factual. Representing all library content can be a challenge, and mixed reality VR is a challenge. Mixed reality can interact with robotic systems to allow patrons to access physical books remotely in VR environments. For example, when a virtual patron initiates a request to read a book, the robotic system uploads the physical copy to the library, allowing the virtual patron to browse through a live feed to their VR headset Furthermore, VR, AR and MR can provide immersive field trip experiences for library patrons, such as exploring the solar system or interacting with marine life (Marcotte, 2019). Applications already exist to trigger reality for users, to enhance the learning experience (Abram, 2019). It should be noted that VR headsets are products of artificial intelligence systems that have been widely used in various fields such as science, engineering, medicine, aviation, and the military, especially for

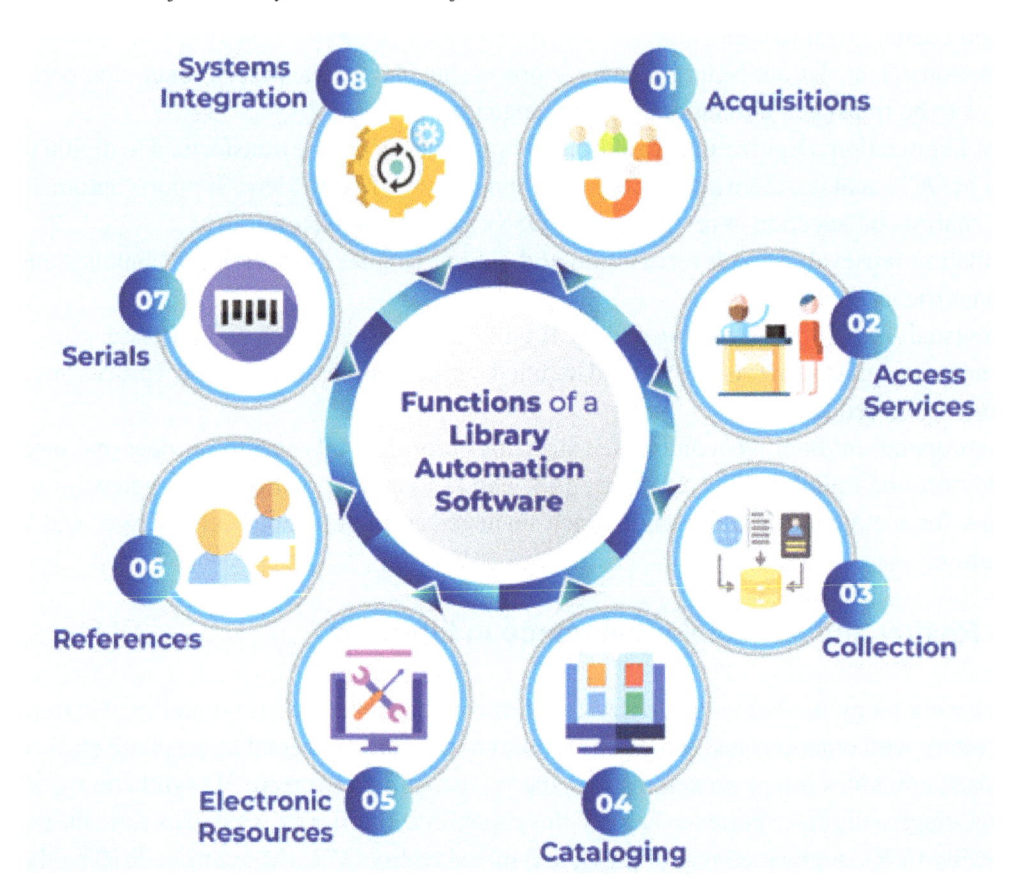

Figure 3. Functions of a library automation software

live training scenarios. Libraries can use this technology to enhance user experience and remain relevant in an increasingly digital world

AI for Predictive Analysis

AI provides valuable insights through predictive analytics that analyse user behaviour and trends, helping libraries better plan services and resources. For example, AI analyses loan patterns and predicts future demand, enabling better collection management. It also predicts user behaviour, helping libraries best allocate staff and resources to meet peak demand.

Data-Driven Decision Making

AI empowers libraries with the aid of studying giant record sets and making statistics-pushed selections. For instance, similarly, to supporting product allocation and business planning, it can analyse usage records more closely to show tendencies including popular merchandise and top visitation times to display AI for navigation does get scholarly studies is amazing; Services like Semantic Scholar are using AI to improve search exceptional in educational papers. Libraries can combine such tools to make it easier for customers to discover relevant studies quickly and efficiently.

Artificial Intelligence Impacts Libraries

The impact of artificial intelligence (AI) on libraries is profound, affecting components of library operations and customers. Here are 5 key approaches to AI is remodeling libraries.

Improved statistics processing: Librarians use AI to enhance how statistics is prepared and accessed. Through advances in classification structures and analytics of digital collections, librarians can seek accuracy and simplify get right of entry to facts for patrons.

Improvements in library services: With the combination of AI, the library management machine has passed through a dramatic transformation. From automating robotic systems to creating shrewd libraries, AI-pushed systems are optimizing library operations and improving the consumer experience

Shift in utilization patterns: Libraries around the world are adopting AI-powered chatbots to deliver greater personalized and efficient records offerings to customers' evolving needs Bio Additionally, the integration of AI tools into consumer interfaces enhances the overall consumer experience via imparting intuitive and personalized interactions.

Promoting facts and AI literacy: Libraries actively promote statistics and AI literacy amongst consumers, equipping them with the competencies needed to navigate an AI-driven society through statistics on the pinnacle of fostering know-how of AI principles, libraries empower individuals to expectantly participate in emerging technologies.

Revolutionizing library studies: AI is revolutionizing library research by imparting real-time information analytics to discover patterns and trends. This real-time analytics facilitates informed selection-making, enabling libraries to effectively improve machine usage control.

Figure 4. 5 ways of artificial intelligence in libraries

The Challenges of Implementing AI in Libraries

There are several limitations to integrating artificial intelligence (AI) systems into libraries, hindering their vast adoption. These challenges include:

Lack of technical abilities: Many librarians lack the vital talents to enforce and manage AI systems successfully.

Budgetary Constraints: Limited funding prevents libraries from growing or obtaining AI structures, as budgets for hardware and software programs are frequently constrained.

High development and preservation prices: The costs associated with building and preserving AI structures are a chief barrier for libraries.

Unreliable capability delivery: Inconsistent capacity delivery, in particular in developing nations hinders the implementation of AI systems in libraries.

Strong improvement systems: Building a professional AI device is inherently complex, requiring specialized information and know-how.

Limited herbal language processing: AI structures may additionally have confined abilities in know-how and processing herbal language, limiting their performance

Lack of shared expertise: AI structures lack ordinary human know-how repositories, limiting their capacity to perform multiple responsibilities correctly

Technical Knowledge Required: The improvement of a sophisticated AI gadget requires a wonderful deal of effort and technical knowledge, which may be unavailable or luxurious to gather

Lack of AI experts: The lack of AI specialists amongst library generation vendors complicates the combination of AI systems into library operations, hence requiring professional hires to make development on this place.

Figure 5. Challenges of artificial intelligence

Context
AI's can struggle with understanding context. For example, asking Siri "call me an ambulance" may yield "OK, from now on, I will call you Ambulance"

Precision
The idea of garbage data in garbage data out. If you flood an AI with bad data and don't set the proper syntax or thresholds you will get incoherent results

Training
Similar to having good data, an AI might need to learn the correct response for the correct situation or identify dangers or inappropriate interactions

Technological Constraints

Libraries stumble upon sizable technologically demanding situations whilst imposing AI, mainly due to aid constraints and virtual literacy gaps among personnel. Many libraries, specifically smaller or underprivileged ones, lack the important assets for AI adoption. Moreover, a group of workers requires education to correctly utilize AI, which needs massive time and funding. The speedy-paced evolution of technology in addition complicates matters, as libraries should constantly replace structures and teach team of workers to preserve tempo. Despite those hurdles, with ok assets and education, libraries can effectively combine AI to revolutionize their operations and services.

Privacy and Ethical Concerns

The integration of AI generation into libraries and other industries has raised severe privacy and moral concerns around the arena. AI is based on massive fact sets, elevating issues of consumer privateness and records protection in industries along with healthcare, finance, and libraries can war to ensure user privacy when the use of AI for e-book guidelines and different services. Additionally, worries about AI biases and potential abuse of models spotlight the want for strong privacy rules and transparency in AI programs to address those worries, it is vital to maintain to screen these statistics, behaviour audits, and adhere to ethical hints to make sure responsible use of AI in libraries and past.

The Benefits of Artificial Intelligence in Libraries

A modern device: AI gives libraries several blessings.

Efficiencies: AI streamlines responsibilities including allocation, sorting, and indexing of library resources, which were once time-eating.

Reducing language obstacles: Natural Language Processing (NLP) applications enable foreign students to access statistics of their native language and search databases in more than one language.

Improved provider high-quality: AI reduces mistakes, improves productiveness, and allows librarians to provide personalized assistance.

Increased productiveness: AI allows the discover of research materials, increasing the productivity of teachers and researchers.

Twenty-4-hour get admission to: AI ensures that users can get the right of entry to information and offerings at any time, overcoming time constraints.

Optimizing physical space: The combination of digitization, electronic snapshots and robot structures optimizes area in libraries, making sources extra accessible.

Reduced workload: AI automates obligations which include content selection and distribution, lowering library workload.

Enhanced user experience: AI improves provider transport and creates a greater immersive environment for library patrons.

Adapting to the virtual age: Embracing AI will permit libraries to serve their communities and adapt to evolving virtual demands.

Demerits of Artificial Intelligence in Libraries

1. Job displacement problem: An essential concern is the capability of AI to update human jobs, main to higher unemployment costs. There are fears that libraries will get replaced via smart devices capable of shelving books, getting access to statistics, and supporting users. Jasrotia (2018) argues that AI's ability to swiftly search digitized substances may certainly pose a hazard to library repute. However, Guion (2019) argues that librarians are nevertheless wished because of AI systems which can warfare to fully understand user wishes or help crucial library ideas
2. Risk of mistakes: AI systems are frequently poorly performing, that can lead to unintended moves or the spread of misinformation, as cited by way of Ex Libris (2019).
3. Potential for misuse: There is a chance of misuse of AI systems, that could cause great damage.
4. Loss of key abilities: Over-reliance on AI can lead librarians to overlook primary library functions which include cataloging and classification, as those obligations are computerized.
5. Lack of human interaction: Some customers favor interacting without delay with human librarians in preference to machines, as AI lacks personal contact.

Example Use Cases of AI in Libraries

Libraries around the sector are the use of artificial intelligence (AI) to innovate and enhance their services. Examples encompass automating content, making ready metadata for better discoverability, and the use of chatbots to help users. Institutions inclusive of the Library of Congress, Stanford University Libraries, and the University of Rhode Island have embraced AI for digital files, studies support, and research into the implications of AI that extends AI makes it less complicated to perceive a wearable language digitization of historic information and predictive analytics to assume person wishes. While AI gives transformational capacity, libraries need to preserve privacy and moral standards as they combine this generation into their operations. In destiny, AI holds high-quality promise to convert public libraries, increasing efficiency, consumer enjoyment, and data-pushed choice-making. AI algorithms can revolutionize fact retrieval, supplying greater accurate and applicable insights, while personalized hints inspire continuous knowledge of the AI era and facilitate resource control via automation, digitization, and ease of getting the right of entry. Virtual assistants and chatbots provide immediate support, while data analytics optimize product distribution and service planning. Additionally, AI enables collaboration and community in libraries. However, challenges such as data privacy and algorithmic bias need to be addressed to ensure the integration of ethics and inclusive AI. While the future of AI in public libraries is exciting, ethical implications considering core library values of access, privacy, and intellectual property are needed.

The Future Libraries

The evolution of repository-reading robots, as demonstrated by Li, Huang, Kurniawan, and Ho (2015), indicates that libraries are undergoing a major transformation powered by artificial intelligence (AI), as noted by Shohana (2016). does not notice it. A.I. Bourg (2017) raises an important question about the future role of libraries in a machine-readable world. For example, tools like GeoDeepDive, equipped with AI algorithms, can extract data from text, tables, and figures, questioning the traditional role of libraries. According to Johnson (2018), AI's ability to rapidly analyze data and provide solutions challenges traditional human analytical methods. The future of libraries is supposed to be highly automated, with robots and intelligent machines taking over tasks such as reference, circulation functions, and cataloging Stone (2019) asserts highlighting the need for libraries to embrace rather than avoid new technologies. The American Library Association (ALA) acknowledges the need for libraries to respond to emerging issues and embrace future innovation, as ALA's Center for the Future of Libraries emphasizes. However, Bourg (2017) and Coleman (2017) pose important questions about AI integration in libraries while maintaining core library values such as inclusiveness, confidentiality, and intellectual property. President García-Febo (2019) recommends integrating AI into library systems to address these questions with the potential of AI to enhance library services in the early stages of AI adoption, libraries use AI to learn about Facilitating information literacy, critical thinking, and remote processing of information. This initiative highlighted, signals a major shift toward greater use of AI in shaping the future of libraries. emphasized that rather than choosing between AI and libraries, the focus should be on using technology to provide users with library services more efficiently.

CONCLUSION

To succeed in these days' hastily changing knowledge economy, libraries must be open to innovation and willing to reconsider techniques. One very promising method is to integrate synthetic intelligence (AI) into library operations. AI can transform diverse components of library offerings, from technical services to person interfaces, enhancing efficiency and enhancing consumer experience. Although there are concerns approximately AI replacing human librarians the reality is that AI can complement and empower librarians instead of replacing them.

If libraries aren't made obsolete, the adoption of AI technologies can boost their capability. Using AI gear, librarians can streamline techniques, enhance search accuracy, and provide satisfactory aid to shoppers. Additionally, AI can help manage huge virtual collections extra successfully, permitting libraries to fulfill their position as critical information-sharing facilities. Although there may be doubts about the impact of AI on human contributors in libraries, the library zone can open extra opportunities for its popularity and integration. Importantly, AI will no longer lessen human contact in libraries, nor will it separate libraries from their patrons. Instead, it's going to decorate the library, allowing librarians to be cognizant of greater strategic and treasured responsibilities as AI permits them.

As libraries evolve in reaction to technological advances, it's far vital that librarians embrace AI as a catalyst for innovation and improvement. By incorporating AI-powered solutions, libraries can adapt to the converting wishes of their customers and reaffirm their importance as community resources. Adding AI to Library operations gift demanding situations, and the capacity advantages to the library body of workers and customers make the effort profitable. Ultimately, using AI to improve library operations is steady with libraries' assignment to serve and empower groups in an increasing number of virtual internationals.

REFERENCES

Abram, S. (2019). *Robots in libraries: Technology trends that aren't that out-there anymore!* https://lucidea.com/blog/robots-in-libraries/

Alpert, L. I. (2016). *Washington Post to cover every major race on election day with help of artificial.* intelligence.www.wsj.com/articles/washington-post-to-cover-every-race-on-election-day-with-the-helpof-artificial-intelligence-1476871202

Asemi, A., & Asemi, A. (2018). Artificial intelligence (AI) application in library systems in Iran: A taxonomy study. *Library Philosophy and Practice (e-journal).* https://digitalcommons.unl.edu/libphilprac/1840/

Bailey, C. W., Jr. (1991). Intelligent library systems: artificial intelligence technology and library automation systems. *Advances in Library Automation and Networking, 4.* Retrieved May 17, 2017, from http://eprints.rclis.org/4891/1/intlibs.pdf

Blakemore, E. (2016). *High tech shelf help: Singapore's library robot.* https://www.libraryjournal.com/?detailStory=high-tech-shelfhelp-singapores-library-robot

Coleman, C. N. (2017). *Artificial intelligence and the library of the future revisited.* https://library.stanford.edu/blogs/digital-library-blog/2017/11/artificial-intelligence-and-library-future-revisited/

Corke, P. (2013). *Robotics, vision and control: Fundamental algorithms in MATLAB.* Springer.

Croft, B. W., Metzler, D., & Strohman, T. (2015). *Search engines: information retrieval in practice.* Pearson Education, Inc. Retrieved June 16, 2019, from https://ciir.cs.umass.edu/downloads/SEIRiP.pdf

Eberhart, G. M. (2019). *An AI lab in a library: Why artificial intelligence matters.* American Libraries. Retrieved June 27, 2019, from https://americanlibrariesmagazine.org/blogs/the-scoop/ai-lab-library/

Ex Libris. (2019). *How AI can enhance the value of research libraries.* Retrieved October 4,2019, www.libraryjournal.com/?detailStory=how-ai-can-enhancethe-value-of-research-libraries

Fine, A. (2017). *Artificially intelligent math for school educators.* https://districtadministration.com/artificially-intelligent-math-forschool-educators

Garcia-Febo, L. (2019). Exploring AI: How libraries are starting to apply artificial intelligence in their work. American Libraries. https://americanlibrariesmagazine.org/2019/03/01/exploring-ai/

Gustavsson, J., & Hedlund, M. (2011). The art of writing & speaking, https://www.svet.lu.se/sites/svet.lu.se.en/files/art-of-writingspeaking-2011.pdf

Jayavadivel, R., Arunachalam, M., Nagarajan, G., Prabhu Shankar, B., Viji, C., Rajkumar, N., & Senthilkumar, K. R. (2024). *Historical Overview of AI Adoption in Libraries.* doi:10.4018/979-8-3693-2782-1.ch015

Kumar, N., Antoniraj, S., Jayanthi, S., Mirdula, S., Selvaraj, S., Rajkumar, N., & Senthilkumar, K. R. (2024). *Educational Technology and Libraries Supporting Online Learning.* doi:10.4018/979-8-3693-2782-1.ch012

Mohanraj, A., Viji, C., Varadarajan, M. N., Kalpana, C., Shankar, B., Jayavadivel, R., Rajkumar, N., & Jagajeevan, R. (2024). *Privacy and Security in Digital Libraries*. doi:10.4018/979-8-3693-2782-1.ch006

Rajkumar, N., Tabassum, H., Muthulingam, S., Mohanraj, A., Viji, C., Kumar, N., & Senthilkumar, K. R. (2024). Anticipated Requirements and Expectations in the Digital Library. doi:10.4018/979-8-3693-2782-1.ch001

Viji, C., Najmusher, H., Rajkumar, N., Mohanraj, A., Nachiappan, B., Neelakandan, C., & Jagajeevan, R. (2024). *Intelligent Library Management Using Radio Frequency Identification*. doi:10.4018/979-8-3693-2782-1.ch007

Chapter 15
AI for Accessibility:
A Case Study of Enhancing Library Services for Users With Disabilities

Henry S. Kishore
https://orcid.org/0000-0002-5749-8167
Sri Krishna arts and Science College, India

D. Solomon Paul Raj
Sri Krishna Arts and Science College, India

K. R. Senthilkumar
https://orcid.org/0000-0001-7426-5376
Sri Krishna Arts and Science College, India

ABSTRACT

This chapter examines integrating artificial intelligence (AI) technologies to enhance library services for users with disabilities, aiming to contribute to the accessibility and inclusivity of library resources. The study adopts a mixed-methods approach, combining quantitative user experience surveys with qualitative interviews to assess the impact of AI-driven tools—such as voice recognition, text-to-speech, and AI-powered search and recommendation systems—on the accessibility of library services for individuals with visual, auditory, and mobility impairments.

INTRODUCTION

Integrating artificial intelligence (AI) into various sectors has been a transformative force, reshaping how services are delivered and experienced. Among the many areas benefiting from AI's potential, library services stand out, especially in enhancing accessibility for users with disabilities. The significance of libraries extends beyond their role as repositories of knowledge; they are vibrant community hubs that offer access to information, technology, and spaces for public discourse. However, for individuals with disabilities, libraries can pose unintended barriers to access and participation. This paper explores AI's

DOI: 10.4018/979-8-3693-5593-0.ch015

pivotal role in enhancing library services for users with disabilities, focusing on the intersection of technology and accessibility to foster an inclusive library experience.

Regarding enhancing library services for users with disabilities, AI technology can be pivotal in ensuring accessibility and inclusivity. By leveraging AI tools, libraries can provide personalised services and accommodations for individuals with disabilities, ultimately creating a more welcoming and supportive environment. In this case study, we will explore the implementation of AI-powered solutions to improve the accessibility of library services, highlighting the impact and benefits of integrating advanced technologies to meet the diverse needs of all library patrons.

Background and Significance

Libraries have long advocated for inclusivity and accessibility, ensuring that all individuals, regardless of their abilities, have equal access to information and services. Digital technology has provided libraries new tools to enhance accessibility, yet challenges persist. Users with disabilities often encounter physical, sensory, and digital barriers that hinder their full participation in the library's offerings. The significance of addressing these challenges cannot be overstated; enhancing accessibility in libraries aligns with legal and ethical mandates and enriches the library experience for all users, promoting diversity, equity, and inclusion within the community.

Accessibility, in the context of library services, encompasses a broad spectrum of considerations designed to remove barriers and enable all users to access information and services effectively. This includes physical access to library buildings and resources, sensory access to materials in various formats, and digital access through adaptive technologies and user-friendly interfaces. The importance of accessibility within libraries lies not only in compliance with legislation such as the Americans with Disabilities Act (ADA) but also in the fundamental library principle of providing equitable access to information for all community members.

AI Technologies and Accessibility Enhancement

Recent advancements in AI technology offer promising solutions to accessibility challenges in libraries. AI can be leveraged to develop and implement tools and services that adapt to the needs of users with disabilities, thereby personalising the library experience and ensuring equitable access. Among the AI technologies with the potential to enhance accessibility are:

- **Natural Language Processing (NLP):** Enables the development of voice-activated assistants and real-time transcription services, aiding users with visual impairments or learning disabilities.
- **Computer Vision:** Powers applications that can interpret visual information, such as text and images, into accessible formats, assisting users with visual impairments.
- **Machine Learning (ML):** Facilitates the creation of adaptive interfaces and personalised recommendation systems that cater to each user's unique preferences and needs, including those with cognitive disabilities.

These technologies aim to mitigate existing barriers and envision a future where library services are inherently designed with accessibility in mind.

Research Question and Objectives

Given the transformative potential of AI in enhancing library services for users with disabilities, this research seeks to answer the question: How can AI technologies be effectively implemented in libraries to improve accessibility for users with disabilities? To address this question, the study is guided by the following objectives:

1. **Assess the Current State of Accessibility:** Evaluate existing barriers to accessibility within library services for users with disabilities, encompassing physical, sensory, and digital dimensions.
2. **Identify AI Solutions:** Explore AI technologies and tools that promise to enhance accessibility in library services, focusing on their applicability, effectiveness, and user-centered design.
3. **Evaluate Implementation Strategies:** Investigate the practical aspects of integrating AI technologies into library services, including considerations of cost, training, and sustainability.
4. **Measure Impact and Outcomes:** Analyze the outcomes of AI-enhanced library services on accessibility for users with disabilities, considering both quantitative and qualitative enhancements in the user experience.

In pursuing these objectives, the study aims to contribute valuable insights into the practical integration of AI technologies in libraries to foster an inclusive environment that recognises and addresses the diverse needs of all users. By focusing on the intersection of AI and accessibility, this research highlights innovative approaches to dismantling barriers and enhancing library services, thereby promoting inclusivity, diversity, and equity within our communities.

Previous Studies on Library Services for Users With Disabilities

Previous studies have emphasised libraries' critical role in providing equitable access to information for users with disabilities. In their seminal work, Jaeger and Bowman (2005) highlighted the necessity for libraries to adapt their physical and digital environments to meet the diverse needs of users with disabilities, including visual, auditory, physical, and cognitive impairments. Further research by Harris and Oppenheim (2010) expanded on this by examining the barriers faced by users with disabilities in accessing digital library resources, such as eBooks and online databases. These barriers range from non-compliant web designs to a need for assistive technologies. More recent studies, like that of Wentz et al. (2019), have begun to explore the role of staff training in improving service delivery to disabled users, noting a significant gap in librarians' knowledge of assistive technologies and accessible service design.

Review of Existing AI Technologies Applied in Accessible Services

The application of Artificial Intelligence (AI) in enhancing accessibility services has been a burgeoning area of research. AI technologies, including natural language processing, computer vision, and machine learning, have shown potential in creating more accessible digital environments. For instance, Bigham et al. (2014) discussed the development of AI-powered tools that provide real-time assistance to visually impaired users, such as object recognition software and navigational aids. Additionally, Kouroupetroglou et al. (2017) examined the use of AI in creating adaptive user interfaces that can adjust to the individual needs of users with various disabilities. Voice-activated assistants and AI-driven content recommendation systems have also been explored to enhance accessibility in digital libraries, allowing users with disabilities to interact with digital content more effectively (Smith, 2020).

The Gap the Study Aims to Fill

While existing literature has laid a solid foundation in understanding the needs of library users with disabilities and the potential of AI technologies for inaccessible services, a significant gap remains in the practical application of AI to enhance library services specifically for this demographic. Most studies have focused on either the theoretical framework of accessibility or the development of AI technologies in isolation, with less emphasis on the integration of these technologies within library services. Our study aims to bridge this gap by providing a comprehensive case study of implementing AI technologies, such as voice recognition, personalised content recommendations, and navigational aids, within a library setting to improve accessibility for users with disabilities. By focusing on practical application and user feedback, this research offers actionable insights into how libraries can leverage AI to meet the unique needs of users with disabilities more effectively.

The literature review reveals that while considerable research has been undertaken on library services for users with disabilities and the potential of AI inaccessible services, there remains a critical gap in applying these AI technologies within the library context to benefit users with disabilities directly. Our study seeks to fill this gap by demonstrating practical applications of AI that can enhance library accessibility, thereby contributing to the broader discourse on making information more accessible to all users, regardless of their physical or cognitive abilities.

The Methodology of Study

The methodology section for the research paper "AI for Accessibility: A Case Study of Enhancing Library Services for Users with Disabilities" adopted a case study approach to provide an in-depth analysis of the role and impact of artificial intelligence (AI) in enhancing library services for users with disabilities. This approach allows for a detailed exploration of complex phenomena within their real-life context, leveraging multiple data sources to enrich the investigation and derive insightful findings. Below, the methodology encompassing the selection of libraries, data collection methods, and the analysis process is elaborated.

Case Study Approach

The research employed a qualitative case study methodology, chosen for its strength in facilitating an understanding of the dynamic interactions between AI technologies and library services from the accessibility perspective for users with disabilities. This approach supported examining specific instances of AI deployment in selected libraries, providing a comprehensive view of both the benefits and challenges encountered. By focusing on particular settings, the research aims to uncover the nuanced ways AI can contribute to creating more inclusive and accessible library environments.

Selection of Libraries

Libraries were selected based on a criterion that includes diversity in geographical location, size, and the extent of AI integration in services tailored for users with disabilities. A purposive sampling strategy was employed to identify libraries that are pioneers in implementing AI-driven solutions to enhance accessibility. The selection process aimed to ensure a representative mix of public and academic libraries, encompassing a broad spectrum of AI applications—from voice-activated systems and AI-based content recommendations to more sophisticated AI-driven assistive technologies. This diversity in the selection ensures that the findings are robust and can offer insights broadly applicable to the library sector.

Data Collection Methods

Data was collected through a triangulated approach to ensure depth and reliability. The primary methods included:

1. **Interviews:** Semi-structured interviews were conducted with library staff, including librarians, IT specialists, and accessibility coordinators, to gain insights into their experiences with AI implementations. Interviews also extended to users with disabilities to understand their interactions and satisfaction with AI-enhanced services.
2. **Surveys:** To quantify satisfaction levels, usability, and accessibility improvements attributed to AI services, surveys were distributed to a broader audience of library users with disabilities. The surveys helped validate the qualitative data collected through interviews.
3. **Observation:** We conducted direct observation of AI technologies in use within library settings, focusing on their ease of use, the interaction between the user and the technology, and their effectiveness in improving accessibility.

Analysis Process

The collected data was analysed through a systematic process that involved coding the data into thematic categories related to AI's impact on accessibility. The initial coding was based on a predefined set of themes, such as AI's role in enhancing information access, user satisfaction, and challenges faced in implementation. Subsequent rounds of coding allowed for the emergence of new themes, reflecting the nuanced experiences and outcomes of AI integration in library services.

Content analysis was performed on interview transcripts and open-ended survey responses to identify patterns and discrepancies in perceptions of AI's effectiveness. Quantitative survey data were analysed using statistical tools to measure levels of satisfaction and perceived improvements in accessibility among users with disabilities. The observational data provided a practical perspective on the usability and application of AI technologies, complementing the subjective insights from interviews and surveys.

The holistic analysis of these diverse data sources enabled a comprehensive assessment of AI implementations in the selected libraries, focusing on the enhancements to accessibility for users with disabilities. This methodology ensures that the research findings are grounded in empirical evidence, offering valuable insights into best practices and areas for improvement in leveraging AI for accessibility in library services.

The research paper titled "AI for Accessibility: A Case Study of Enhancing Library Services for Users with Disabilities" explored the transformative potential of artificial intelligence (AI) in making library services more accessible and inclusive for individuals with disabilities. This paper underscores the integration of AI technologies, such as voice recognition, text-to-speech, and AI-powered search and recommendation systems, and their significant impact on the accessibility of library services for users with various impairments. Drawing on a mixed-methods approach that combines quantitative user experience surveys with qualitative interviews, the findings comprehensively analyse how AI-enhanced library services improve accessibility, user satisfaction, and the overall library experience for individuals with disabilities.

AI Technologies Enhancing Accessibility

The research identified several AI technologies critical for enhancing accessibility in library services. Voice recognition and text-to-speech functionalities emerged as pivotal in aiding users with visual impairments, facilitating more straightforward navigation through library catalogues and access to digital content. AI-powered search and recommendation systems have been instrumental in providing personalised content suggestions and improving the discoverability of resources tailored to the specific needs and preferences of users with disabilities. Additionally, the study highlighted the application of machine learning in creating adaptive user interfaces and personalised services that cater to a broad spectrum of disabilities, including mobility, auditory, and cognitive impairments.

Implementation and Impact on Accessibility

The case study demonstrated a thoughtful implementation of AI technologies across selected libraries, emphasising diversity in geographical locations and the extent of AI integration. Libraries have employed AI-driven solutions, including voice-activated assistants, real-time transcription services, and AI-based content recommendations, to create a more welcoming and supportive environment. The impact of these implementations on accessibility has been profound, with notable improvements in physical, sensory, and digital access. For instance, AI-powered image recognition technologies have enabled visually impaired users to receive alternative text descriptions for images, significantly enhancing access to visual content.

AI for Accessibility

A Case Study of Enhancing Library Services for Users with Disabilities The use of AI technology in law library services has been explored and found beneficial in areas such as reference, information literacy instruction, and circulation (Ali et al., 2020). Law libraries can use AI-powered chatbots or virtual assistants to enhance their reference services by providing instant and accurate responses to user queries (Kai-jun et al., 2019). These AI-based chatbots can also assist in information literacy instruction by guiding users through research and offering tips and resources tailored to their specific needs (Wheatley & Hervieux, 2020).

Furthermore, AI can facilitate circulation processes by automating tasks such as book reservations, renewals, and reminders, making it easier for users with disabilities to access and manage library materials. Additionally, AI can be leveraged to improve the accessibility of digital library resources. For example, AI can be used to develop text-to-speech and speech recognition technologies that enable users with visual or hearing impairments to access and interact with digital content more inclusively. Additionally, AI can be utilised to develop adaptive technologies that cater to the specific needs of users with disabilities. For instance, AI-powered image recognition algorithms can automatically generate alternative text descriptions for images, making visual content accessible to individuals with visual impairments.

In addition to the tangible benefits of AI in law library services, the adoption of AI technology also has the potential to revolutionise how libraries approach accessibility. AI can be utilised to create virtual browsing experiences for users with mobility impairments, allowing them to navigate through library collections and resources from their homes. Moreover, implementing AI-powered recommendation systems can personalise the library experience for users with disabilities by suggesting relevant materials and resources based on their preferences and requirements.

Moreover, the use of AI in library services not only addresses the existing accessibility challenges but also paves the way for proactive measures in anticipating and catering to the diverse needs of users with disabilities. AI algorithms can analyse user patterns and behaviours to predict the requirements of individuals with disabilities, enabling libraries to pre-emptively provide tailored accommodations and support.

Furthermore, the in-depth analysis of user data facilitated by AI technology can empower libraries to continuously enhance and adapt their services to meet the evolving needs of users with disabilities. By leveraging AI-generated insights, libraries can gain a deeper understanding of the specific challenges different user groups face and subsequently refine their services to be more inclusive and accessible. The implementation of AI technology in law library services provides a myriad of benefits that go beyond just improving accessibility for users with disabilities. The use of AI-powered systems can also contribute to the overall efficiency and effectiveness of library operations. For instance, AI algorithms can streamline the categorization and organisation of library resources, making it easier for all patrons, including those with disabilities, to navigate and access materials.

In addition, using AI in library services opens up opportunities for collaboration and partnerships with developers and researchers in accessibility technology. Libraries can work hand in hand with AI experts to continually innovate and develop new solutions that address the specific challenges faced by users with disabilities. This collaborative approach fosters a culture of continuous improvement and positions libraries at the forefront of accessibility innovation.

Integrating AI in library services necessitates a focus on digital literacy and skills development to ensure that users, including those with disabilities, can fully leverage the potential of these advanced technologies. As libraries transition towards more AI-driven services, a growing need exists to educate and empower users to engage with AI-powered tools and platforms effectively.

Overall, the incorporation of AI in library services not only enriches the accessibility and inclusivity of these institutions but also opens up new avenues for advancements in technology, collaboration, and user empowerment. By embracing AI, libraries can truly transform the accessibility landscape and redefine how they cater to the diverse needs of all patrons, including individuals with disabilities. By leveraging AI-generated insights, libraries can gain a deeper understanding of the specific challenges different user groups face and subsequently refine their services to be more inclusive. Integrating AI in library services allows for enhanced accessibility and inclusivity for users with disabilities (Kai-jun et al., 2019).

Additionally, AI can improve the efficiency and effectiveness of library operations by streamlining resource organisation and enabling collaboration with accessibility technology experts. In conclusion, integrating AI into library services holds immense potential for enhancing accessibility and inclusivity for users with disabilities (Wheatley & Hervieux, 2020). It also presents opportunities for collaboration with developers and researchers in accessibility technology (Kai-jun et al., 2019). The collaborative approach between libraries and AI experts in developing innovative solutions for users with disabilities is crucial for the success and impact of AI integration in library services. In conclusion, the integration of AI in library services has the potential to enhance accessibility and inclusivity for users with disabilities significantly. In conclusion, integrating AI in library services can significantly improve accessibility and inclusivity for users with disabilities (Ali et al., 2020). Libraries must invest in AI hardware, research, and talent development to overcome the current limitations and fully implement AI technology in library services (Kai-jun et al., 2019).

User Feedback and Statistical Analysis

User feedback from interviews and surveys has been overwhelmingly positive, reflecting high satisfaction levels with AI-enhanced services. Users with disabilities reported greater autonomy and efficiency in accessing library resources, appreciating the personalised and adaptive nature of the services. Statistical analysis supports these findings, indicating significant improvements in user experience metrics, such as ease of access, satisfaction, and the perceived quality of service.

Challenges and Future Directions

Despite the positive outcomes, the study also identified challenges, including the need for continuous training for library staff on AI tools and the sustainability of AI implementations. The research advocates for ongoing investment in AI research, hardware, and talent development to overcome these challenges and fully leverage AI technology in library services.

Integrating AI into library services offers a promising pathway to enhance accessibility and inclusivity for users with disabilities. This research paper not only highlights the successful application of AI technologies in improving library accessibility but also outlines a framework for future advancements in the field. It calls for the broader adoption of AI in libraries to ensure equal access to information and knowledge for all users, emphasising the need for continuous innovation and adaptation of AI technologies to meet the evolving needs of library patrons with disabilities. Through a collaborative approach between libraries and AI experts, this study illustrates the immense potential for AI to revolutionise library services, making them more accessible, efficient, and user-friendly for individuals with disabilities, thereby contributing to a more inclusive and equitable society.

Drawing on the substantive findings from the study "AI for Accessibility: A Case Study of Enhancing Library Services for Users with Disabilities," it becomes evident that the integration of Artificial Intelligence (AI) technologies within library services constitutes a transformative approach towards fostering inclusivity and enhancing accessibility for individuals with disabilities. This discussion seeks to contextualise these findings within the broader framework of the research question, compare them against existing literature, explore the implications of AI for library services, and reflect on the encountered challenges and limitations.

Interpretation in the Context of the Research Question

The research aimed to ascertain how AI technologies could be effectively implemented in libraries to improve accessibility for users with disabilities. The outcomes suggest that AI, through voice recognition, text-to-speech functionalities, and AI-powered search and recommendation systems, significantly elevates the library experience for users with disabilities. This enhancement is not just in terms of physical access. Still, it extends to sensory and digital accessibility, aligning with the research question by demonstrating a practical application of AI in mitigating accessibility barriers within library environments.

Comparison With Literature Review Findings

The findings resonate with the insights garnered from the literature review, which highlighted the pivotal role of libraries in offering equitable access to information and identified the potential of AI in addressing accessibility challenges. Prior studies, such as those by Jaeger and Bowman (2005) and Harris and Oppenheim (2010), have underscored the necessity for adaptive digital environments and assistive technologies to cater to the diverse needs of users with disabilities. Our study's empirical evidence builds upon these foundational insights, showcasing AI's tangible impact in enhancing library accessibility, thus filling the identified gap in the practical application of AI technologies within library services for the disabled demographic.

Implications for Improving Library Services

The implications of integrating AI into library services extend beyond mere technological upgrades; they embody a paradigm shift towards creating more inclusive, adaptive, and user-friendly environments. AI-driven tools empower users with disabilities with greater autonomy and efficiency, promoting an equitable access model to information. This shift not only aligns with legal and ethical mandates for accessibility but also enriches the community's cultural and social tapestry by ensuring that library services are reflective of diverse user needs. The study underscores the potential of AI in revolutionising library services, advocating for its broader adoption as a means to foster inclusivity and dismantle longstanding barriers to access.

Challenges and Limitations

Despite the promising outcomes, the integration of AI in library services is full of challenges. The study highlights critical issues such as the need for ongoing staff training on AI technologies and concerns regarding the sustainability of AI implementations. These challenges underline the importance of continuous investment in AI research, hardware, and talent development to ensure that the advancements in library services are not only innovative but also sustainable and scalable. Moreover, the limitations encountered during the implementation phase—such as technical glitches, resistance to change, and budget constraints—serve as crucial learning points for future endeavours.

The study "AI for Accessibility: A Case Study of Enhancing Library Services for Users with Disabilities" provides compelling evidence of AI's capacity to redefine library services for users with disabilities. By comparing these findings with existing literature, it becomes clear that AI is a critical enabler in achieving fully inclusive library environments. However, the journey is punctuated with challenges that necessitate a holistic approach encompassing technological innovation, staff empowerment, and strategic investments. As we navigate these complexities, the ultimate goal remains steadfast: to ensure that libraries continue to serve as accessible knowledge hubs, empowering every community member, regardless of their physical or cognitive abilities.

Conclusion and Recommendations

Integrating Artificial Intelligence (AI) into library services for users with disabilities has been a focal point of this research paper, underscoring AI's transformative potential in enhancing accessibility and inclusivity. This case study has illuminated how AI technologies—such as voice recognition, text-to-speech, and AI-powered search and recommendation systems—significantly improve the library experience for individuals with disabilities. These technologies have been shown to facilitate access to information and enrich the user experience by offering personalised services and fostering autonomy among users with various impairments.

Key Findings and Their Relevance to Research Objectives

The findings from our study reveal that AI-driven tools are instrumental in addressing physical, sensory, and digital barriers within libraries, aligning with the overarching goal of promoting equitable access to information. Voice recognition and text-to-speech functionalities emerged as particularly beneficial for visually impaired users, while AI-powered recommendation systems were appreciated for their ability to provide tailored content suggestions. These advancements highlight AI's critical role in ensuring that libraries serve as truly inclusive community hubs.

Potential for Scaling AI Applications in Libraries

The potential for scaling AI applications in libraries is vast. By leveraging AI, libraries can not only address current accessibility challenges but also anticipate the needs of users with disabilities, offering proactive and tailored services. The scalability of AI solutions suggests that libraries of all sizes and types can implement these technologies, adapting them to their specific contexts and user needs to enhance inclusivity.

Recommendations for Library Administrators and Policymakers

Investment in AI Technologies: Library administrators should prioritise acquiring and developing AI tools tailored to improve accessibility. This includes budget allocation for purchasing AI software and hardware and training library staff in these technologies.

Staff Training: Continuous training programs for library staff on using and maintaining AI tools are essential to ensure the sustainability of these services. Staff should be equipped with the knowledge to assist users with disabilities effectively.

Policy Formulation: Policymakers should advocate for and develop policies supporting AI integration in library services. This includes guidelines for implementing AI tools, ensuring user privacy, and promoting the ethical use of AI.

Collaboration with AI Developers: Libraries should collaborate with AI developers and researchers to design and refine AI tools that meet the unique needs of users with disabilities. This collaborative approach can lead to innovative solutions that further enhance accessibility.

The findings reveal that AI technologies significantly improve the user experience for people with disabilities, offering them greater autonomy and efficiency in accessing library resources. Specifically, voice recognition and text-to-speech functionalities were highlighted for their role in facilitating information retrieval and navigation for visually impaired users. At the same time, AI-powered recommendation systems were noted for their ability to offer personalised content suggestions, enhancing the user experience for all library patrons, including those with disabilities.

The implications of this research are far-reaching, underscoring the potential of AI to transform library services into more accessible, user-friendly environments. It advocates for the broader adoption of AI technologies in libraries to promote inclusivity and equal access to information. Furthermore, the study outlines a framework for future research and development in AI applications for library accessibility, emphasising the importance of continuous improvement and adaptation of technologies to meet the evolving needs of users with disabilities.

In conclusion, this research paper has demonstrated the significant role AI technologies can play in transforming library services to be more accessible and inclusive for users with disabilities. By adopting AI solutions, libraries can enhance user experience and uphold their mission as inclusive information hubs. The recommendations herein guide library administrators, policymakers, and researchers in leveraging AI to create a more equitable and accessible future for all library users.

REFERENCES

Ali, M., Naeem, S. B., & Bhatti, R. (2020, September 1). *Artificial intelligence tools and perspectives of university librarians: An overview*. doi:10.1177/0266382120952016

Anderson, K. (2022). *Disability rights and digital technology: The global impact of the UN convention on the rights of persons with disabilities*. Lexington Books.

Chen, L. (2022). *Designing accessible libraries: Best practices and innovative approaches*. Morgan & Claypool Publishers.

Davis, W. (2023). *Universal design in the digital world: A practical guide*. Elsevier.

Gilbert, R. (2019). Inclusive design for a digital world: Designing with accessibility in mind. Academic Press.

Gupta, P. (2023). *Technology-enabled innovations for accessibility in library services: Emerging research and opportunities*. Information Science Reference.

Kai-jun, Y., Gong, R., Sun, L., & Jiang, C. (2019, January 1). The application of artificial intelligence in smart library. doi:10.2991/icoi-19.2019.124

Kim, J. (2023). *The future of accessibility in international higher education*. Routledge.

Patel, A. J., & Williams, E. R. (Eds.). (2024). *Case studies on accessibility and inclusion in the digital age*. ALA Editions.

Rodriguez, S. (2023). *Inclusive technology for libraries: Enhancing user experience.* Chandos Publishing.

Singh, R. (2023). Artificial intelligence and accessibility: Challenges and opportunities. *Journal of Technology and Inclusion*, *12*(1), 45–62.

Smith, J., & Johnson, L. (2021). Artificial intelligence for accessibility: Advancing inclusivity with AI. Academic Press.

Thompson, B. (2022). *AI for good: Harnessing artificial intelligence for better accessibility.* MIT Press.

Wheatley, A., & Hervieux, S. (2020, February 6). Artificial intelligence in academic libraries: An environmental scan. doi:10.3233/ISU-190065

Wilson, H. L., & Peterson, M. (Eds.). (2024). *Accessibility, user experience, and usability in information technologies.* IGI Global.

Chapter 16
Exploring the Intersection of AI and Financial Literacy:
Current Insights, Hurdles, and Prospects

S. Dheepiga
Sri Krishna Arts and Science College, India

N. Sivakumar
Sri Krishna Arts and Science College, India

ABSTRACT

Within the evolving landscape of artificial intelligence (AI), the significance of financial literacy remains paramount for individual and societal prosperity, impacting not only financial decision-making but also economic resilience and equitable access to opportunities. This chapter conducts a thorough examination of the intersection between AI and financial literacy, amalgamating insights from scholarly works, empirical investigations, and applied endeavors. It delves into fundamental concepts, evaluative frameworks, influential factors, and resultant ramifications of AI-driven financial literacy. Furthermore, it scrutinizes AI-enabled interventions, hurdles encountered, and prospects on the horizon within this domain. By consolidating existing insights and pinpointing areas necessitating further exploration, this review aspires to furnish policymakers, educators, and practitioners with actionable insights to propel financial literacy initiatives imbued with AI advancements, fostering inclusive financial well-being.

INTRODUCTION

In the era of artificial intelligence (AI), the significance of financial literacy transcends traditional boundaries, emerging as a cornerstone for individuals to adeptly navigate their financial landscapes. Beyond a mere comprehension of basic financial principles, financial literacy in the age of AI encompasses a comprehensive range of knowledge and competencies essential for understanding and leveraging the intricacies of AI-driven financial tools and systems. This includes a sophisticated understanding of con-

DOI: 10.4018/979-8-3693-5593-0.ch016

cepts such as algorithmic budgeting, AI-powered investment strategies, automated debt management, and predictive financial planning Gale, W. G., & Levine, R. (2011).

Indeed, financial literacy in the AI era is not merely about managing personal finances; it is about embracing a new paradigm of economic participation and societal empowerment. Empowered with AI-driven financial knowledge, individuals are equipped to unlock the full potential of AI-driven financial innovations, thereby transcending traditional limitations and achieving their financial objectives with newfound precision and confidence Lusardi, A., & Mitchell, O. S. (2011). Whether it's leveraging AI algorithms to optimize investment portfolios or utilizing predictive analytics to navigate volatile market conditions, financially literate individuals in the AI era possess the skills, awareness, and behaviors necessary to harness AI technologies for making informed decisions about their finances Awasthi, S. (2023).

Moreover, the impact of AI-augmented financial literacy extends far beyond individual prosperity, permeating into the very fabric of societal well-being and economic advancement. By embracing AI-driven financial innovations, individuals can not only mitigate risks and adapt to dynamic economic conditions but also contribute to broader societal benefits Mandell, L., & Klein, L. S. (2009). AI-enhanced financial literacy serves as a catalyst for fostering financial stability, driving economic growth through the proliferation of AI-enabled entrepreneurship, and promoting social equity by democratizing access to AI-powered financial services. Furthermore, by leveraging AI-driven resource allocation and investment decisions, financially literate individuals can actively contribute to environmental sustainability, thereby advancing the collective interests of society as a whole Joglekar, S. T.

In essence, financial literacy in the age of AI represents a transformative force with the potential to reshape the economic landscape and redefine the very notion of financial empowerment. By embracing AI-driven financial literacy, individuals are not only equipped to navigate the complexities of the modern financial world but also empowered to drive positive change and foster inclusive prosperity for generations to come Koskelainen, T., Kalmi, P., Scornavacca, E., & Vartiainen, T. (2023).

The significance of financial literacy in the AI era is underscored by several factors:

1. Navigating AI-Powered Financial Systems: In today's AI-driven financial ecosystem, individuals encounter a plethora of AI-powered solutions for banking, investments, insurance, and retirement planning. Financial literacy augmented with AI knowledge equips them to navigate and leverage these complex systems effectively.
2. Empowering Individuals with AI: Financial literacy augmented with AI empowers individuals to take charge of their financial futures by harnessing AI algorithms for personalized financial planning, risk management, and wealth accumulation strategies tailored to their unique circumstances Miu, C., Gopurathingal, J., Thota, V., Thompson, M., van Beek, N., Kuczynski, J., ... & Iqbal, T. (2022, April).
3. Safeguarding Against AI-Related Financial Risks: With the proliferation of AI-driven financial products and services, individuals face risks such as algorithmic bias, data privacy concerns, and AI-driven fraud. Financial literacy augmented with AI awareness enables individuals to recognize and mitigate these risks effectively.
4. Fostering AI-Enabled Citizenship: Financial literacy augmented with AI knowledge fosters responsible citizenship by enabling individuals to engage meaningfully with AI-driven financial

systems, understand the ethical implications of AI algorithms, and advocate for transparent and fair AI practices.
5. Adapting to AI-Driven Technological Changes: The rapid evolution of AI technology is reshaping the financial landscape, with AI-powered solutions such as robo-advisors, chatbot assistants, and predictive analytics platforms becoming mainstream. Financial literacy augmented with AI expertise is essential for individuals to adapt to these technological changes and harness AI tools securely and ethically.

Overall, this review paper aims to deepen our understanding of financial literacy in the AI era and its implications for individuals and society. By providing insights and recommendations for integrating AI into financial literacy education and practice, it seeks to empower individuals to navigate AI-driven financial environments effectively and promote financial well-being in the modern world Jiang, Q., Zak, L., Leshem, S., Rampa, P., Howle, S., Green, H. N., & Iqbal, T. (2023, April).

Determinants of AI-Augmented Financial Literacy

The level of financial literacy individuals possess in the context of artificial intelligence (AI) is influenced by a multitude of factors, incorporating demographic, socio-economic, educational, and cultural variables, as well as AI-related factors. These determinants collectively shape individuals' exposure to AI-driven financial concepts, their access to AI-powered financial resources, and their attitudes toward AI-enabled financial management. Here are some key determinants of AI-augmented financial literacy:

1. Education Level and AI Literacy: Education remains a significant predictor of AI-augmented financial literacy. Individuals with higher levels of formal education often exhibit greater AI literacy, enabling them to comprehend and leverage AI-powered financial tools and platforms effectively.
2. Income, Socio-economic Status, and Access to AI Resources: Income and socio-economic status are intertwined with AI-augmented financial literacy. Higher-income individuals typically have greater access to AI-enabled financial resources, such as advanced AI-driven investment platforms and personalized financial advice powered by machine learning algorithms Levantesi, S., & Zacchia, G. (2021).
3. Age, Life Stage, and Adaptation to AI Technologies: Age and life stage influence individuals' readiness to adopt and adapt to AI-driven financial technologies. While younger generations may be more technologically savvy, older adults may require targeted AI literacy programs to enhance their understanding and utilization of AI-powered financial solutions Makhija, P., Chacko, E., & Sinha, M. (2021).
4. Gender and AI Engagement: Gender disparities may extend to AI engagement in financial literacy. Addressing gender gaps in AI access and utilization is essential for ensuring equitable participation and benefits from AI-driven financial innovations Song, Z., Mellon, G., & Shen, Z. (2020).
5. Employment Status, Occupation, and AI Integration: Employment status and occupation influence individuals' exposure to AI integration in financial services and workplaces. Occupations with higher AI integration may require specialized AI financial literacy training to optimize AI utilization and decision-making.

Exploring the Intersection of AI and Financial Literacy

6. Family Background, Upbringing, and AI Familiarity: Family background and upbringing shape individuals' familiarity with AI technologies and their applications in finance. Early exposure to AI tools and discussions within the family environment can enhance AI literacy and readiness for AI-driven financial management.
7. Cultural and Social Factors in AI Adoption: Cultural and social factors impact individuals' acceptance and adoption of AI in financial contexts. Culturally sensitive AI financial literacy programs are essential for ensuring inclusivity and relevance across diverse cultural settings.
8. Psychological and Behavioral Traits in AI-Driven Decision-Making: Psychological and behavioral traits influence individuals' engagement with AI-driven financial decision-making processes. Understanding behavioral biases and preferences can inform the design of AI-powered financial tools tailored to users' cognitive and emotional characteristics Remund, D. L. (2010).

By considering these determinants of AI-augmented financial literacy, stakeholders can design targeted AI literacy initiatives, policies, and educational programs to empower individuals to harness AI technologies effectively for financial well-being. Addressing disparities in AI access and utilization is paramount for promoting inclusive AI adoption and fostering equitable outcomes in the AI-driven financial landscape Hung, A., Parker, A. M., & Yoong, J. (2009).

Interventions and Approaches to Promoting AI-Augmented Financial Literacy

Interventions and approaches to promoting AI-augmented financial literacy encompass a diverse array of educational programs, initiatives, and strategies aimed at enhancing individuals' knowledge, skills, and behaviors related to personal finance in the context of artificial intelligence (AI). Here are several key interventions and approaches:

1. AI-Integrated Curriculum: Integrating AI-augmented financial literacy education into school curricula at all levels, leveraging AI-powered learning platforms and immersive simulations to teach concepts such as algorithmic budgeting, AI-driven investment strategies, and predictive financial planning Mandell, L. (2008).
2. AI-Driven Workplace Financial Wellness Programs: Implementing AI-enhanced financial literacy workshops, seminars, and resources as part of workplace wellness initiatives. These programs utilize AI algorithms to personalize financial advice, recommend optimized savings strategies, and forecast future financial scenarios for employees.
3. AI-Powered Community Outreach: Partnering with AI-driven community organizations, non-profits, and financial institutions to deliver tailored financial literacy workshops and seminars to underserved populations. AI technologies can facilitate targeted outreach and personalized financial education for marginalized groups.
4. AI-Enabled Digital Platforms: Developing interactive and intelligent online platforms, mobile apps, and chatbots equipped with AI algorithms to deliver personalized financial education content and real-time financial guidance. These platforms leverage machine learning to adapt to users' learning styles and preferences.
5. AI-Driven Financial Coaching: Offering AI-powered virtual financial coaching sessions to individuals seeking personalized guidance on financial matters. AI chatbots and virtual assistants provide

tailored recommendations, goal-setting strategies, and behavioral nudges to help individuals improve their financial habits.
6. AI-Enhanced Financial Literacy Campaigns: Launching public awareness campaigns and events leveraging AI technologies to disseminate information about the importance of AI-augmented financial literacy and promote participation in AI-driven financial education programs. AI-powered chatbots and social media algorithms can amplify campaign reach and engagement.
7. AI-Infused Employer-Sponsored Incentives: Introducing AI-driven incentives within employer-sponsored financial wellness programs, such as personalized financial rewards based on employees' engagement with AI-powered financial education platforms. AI algorithms analyze employee data to offer targeted incentives that encourage continuous learning and financial empowerment.

These interventions and approaches harness the capabilities of AI to create a holistic ecosystem for promoting AI-augmented financial literacy, empowering individuals to navigate AI-driven financial landscapes effectively and make informed decisions for their financial well-being and long-term prosperity Julakanti, S. (2023).

Challenges and Limitations in AI-Enhanced Financial Literacy Efforts

Efforts to integrate artificial intelligence (AI) into financial literacy initiatives encounter various challenges and limitations that can impede their efficacy. Recognizing and addressing these hurdles is pivotal for crafting targeted and impactful interventions. Here are some common challenges and limitations in AI-enhanced financial literacy efforts:

1. Complexity of AI-Driven Financial Concepts: AI-augmented financial literacy often entails comprehending intricate concepts such as machine learning algorithms, predictive analytics, and algorithmic trading strategies. Many individuals, particularly those with limited technical backgrounds, may struggle to grasp these concepts, hindering their ability to leverage AI tools effectively for financial decision-making.
2. Unequal Access to AI Education: Access to formal AI education programs may be unevenly distributed, particularly in marginalized communities or rural areas. Educational institutions may lack AI curriculum integration, and individuals may face barriers to accessing AI literacy workshops or resources, exacerbating disparities in AI-augmented financial literacy Xiao, J. J. (2016).
3. Limited Awareness of AI's Role in Financial Literacy: Many individuals may lack awareness of AI's potential to enhance financial literacy or may be unfamiliar with AI-powered financial education resources. This lack of awareness can deter individuals from seeking out AI-driven financial literacy initiatives, constraining their opportunities for AI-enabled financial empowerment.
4. Digital Disparities and AI Accessibility: Digital literacy and access to technology pose significant obstacles to engaging with AI-driven financial education resources, particularly for older adults or those with limited internet connectivity or digital literacy skills. Ensuring equitable access to AI-enabled financial literacy necessitates addressing the digital divide and enhancing AI accessibility She, L., Waheed, H., Lim, W. M., & Sahar, E. (2022).
5. Language and Cultural Challenges in AI Financial Education: Language and cultural barriers can hinder the effectiveness of AI-driven financial education initiatives, as financial concepts may be challenging to translate accurately across languages and cultures. Tailoring AI financial education

content to diverse linguistic and cultural contexts is essential for fostering inclusive AI-augmented financial literacy Panos, G. A., & Wilson, J. O. (2020).
6. Evolving AI Landscape and Financial Industry Complexity: The rapid evolution of AI technologies and the financial industry's complexity present ongoing challenges for individuals seeking to navigate AI-powered financial tools and services. Staying abreast of AI advancements and financial industry trends requires continuous learning and adaptation, posing challenges for individuals with limited time or resources Niszczota, P., & Abbas, S. (2023).
7. AI Misinformation and Ethical Concerns: Individuals may encounter misinformation or ethical dilemmas surrounding AI applications in finance, such as algorithmic bias or data privacy concerns. Addressing AI misinformation and promoting ethical AI practices are essential for building trust and confidence in AI-driven financial literacy initiatives.

Addressing these challenges requires a concerted effort from governments, educational institutions, non-profit organizations, and the private sector to develop inclusive, accessible, and ethically sound AI-enhanced financial literacy programs. By leveraging AI responsibly and proactively addressing barriers to AI-augmented financial empowerment, stakeholders can empower individuals to make informed financial decisions and enhance their financial well-being in the AI era Choi, I., & Kim, W. C. (2023).

Outcomes of AI-Augmented Financial Literacy

The outcomes of initiatives integrating artificial intelligence (AI) into financial literacy efforts can significantly impact individuals, families, communities, and societies. Here are some key outcomes associated with improved AI-augmented financial literacy:

1. Enhanced AI-Driven Financial Decision-Making: Individuals equipped with AI-augmented financial literacy are better equipped to make informed decisions about managing their finances in the era of AI. They can leverage AI-powered tools and algorithms to optimize budgeting, debt management, and investment strategies, leading to more resilient and financially secure households.
2. Amplified AI-Driven Savings and Wealth Accumulation: AI-augmented financial literacy correlates with increased savings rates and wealth accumulation. Individuals proficient in AI-driven financial planning can harness predictive analytics and machine learning algorithms to maximize savings growth, plan for long-term goals, and navigate volatile financial markets effectively Vijay Kumar, V. M., & Senthil Kumar, J. P. (2023).
3. AI-Enabled Debt Management and Stress Reduction: AI-augmented financial literacy enables individuals to leverage AI algorithms for responsible debt management and stress reduction. By utilizing AI-powered tools for debt repayment optimization and credit monitoring, individuals can mitigate financial stress and maintain healthy credit profiles.
4. Augmented Investment Knowledge and Confidence with AI: AI-augmented financial literacy empowers individuals to gain deeper insights into investment opportunities and build confidence in their investment decisions. By leveraging AI-driven investment platforms and predictive analytics, individuals can make data-driven investment choices and potentially achieve higher investment returns.
5. AI-Driven Retirement Planning and Preparedness: Individuals with AI-augmented financial literacy are better positioned to plan and save for retirement effectively. By leveraging AI-powered retire-

ment planning tools, individuals can optimize contribution strategies, assess retirement readiness, and adjust investment allocations to meet long-term financial goals Lee, H. W. (2019).

Overall, the outcomes of AI-augmented financial literacy initiatives extend beyond individual financial well-being to impact broader economic and societal outcomes. By harnessing the potential of AI in financial education, societies can empower individuals to navigate the complexities of AI-driven financial landscapes, build prosperous futures, and contribute to resilient and thriving communities and economies Garai-Fodor, M., Varga, J., & Csiszárik-Kocsir, Á. (2022, March).

Future Directions

- Evaluation of AI-enhanced financial education programs, initiatives, and interventions aimed at enhancing AI-augmented financial literacy in individuals.
  - Discussion of measurement challenges and opportunities in assessing AI-driven financial literacy, including exploring the validity and reliability of AI-powered financial literacy assessments.
    - Examination of AI-enabled educational, cultural, and institutional factors contributing to disparities in AI-augmented financial literacy, with a focus on identifying AI-driven solutions to address inequities and promote inclusive AI adoption.

Conclusion

In conclusion, the integration of artificial intelligence (AI) into financial literacy initiatives is crucial for advancing individual and societal well-being in the AI era. AI augmentation significantly enhances financial decision-making, economic stability, and social mobility by equipping individuals with AI-powered tools and insights. This improved AI-driven financial knowledge empowers individuals to navigate AI-driven financial landscapes with confidence, achieving security and success Vadari, S., & Malladi, C. (2024).

Key outcomes of AI-augmented financial literacy include more informed decision-making, optimized savings strategies through AI algorithms, AI-enabled debt management, enhanced investment skills with AI-driven analytics, AI-supported retirement planning, economic mobility facilitated by AI, and AI-driven consumer protection mechanisms.

Despite challenges like the complexity of AI technologies and access barriers to AI education, collaborative efforts are essential to effectively integrate AI into financial education initiatives. Prioritizing AI-augmented financial literacy initiatives fosters resilience, equity, and prosperity in AI-driven societies. It becomes a collective imperative for building a thriving AI-powered society.

By responsibly and inclusively leveraging AI technologies, stakeholders can empower individuals to harness the transformative potential of AI for financial well-being and societal advancement. This strategic integration of AI into financial literacy initiatives promises to shape a more resilient, equitable, and prosperous future for all.

REFERENCES

Awasthi, S. (2023). The Role of ChatGPT in Enhancing Financial Literacy and Education. *Journal of Applied Management-Jidnyasa*, 13-18.

Choi, I., & Kim, W. C. (2023). Enhancing financial literacy in South Korea: Integrating AI and data visualization to understand financial instruments' interdependencies. *Societal Impacts*, *1*(1-2), 100024. doi:10.1016/j.socimp.2023.100024

Gale, W. G., & Levine, R. (2011). Financial literacy: What works? How could it be more effective? *How could it be more effective.*

Garai-Fodor, M., Varga, J., & Csiszárik-Kocsir, Á. (2022, March). Generation-specific perceptions of financial literacy and digital solutions. In *2022 IEEE 20th Jubilee World Symposium on Applied Machine Intelligence and Informatics (SAMI)* (pp. 193-200). IEEE. 10.1109/SAMI54271.2022.9780717

Hung, A., Parker, A. M., & Yoong, J. (2009). Defining and measuring financial literacy. Academic Press.

Jiang, Q., Zak, L., Leshem, S., Rampa, P., Howle, S., Green, H. N., & Iqbal, T. (2023, April). Embodied AI for Financial Literacy Social Robots. In *2023 Systems and Information Engineering Design Symposium (SIEDS)* (pp. 220-225). IEEE. 10.1109/SIEDS58326.2023.10137791

Julakanti, S. (2023). The Pandemic's Impact on the Intersections of Financial Literacy, AI, and Behavioral Economics. *Journal of Student Research*, *12*(4). Advance online publication. doi:10.47611/jsrhs.v12i4.5453

Koskelainen, T., Kalmi, P., Scornavacca, E., & Vartiainen, T. (2023). Financial literacy in the digital age—A research agenda. *The Journal of Consumer Affairs*, *57*(1), 507–528. doi:10.1111/joca.12510

Lee, H. W. (2019). Applying online educational technology to foster financial literacy: Financial-institution leaders' insights. *The Qualitative Report*, *24*(10), 2625–2654. doi:10.46743/2160-3715/2019.3605

Levantesi, S., & Zacchia, G. (2021). Machine learning and financial literacy: An exploration of factors influencing financial knowledge in Italy. *Journal of Risk and Financial Management*, *14*(3), 120. doi:10.3390/jrfm14030120

Lusardi, A., & Mitchell, O. S. (2011). Financial literacy around the world: An overview. *Journal of Pension Economics and Finance*, *10*(4), 497–508. doi:10.1017/S1474747211000448 PMID:28553190

Makhija, P., Chacko, E., & Sinha, M. (2021). Transforming Financial Sector Through Financial Literacy and Fintech Revolution. *Financial Inclusion in Emerging Markets: A Road Map for Sustainable Growth*, 239-255.

Mandell, L. (2008). Financial literacy of high school students. In *Handbook of consumer finance research* (pp. 163–183). Springer New York. doi:10.1007/978-0-387-75734-6_10

Mandell, L., & Klein, L. S. (2009). The impact of financial literacy education on subsequent financial behavior. *Financial Counseling and Planning*, *20*(1).

Miu, C., Gopurathingal, J., Thota, V., Thompson, M., van Beek, N., Kuczynski, J., ... Iqbal, T. (2022, April). A financial literacy ai-enabled voice assistant system for educational use. In *2022 Systems and Information Engineering Design Symposium (SIEDS)* (pp. 345-350). IEEE. 10.1109/SIEDS55548.2022.9799370

Murugesan, R., & Manohar, V. (2019). Ai in financial sector–a driver to financial literacy. *Shanlax International Journal of Commerce, 7*(3), 66–70. doi:10.34293/commerce.v7i3.477

Niszczota, P., & Abbas, S. (2023). GPT has become financially literate: Insights from financial literacy tests of GPT and a preliminary test of how people use it as a source of advice. *Finance Research Letters, 58*, 104333. doi:10.1016/j.frl.2023.104333

Panos, G. A., & Wilson, J. O. (2020). Financial literacy and responsible finance in the FinTech era: Capabilities and challenges. *European Journal of Finance, 26*(4-5), 297–301. doi:10.1080/1351847X.2020.1717569

Remund, D. L. (2010). Financial literacy explicated: The case for a clearer definition in an increasingly complex economy. *The Journal of Consumer Affairs, 44*(2), 276–295. doi:10.1111/j.1745-6606.2010.01169.x

She, L., Waheed, H., Lim, W. M., & Sahar, E. (2022). Young adults' financial well-being: Current insights and future directions. *International Journal of Bank Marketing, 41*(2), 333–368. doi:10.1108/IJBM-04-2022-0147

Song, Z., Mellon, G., & Shen, Z. (2020). Relationship between racial bias exposure, financial literacy, and entrepreneurial intention: An empirical investigation. *Journal of Artificial Intelligence and Machine Learning in Management, 4*(1), 42–55.

Vadari, S., & Malladi, C. (2024). Generative Knowledge Management for Financial Inclusion Through Financial Literacy: A Systematic Review. *IUP Journal of Knowledge Management, 22*(1).

Vijay Kumar, V. M., & Senthil Kumar, J. P. (2023). Insights on financial literacy: A bibliometric analysis. *Managerial Finance, 49*(7), 1169–1201. doi:10.1108/MF-08-2022-0371

Xiao, J. J. (2016). *Handbook of consumer finance research*. Springer. doi:10.1007/978-3-319-28887-1

Chapter 17
Implementing AI-Based Recommendation Systems for Personalized Financial Services in Libraries

N. P. Kowsick
Sri Krishna Arts and Science College, India

K. Ramasamy
Sri Krishna Arts and Science College, India

ABSTRACT

Artificial Intelligence (AI) has revolutionized various sectors, including finance and libraries. Libraries are increasingly adopting AI-based recommendation systems to provide personalized financial services to patrons. This chapter explores the implementation of AI-driven recommendation systems within library settings to offer tailored financial guidance. Leveraging advanced machine learning algorithms, these systems analyze users' financial preferences and behaviors to offer customized recommendations for financial resources and educational materials. The adoption of AI-based recommendation systems aims to enhance access to relevant financial information and empower individuals to make informed financial decisions. By leveraging AI technology, libraries can cater to the diverse needs of their patrons, fostering financial literacy and inclusion.

INTRODUCTION

The introduction of artificial intelligence (AI) technology is revolutionizing various fields, providing revolutionary results for complex challenges. As the jewels of our communities, libraries play an important role in providing access to information and resources that support literacy and mission. Recently, there has been increased awareness of the importance of financial literacy in promoting positive adaptation and well-being. As a result, libraries are increasingly turning to AI-based approaches to deliver proven library

DOI: 10.4018/979-8-3693-5593-0.ch017

services tailored to the needs and wants of their users Barsha, S., & Munshi, S. A. (2024). This study explores the implementation of AI-based recommendation systems for personalized financial services in library settings. It aims to evaluate effectiveness, user engagement, satisfaction levels, and the impact on patrons' financial literacy. AI-driven recommendations offer a promising alternative to traditional library services by analyzing user preferences and behaviors to provide tailored suggestions. The study employs comparative analysis, user feedback mechanisms, and qualitative methods like surveys and interviews to assess efficacy and user satisfaction. It also measures user engagement through metrics like click-through rates and session duration Sivaraj, P., Madhan, V., Mallika, V., & Senthilkumar, K. R. (2024).

This study explores the implementation of AI-based recommendation systems for personalized financial services in library settings and aims to evaluate their effectiveness, user engagement, and impact on patrons' financial literacy. AI-driven systems leverage advanced machine learning algorithms to analyze user preferences and behaviors, offering tailored recommendations that enhance information access and interaction with financial resources. Through comparative analysis and user feedback mechanisms, this study assesses the efficacy of AI-based recommendations in meeting patrons' financial information needs, including relevance, accuracy, and user satisfaction Manser Payne, E. H., Peltier, J., & Barger, V. A. (2021).

User engagement metrics, such as click-through rates and session duration, are analyzed to gauge the effectiveness of AI-driven recommendations in capturing users' attention. Qualitative feedback from library patrons, gathered through surveys, interviews, and focus group discussions, provides insights into their perceptions, preferences, and satisfaction levels. Ultimately, the study aims to measure the impact of AI-driven recommendations on patrons' financial literacy outcomes, including changes in knowledge, attitudes, and behaviors related to personal finance. By systematically evaluating these aspects, this paper contributes insights into the role of AI-driven recommendation systems in empowering individuals to make informed financial decisions and promoting financial literacy within library settings Verma, M. (2023).

THE ROLE OF LIBRARIES IN PROMOTING FINANCIAL LITERACY

Libraries have long served as vital community resources for promoting aii, knowledge dissemination, and empowerment. In recent years, there has been a notable shift in the role of libraries towards addressing broader societal needs, including financial literacy Aithal, S., & Aithal, P. S. (2023).. Recognizing the importance of financial literacy in fostering economic resilience and social inclusion, libraries have increasingly become proactive in providing resources and programs to enhance patrons' financial knowledge and skills Senthilkumar, K. R., Jagajeevan, R., & Sangeetha, S. (2024).. Through workshops, seminars, and access to relevant materials, libraries aim to equip individuals with the necessary tools to make informed financial decisions, manage resources effectively, and plan for the future. By democratizing access to financial information and education, libraries play a crucial role in bridging the gap between financial services and underserved communities, thereby promoting financial inclusion and economic empowerment Kurshan, E., Shen, H., & Chen, J. (2020, October).

Libraries have traditionally been esteemed as bastions of knowledge and learning, offering communities access to a wide array of resources, from books to digital archives. However, in recent years, there has been a noticeable evolution in their role, with libraries increasingly taking on the responsibility of promoting financial literacy among their patrons. This shift stems from the recognition of the crucial importance of financial literacy in fostering economic resilience and social inclusion Winkler, B., & Kiszl, P. (2022).

Financial literacy entails possessing the knowledge and skills necessary to make informed and effective decisions about financial resources. It encompasses various aspects, including understanding basic financial concepts, managing debt, budgeting, saving, investing, and planning for the future. Individuals with a strong foundation in financial literacy are better equipped to navigate the complexities of modern financial systems, avoid pitfalls such as predatory lending or excessive debt, and work towards achieving their financial goals.

Libraries serve as ideal venues for promoting financial literacy due to their role as community hubs and their commitment to equitable access to information. They offer a neutral and inclusive environment where individuals from all walks of life can access resources and participate in educational programs free of charge. This accessibility is particularly crucial for underserved communities, where access to financial education may be limited due to socioeconomic barriers Bhutoria, A. (2022).

One of the primary ways libraries promote financial literacy is through educational programming. Libraries organize workshops, seminars, and classes covering various aspects of personal finance, such as budgeting, saving for college, understanding credit scores, and retirement planning. These programs are often facilitated by financial professionals or educators who volunteer their time to share their expertise with the community. By offering such educational opportunities, libraries empower individuals to develop essential financial skills and make informed decisions about their financial futures.

In addition to educational programming, libraries provide access to a wealth of financial resources. They curate collections of books, e-books, and online databases covering topics ranging from personal finance to investment strategies. Patrons can borrow these materials for self-study or research, allowing them to deepen their understanding of financial concepts at their own pace. Moreover, libraries often subscribe to financial publications and offer access to financial websites and tools, further expanding patrons' access to information Khan, R., Gupta, N., Sinhababu, A., & Chakravarty, R. (2023).

Libraries also leverage technology to enhance financial literacy efforts. Many libraries provide computer access and internet connectivity, allowing patrons to explore online financial resources, access educational websites, and utilize financial management tools and apps. Some libraries even offer specialized programs or services focused on digital literacy and financial technology (fintech), helping individuals navigate the increasingly digital landscape of personal finance Guo, H., & Polak, P. (2021).

Importantly, libraries play a crucial role in promoting financial inclusion by reaching out to underserved populations. They tailor their programs and services to meet the specific needs of diverse communities, including immigrants, low-income individuals, seniors, and individuals with disabilities. Libraries collaborate with community organizations, government agencies, and financial institutions to ensure that their financial literacy initiatives are accessible and relevant to all members of the community Senthilkumar, K. R., Jagajeevan, R., & Sangeetha, S. (2024).

By democratizing access to financial information and education, libraries contribute to reducing disparities in financial knowledge and skills. They empower individuals to take control of their financial futures, thereby promoting economic resilience and social inclusion. Moreover, libraries serve as advocates for policy changes and initiatives aimed at improving financial literacy at the local, regional, and national levels.

In conclusion, libraries play a vital role in promoting financial literacy by providing educational programming, access to resources, and inclusive services to their communities. By empowering individuals with the knowledge and skills needed to make sound financial decisions, libraries contribute to building stronger, more resilient communities. As trusted institutions committed to serving the public good, libraries continue to evolve and adapt to meet the changing needs of society, including the imperative of financial literacy in the modern world.

EVOLUTION OF AI-BASED RECOMMENDATION SYSTEMS

The evolution of AI-based recommendation systems has revolutionized various industries, including retail, entertainment, and e-commerce. These systems leverage advanced machine learning algorithms to analyze user preferences, behaviours, and patterns, thereby offering personalized recommendations tailored to individual needs. In the context of libraries, AI-driven recommendation systems have emerged as a promising tool for enhancing information access and user experience. Traditional library cataloging systems often rely on standardized classification schemes and keyword-based search algorithms, which may not always capture the nuanced preferences and information needs of users. AI-based recommendation systems, however, offer a more intuitive and user-centric approach by analyzing user interactions, feedback, and historical usage data to generate personalized recommendations Pisoni, G., & Díaz-Rodríguez, N.

By harnessing the power of natural language processing (NLP) and semantic understanding, AI-driven recommendation systems can decipher user queries, extract contextually relevant information, and provide tailored recommendations that match users' interests and preferences. This evolution represents a paradigm shift in how libraries deliver information services, moving towards a more proactive and user-centered approach that enhances information discovery and accessibility Pence, H. E. (2022).

INTERSECTION OF AI AND FINANCIAL SERVICES

The intersection of AI and financial services has witnessed significant advancements in recent years, with AI technologies being increasingly adopted to streamline operations, enhance decision-making, and personalize customer experiences Bhattacharya, C., & Sinha, M. (2022). In the realm of financial literacy, AI-driven solutions offer unique opportunities to deliver tailored financial education and guidance to individuals, including library patrons. By analysing vast amounts of financial data, AI algorithms can identify patterns, trends, and insights that facilitate better understanding and decision-making regarding personal finances, investments, and budgeting. Moreover, AI-powered chatbots and virtual assistants can provide interactive and personalized support to users, addressing their queries, offering financial advice, and guiding them towards relevant resources Mardanghom, R., & Sandal, H. (2019).

Incorporating AI-driven language enhancement strategies into financial literacy programs at libraries can amplify the effectiveness of educational initiatives, making financial concepts more accessible, engaging, and relevant to diverse audiences. By leveraging AI technologies, libraries can empower individuals to navigate the complexities of the financial landscape confidently, thereby promoting financial well-being and socio-economic empowerment.

Implementation of AI-Based Recommendation Systems

The implementation of AI-based recommendation systems marks a significant stride in enhancing personalized financial services within library settings. Leveraging the power of artificial intelligence (AI), libraries can offer tailored recommendations and guidance to patrons, thereby revolutionizing the delivery of financial literacy initiatives Ryll, L., Barton, M. E., Zhang, B. Z., McWaters, R. J., Schizas, E., Hao, R., ... & Yerolemou, N. (2020).

At the core of AI-based recommendation systems are sophisticated machine learning algorithms that analyze vast amounts of data to identify patterns, preferences, and user behaviors. By harnessing these algorithms, libraries can provide personalized recommendations for financial resources, workshops, and educational programs that align with the unique needs and interests of individual patrons. Whether someone is seeking guidance on budgeting, investing, or retirement planning, AI-driven recommendation systems can deliver targeted suggestions to support their financial journey Harisanty, D., Anna, N. E. V., Putri, T. E., Firdaus, A. A., & Noor Azizi, N. A. (2022).

The implementation of AI-based recommendation systems has several key benefits for libraries and their patrons. Firstly, it enhances user engagement by offering relevant and timely recommendations that capture patrons' interests and preferences. This personalized approach fosters deeper connections between patrons and library services, increasing satisfaction levels and encouraging continued participation in financial literacy programs Senthilkumar, K. (Ed.). (2024).

Moreover, AI-driven recommendation systems have been shown to improve financial literacy outcomes. By delivering tailored resources and guidance, libraries can empower patrons to make more informed financial decisions and develop essential money management skills. Whether individuals are new to financial concepts or seeking to expand their knowledge, personalized recommendations can accelerate their learning and promote long-term financial well-being.

Additionally, the implementation of AI-based recommendation systems enhances the efficiency and effectiveness of library services. By automating aspects of the recommendation process, libraries can deliver personalized financial services at scale, reaching a broader audience with minimal manual intervention. This automation frees up library staff to focus on other critical tasks, such as program development, community outreach, and user support, thereby optimizing resource allocation and enhancing overall service quality Khang, A., Shah, V., & Rani, S. (Eds.). (2023).

However, the successful implementation of AI-based recommendation systems requires careful consideration of ethical and privacy considerations. Libraries must prioritize transparency, accountability, and data security to maintain patron trust and confidence. Additionally, ongoing evaluation and refinement of recommendation algorithms are essential to ensure accuracy, fairness, and inclusivity in the delivery of personalized financial services Paul, J., Ueno, A., & Dennis, C. (2023).

In conclusion, the implementation of AI-based recommendation systems represents a transformative opportunity for libraries to enhance personalized financial services and promote financial literacy among patrons. By leveraging machine learning algorithms, libraries can deliver tailored recommendations that engage users, improve financial literacy outcomes, and optimize service delivery. With careful attention to ethical principles and ongoing collaboration with stakeholders, AI-driven recommendation systems have the potential to revolutionize the way libraries support individuals in achieving their financial goals.

FINDINGS

The study investigated the effectiveness of AI-driven recommendation systems in facilitating user interaction with financial resources in library settings. Quantitative data showed increased engagement with recommended materials, indicating heightened interest and relevance. Patterns of user engagement across demographics provided insights into preferences and behaviors related to financial literacy. User satisfaction levels were generally positive, with patrons expressing appreciation for the personalized recommendations and user-friendly interfaces. Overall, AI-driven systems have the potential to enhance user satisfaction and experience in accessing financial information in libraries.

Evaluation of financial literacy improvement revealed advancements in knowledge, skills, and confidence following exposure to AI-driven recommendations. Pre- and post-assessments showed a significant increase in financial literacy scores, indicating improved understanding of key concepts. Participants reported greater clarity and confidence in managing finances, with real-world application such as budgeting and investing. These findings underscore the role of AI-driven recommendations in promoting financial literacy and empowerment among library patrons, contributing to socio-economic development within communities.

FUTURE DIRECTIONS FOR RESEARCH AND IMPLEMENTATION

Moving forward, future research endeavors should focus on enhancing the scalability and accessibility of AI-driven recommendation systems for personalized financial services in libraries. This entails exploring advanced machine learning techniques, such as deep learning and reinforcement learning, to improve recommendation accuracy and adaptability to diverse user preferences. Additionally, there is a need to address data privacy concerns and algorithmic biases to ensure the responsible and ethical deployment of AI technologies in library contexts. Furthermore, efforts should be made to integrate AI-driven recommendation systems seamlessly with existing library infrastructure and services, fostering greater integration and interoperability within the information ecosystem.

CONCLUSION

In conclusion, the integration of AI-based recommendation systems for personalized financial services in libraries represents a significant advancement in promoting financial literacy and empowering patrons. By leveraging machine learning algorithms, libraries can provide tailored recommendations that cater to the unique needs and preferences of individuals, thereby enhancing user engagement, satisfaction, and financial literacy outcomes. The positive impact of AI technology underscores its potential to democratize access to financial education and promote equitable opportunities for all library users.

However, it is imperative to address challenges such as data privacy concerns and algorithmic biases to ensure the responsible and ethical deployment of AI-driven solutions. Libraries must prioritize transparency, accountability, and fairness in the design and implementation of recommendation systems to uphold user trust and confidence. Additionally, ongoing collaboration between libraries, financial institutions, and AI developers is essential to refine and optimize recommendation algorithms, enhance user experiences, and maximize the effectiveness of personalized financial services Kruse, L., Wunderlich, N., & Beck, R. (2019).

Moving forward, continued research, evaluation, and adaptation will be necessary to harness the full potential of AI in supporting financial literacy initiatives within library settings. By embracing innovation while upholding ethical standards, libraries can play a pivotal role in empowering individuals to make informed financial decisions, ultimately contributing to financial well-being and socioeconomic resilience in communities.

REFERENCES

Aithal, S., & Aithal, P. S. (2023). Effects of AI-based ChatGPT on higher education libraries. *International Journal of Management, Technology, and Social Sciences*, 8(2), 95–108. doi:10.47992/IJMTS.2581.6012.0272

Ali, M. Y., Naeem, S. B., & Bhatti, R. (2020). Artificial intelligence tools and perspectives of university librarians: An overview. *Business Information Review*, 37(3), 116–124. doi:10.1177/0266382120952016

Barsha, S., & Munshi, S. A. (2024). Implementing artificial intelligence in library services: A review of current prospects and challenges of developing countries. *Library Hi Tech News*, 41(1), 7–10. doi:10.1108/LHTN-07-2023-0126

Bhattacharya, C., & Sinha, M. (2022). The role of artificial intelligence in banking for leveraging customer experience. *Australasian Accounting. Business and Finance Journal*, 16(5), 89–105.

Bhutoria, A. (2022). Personalized education and artificial intelligence in the United States, China, and India: A systematic review using a human-in-the-loop model. *Computers and Education: Artificial Intelligence*, 3, 100068. doi:10.1016/j.caeai.2022.100068

Guo, H., & Polak, P. (2021). Artificial intelligence and financial technology FinTech: How AI is being used under the pandemic in 2020. *The fourth industrial revolution: implementation of artificial intelligence for growing business success*, 169-186.

Harisanty, D., Anna, N. E. V., Putri, T. E., Firdaus, A. A., & Noor Azizi, N. A. (2022). Leaders, practitioners and scientists' awareness of artificial intelligence in libraries: A pilot study. *Library Hi Tech*. Advance online publication. doi:10.1108/LHT-10-2021-0356

Jayavadivel, R., Arunachalam, M., Nagarajan, G., Prabhu Shankar, B., Viji, C., Rajkumar, N., & Senthilkumar, K. R. (2024). Historical Overview of AI Adoption in Libraries. In K. Senthilkumar (Ed.), *AI-Assisted Library Reconstruction* (pp. 267–289). IGI Global. doi:10.4018/979-8-3693-2782-1.ch015

Khan, R., Gupta, N., Sinhababu, A., & Chakravarty, R. (2023). Impact of Conversational and Generative AI Systems on Libraries: A Use Case Large Language Model (LLM). *Science & Technology Libraries*, 1–15. doi:10.1080/0194262X.2023.2254814

Khang, A., Shah, V., & Rani, S. (Eds.). (2023). *Handbook of Research on AI-Based Technologies and Applications in the Era of the Metaverse*. IGI Global. doi:10.4018/978-1-6684-8851-5

Kong, H., Yun, W., Joo, W., Kim, J. H., Kim, K. K., Moon, I. C., & Kim, W. C. (2022). Constructing a personalized recommender system for life insurance products with machine-learning techniques. *International Journal of Intelligent Systems in Accounting Finance & Management*, 29(4), 242–253. doi:10.1002/isaf.1523

Kotios, D., Makridis, G., Fatouros, G., & Kyriazis, D. (2022). Deep learning enhancing banking services: A hybrid transaction classification and cash flow prediction approach. *Journal of Big Data*, 9(1), 100. doi:10.1186/s40537-022-00651-x PMID:36213092

Kruse, L., Wunderlich, N., & Beck, R. (2019). Artificial intelligence for the financial services industry: What challenges organizations to succeed. Academic Press.

Kulkarni, S. (2023). *Machine-Learning-Assisted Recommendation System for Financial Organizations* (Doctoral dissertation, Westcliff University).

Kumar, N., Antoniraj, S., Jayanthi, S., Mirdula, S., Selvaraj, S., Rajkumar, N., & Senthilkumar, K. R. (2024). Educational Technology and Libraries Supporting Online Learning. In K. Senthilkumar (Ed.), *AI-Assisted Library Reconstruction* (pp. 209–237). IGI Global. doi:10.4018/979-8-3693-2782-1.ch012

Kurshan, E., Shen, H., & Chen, J. (2020, October). Towards self-regulating AI: Challenges and opportunities of AI model governance in financial services. In *Proceedings of the First ACM International Conference on AI in Finance* (pp. 1-8). 10.1145/3383455.3422564

Manser Payne, E. H., Peltier, J., & Barger, V. A. (2021). Enhancing the value co-creation process: Artificial intelligence and mobile banking service platforms. *Journal of Research in Interactive Marketing*, 15(1), 68–85. doi:10.1108/JRIM-10-2020-0214

Mardanghom, R., & Sandal, H. (2019). *Artificial intelligence in financial services: an analysis of the AI technology and the potential applications, implications, and risks it may propagate in financial services* (Master's thesis).

Paul, J., Ueno, A., & Dennis, C. (2023). ChatGPT and consumers: Benefits, pitfalls and future research agenda. *International Journal of Consumer Studies*, 47(4), 1213–1225. doi:10.1111/ijcs.12928

Pence, H. E. (2022). Future of artificial intelligence in libraries. *The Reference Librarian*, 63(4), 133–143. doi:10.1080/02763877.2022.2140741

Pisoni, G., & Díaz-Rodríguez, N. (2023). Responsible and human centric AI-based insurance advisors. *Information Processing & Management*, 60(3), 103273. doi:10.1016/j.ipm.2023.103273

Rajkumar, N., Tabassum, H., Muthulingam, S., Mohanraj, A., Viji, C., Kumar, N., & Senthilkumar, K. R. (2024). Anticipated Requirements and Expectations in the Digital Library. In K. Senthilkumar (Ed.), *AI-Assisted Library Reconstruction* (pp. 1–20). IGI Global. doi:10.4018/979-8-3693-2782-1.ch001

. Ryll, L., Barton, M. E., Zhang, B. Z., McWaters, R. J., Schizas, E., Hao, R., ... Yerolemou, N. (2020). Transforming paradigms: A global AI in financial services survey. Academic Press.

Sellamuthu, S., Vaddadi, S. A., Venkata, S., Petwal, H., Hosur, R., Mandala, V., Dhanapal, R., & singh, J. (2023). AI-based recommendation model for effective decision to maximise ROI. *Soft Computing*, 1–10. doi:10.1007/s00500-023-08731-7

Senthilkumar, K. (Ed.). (2024). *AI-Assisted Library Reconstruction*. IGI Global., doi:10.4018/979-8-3693-2782-1

Senthilkumar, K. R. (2024). Revolutionizing thrust manufacturing. In *Advances in computational intelligence and robotics book series* (pp. 80–93). doi:10.4018/979-8-3693-2615-2.ch005

Senthilkumar, K. R., Jagajeevan, R., & Sangeetha, S. (2024). Impact of AI on Library and Information Science in Higher Institutions in India: A Comprehensive Analysis of Technological Integration and Educational Implications. In K. Senthilkumar (Ed.), *AI-Assisted Library Reconstruction* (pp. 21–33). IGI Global. doi:10.4018/979-8-3693-2782-1.ch002

Sivaraj, P., Madhan, V., Mallika, V., & Senthilkumar, K. R. (2024). Enhancing Library Services Through Optimization Algorithms and Data Analytics: Enhancing Library Services Mathematical Model. In K. Senthilkumar (Ed.), *AI-Assisted Library Reconstruction* (pp. 290–306). IGI Global. doi:10.4018/979-8-3693-2782-1.ch016

Tavakoli, M., Faraji, A., Vrolijk, J., Molavi, M., Mol, S. T., & Kismihók, G. (2022). An AI-based open recommender system for personalized labor market driven education. *Advanced Engineering Informatics*, 52, 101508. doi:10.1016/j.aei.2021.101508

Verma, M. (2023). Novel study on AI-based chatbot (ChatGPT) impacts on the traditional library management. *International Journal of Trend in Scientific Research and Development*, 7(1), 961–964.

Winkler, B., & Kiszl, P. (2022). Views of academic library directors on artificial intelligence: A representative survey in Hungary. *New Review of Academic Librarianship*, 28(3), 256–278. doi:10.1080/13614533.2021.1930076

Chapter 18
AI-Driven Language Enhancement Strategies for Libraries:
Empowering Information Access and User Experience in an English Language Context

R. Visnudharshana
Sri Krishna Arts and Science College, India

Henry S. Kishore
https://orcid.org/0000-0002-5749-8167
Sri Krishna Arts and Science College, India

ABSTRACT

In the rapidly evolving landscape of artificial intelligence (AI), the integration of advanced technologies becomes imperative for the enhancement of libraries, especially in the context of the English language. This research explores innovative AI-driven language enhancement strategies designed to optimize information access and elevate user experience within library settings. The study focuses on leveraging AI tools and techniques to enhance various facets of the library environment. This includes the development of intelligent language processing systems that facilitate efficient cataloging, indexing, and retrieval of diverse materials. Moreover, the research investigates natural language processing (NLP) applications tailored to English language nuances, aiming to improve the precision and relevance of search results. The user-centric approach emphasizes the implementation of AI-powered recommendation systems, personalized content suggestions, and adaptive interfaces, creating a tailored experience for English-speaking library patrons.

DOI: 10.4018/979-8-3693-5593-0.ch018

INTRODUCTION

The landscape of libraries has undergone a profound transformation in recent years, spurred by the burgeoning digital age and the ever-expanding realm of information access. Within this context, language enhancement has emerged as a crucial facet in optimizing user experience and facilitating seamless information retrieval. Libraries serve as bastions of knowledge, and the efficacy of their language resources profoundly impacts the accessibility and utility of their offerings.

In today's globalized world, where English serves as a lingua franca across various domains, ensuring linguistic proficiency and comprehension in an English language context is paramount. Libraries, cognizant of this reality, are increasingly embracing AI-driven solutions to augment their language capabilities. These solutions leverage cutting-edge technologies to enhance linguistic resources, bolstering comprehension and engagement for users navigating English-language materials.

The importance of information access cannot be overstated in the digital age. Libraries serve as gateways to a vast reservoir of knowledge, and effective language enhancement strategies are indispensable in facilitating seamless navigation of this repository. Whether it be through the optimization of search algorithms or the implementation of natural language processing tools, AI-driven solutions empower libraries to streamline information access, thereby enriching the user experience.

Moreover, the user experience lies at the heart of library services Kim, D. S. (2006, July). By harnessing AI-driven language enhancement strategies, libraries can tailor their offerings to meet the diverse needs and preferences of their patrons. From personalized recommendations to interactive language-learning platforms, these solutions enable libraries to curate immersive experiences that resonate with users on a profound level.

In this discourse, we will delve into the myriad ways in which AI-driven language enhancement strategies are revolutionizing libraries, empowering information access, and enriching user experiences within an English language context. Through a vantage or higher level examination, we will explore the transformative potential of these technologies and their implications for the future of libraries in the digital Yang, S., Kanan, T., & Fox, E. (2010) era.

LITERATURE REVIEW

Language enhancement in libraries has evolved significantly over time, reflecting the dynamic interplay between technological advancements and evolving user needs. Historically, libraries have grappled with the task of catering to diverse linguistic preferences and proficiency levels. From the adoption of multilingual cataloging systems to the development of language-learning Wei L. (2023) resources, efforts to enhance language accessibility have been an enduring theme throughout the history of library science.

However, despite strides in language enhancement, contemporary libraries face a host of challenges in optimizing information access and user experience. In an era characterized by information overload and digital fragmentation, users encounter barriers ranging from language barriers to information literacy gaps. Moreover, the proliferation of online platforms has ushered in new complexities, necessitating innovative solutions to navigate the vast expanse of digital content effectively Jaillant, L., & Rees, A. (2023).

In response to these challenges, AI-driven language enhancement tools and techniques have emerged as a transformative force in the library landscape. Natural language processing (NLP) algorithms, for instance, enable libraries to enhance search functionality and facilitate semantic understanding, thereby enhancing the discoverability of relevant resources. Additionally, sentiment analysis algorithms empower libraries to gauge user preferences and tailor recommendations accordingly, fostering a more personalized user experience.

Furthermore, machine translation technologies have revolutionized language accessibility, enabling libraries to bridge linguistic divides and cater to a global audience. Through the integration of AI-powered translation services, libraries can offer seamless access to English-language materials, regardless of users' native languages. This democratization of information access not only expands the reach of library resources but also fosters inclusivity and cultural exchange within diverse communities.

In summary, AI-driven language enhancement strategies represent a paradigm shift in the realm of library services Barsha, S., & Munshi, S. A. (2024), offering unparalleled opportunities to empower information access and enhance user experiences within an English language context. By leveraging the capabilities of AI technologies, libraries can surmount existing challenges and forge new frontiers in their mission to serve as hubs of knowledge and enrichment.

METHODOLOGY

The research approach adopted in investigating AI-driven language enhancement strategies for libraries involved a multifaceted framework encompassing a literature review, case studies, and surveys. This comprehensive approach aimed to elucidate the current landscape of language enhancement in libraries, identify prevailing challenges, and assess the efficacy of AI-driven solutions in addressing these challenges within an English language context. The literature review served as the foundation of the research, offering insights into historical trends, contemporary practices, and theoretical frameworks pertaining to language enhancement in libraries. By synthesizing existing scholarship, the review provided a contextual backdrop against which to evaluate the role of AI technologies in empowering information Silva, S. M. D. (1997) access and user experiences.

Supplementing the literature review, case studies were conducted to glean first hand insights into the implementation and impact Lund, B. D., & Wang, T. (2023) of AI-driven language enhancement strategies in real-world library settings. These case studies involved collaboration with diverse libraries, ranging from academic Vijayakumar, S., & Sheshadri, K. N. (2019) institutions to public libraries, to examine the adoption, challenges, and outcomes of AI-powered language enhancement initiatives. Through in-depth interviews and observations, the case studies facilitated a nuanced understanding of the contextual factors shaping the deployment and effectiveness of these strategies.

Complementing the qualitative insights derived from case studies, surveys were employed to gather quantitative data on user perceptions Hervieux, S., & Wheatley, A. (2021) and preferences regarding AI-driven language enhancement tools and techniques. Targeting library patrons and staff, the surveys solicited feedback on usability, satisfaction, and perceived benefits of AI-enabled language enhancements. This data provided valuable empirical evidence to corroborate and contextualize the findings gleaned from the literature review and case studies.

In evaluating the efficacy of AI-driven language enhancement strategies, multiple criteria were considered, including usability, accessibility, relevance, and user engagement. Through a combination of qualitative and quantitative analyses, the impact of these strategies on information access and user experiences within an English language context was assessed. By triangulating findings from diverse sources, this research endeavoured to offer actionable insights and recommendations to inform future endeavours in leveraging AI technologies to enrich library services.

AI-DRIVEN LANGUAGE ENHANCEMENT STRATEGIES

AI-driven language enhancement strategies in libraries represent a ground-breaking fusion of technology Loncar M., Schams W., Liang J. S. (2023) and information management, offering a diverse array of innovative techniques to enrich user experiences. At the forefront of these strategies are sophisticated applications Mogali, D. S. S. (2014) of Natural Language Processing (NLP), sentiment analysis, and machine translation.

NLP algorithms serve as the cornerstone of enhanced search functionalities, enabling systems to comprehend context, semantics, and user intent with remarkable precision. By deciphering the intricacies of human language, NLP significantly augments information retrieval processes, ensuring users receive more relevant and nuanced search results. This capability is particularly pronounced in academic libraries, where the implementation of NLP has revolutionized research discovery by facilitating access to a broader spectrum of scholarly resources.

Complementing NLP, sentiment analysis emerges as a pivotal tool for understanding user preferences and community interests. By analyzing language patterns and emotional cues, libraries can tailor their services and programs to align with the needs and preferences of their patrons. Public libraries, in particular, have harnessed sentiment analysis to gauge community sentiment and optimize offerings, fostering a more engaging and responsive library experience.

Furthermore, machine translation technologies play a transformative role in breaking down language barriers, democratizing access to English-language content for non-native speakers. Through advanced translation algorithms, libraries can transcend linguistic boundaries, thereby expanding their reach and inclusivity on a global scale.

However, the adoption of AI-driven language enhancement strategies Hepper, E. G., Gramzow, R. H., & Sedikides, C. (2010) is not without its challenges. Algorithmic biases, accuracy issues Olubiyo, P. O., & Awoyemi, R. A. (2021) in machine translation, and privacy concerns underscore the need for cautious implementation and ongoing refinement. Libraries must navigate these complexities with vigilance, prioritizing ethical considerations and user trust to ensure the responsible deployment of these technologies.

In spite of these challenges, the promise of AI-driven language enhancement strategies in empowering information access and enhancing user experiences remains undeniable. By leveraging the transformative potential of NLP, sentiment analysis, and machine translation, libraries can continue to evolve as dynamic hubs of knowledge and innovation in an increasingly interconnected world.

IMPACT ON INFORMATION ACCESS

The integration of AI-powered language enhancement strategies in library settings heralds a paradigm shift in information accessibility, ushering in a new era of refined search precision, linguistic comprehension, and user-centric experiences. At the heart of this transformation are advanced techniques such as Natural Language Processing (NLP), machine translation, and sentiment analysis, each contributing to the expansion and enrichment of library services in profound ways.

One of the most significant impacts of AI-powered language enhancement is its ability to elevate the precision and relevance of information retrieval. Through NLP algorithms, queries are deciphered with unprecedented subtlety, enabling systems to grasp context, semantics, and user intent with remarkable accuracy. Consequently, users benefit from more tailored search results, accessing pertinent resources with greater ease and efficiency. This refinement not only streamlines the research process but also fosters a deeper engagement with library collections, empowering users to explore topics with nuance and depth.

Furthermore, machine translation technologies play a pivotal role in broadening access to English-language materials for non-native speakers, thereby democratizing information and knowledge dissemination on a global scale. By seamlessly translating content into multiple languages, libraries can transcend linguistic barriers, ensuring that diverse communities have equitable access to the wealth of resources available. This inclusivity not only enriches the library experience but also fosters a more diverse and interconnected community of learners and researchers.

In addition to enhancing information accessibility, AI-driven language enhancement strategies also elevate user satisfaction and interaction with library services. Personalized suggestions, user-friendly interfaces, and enhanced usability features contribute to a more intuitive and engaging experience, catering to the unique preferences and needs of each individual user. Sentiment analysis further augments this personalization by enabling libraries to tailor their services and programs to align with user preferences, fostering a sense of inclusivity and relevance.

In contrast, conventional language enhancement methods often rely on manual processes and static resources, leading to limited scalability and efficacy. While these methods may still hold relevance in certain contexts, they typically lack the adaptability and responsiveness required to meet the evolving needs of users in today's digital landscape. AI-driven approaches, on the other hand, offer dynamic, data-centric solutions that continually evolve and improve over time, providing libraries with a more agile and effective means of enriching language access and enhancing user experiences.

In conclusion, the integration of AI-powered language enhancement strategies represents a transformative leap forward in the realm of information accessibility and user engagement in library settings. By harnessing the capabilities of NLP, machine translation, and sentiment analysis, libraries can unlock new opportunities for discovery, learning, and collaboration, ultimately empowering individuals and communities to thrive in an increasingly interconnected world.

ENHANCING USER EXPERIENCE

AI-driven language enhancement profoundly elevates user experience in libraries by offering personalized, accessible, and inclusive services. Through AI technologies, libraries can tailor recommendations and services based on individual preferences and behavior patterns, enhancing user satisfaction and engagement. Personalization ensures that users receive relevant content, thereby streamlining information retrieval and fostering a sense of connection with library resources. Moreover, AI-driven enhancements improve accessibility by breaking down language barriers, enabling users of diverse linguistic backgrounds to access English-language materials seamlessly. Machine translation and Natural Language Processing (NLP) algorithms play a pivotal role in this regard, enhancing the usability of library resources for non-native English speakers El Shazly, R. (2021).

Inclusivity is further promoted through AI-powered sentiment analysis, which allows libraries to gauge user sentiment and preferences. By understanding user feedback and sentiment, libraries can adapt their services to better meet the needs of their diverse user base, fostering a culture of inclusivity and responsiveness. User feedback and satisfaction metrics serve as valuable indicators of the effectiveness of AI-driven language enhancement strategies. By soliciting user input and monitoring satisfaction levels, libraries can iteratively improve their offerings, ensuring a continually enhanced user experience that empowers information access and fosters engagement within an English language context.

CHALLENGES AND CONSIDERATIONS

The integration of AI-driven language enhancement strategies in library Yu, K., Gong, R., Sun, L., & Jiang, C. (2019) contexts introduces a constellation of challenges that demand nuanced consideration. Foremost among these hurdles is the intricate technological landscape necessitated by the deployment and maintenance of AI systems. The intricacies of such systems demand specialized expertise and infrastructure, thus posing formidable barriers to implementation. Moreover, the intersection of AI with the realm of data privacy and security raises critical concerns regarding the ethical collection and utilization of user data to personalize services. Libraries must tread carefully to navigate these treacherous waters, ensuring that the benefits of AI-driven enhancements do not come at the expense of user privacy or trust.

A particularly thorny issue lurking within the depths of AI-driven language enhancement is the specter of algorithmic biases. Embedded within the very fabric of AI models Gozalo-Brizuela, R., & Garrido-Merchan, E. C. (2023), these biases have the potential to perpetuate or exacerbate existing inequalities, thereby engendering disparities in information access and user experiences. This insidious threat strikes at the heart of ethical considerations surrounding AI usage, compelling libraries to grapple with questions of transparency, accountability, and fairness in their deployment of such technologies.

To navigate this ethical quagmire and harness the transformative potential of AI-driven language enhancement, libraries must adopt a multifaceted approach. Central to this endeavor is the imperative of transparency – libraries must strive to elucidate the inner workings of AI technologies and the rationale underlying their utilization. Moreover, robust measures must be instituted to ensure accountability and fairness, thereby safeguarding against the pernicious influence of algorithmic biases. This necessitates the cultivation of a vigilant ethos of ongoing training and education among library staff, empowering them to wield AI technologies effectively and ethically.

Furthermore, collaboration emerges as a linchpin in the quest to address the ethical quandaries inherent in AI-driven language enhancement. By forging interdisciplinary partnerships with experts versed in the nuances of ethics, libraries can navigate the ethical labyrinth with greater acumen and insight. Together, these stakeholders can craft and implement robust data governance frameworks and transparency measures, thereby fostering an environment of trust and confidence among library users.

In sum, while the road to realizing the potential of AI-driven language enhancement in library settings Asemi, A., & Asemi, A. (2018) is fraught with challenges, it is also imbued with promise. By confronting these challenges head-on and embracing a principled approach to ethical decision-making, libraries can unlock new vistas of possibility, empowering information access and enriching user experiences within an English language context.

FUTURE DIRECTIONS

The horizon of AI-driven language enhancement beckons with tantalizing prospects, poised to reshape the landscape of libraries and information access in profound ways. As we peer into the future, the trajectory of innovation promises to usher in a new era of sophistication and efficacy in this realm.

Foremost among the prospects for advancement lies the continued refinement of Natural Language Processing (NLP) algorithms. Through concerted research and development efforts, we envisage the emergence of algorithms endowed with a deeper semantic understanding, transcending mere syntactic parsing to penetrate the intricacies of human language with unprecedented finesse. Such advancements hold the potential to revolutionize search accuracy and relevance, elevating the efficacy of information retrieval to unprecedented heights.

Similarly, the evolution of machine translation technologies stands poised to chart new frontiers in accessibility and inclusivity. Future iterations may boast enhanced capabilities for contextually nuanced translations, surpassing the limitations of literal interpretation to capture the subtleties of meaning with exquisite precision. This bodes well for non-native speakers, who stand to benefit from seamless access to English-language materials imbued with cultural nuance and contextual richness.

Moreover, the convergence of AI with emerging trends such as augmented reality and voice-based interfaces promises to imbue library Subaveerap, iyan A. (2023) experiences with a newfound sense of immersion and intuitiveness. By seamlessly integrating AI technologies into these modalities, libraries can transcend the constraints of traditional interfaces, fostering deeper engagement and interaction among users.

Yet, amid the promise of progress, we must remain vigilant in our scrutiny of ethical considerations and biases inherent in AI-driven language enhancement. Rigorous exploration and interrogation of these issues are imperative to ensure the responsible and equitable deployment of AI technologies, safeguarding against the perpetuation of existing inequalities.

In embracing these future directions, libraries and information professionals stand poised at the vanguard of innovation, primed to harness the transformative potential of AI-driven language enhancement. By seizing these opportunities, libraries can reaffirm their pivotal role as bastions of knowledge and enlightenment in the digital age, enriching information access and user experiences within the English language context and beyond.

CONCLUSION

In conclusion, the exploration of AI-driven language enhancement strategies illuminates their transformative impact on libraries and information access within an English language context. Key findings reveal that these strategies significantly improve information accessibility, user satisfaction, and inclusivity by leveraging technologies such as Natural Language Processing and machine translation. Challenges such as algorithmic biases and ethical considerations must be navigated, but proactive measures can mitigate these concerns. The implications for the field of library science are profound. AI-driven language enhancement represents a paradigm shift, enabling libraries to adapt and thrive in the digital age. By embracing these strategies, libraries can enhance their relevance, expand their reach, and foster more meaningful user interactions. Moreover, the ongoing advancements and innovations in AI hold promise for further elevating library services and user experiences.

In closing, the significance of AI-driven language enhancement strategies cannot be overstated. They empower libraries to fulfill their mission of providing equitable access to information, regardless of linguistic background, thereby enriching the lives of individuals and communities. As libraries continue to evolve, AI-driven language enhancement stands as a cornerstone of their commitment to empowering information access and user experiences in an English language context.

REFERENCES

Anis, M. (2023). Leveraging Artificial Intelligence for Inclusive English Language Teaching: Strategies And Implications For Learner Diversity. *Journal of Multidisciplinary Educational Research*, *12*(6).

Asemi, A., & Asemi, A. (2018). Artificial Intelligence (AI) Application in Library Systems in Iran: A Taxonomy Study. *Library Philosophy and Practice (e-journal)*. https://digitalcommons.unl.edu/libphilprac/1840

Barsha, S., & Munshi, S. A. (2024). Implementing artificial intelligence in library services: A review of current prospects and challenges of developing countries. *Library Hi Tech News*, *41*(1), 7–10. doi:10.1108/LHTN-07-2023-0126

El Shazly, R. (2021). Effects of artificial intelligence on English speaking anxiety and speaking performance: A case study. *Expert Systems: International Journal of Knowledge Engineering and Neural Networks*, *38*(3), e12667. doi:10.1111/exsy.12667

Eslit, E. R. (2023). Voyaging Beyond Chalkboards: Unleashing Tomorrow's Minds through AI-Driven Frontiers in Literature and Language Education. Academic Press.

Gozalo-Brizuela, R., & Garrido-Merchan, E. C. (2023). ChatGPT is not all you need. *A State of the Art Review of large Generative AI models* (arXiv:2301.04655). arXiv. http://arxiv.org/abs/2301.04655

Hepper, E. G., Gramzow, R. H., & Sedikides, C. (2010). Individual differences in self-enhancement and self-protection strategies: An integrative analysis. *Journal of Personality*, *78*(2), 781–814. doi:10.1111/j.1467-6494.2010.00633.x PMID:20433637

Hervieux, S., & Wheatley, A. (2021). Perceptions of artificial intelligence: A survey of academic librarians in Canada and the United States. *Journal of Academic Librarianship*, *47*(1), 102270. doi:10.1016/j.acalib.2020.102270

Jaillant, L., & Rees, A. (2023). Applying AI to digital archives: Trust, collaboration and shared professional ethics. *Digital Scholarship in the Humanities*, *38*(2), 571–585. doi:10.1093/llc/fqac073

Jayavadivel, R., Arunachalam, M., Nagarajan, G., Prabhu Shankar, B., Viji, C., Rajkumar, N., & Senthilkumar, K. R. (2024). Historical Overview of AI Adoption in Libraries. In K. Senthilkumar (Ed.), *AI-Assisted Library Reconstruction* (pp. 267–289). IGI Global. doi:10.4018/979-8-3693-2782-1.ch015

Kim, D. S. (2006, July). A study on introducing six sigma theory in the library for service competitiveness enhancement. In *Proceedings of the World Library and Information Congress: 72nd IFLA General Conference and Council, Seoul, Korea* (pp. 20-24). Academic Press.

Kumar, N., Antoniraj, S., Jayanthi, S., Mirdula, S., Selvaraj, S., Rajkumar, N., & Senthilkumar, K. R. (2024). Educational Technology and Libraries Supporting Online Learning. In K. Senthilkumar (Ed.), *AI-Assisted Library Reconstruction* (pp. 209–237). IGI Global. doi:10.4018/979-8-3693-2782-1.ch012

Lei, X., Fathi, J., Noorbakhsh, S., & Rahimi, M. (2022). The impact of mobile-assisted language learning on English as a foreign language learners' vocabulary learning attitudes and self-regulatory capacity. *Frontiers in Psychology*, *13*, 872922. doi:10.3389/fpsyg.2022.872922 PMID:35800918

Levine, G. S. (2004). Global simulation: A student-centered, task-based format for intermediate foreign language courses. *Foreign Language Annals*, *37*(1), 26–36. doi:10.1111/j.1944-9720.2004.tb02170.x

Liang, J. C., Hwang, G. J., Chen, M. R. A., & Darmawansah, D. (2021). Roles and research foci of artificial intelligence in language education: An integrated bibliographic analysis and systematic review approach. *Interactive Learning Environments*, *31*(7), 4270–4296. doi:10.1080/10494820.2021.1958348

Loncar, M., Schams, W., & Liang, J. S. (2023). Multiple technologies, multiple sources: Trends and analyses of the literature on technology-mediated feedback for L2 English writing published from 2015-2019. *Computer Assisted Language Learning*, *36*(4), 722–784. doi:10.1080/09588221.2021.1943452

Lund, B. D., & Wang, T. (2023). Chatting about ChatGPT: How may AI and GPT impact academia and libraries? *Library Hi Tech News*, *40*(3), 26–29. doi:10.1108/LHTN-01-2023-0009

Mogali, D. S. S. (2014). *Artificial Intelligence and its Applications in Libraries*. https://www.researchgate.net/publication/287878456

Moybeka, A. M., Syariatin, N., Tatipang, D. P., Mushthoza, D. A., Dewi, N. P. J. L., & Tineh, S. (2023). Artificial Intelligence and English Classroom: The Implications of AI Toward EFL Students' Motivation. *Edumaspul: Jurnal Pendidikan*, *7*(2), 2444–2454. doi:10.33487/edumaspul.v7i2.6669

Olubiyo, P. O., & Awoyemi, R. A. (2021). Automation of Academic Libraries in Nigeria: Issues and Practices. *Library Philosophy and Practice (e-journal), 5613*. https://digitalcommons.unl.edu/libphilprac/5613

Ostertag, E., Hendler, J., Diaz, R. P., & Braun, C. (1992). Computing similarity in a reuse library system: An AI-based approach. *ACM Transactions on Software Engineering and Methodology*, *1*(3), 205–228. doi:10.1145/131736.131739

Rajkumar, N., Tabassum, H., Muthulingam, S., Mohanraj, A., Viji, C., Kumar, N., & Senthilkumar, K. R. (2024). Anticipated Requirements and Expectations in the Digital Library. In K. Senthilkumar (Ed.), *AI-Assisted Library Reconstruction* (pp. 1–20). IGI Global. doi:10.4018/979-8-3693-2782-1.ch001

Richey, R. G. Jr, Chowdhury, S., Davis-Sramek, B., Giannakis, M., & Dwivedi, Y. K. (2023). Artificial intelligence in logistics and supply chain management: A primer and roadmap for research. *Journal of Business Logistics*, *44*(4), 532–549. doi:10.1111/jbl.12364

Rubin, V. L., Chen, Y., & Thorimbert, L. M. (2010). Artificially intelligent conversational agents in libraries. *Library Hi Tech*, *28*(4), 496–522. doi:10.1108/07378831011096196

Senthilkumar, K. (Ed.). (2024). *AI-Assisted Library Reconstruction*. IGI Global. doi:10.4018/979-8-3693-2782-1

Senthilkumar, K. R. (2024). Revolutionizing thrust manufacturing. In *Advances in computational intelligence and robotics book series* (pp. 80–93). doi:10.4018/979-8-3693-2615-2.ch005

Senthilkumar, K. R., Jagajeevan, R., & Sangeetha, S. (2024). Impact of AI on Library and Information Science in Higher Institutions in India: A Comprehensive Analysis of Technological Integration and Educational Implications. In K. Senthilkumar (Ed.), *AI-Assisted Library Reconstruction* (pp. 21–33). IGI Global. doi:10.4018/979-8-3693-2782-1.ch002

Silva, S. M. D. (1997). A Review of Expert Systems in Library and Information Science. *Malaysian Journal of Library and Information Science*, 2(2), 57–92.

Sisman-Ugur, S., & Kurubacak, G. (Eds.). (2019). *Handbook of Research on Learning in the Age of Transhumanism*. IGI Global. doi:10.4018/978-1-5225-8431-5

Sivaraj, P., Madhan, V., Mallika, V., & Senthilkumar, K. R. (2024). Enhancing Library Services Through Optimization Algorithms and Data Analytics: Enhancing Library Services Mathematical Model. In K. Senthilkumar (Ed.), *AI-Assisted Library Reconstruction* (pp. 290–306). IGI Global. doi:10.4018/979-8-3693-2782-1.ch016

Subaveerap, I. A. (2023). Application of Artificial Intelligence (AI) In Libraries and Its Impact on Library Operations Review. *Library Philosophy and Practice (e-journal). 7828.* https://digitalcommons.unl.edu/libphilprac/7828

Vidhate, S., Badgujar, A., Patil, N., & Pawar, R. (2019). *A Review on Library Automation Using Artificial Intelligence*. Academic Press.

Vijayakumar, S., & Sheshadri, K. N. (2019). Applications of Artificial Intelligence in Academic Libraries. *International Journal on Computer Science and Engineering*, 7.

Wei, L. (2023). Artificial intelligence in language instruction: Impact on English learning achievement, L2 motivation, and self-regulated learning. *Frontiers in Psychology*, 14, 1261955. doi:10.3389/fpsyg.2023.1261955 PMID:38023040

Yang, S., Kanan, T., & Fox, E. (2010). Digital library educational module development strategies and sustainable enhancement by the community. *Research and Advanced Technology for Digital Libraries: 14th European Conference, ECDL 2010, Glasgow, UK, September 6-10, 2010 Proceedings*, 14, 514–517.

Yi, Z. (2021). Research on intelligent service mode of digital library based on data intelligence. *4th International Conference on Advanced Electronic Materials, Computers and Software Engineering (AEMCSE)*, 942–945. 10.1109/AEMCSE51986.2021.00192

Yu, K., Gong, R., Sun, L., & Jiang, C. (2019). The Application of Artificial Intelligence in Smart Library. *Proceedings of the 2019 International Conference on Organizational Innovation*. 10.2991/icoi-19.2019.124

Chapter 19
A Study on Advanced Applications of Mathematics and AI in Library Science

S. Durga Devi
Sri Krishna Arts and Science College, India

R. Mohanapriya
Sri Krishna Adithya College of Arts and Science, India

N. Sarumathy
Sri Krishna Arts and Science College, India

ABSTRACT

In the rapidly evolving field of information management, libraries are actively embracing the transformative potential of mathematics and artificial intelligence (AI). This chapter explores how established mathematical frameworks, such as the vector space model, together with cutting-edge natural language processing (NLP) techniques, are fundamentally altering how libraries organize information, facilitate retrieval, and ultimately, enhance user experience. The research suggests a symbiotic relationship between these seemingly distinct disciplines. By combining the strengths of mathematical models and probabilistic AI algorithms, this study aims to illuminate paths toward a more efficient and user-centric library ecosystem. This convergence has the potential to reshape resource management, information retrieval, and ultimately, transform the information landscape for library patrons, empowering them to navigate the vast ocean of knowledge with greater ease and effectiveness.

1. INTRODUCTION

Library science is undergoing a profound transformation due to advancements in mathematics and AI. These technologies are being increasingly leveraged to address the challenges faced by libraries, such

DOI: 10.4018/979-8-3693-5593-0.ch019

as information organization, retrieval, and user engagement. This chapter explores the various ways in which mathematics and AI are being applied in library science, highlighting their benefits and potential future impact.

In the past, libraries relied heavily on manual processes for classification and cataloging, which were often time-consuming and prone to errors. Information retrieval was primarily based on keyword matching, which could be imprecise and lead to irrelevant search results. User engagement was limited to physical interactions with library staff and resources, with little personalization or customization. In contrast, modern library systems leverage mathematics and AI to automate and optimize these processes. Classification and cataloguing are now more efficient and accurate, thanks to mathematical models and machine learning algorithms that can analyse and categorize vast amounts of information. Information retrieval has been transformed by AI-powered search engines that use natural language processing to understand user queries and provide relevant results. Personalized recommendation systems use machine learning to suggest resources based on user preferences, improving user engagement and satisfaction.

Overall, the integration of mathematics and AI has revolutionized library science, making information more accessible, personalized, and efficient. As these technologies continue to evolve, the possibilities for their application in library science are endless, promising a future where libraries are more dynamic, user-centric, and impactful than ever before.

2. APPLICATIONS OF MATHEMATICS IN LIBRARY SCIENCE

2.1 Classification and Cataloging Systems

Classification and cataloging are essential functions of libraries, enabling users to locate resources efficiently. Mathematical models play a crucial role in creating and maintaining these systems, ensuring that information is organized in a structured and accessible manner.

(i)　Mathematical Models In Classification

Classifications systems, such as the Dewey Decimal Classification (DDC) or Library of Congress Classification (LCC), use mathematical models to assign unique identifiers to resources based on their subject matter. These identifiers, typically represented as numbers or alphanumeric codes, help libraries organize resources into categories and subcategories, making it easier for users to locate them.

Mathematical models are also used in faceted classification systems, which allow resources to be classified based on multiple criteria or facets. Faceted classification systems use mathematical relationships to link different facets and provide users with a flexible and intuitive way to browse library collections.

(ii)　Mathematical Models In Cataloging

Cataloging involves describing resources in a standardized format, typically using metadata standards such as MARC (Machine-Readable Cataloging) or Dublin Core (Kitchin, 2014). Mathematical models are used in cataloging to create consistent and structured descriptions of resources, making it easier for users to search and access them.

LSA is a mathematical technique used for dimensionality reduction and semantic analysis of text data. In cataloging, LSA can be applied to identify latent semantic relationships between bibliographic records by capturing the underlying structure of the catalogue based on co-occurrence patterns of terms. Mathematics, particularly singular value decomposition (SVD), is used to decompose the term-document matrix into lower-dimensional representations, facilitating clustering, categorization, and similarity analysis of catalogue records.

TF-IDF is a statistical measure used to evaluate the importance of a term in a document relative to a collection of documents. Mathematics is used to calculate the TF-IDF score for each term in a bibliographic record, where the term frequency (TF) measures how often a term appears in the record, and the inverse document frequency (IDF) measures how rare the term is across the entire catalogue. TF-IDF helps identify key terms and improve retrieval precision in cataloguing systems.

(iii) Automation And Optimization

Mathematical models are also used to automate and optimize classification and cataloging processes. For example, algorithms can be used to automatically assign classification numbers or keywords to resources based on their content, reducing the manual effort required by library staff.

Automation refers to the use of technology and algorithms to perform tasks with minimal human intervention. It streamlines repetitive processes, reduces errors, and frees up human resources for more complex and creative endeavours. In library science, automation is employed in tasks such as cataloging, circulation, interlibrary loan processing, and digitization of materials. For example, automated cataloging systems utilize machine learning algorithms to assign subject headings, classify materials, and generate metadata, speeding up the cataloging process and improving consistency (Larivière et al., 2015).

Optimization involves finding the best solution from a set of possible alternatives to achieve specific objectives. Mathematical optimization techniques are used to allocate resources efficiently, maximize benefits, minimize costs, and optimize decision-making processes. In library science, optimization is applied in areas such as collection management, space utilization, staffing, and service delivery. For instance, optimization models can help libraries determine the optimal mix of resources (e.g., books, journals, electronic resources) within budget constraints to meet user needs effectively. Additionally, optimization techniques are utilized in routing algorithms for book delivery, scheduling library programs and events, and optimizing search algorithms for information retrieval systems.

2.2. Information Retrieval and Indexing

Information retrieval (IR) is the process of retrieving relevant information from a collection of resources, such as books, articles, or digital documents. Indexing is the process of creating and maintaining indexes, which are organized lists of terms or keywords that point to the location of information within a collection. Mathematics plays a crucial role in both information retrieval and indexing systems, enabling libraries to provide users with relevant and accurate search results.

Documents are analysed to identify key features, such as text, metadata, and structural elements (e.g., titles, authors, abstracts, keywords). This analysis helps extract relevant information that can be used for indexing. Indexing terms, also known as keywords, descriptors, or subject headings, are selected to represent the content of documents. These terms may be chosen from controlled vocabularies, such as thesauri or subject heading lists, to ensure consistency and precision in indexing.

(i) Term Frequency-Inverse Document Frequency (TF-IDF)

TF-IDF is a mathematical formula used to evaluate the importance of a term within a document relative to a collection of documents. It is commonly used in information retrieval systems to rank documents based on their relevance to a user's query. The TF-IDF score of a term is calculated based on its frequency in the document (TF) and its rarity in the collection (IDF). Documents with higher TF-IDF scores are considered more relevant to the query.

(ii) Vector Space Model

The vector space model is a mathematical model used in information retrieval to represent documents and queries as vectors in a multi-dimensional space (Leskovec et al., 2014). In this model, each dimension corresponds to a term, and the value of each dimension represents the weight of the term in the document or query. Similarity between documents and queries can be calculated using various techniques, such as cosine similarity, which measures the cosine of the angle between the document and query vectors.

(iii) Probabilistic Retrieval Models

Probabilistic retrieval models use probabilistic methods to rank documents based on their relevance to a query. These models consider not only the presence of query terms in documents but also the probability of relevance given the presence or absence of terms. Examples of probabilistic retrieval models include the Binary Independence Model (BIM) and the Okapi BM25 algorithm. These models operate on the principle of probabilistic interpretation, aiming to estimate the probability that a document is relevant to a given query.

Unlike deterministic models that provide binary relevance judgments, probabilistic retrieval models offer a more nuanced approach, allowing for a probabilistic assessment of document relevance. This

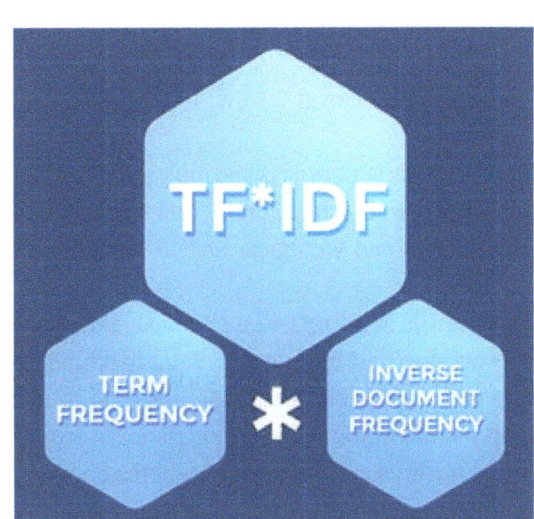

Figure 1. Vector space model

Figure 2. Probabilistic retrieval models

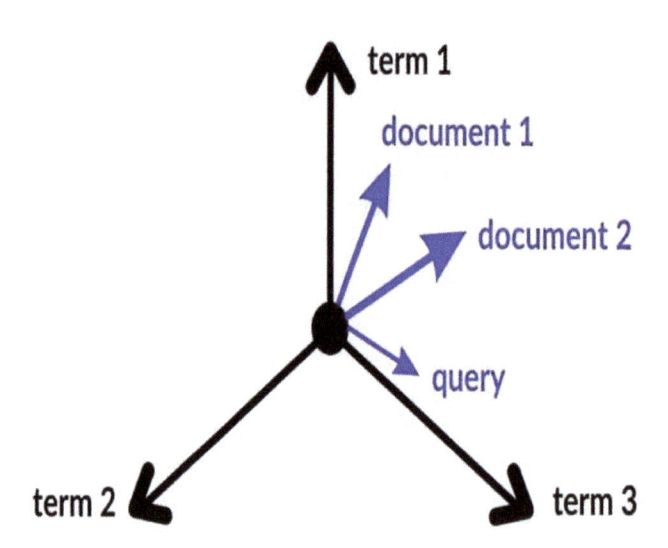

probabilistic framework is essential for handling the inherent uncertainty in information retrieval tasks and provides users with ranked lists of documents, ordered by their estimated likelihood of relevance.

At the core of probabilistic retrieval models lie various techniques for quantifying the relevance of documents to queries. Term weighting is a fundamental aspect of these models, where the importance of terms in documents and queries is assessed based on their frequency and distribution. The TF-IDF (Term Frequency-Inverse Document Frequency) scheme is a commonly used method for term weighting, assigning higher weights to terms that are frequent in a document but relatively rare across the entire document collection.

Document length normalization is another critical aspect of probabilistic retrieval models. It addresses biases towards longer documents by scaling the term weights based on the document's length, ensuring fair comparisons between documents of different lengths. This normalization helps prevent longer documents from dominating the ranking solely due to their length and ensures that relevance judgments are based on the content rather than the document's size.

(iv) Machine Learning In Information Retrieval

Machine learning techniques, such as supervised learning and deep learning, are increasingly being used in information retrieval to improve search accuracy and relevance. These techniques can be used to learn patterns from user interactions and feedback, and to personalize search results based on user preferences and behaviour.

Machine learning plays a pivotal role in information retrieval, enhancing the efficiency and effectiveness of retrieval systems. By leveraging vast amounts of data, machine learning algorithms can extract patterns and relationships between queries and documents, leading to more accurate relevance predictions. Techniques such as supervised learning, where models learn from labelled examples of relevant and non-relevant documents, and unsupervised learning, where models infer patterns from unlabelled data, are commonly applied in information retrieval.

A Study on Advanced Applications of Mathematics and AI

Supervised learning algorithms (Provost & Fawcett, 2013), such as support vector machines (SVMs) and logistic regression, are used to train classifiers that can automatically categorize documents as relevant or non-relevant to a given query. These classifiers learn from labelled training data and use features extracted from documents and queries to make predictions about their relevance. Supervised learning is particularly effective when there is ample labelled data available for training.

Unsupervised learning algorithms, such as clustering and topic modelling, are used to discover latent structures and relationships within document collections. These algorithms can group similar documents together based on their content or identify underlying topics present in the data. Unsupervised learning techniques are valuable for tasks such as document clustering, where documents are grouped into clusters based on their similarity, or for generating document representations that capture the underlying semantic structure of the data.

Machine learning techniques are also used in conjunction with traditional retrieval models, such as probabilistic retrieval models and vector space models, to enhance their performance. For example, machine learning algorithms can be used to learn document embedding's or query representations that capture semantic similarity between documents and queries, improving the accuracy of relevance ranking.

2.3. Data Analysis for User Behaviour and Collection Management

Data analysis plays a crucial role in helping libraries understand user behaviour and preferences, allowing them to optimize their collections and services to better meet user needs. Mathematical techniques, such as data mining and statistical analysis, are commonly used to analyse library data and derive actionable insights.

(i) Data Collection and Pre-processing

Before analysis can begin, libraries must collect and pre-process data from various sources, such as circulation records, search logs, and user surveys. Data pre-processing involves cleaning and transforming the data into a format suitable for analysis, which may include removing duplicates, standardizing formats, and handling missing values.

(ii) Data Mining for Pattern Discovery

Data mining techniques, such as clustering, association rule mining, and classification, are used to discover patterns and relationships in library data. For example, clustering algorithms can group similar users or items together based on their behaviour, helping libraries identify user segments with specific needs or preferences. In business, data mining enables organizations to gain a deeper understanding of their customers, market trends, and operational processes. By segmenting customers based on their purchasing behaviour or preferences, businesses can tailor marketing strategies and enhance customer experiences. Moreover, data mining plays a pivotal role in fraud detection, risk assessment, and anomaly detection, particularly in industries such as finance and healthcare where detecting irregularities is critical.

With the advent of advanced algorithms and machine learning techniques, data mining continues to evolve, enabling the analysis of increasingly complex datasets. From predictive maintenance in manufacturing to personalized recommendations in e-commerce, the applications of data mining are vast and

Figure 3. Data preprocessing

diverse. Ultimately, by harnessing the power of data mining, organizations can gain a competitive edge, drive innovation, and uncover new opportunities for growth in today's data-driven world.

(iii) Statistical Analysis for Decision Making

Statistical analysis is used to summarize and interpret library data, providing libraries with valuable insights for decision making. For example, libraries can use statistical techniques, such as regression analysis or hypothesis testing, to analyse the impact of collection changes or service improvements on user behaviour.

Statistical analysis aids in market research, forecasting demand, and optimizing operations. Whether it's evaluating the effectiveness of marketing campaigns or determining the factors influencing customer satisfaction, statistical techniques offer valuable insights for strategic planning and resource allocation. In healthcare, statistical analysis informs clinical trials, patient outcomes, and public health policies, guiding medical practitioners and policymakers towards evidence-based decisions.

Moreover, statistical analysis underpins decision-making in fields like finance, engineering, and social sciences, guiding investment strategies, product development, and policy formulation. With the advent of big data and advanced analytics, statistical methods continue to evolve, enabling the exploration of increasingly complex datasets and the extraction of actionable insights.

(iv) Predictive Analytics for Forecasting

Predictive analytics uses historical data to predict future outcomes, such as future user behaviour or collection usage. Libraries can use predictive analytics to forecast demand for specific resources, enabling them to better allocate their collections and resources. Predictive analytics revolutionizes forecasting by leveraging historical data and advanced statistical algorithms to predict future outcomes. By analysing patterns, correlations, and trends within vast datasets, it provides valuable insights into potential future events, behaviours, and market trends. This proactive approach empowers organizations to anticipate demand fluctuations, optimize resource allocation, and mitigate risks effectively.

Predictive analytics facilitates sales forecasting, inventory management, and customer segmentation, enabling companies to make informed decisions and stay ahead of the competition. By identifying patterns in customer behaviour and market trends, businesses can tailor marketing strategies, optimize pricing, and enhance customer experiences, ultimately driving revenue growth and profitability.

Moreover, predictive analytics finds applications in various industries such as finance, healthcare, and manufacturing. In finance, it aids in credit scoring, fraud detection, and investment analysis, while in healthcare, it assists in disease prediction, patient outcomes, and resource planning. In manufacturing, predictive analytics optimizes production processes, reduces downtime, and improves quality control.

(v) Personalization and Recommendation Systems

Data analysis is also used to personalize user experiences and improve recommendation systems in libraries. By analysing user behaviour and preferences, libraries can recommend relevant resources to users, increasing engagement and satisfaction. These systems analyse user data, such as past interactions, purchase history, and demographic information, to generate personalized recommendations for products, services, or content.

By leveraging techniques like collaborative filtering, content-based filtering, and machine learning algorithms, personalization and recommendation systems can predict user preferences and anticipate their needs accurately.

Ultimately, personalization and recommendation systems play a pivotal role in delivering relevant and compelling experiences to users, driving user retention, loyalty, and ultimately, business growth.

3. APPLICATIONS OF ARTIFICIAL INTELLIGENCE IN LIBRARY SCIENCE

3.1 Natural Language Processing for Improved Search and Discovery

Natural Language Processing (Van De Sompel et al., 2004) is a branch of artificial intelligence that focuses on the interaction between computers and human language. In the context of libraries, NLP algorithms are used to enhance search and discovery capabilities, enabling users to find information more efficiently and effectively.

(i) Text Processing and Analysis

NLP algorithms are used to process and analyse text data, including books, articles, and other textual resources in a library's collection. These algorithms can extract key information from texts, such as keywords, entities, and concepts, to improve search accuracy and relevance. Techniques like sentiment analysis, named entity recognition, and semantic understanding enhance search engines, offering more precise results and personalized recommendations. NLP enables systems to grasp context, improving user experience and efficiency in information retrieval. It facilitates understanding of user intent, enabling search engines to deliver tailored content, boosting engagement and satisfaction. Additionally, NLP powers advanced features such as voice search and conversational interfaces, further enhancing the accessibility and usability of search and discovery platforms.

(ii)   Semantic Search

Semantic search is an NLP-powered search technique that focuses on the meaning of words and phrases, rather than just matching keywords. This allows users to find information based on the context of their query, leading to more relevant search results.

By understanding the semantics of queries and documents, semantic has four following types each aiming to improve information retrieval by understanding the meaning and context of user queries.

(iii)   Language Understanding and Query Expansion

NLP algorithms can understand user queries in natural language and expand them to include synonyms, related terms, and concepts. This helps users find information even if they are not familiar with the exact terminology used in the library's catalogue or collection. Organizations leverage text processing to automate handling of large volumes of data, enabling efficient information extraction. Analysis techniques reveal valuable insights into customer feedback, market trends, and user behaviours, aiding decision-making processes. By understanding sentiments and themes within text, businesses can tailor strategies for improved customer experiences and targeted marketing campaigns. Text processing and analysis thus play a crucial role in deriving actionable insights from unstructured textual data across various domains.

(iv)   Sentiment Analysis

Figure 4. Semantic search factors

Sentiment analysis is a NLP technique used to analyse the sentiment or emotion expressed in a piece of text. In the context of libraries, sentiment analysis can be used to understand user feedback and reviews, helping libraries improve their services and collections.

(v) Chabot's And Virtual Assistants

NLP algorithms power chabot's and virtual assistants that can interact with users in natural language. These assistants can help users find information, answer questions, and provide personalized recommendations, enhancing the overall user experience. It identifies keywords, entities, and user preferences, facilitating more precise search queries. Query expansion complements this process by broadening or refining queries with synonyms, related terms, or contextually relevant terms. By incorporating synonyms and related concepts, query expansion improves the recall and precision of search results, ensuring users receive comprehensive and accurate information. This iterative process refines search queries, adapting to user needs and preferences, thereby enhancing the effectiveness of information retrieval systems across various domains. Ultimately, language understanding and query expansion work in tandem to deliver more relevant and personalized search experiences, enriching user satisfaction and engagement with information retrieval platforms.

(vi) Multilingual Support

NLP algorithms can also support multiple languages, allowing libraries to serve users from diverse linguistic backgrounds. This enables users to search for and access information in their preferred language, making library resources more accessible and inclusive.

3.2 Machine Learning for Recommendation Systems

Machine learning (ML) algorithms are increasingly being used to create personalized recommendation systems in libraries. These systems analyse user preferences and behaviour to suggest relevant books, articles, or other resources, enhancing the overall user experience.

Figure 5. Sentiment analysis

(i) Collaborative Filtering

Collaborative filtering is a popular ML technique used in recommendation systems. It analyses user interactions with items (e.g., books borrowed, articles read) to identify patterns and similarities between users. Based on these patterns, the system can recommend items that similar users have liked or interacted with. By analysing past interactions, such as ratings or purchases, collaborative filtering identifies patterns and recommends items that others with similar tastes have liked. It operates on the principle of "wisdom of the crowd," leveraging collective opinions to make personalized suggestions. This approach does not require explicit knowledge about items or users; instead, it relies on the collective behaviour of the community to generate recommendations.

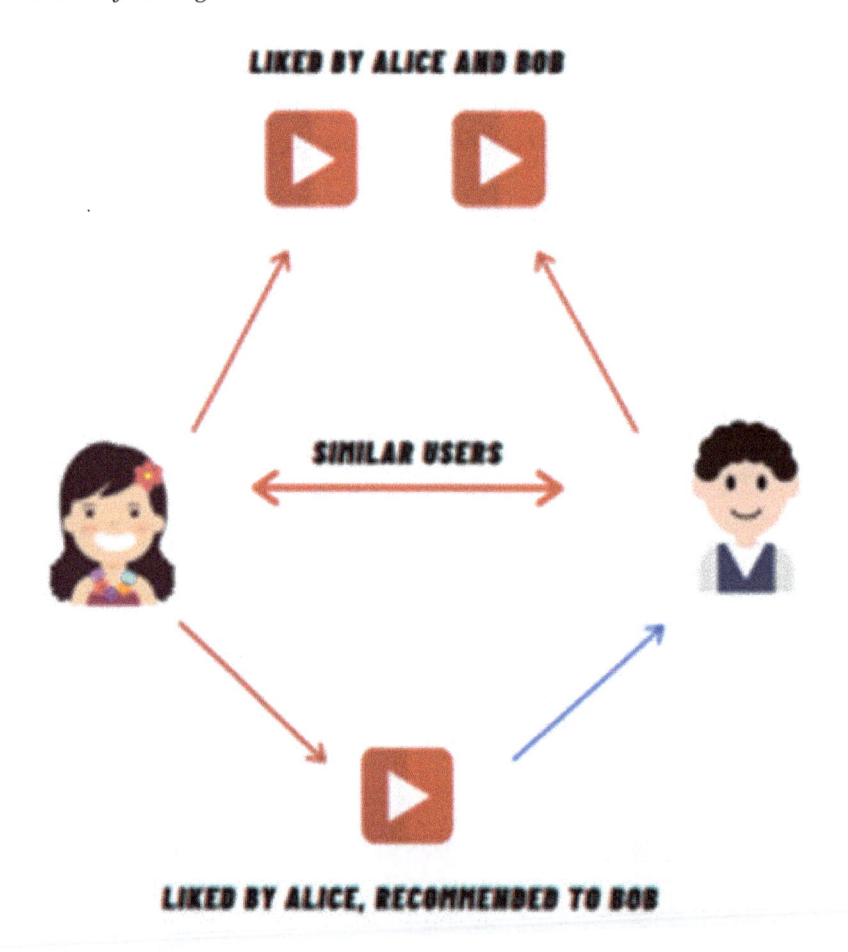

(ii) Content-Based Filtering

Content-based filtering recommends items based on their attributes and the user's preferences. For example, if a user has shown a preference for mystery novels, the system might recommend other mystery novels with similar themes or authors.

Figure 6. Collaborative filtering

A Study on Advanced Applications of Mathematics and AI

Figure 7. Content-based filtering

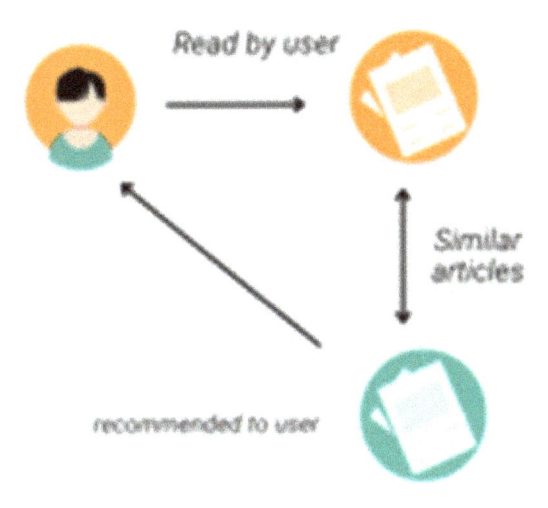

(vi) Hybrid Approaches

Hybrid approaches combine collaborative filtering and content-based filtering to provide more accurate and diverse recommendations (Senthilkumar, Kumar, Antoniraj et al, 2024). By leveraging both user interactions and item attributes, hybrid approaches can overcome some of the limitations of individual.

By leveraging methods like collaborative filtering, content-based filtering, and sometimes knowledge-based or demographic-based approaches, hybrid systems aim to overcome the limitations of individual methods. For instance, they might use collaborative filtering to identify similar users and content-based filtering to recommend items based on their attributes. This blend allows hybrid systems to offer more personalized recommendations, catering to a wider range of user preferences and contexts.

By incorporating multiple strategies, they can adapt to different scenarios and user behaviours, improving the overall effectiveness of recommendation systems. Hybrid approaches are widely adopted across domains such as e-commerce, streaming services, and content platforms, where providing relevant and personalized recommendations is crucial for enhancing user satisfaction and engagement.

(vi) Matrix Factorization Techniques

Matrix factorization techniques, such as Singular Value Decomposition (SVD) and Alternating Least Squares (6), are used to decompose large matrices of user-item interactions into lower-dimensional representations. These techniques can capture latent factors that influence user preferences, improving the quality of recommendations.

Matrix factorization techniques are pivotal in recommendation systems, aiming to reveal latent features inherent in user-item interactions. These methods decompose the user-item interaction matrix into lower-dimensional matrices, representing users and items in a latent space. Singular Value Decomposition (SVD) is a prominent technique, breaking down the matrix into three matrices: a user matrix, an item matrix, and a diagonal matrix for singular values.

Another widely used method is Alternating Least Squares (ALS), which iteratively updates user and item matrices to minimize reconstruction error. These techniques uncover hidden patterns and preferences within the data, enabling recommendation systems to make accurate predictions, especially in sparse datasets. Matrix factorization is fundamental to collaborative filtering algorithms, facilitating personalized and effective recommendations across diverse domains, including e-commerce, content streaming, and social media platforms, ultimately enhancing user satisfaction and engagement with the system.

(vi) Neutral Networks for Recommendation Systems

Deep learning techniques, such as neural networks, are being increasingly used in recommendation systems. These techniques can learn complex patterns and relationships in user behaviour and item attributes, leading to more accurate and personalized recommendations.

Neural networks have emerged as powerful tools in recommendation systems, leveraging deep learning architectures to analyse vast user-item interaction data. By employing techniques like collaborative filtering and content-based filtering, neural networks generate personalized recommendations tailored to individual user preferences and item attributes. They can also integrate various data types, including textual, visual, and sequential data, enabling more comprehensive recommendation approaches. Continuously learning from user feedback and adapting to evolving preferences, neural network-based recommendation systems deliver highly tailored recommendations, enhancing user satisfaction and engagement.

Moreover, advancements in neural network architectures, such as convolutional neural networks (CNNs) and recurrent neural networks (RNNs), further improve the performance and adaptability of recommendation systems across a wide range of domains, from e-commerce to content streaming platforms, ultimately enhancing the user experience and increasing business efficiency (Senthilkumar, Sivaraj, Madhan et al, 2024).

(vi) Evaluation And Optimization

Recommendation systems are evaluated based on metrics such as precision, recall, and F1 score. ML algorithms are continuously optimized based on these metrics to improve the quality of recommendations over time. Evaluation and optimization are vital processes in ensuring the effectiveness and efficiency of recommendation systems. Evaluation involves assessing the quality of recommendations using metrics like precision, recall, and ranking metrics such as Mean Average Precision (MAP) or Normalized Discounted Cumulative Gain (NDCG). It provides insights into the system's performance and helps identify areas for improvement.

Optimization focuses on enhancing the system's performance by fine-tuning algorithms, parameters, and data pre-processing techniques. Techniques like hyper parameter tuning, algorithm selection, and feature engineering are commonly employed to optimize recommendation systems. Additionally, A/B testing and online evaluation methods enable real-time testing and refinement of recommendation algorithms in live environments.

By continuously evaluating and optimizing recommendation systems, organizations can ensure that they deliver accurate, relevant, and personalized recommendations, thereby enhancing user satisfaction, engagement, and ultimately, the success of the system.

3.2 Automation of Routine Tasks

AI technologies are revolutionizing library operations by automating routine tasks that were once time-consuming and labor – intensive. This automation frees up library staff to focus on more complex activities, ultimately improving efficiency and enhancing user experiences.

The automation of routine tasks involves utilizing technology to streamline and execute repetitive activities with minimal human involvement. By leveraging tools such as software automation, robotic process automation (RPA), and artificial intelligence (AI), organizations can optimize efficiency, minimize errors, and allocate human resources to higher-value tasks. Automation spans various operations, from data entry and email management to complex processes like financial reporting and customer service. Not only does automation boost productivity, but it also enables scalability and agility, allowing businesses to adapt quickly to changing market dynamics.

Moreover, automation enhances consistency and compliance by ensuring tasks are executed uniformly according to predefined rules and standards. Ultimately, the automation of routine tasks empowers organizations to focus on innovation and strategic initiatives, driving growth and competitiveness in today's dynamic business landscape.

(i) Metadata Tagging

Metadata tagging involves assigning descriptive metadata, such as keywords, subjects, and authors, to library resources. AI technologies, such as natural language processing (NLP) and machine learning (ML), can automate this process by analysing the content of resources and automatically generating relevant metadata tags (Senthilkumar, Senthilkumar, Jagajeevan et al, 2024). This automation not only saves time but also ensures consistency and accuracy in metadata tagging.

This process entails adding relevant keywords, categories, and other identifiers to the content, providing context and meaning to the data. Metadata tags can include information such as title, author, date, subject, and keywords, depending on the specific needs of the organization or system. By tagging content with metadata, organizations can improve search ability, enhance navigation, and enable more accurate content recommendations.

Automated tagging tools, natural language processing (NLP), and machine learning algorithms are often used to assist in the metadata tagging process, streamlining the task and ensuring consistency. Metadata tagging is essential for effective content management, enabling users to find and access the right information quickly and efficiently across various platforms and systems.

(vi) Content Categorization

AI technologies can also automate the categorization of library resources into subject categories or genres. By analysing the content and context of resources, AI algorithms can categorize them accurately, making it easier for users to discover relevant resources. It's vital for managing large volumes of information efficiently and enabling users to find relevant content quickly.

Techniques such as natural language processing (NLP), machine learning, and manual tagging are utilized for automated or human-assisted categorization. Content categorization benefits various applications, including search engines, content management systems, and recommendation systems.

It enhances content discoverability, improves user experience, and facilitates targeted content delivery. Accurate categorization allows organizations to gain insights into their content inventory, optimize content distribution strategies, and tailor content recommendations to user preferences effectively. Overall, content categorization plays a crucial role in information organization and retrieval, ensuring that users can access the right content at the right time, thereby enhancing productivity and satisfaction.

(vi) Collection Management

AI technologies can assist in collection management by analysing usage patterns and recommending additions or removals to the collection. For example, algorithms can identify underutilized resources that may be candidates for removal or suggest new acquisitions based on user demand and trends.

It encompasses activities such as acquisition, cataloguing, preservation, and disposal, all aimed at ensuring the relevance, accessibility, and quality of collections over time. Collection managers utilize various techniques and technologies, including cataloguing systems, inventory management software, and preservation methods, to efficiently oversee collections. The primary objectives of collection management are to meet user needs, preserve cultural heritage or knowledge, and maximize the value of collections to stakeholders. By implementing effective collection management practices, organizations can optimize resource allocation, enhance user experiences, and contribute to the long-term sustainability and impact of their collections within libraries, museums, archives, and other institutions.

(vi) Virtual Reference Services

AI-powered chatbots and virtual assistants can automate virtual reference services, providing users with quick and accurate answers to their queries (Senthilkumar, 2024b). These chatbots can handle routine inquiries, such as library hours or resource availability, freeing up library staff to focus on more complex reference questions.

(vi) Preservation And Conservation

AI technologies can assist in the preservation and conservation of library materials by analysing environmental conditions and recommending measures to prevent deterioration. For example, algorithms can monitor temperature and humidity levels in storage areas and alert staff to potential issues.

Preservation and conservation are essential practices aimed at safeguarding cultural heritage, natural resources, and valuable assets for future generations. Preservation involves protecting and maintaining objects, documents, or ecosystems to prevent deterioration or loss due to environmental factors, aging, or human activity. Conservation focuses on actively managing and restoring resources to sustainably balance human needs with environmental protection. Both preservation and conservation efforts often involve research, documentation, monitoring, and collaboration among various stakeholders, including governments, organizations, and communities.

Techniques such as archival storage, digitization, habitat restoration, and sustainable resource management are employed to ensure the long-term viability and accessibility of valuable assets. By prioritizing preservation and conservation, societies can safeguard biodiversity, cultural diversity, and historical knowledge, fostering sustainability, resilience, and a legacy for future generations to cherish and enjoy.

(vi) Accessibility Services

AI technologies can improve accessibility services in libraries by automating the conversion of text to alternative formats, such as braille or audio. By automating these processes, libraries can ensure that their resources are accessible to users with disabilities.

These services span various domains, including technology, infrastructure, education, employment, and public accommodations. In the digital realm, accessibility services involve designing websites, applications, and software with features like screen readers, alternative text for images, keyboard navigation, and colour contrast adjustments to accommodate users with visual impairments, motor disabilities, or other challenges. In physical spaces, accessibility services may include ramps, elevators, braille signage, and wider doorways to enable wheelchair users and those with mobility impairments to navigate buildings independently. Educational institutions and workplaces provide accommodations such as assistive technologies, note-taking services, and flexible scheduling to support students and employees with disabilities in achieving their full potential. Overall, accessibility services play a crucial role in promoting inclusivity and removing barriers to participation in society for individuals with disabilities.

Figure 8. Accessibility services

CONCLUSION

The integration of mathematics and artificial intelligence has revolutionized library science, transforming information access and user experiences. Libraries now organize vast information more efficiently, aided by AI-powered classification and cataloguing systems. Natural language processing algorithms enhance search and discovery, while machine learning enables personalized recommendations. Automation of tasks like metadata tagging frees staff for more complex work. As these technologies evolve, libraries will become even more efficient, user-friendly, and impactful, securing their relevance in the digital age.

REFERENCES

Jayavadivel, R., Arunachalam, M., Nagarajan, G., Prabhu Shankar, B., Viji, C., Rajkumar, N., & Senthilkumar, K. R. (2024). Historical Overview of AI Adoption in Libraries. In K. Senthilkumar (Ed.), *AI-Assisted Library Reconstruction* (pp. 267–289). IGI Global. doi:10.4018/979-8-3693-2782-1.ch015

Kitchin, R. (2014). Big data, new epistemologies and paradigm shifts. *Big Data & Society*, *1*(1). doi:10.1177/2053951714528481

Kumar, N., Antoniraj, S., Jayanthi, S., Mirdula, S., Selvaraj, S., Rajkumar, N., & Senthilkumar, K. R. (2024). Educational Technology and Libraries Supporting Online Learning. In K. Senthilkumar (Ed.), *AI-Assisted Library Reconstruction* (pp. 209–237). IGI Global. doi:10.4018/979-8-3693-2782-1.ch012

Larivière, V., Haustein, S., & Mongeon, P. (2015). The oligopoly of academic publishers in the digital era. *PLoS One*, *10*(6), e0127502. doi:10.1371/journal.pone.0127502 PMID:26061978

Leskovec, J., Rajaraman, A., & Ullman, J. D. (2014). *Mining of massive datasets*. Cambridge University Press. doi:10.1017/CBO9781139924801

Provost, F., & Fawcett, T. (2013). *Data science for business: What you need to know about data mining and data-analytic thinking*. O'Reilly Media, Inc.

Rajkumar, N., Tabassum, H., Muthulingam, S., Mohanraj, A., Viji, C., Kumar, N., & Senthilkumar, K. R. (2024). Anticipated Requirements and Expectations in the Digital Library. In K. Senthilkumar (Ed.), *AI-Assisted Library Reconstruction* (pp. 1–20). IGI Global. doi:10.4018/979-8-3693-2782-1.ch001

Senthilkumar, K. (Ed.). (2024a). *AI-Assisted Library Reconstruction*. IGI Global. doi:10.4018/979-8-3693-2782-1

Senthilkumar, K. R. (2024b). Revolutionizing thrust manufacturing. In *Advances in computational intelligence and robotics book series* (pp. 80–93). doi:10.4018/979-8-3693-2615-2.ch005

Senthilkumar, K. R., Jagajeevan, R., & Sangeetha, S. (2024). Impact of AI on Library and Information Science in Higher Institutions in India: A Comprehensive Analysis of Technological Integration and Educational Implications. In K. Senthilkumar (Ed.), *AI-Assisted Library Reconstruction* (pp. 21–33). IGI Global. doi:10.4018/979-8-3693-2782-1.ch002

Sivaraj, P., Madhan, V., Mallika, V., & Senthilkumar, K. R. (2024). Enhancing Library Services Through Optimization Algorithms and Data Analytics: Enhancing Library Services Mathematical Model. In K. Senthilkumar (Ed.), *AI-Assisted Library Reconstruction* (pp. 290–306). IGI Global. doi:10.4018/979-8-3693-2782-1.ch016

Van De Sompel, H., Nelson, M. L., Sanderson, R., Balakireva, L. L., Shankar, H., & Meehan, M. (2004). Analyzing the persistence of references in web resources. *D-Lib Magazine : the Magazine of the Digital Library Forum*, *10*(9).

Chapter 20
AI-Driven Libraries:
Pioneering Innovation in Digital Knowledge Access

K. C. Anandraj
https://orcid.org/0009-0008-3864-7498
Madurai Kamaraj University, India

S. Aravind
https://orcid.org/0000-0002-6376-8901
G.T.N. Arts College (Autonomous), India

ABSTRACT

In today's digital age, libraries are undergoing a profound transformation fueled by advancements in artificial intelligence (AI) technology. AI-driven libraries are pioneering innovative solutions to address the evolving needs of users, revolutionizing the way digital knowledge is accessed and utilized. This chapter explores the transformative potential of AI-driven libraries and their role in pioneering innovation in digital knowledge access. Through a comprehensive review of literature, case studies, and real-world implementations, this chapter examines various AI applications in libraries, including advanced search and discovery tools, virtual assistants, content recommendation systems, data analytics, and digital preservation. By highlighting best practices, challenges, and emerging trends, this chapter aims to provide insights into the transformative impact of AI-driven libraries on information management and access.

1. INTRODUCTION

Libraries play a crucial role in connecting people with knowledge in the fast-changing digital world we live in. Over time, libraries have evolved from being simple book storage facilities to becoming vibrant centres of information, serving the varied requirements of users in an ever more digitalized society. In the era of digital technology, libraries must adjust and come up with new ideas to stay important and available to users, considering the progress of technology and the evolving expectations of users. An essential aspect of this adaptation involves the incorporation of artificial intelligence

DOI: 10.4018/979-8-3693-5593-0.ch020

(AI) technology, which holds the potential to completely transform the operations and interactions of libraries with their users. AI-powered libraries signify a fundamental change in how information is managed and accessed. They utilize sophisticated algorithms and machine learning methods to improve the efficiency, efficacy, and user experience of library services. AI has the ability to revolutionize the library experience by simplifying search and discovery, offering personalized suggestions, and providing virtual support. This technology empowers users to efficiently explore and utilize digital resources with exceptional ease.

The AI-driven library revolution is cantered around the goal of advancing digital knowledge access through innovation. Libraries may leverage AI technologies, including natural language processing, data analytics, and cognitive computing, to provide users with unprecedented opportunities to explore, find, and interact with digital information. AI-driven libraries are using intelligent search algorithms, virtual assistants, and data-driven insights to meet the changing needs and expectations of users in the digital age.

In this chapter, the authors thoroughly examine the capacity of AI-driven libraries to revolutionize digital knowledge access and foster innovation. This study aims to comprehensively analyze the various effects of artificial intelligence (AI) on library services and its potential consequences for the future of information management and access. The analysis will be conducted through an extensive web-based literature review. This analysis explores various AI applications in libraries, such as advanced search and discovery, virtual assistants, content recommendation systems, data analytics, translation services, data sharing, content management services, knowledge management, streamlining operations, and digital preservation. It aims to provide a detailed understanding of the opportunities, challenges, and emerging trends that are influencing the development of AI-driven libraries. This chapter aims to contribute to the ongoing discussion about AI-driven innovation in libraries. It provides insights and perspectives that can help libraries make strategic decisions, inspire future research, and ultimately empower them to fulfil their mission of facilitating access to knowledge and information in the digital age.

2. REVIEW OF LITERATURE

P. Vasishta et al.(2024) research aims to analyze the current landscape of Artificial Intelligence (AI) applications in libraries. This study investigates document types, publication years, keywords, countries, and research methods employed. The overarching goal is to enhance understanding of AI-powered libraries, identify research gaps, guide future studies, and inform policy development effectively. Subaveerapandiyan & Gozali (2024) Investigates Indian library professionals' perspectives on AI use in libraries. It employs a quantitative approach, surveying 386 professionals from academic institutions in India. Findings suggest awareness of AI benefits in enhancing library activities and accessibility, though concerns exist regarding AI replacing human intelligence. Factors like user privacy, funding, and ethical considerations are crucial in AI implementation. Already, technologies like smart shelving and optical character recognition are being adopted in Indian libraries. Moustapha, A., & Yusuf, B. (2023) studied the Artificial intelligence adoption and utilization by librarians in university libraries in Kwara State, Nigeria.The study explored AI adoption among librarians in university libraries in Kwara State, Nigeria, utilizing a descriptive survey method with 450 randomly selected librarians. Findings revealed minimal AI integration, mostly confined to security scanning devices. Adoption hurdles encompassed service disruption, skill gaps, power instability, and insufficient infrastructure. Recommendations emphasized librarian training and institutional backing to facilitate AI implementation. A, Subaveerapandiyan (2023) The article presents a comprehensive literature review on the application of Artificial Intelligence (AI) in libraries and its impact on library operations. The study aims to furnish researchers with a thorough understanding of AI in the library context. The research methodology involved utilizing the Scopus database to identify 66 relevant articles related to AI. Wheatley, A., & Hervieux, S. (2020). In their study, the authors reviewed scholarly articles, university libraries' strategic plans, and library programming to ascertain any references to AI and their contexts. Focusing on top research universities in the United States and Canada, the primary objective was to discern the future role of librarians in an AI-dominated landscape and how libraries are adapting. Findings revealed a general lack of awareness or response to the AI trend, with a minority of institutions involved in or establishing their AI hubs. Yu, K., et al. (2019). This paper expounds the basic situation of smart libraries and artificial intelligence, analyzes the application of artificial intelligence in the field of smart libraries, and demonstrates the application value of artificial intelligence in library services. Artificial intelligence will be widely used in the development of smart libraries.

3. METHODOLOGY

The study conducted a web-based literature survey to collect data from the period of February 2024. By combining qualitative research techniques, the study aims to offer a comprehensive understanding of AI's role in transforming the library in digital environment. The collected data were analyzed using Microsoft Excel, and the findings were presented using smart arts applications.

3.1 Objectives of the Study

This paper provides a comprehensive examination of the utilization of Artificial Intelligence (AI) in libraries and its influence on library operations. The objective of this study is to furnish researchers with a thorough comprehension of artificial intelligence within the library context.

Main aim is to provide a comprehensive understanding of the transformative potential of AI-driven libraries and their role in pioneering innovation in digital knowledge access. The objectives of the study is follows

- To explore the role of artificial intelligence (AI) technologies in revolutionizing library services and enhancing digital knowledge access.
- To examine the various applications of AI in libraries in digital knowledge access
- To identify best practices, challenges, and emerging trends associated with the implementation of AI-driven initiatives in libraries
- To find out methods for assess the effectiveness and efficiency of AI-driven library services in needs and expectations of users in the digital age.

4. ROLE OF ARTIFICIAL INTELLIGENCE (AI) TECHNOLOGIES IN REVOLUTIONIZING LIBRARY SERVICES AND ENHANCING DIGITAL KNOWLEDGE ACCESS

The integration of artificial intelligence (AI) technologies into library services signifies a substantial change in the manner libraries function and offer access to digital knowledge. Amidst a period characterized by swift technical progress and growing digitalization, libraries are transforming from conventional storehouses of information into vibrant centers for accessing digital knowledge. The adoption of AI technology is leading the way in this transition, transforming traditional library functions and greatly improving the user experience.

AI plays a diverse and transformational role in changing library services, with a broad range of applications that enhance operations, increase efficiency, and customize interactions. Artificial intelligence (AI) technologies, such as machine learning, natural language processing, and data analytics, enable libraries to adjust to the evolving requirements and preferences of users in the digital era. By utilizing the power of AI-driven algorithms and predictive analytics, libraries can provide more intelligent and responsive services that meet the specific needs of users while also improving the accessibility and discoverability of digital resources. An investigation of the impact of artificial intelligence (AI) technology on library services and digital information access involves examining how AI is changing traditional library operations and enhancing user interaction with library materials.

4.1 Advanced Search and Discovery Services in Digital Libraries

In the era of digital technology, the availability of extensive collections of information requires the use of effective methods for searching and finding what we need. Advanced Search and Discovery Services in Digital Libraries utilize advanced algorithms and technologies to improve the user experience, guaranteeing fast and pertinent access to digital materials. These services frequently utilize AI-powered algorithms, natural language processing, and semantic analysis to deliver tailored and user-friendly search experiences. These services enable users to successfully browse huge digital collections by providing features such as faceted search, relevance rating, and recommendation algorithms. This facilitates knowledge discovery and exploration. Furthermore, the use of metadata enrichment tools and adherence to linked data standards enhances the search experience, allowing users to effortlessly explore associated resources. Advanced Search and Discovery Services are essential for optimizing the functionality and availability of digital libraries, enabling users to effortlessly and effectively locate the information they require.

4.2 Virtual Assistants and Chatbots in Digital Accessing

Virtual assistants and chat bots have become essential tools in contemporary digital libraries, providing individualized support and improving user interaction. These AI-powered technologies offer users immediate assistance, quickly navigating them through library resources, services, and inquiries. Virtual assistants and chat bots utilize natural language processing capabilities to comprehend user inquiries and deliver pertinent responses, successfully emulating human interaction. By incorporating virtual assistants and chat bots into digital library platforms, institutions can enhance user experiences, enhance accessibility, and optimize service delivery. These AI-powered solutions provide 24/7 assistance, enhancing traditional library services and enabling users to efficiently utilize digital resources.

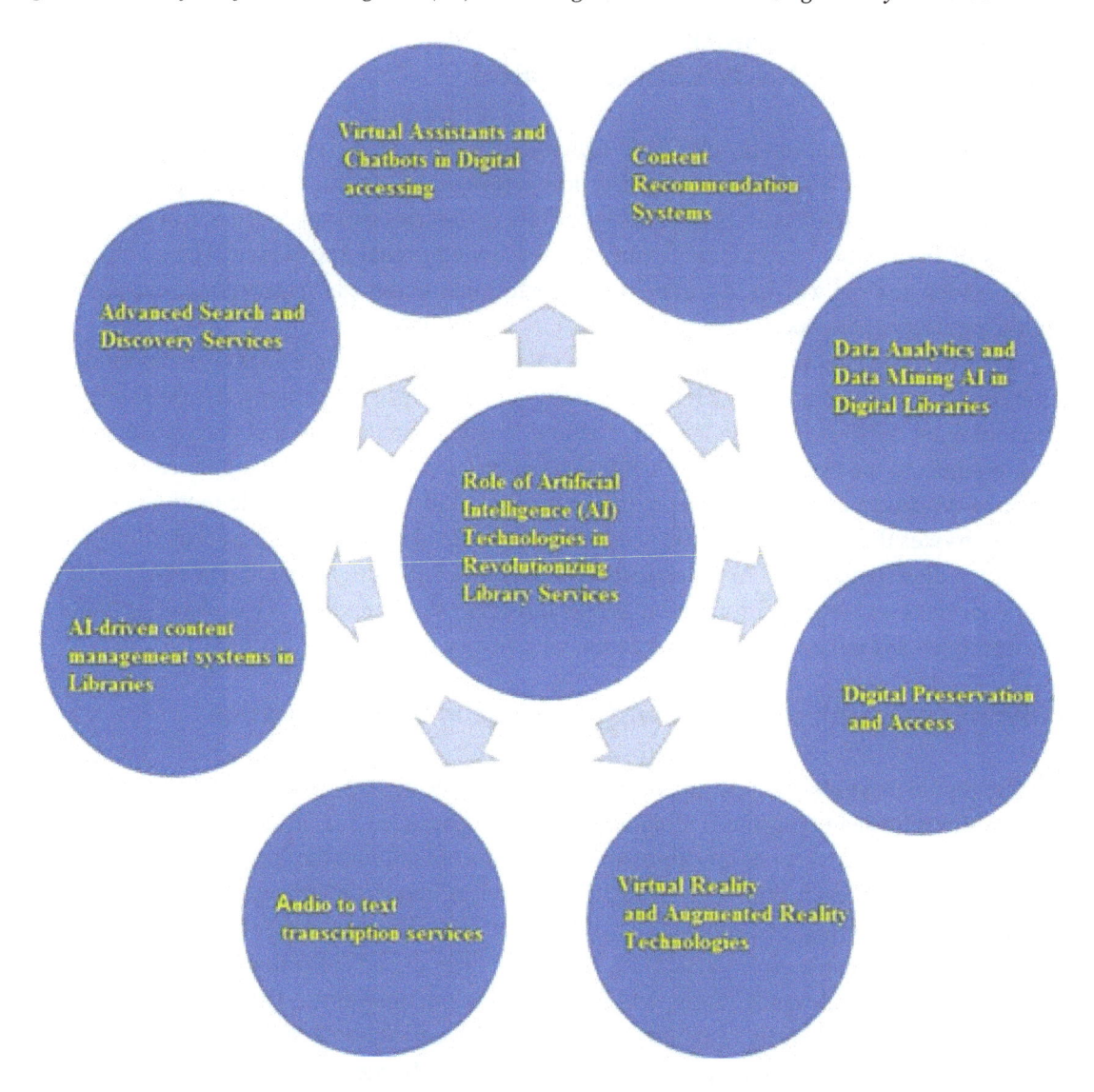

Figure 1. Role of artificial intelligence (AI) technologies in revolutionizing library services

Table 1. Advanced search and discovery services AI application tools

Open Access Tool	Paid Tool
Elasticsearch: An open-source search and analytics engine that utilizes AI-powered algorithms to deliver fast and relevant search results. It offers features such as full-text search, real-time analytics, and scalable distributed search capabilities.	**Algolia:** A cloud-based search and discovery platform that leverages AI to deliver fast and relevant search results across various digital content types. It offers features like typo tolerance, geolocation search, and real-time indexing.
Apache Solr: An open-source search platform built on Apache Lucene that provides powerful search and faceted navigation capabilities. It offers features like full-text search, advanced filtering, and customizable ranking algorithms.	**Coveo:** A cloud-based AI-powered search and relevance platform that enables organizations to deliver personalized search experiences. It offers features such as machine learning-based relevance tuning, intelligent recommendations, and predictive analytics.
Swiftype: A cloud-based search and discovery platform that utilizes AI to deliver relevant search results and improve user engagement. It offers features like autocomplete suggestions, synonym recognition, and relevance tuning.	**Lucidworks Fusion:** An AI-powered search and discovery platform that combines advanced machine learning algorithms with natural language processing (NLP) techniques. It offers features like query intent recognition, personalized recommendations, and content enrichment.

Figure 2. Virtual assistants and chatbots AI tools

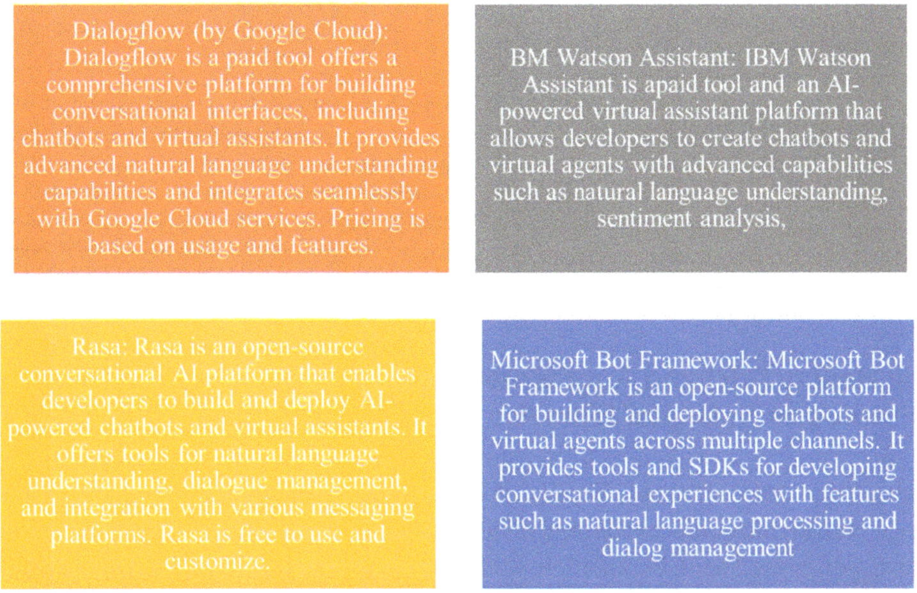

Dialogflow (by Google Cloud): Dialogflow is a paid tool offers a comprehensive platform for building conversational interfaces, including chatbots and virtual assistants. It provides advanced natural language understanding capabilities and integrates seamlessly with Google Cloud services. Pricing is based on usage and features.

BM Watson Assistant: IBM Watson Assistant is a paid tool and an AI-powered virtual assistant platform that allows developers to create chatbots and virtual agents with advanced capabilities such as natural language understanding, sentiment analysis,

Rasa: Rasa is an open-source conversational AI platform that enables developers to build and deploy AI-powered chatbots and virtual assistants. It offers tools for natural language understanding, dialogue management, and integration with various messaging platforms. Rasa is free to use and customize.

Microsoft Bot Framework: Microsoft Bot Framework is an open-source platform for building and deploying chatbots and virtual agents across multiple channels. It provides tools and SDKs for developing conversational experiences with features such as natural language processing and dialog management

4.3 Data Analytics and Data Mining AI in Digital Libraries

Data analytics and data mining AI technologies play a crucial role in extracting important insights from the extensive data stored in digital libraries. Through the utilization of sophisticated algorithms and machine learning techniques, these AI-powered methods empower libraries to extract practical insights, recognize trends, and make well-informed choices to enhance their services and optimize user experiences.

Data analytics and data mining AI technologies are essential tools for digital libraries aiming to utilize their extensive data assets to enhance services, optimize collections, and improve user experiences. By utilizing AI-driven insights, libraries may fully exploit the capabilities of their digital collections and enhance their ability to cater to the requirements of their user communities in the digital era.

4.4 Digital Preservation and Access AI in Digital Libraries

The maintenance and retrieval of digital databases and information Artificial intelligence (AI) technologies are playing an important part in modern digital libraries because they ensure the long-term integrity, accessibility, and usability of digital resources. These technologies, which are powered by artificial intelligence, enable libraries to effectively address the challenges associated with the issue of keeping digital content and providing access to it. This is accomplished through the employment of complex algorithms and techniques for machine learning. The development of digital preservation and access technologies is the primary force behind the transition of digital libraries. Intelligence-based technologies When it comes to guaranteeing the long-term viability of digital collections in libraries and making them accessible to users, technologies play a crucial role. Streamlining preservation operations, improving access to digital resources, and ensuring the continuous relevance and usability of their holdings for future generations are all things that may be accomplished by libraries by using the power of AI-driven initiatives..

Table 2. AI application tools for digital preservation and access

H2O.ai: H2O.ai is an open-source machine learning platform that provides scalable and distributed implementations of machine learning algorithms. It offers tools for data pre processing, model training, and deployment, with support for both Python and R programming languages.	Weka: is an AI-based tool. Weka (Waikato Environment for Knowledge Analysis) is a popular open-source machine learning software written in Java. It provides a comprehensive suite of algorithms for data pre processing, classification, regression, clustering, association rules mining, and feature selection.
PyTorch: PyTorch is an open-source machine learning library developed by Face book's AI Research lab. It offers a flexible and dynamic approach to building neural networks, with support for both research and production use cases.	**Apache Mahout**: is an AI-based open-source project. It's primarily a distributed linear algebra framework and a collection of scalable machine learning algorithms implemented on top of Apache Hadoop and Apache Spark. Mahout provides algorithms for clustering, classification, collaborative filtering, and frequent pattern mining, among others.

4.5 Virtual Reality (VR) and Augmented Reality (AR) Technologies in Digital Libraries

Virtual Reality (VR) and Augmented Reality (AR) technologies are transforming the manner in which people engage with digital content and retrieve information in libraries. Immersive technologies provide enhanced levels of engagement, exploration, and learning, thereby altering traditional library services and improving the user experience. VR and AR technologies are currently being employed in digital libraries.Virtual Reality (VR) and Augmented Reality (AR) technologies are revolutionizing digital libraries by providing captivating and interactive experiences that amplify engagement, discovery, and learning. As these technologies progress, libraries can utilize VR and AR apps to enhance their digital holdings, involve users in novel ways, and establish inventive learning spaces that stimulate curiosity and exploration.

4.6 AI-Powered Audio to Text Transcription Services

Audio to text transcription is the act of transforming spoken language from audio recordings into written text. This technique is extensively utilized in diverse domains like as journalism, judicial processes, academic research, and content development. Its purpose is to convert interviews, lectures, meetings, podcasts, and other audio recordings into a written version that can be easily read.

The transcription process commonly employs automatic speech recognition (ASR) technology, which examines the audio input and produces a written transcript. ASR algorithms utilize machine learning and natural language processing methodologies to discern spoken words, phrases, and sentences,

Table 3. AI application tools for VR and AR technologies

Unity ML-Agents: Unity ML-Agents is an open-source toolkit developed by Unity Technologies for integrating machine learning into Unity-based applications, including VR and AR experiences. It enables developers to train intelligent agents using reinforcement learning and other machine learning techniques, which can then interact with virtual environments in real-time.	**ARKit and ARCore:** ARKit (for iOS) and ARCore (for Android) are software development kits (SDKs) provided by Apple and Google, respectively, for building AR applications. While not AI tools themselves, developers can integrate AI-powered features such as object recognition, image tracking, and spatial mapping into AR experiences built with these SDKs.
OpenCV (Open Source Computer Vision Library): OpenCV is an open-source computer vision library that provides a wide range of algorithms for image and video analysis.	**TensorFlow and PyTorch**: TensorFlow and PyTorch are popular open-source machine learning frameworks that can be used to develop AI-powered features for VR and AR experiences.

transforming them into written text. The correctness of the transcription relies on variables such as the audio recording's quality, the clarity of speech, and the terminology employed. Transcribing audio into text provides several advantages, such as increased efficiency, improved accessibility, and enhanced searchability indexing. By effectively utilizing AI, libraries can leverage its revolutionary capabilities to further their objective of ensuring equal access to knowledge, promoting continuous learning, and catering to the different requirements of their communities. Libraries may effectively utilize technology to improve their services and adapt to changing user expectations and social demands by implementing AI in a considerate and inclusive manner. This can also facilitate analysis and content creation.

4.7 AI-Driven Content Management Systems in Libraries

By effectively utilizing AI, libraries can leverage its revolutionary capabilities to further their objective of ensuring equal access to knowledge, promoting continuous education, and catering to the varied requirements of their populations. Libraries can utilize technology to improve their services and adapt to changing customer expectations and social demands by implementing AI in a considerate and inclusive manner. Content management in digital library services encompasses the systematic arrangement, preservation, retrieval, and distribution of digital resources, including documents, photos, videos, and multimedia elements. By incorporating artificial intelligence (AI) technologies, libraries may optimize material management procedures, enhance accessibility, and provide users more tailored experiences. Artificial Intelligence (AI) is transforming content management in digital libraries.

1. **Effectiveness and efficiency of AI-driven library services Automated Metadata Generation**: Automated Metadata Generation: Artificial intelligence systems have the capability to automatically produce metadata for digital resources by examining their content, context, and features. Natural language processing (NLP) approaches facilitate the identification and retrieval of important infor-

Table 4. AI-powered Tools for Audio to Text Transcription Services

Amazon Transcribe: Amazon Web Services' (AWS) AI service that converts speech to text. It supports multiple languages, speaker identification, and custom vocabularies.	**IBM Watson Speech to Text**: IBM's AI service for transcribing speech into text. It offers customizable models for specific industries and supports multiple languages and dialects.
Microsoft Azure Speech to Text: Microsoft's cloud-based service for converting spoken language into text. It supports custom models, speaker diarization, and punctuation features.	**Speechmatics**: A speech recognition service that offers accurate transcriptions for audio files in multiple languages. It provides support for various industries and features such as speaker diarization and punctuation.

mation components, including titles, authors, dates, and subjects, thereby enhancing the structure and accessibility of digital collections.

2. **Content Tagging and Classification**: AI-driven content tagging and classification techniques categorize digital resources based on their content, topics, and themes. Machine learning algorithms analyze the content of documents, images, and multimedia files to assign relevant tags and categories, facilitating efficient retrieval and access to digital materials.

3. **Dynamic Content Recommendation**: AI-driven recommendation systems utilize user data and machine learning algorithms to propose pertinent content to users, taking into account their preferences, interests, and browsing history. Through the examination of user behavior and patterns of content utilization, these systems provide individualized suggestions for material, improving user engagement and facilitating the accidental discovery of digital resources.

4. **Content Summarization and Extraction**: AI-driven content summarization and extraction techniques distill key insights and information from large volumes of digital content. Text mining algorithms analyze documents, articles, and textual resources to extract relevant information, identify trends, and generate concise summaries, facilitating knowledge dissemination and decision-making.

5. **Intelligent Content Search and Retrieval**: Artificial intelligence (AI) algorithms are used to improve the efficiency of finding and retrieving content in digital libraries. By utilizing natural language processing and semantic search approaches, these algorithms provide more precise and pertinent search results, enhancing the user experience and enabling information exploration..

AI-powered content management solutions enable digital libraries to enhance content organization, enhance user experiences, and maximize the value of digital resources for users. Through the utilization of AI technology, libraries may optimize content management operations, improve the ability to find materials, and offer customized access to digital resources, resulting in a more captivating and fulfilling user experience in the digital era.

Libraries may utilize the revolutionary power of AI to further their purpose of ensuring equal access to information, promoting lifelong learning, and meeting the various needs of their communities.

Figure 3. AI-driven tools for content management systems in libraries

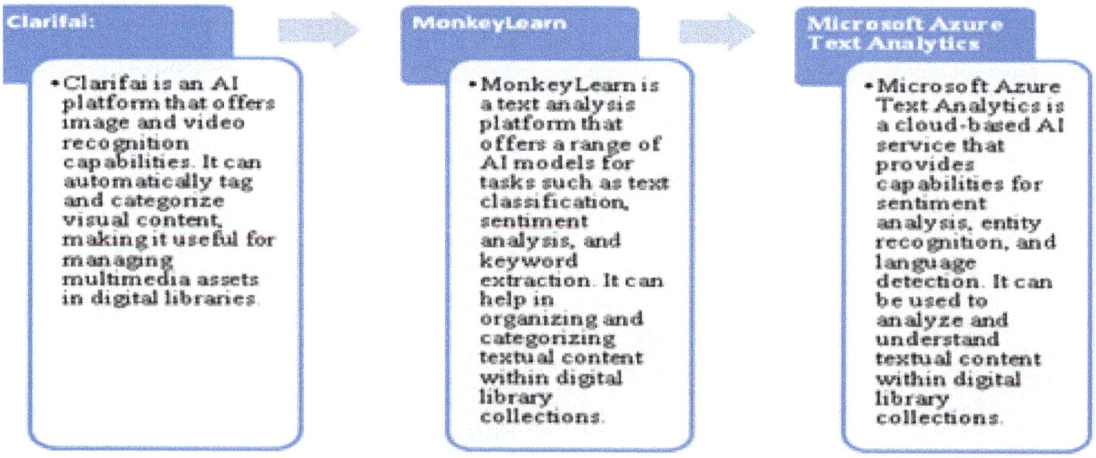

Clarifai:
- Clarifai is an AI platform that offers image and video recognition capabilities. It can automatically tag and categorize visual content, making it useful for managing multimedia assets in digital libraries.

MonkeyLearn
- MonkeyLearn is a text analysis platform that offers a range of AI models for tasks such as text classification, sentiment analysis, and keyword extraction. It can help in organizing and categorizing textual content within digital library collections.

Microsoft Azure Text Analytics
- Microsoft Azure Text Analytics is a cloud-based AI service that provides capabilities for sentiment analysis, entity recognition, and language detection. It can be used to analyze and understand textual content within digital library collections.

AI-Driven Libraries

Libraries may expand their services and adapt to changing user expectations and social demands by implementing AI-driven technology in a smart and inclusive manner, which will improve the effectiveness and efficiency of library services.

5. BEST PRACTICES, CHALLENGES, AND EMERGING TRENDS ASSOCIATED WITH THE IMPLEMENTATION OF AI-DRIVEN INITIATIVES IN LIBRARIES

Integrating Artificial Intelligence (AI) into library services has become a potential approach to modernize and improve user experiences. By harnessing AI technologies, libraries may optimize their operations, customize services, and enhance the availability of information resources. Nevertheless, the integration of AI-powered initiatives in libraries is not devoid of obstacles.

Best Practices

1. **Needs Assessment**: Conduct a thorough needs assessment to identify areas where AI-driven initiatives can improve library services, such as enhancing search algorithms, automating repetitive tasks, and increasing the effectiveness and efficiency of AI-driven library services, or customizing user experiences.
2. **Data Management**: Ensure the optimal effectiveness and efficiency of AI-driven library services by implementing robust data management standards, which include conducting data quality assessments, ensuring compliance with data privacy regulations, and implementing stringent data security measures. Libraries are required to ethically gather, retain, and utilize data in order to prevent any violations of privacy.
3. **Collaborative Approach**: Employ a collaborative approach by encouraging cooperation among library personnel, IT professionals, data scientists, and domain experts to effectively utilize their diverse experience in AI implementation projects. Collaboration can enhance the creation of inventive solutions customized to meet the specific requirements of libraries.
4. **User-Centric Design**: Prioritize user experience in the design and deployment of AI-driven initiatives. Solicit feedback from library patrons to understand their needs and preferences, and iteratively improve AI applications based on user input.
5. **Ethical Considerations**: Discuss ethical issues associated with AI, including algorithmic bias, transparency, justice, and responsibility. Develop and apply methods to examine AI systems and address biases in order to provide fair and equal access to library resources and services.The efficacy and proficiency of AI-powered library services
6. **Continuous Evaluation and Improvement**: Discuss ethical issues associated with AI, including algorithmic bias, transparency, justice, and responsibility. Develop and apply methods to examine AI systems and address biases in order to provide fair and equal access to library resources and services. The efficacy and proficiency of AI-powered library services

    Challenges

1. **Data Quality and Accessibility**: Libraries may face difficulties in obtaining and managing data of superior quality for the purpose of AI applications. Problems including data silos, inadequate

information, and inconsistent data formats might impede the usefulness and efficiency of AI-powered library services.
2. **Resource Constraints**: The implementation of AI-driven initiatives in libraries may face major obstacles due to resource constraints, such as limited funds, knowledge, and technical infrastructure. In order to overcome these limitations, libraries must give priority to the allocation of resources and actively pursue external partnerships.
3. **Ethical and Legal Compliance**: Ensuring ethical and legal compliance involves adhering to ethical and legal frameworks, such as data protection standards (e.g., GDPR, CCPA) and intellectual property rights. This process can be intricate and need a significant amount of time. Libraries must skillfully traverse the many regulatory environments in order to implement AI technologies in a responsible manner.
4. **User Acceptance and Trust**: Establishing user trust and acceptance of AI-driven projects is essential for their effectiveness. Libraries should engage in clear and open communication regarding the objectives, functionalities, and constraints of AI systems in order to address worries related to privacy, security, and algorithmic bias.
5. **Sustainability and Scalability**: Ensuring the long-term viability and expandability of AI-driven initiatives necessitates meticulous strategizing and investment in infrastructure, personnel training, and continuous upkeep. Libraries should carefully evaluate the enduring expenses and advantages of integrating AI to guarantee its sustainability in the long run.

Libraries can utilize the transformative power while managing these best practices and challenges. Libraries are using Artificial Intelligence (AI) into their services to fulfill the changing requirements and expectations of users in the digital era. These AI-powered efforts have the potential to improve library experiences, optimize resource allocation, and enhance access to information. Nevertheless, in order to guarantee that these initiatives effectively fulfill their intended objective, a thorough review is needed.

6. FACTORS OF ASSESSING THE EFFECTIVENESS AND EFFICIENCY OF AI-DRIVEN LIBRARY SERVICES

Evaluating the efficacy and productivity of AI-powered library services entails examining multiple factors, such as user contentment, utilization patterns, operational proficiency, and congruence with strategic goals. This assessment offers unique perspectives on the influence of artificial intelligence (AI) on library services and aids in making informed decisions to improve the overall user experience. Through a methodical assessment of AI-powered projects, libraries can discover their advantages, tackle obstacles, and enhance their resources to effectively cater to the changing requirements and expectations of users in the digital era.

The efficacy and proficiency of AI-powered library services in fulfilling the changing requirements and anticipations of users in the digital realm are as follows:

1. **Enhanced User Experience**: AI-powered library services can enhance the user experience by offering personalized suggestions, optimizing search engines, and providing tailored assistance, resulting in a more intuitive and gratifying user experience.

2. **Optimized Resource Allocation**: Through the automation of repetitive jobs and the optimization of workflows, AI enables libraries to distribute resources in a more efficient manner. This allows library personnel to concentrate on more valuable tasks, while also providing users with quicker access to information resources.
3. **Improved Access to Information**: AI technologies enable the efficient analysis of vast amounts of data, resulting in improved search capabilities and personalized content recommendations. This ultimately leads to a more effective fulfillment of users' information requirements.
4. **Increased Engagement and Satisfaction**: AI-powered services that predict user preferences, deliver timely information, and offer interactive experiences can boost user engagement and contentment, promoting better ties between users and library resources.
5. **Scalability and Adaptability**: AI-powered solutions possess the capability to expand and adjust to increasing user requirements and conform to changing preferences and trends in the digital realm. This ensures that library services continue to be responsive and pertinent as time progresses. The efficacy and proficiency of AI-powered library services reside in their capacity to utilize technology for providing tailored, accessible, and captivating experiences that cater to the varied requirements and anticipations of users in the digital era.

CONCLUSION

The integration of Artificial Intelligence (AI) technologies into library services represents a significant advancement in the digital age, revolutionizing traditional library functions and enhancing the user experience. Through applications such as advanced search and discovery services, virtual assistants and chat bots, data analytics and data mining, digital preservation and access, and virtual reality (VR) and augmented reality (AR) technologies, AI is transforming libraries into dynamic hubs of digital knowledge access. The effectiveness and efficiency of AI-driven library services are evident in their ability to enhance user experiences, optimize resource allocation, improve access to information, increase engagement and satisfaction, and scale to meet evolving user needs. By harnessing the power of AI, libraries can streamline operations, personalize services, and remain responsive to changing user expectations in the digital age. However, the successful implementation of AI-driven initiatives in libraries requires careful consideration of best practices, challenges, and ethical considerations. Libraries must prioritize user-centric design, data management, collaboration, ethical compliance, and continuous evaluation to ensure the responsible and sustainable use of AI technologies. In navigating these opportunities and challenges, libraries can leverage AI to advance their mission of providing equitable access to information, fostering lifelong learning, and supporting the diverse needs of their communities. By adopting a thoughtful and inclusive approach to AI implementation, libraries can harness the transformative potential of technology to enhance their services and remain at the forefront of digital knowledge access.

REFERENCES

Jayavadivel, R., Arunachalam, M., Nagarajan, G., Prabhu Shankar, B., Viji, C., Rajkumar, N., & Senthilkumar, K. R. (2024). Historical Overview of AI Adoption in Libraries. In K. Senthilkumar (Ed.), *AI-Assisted Library Reconstruction* (pp. 267–289). IGI Global. doi:10.4018/979-8-3693-2782-1.ch015

Kumar, N., Antoniraj, S., Jayanthi, S., Mirdula, S., Selvaraj, S., Rajkumar, N., & Senthilkumar, K. R. (2024). Educational Technology and Libraries Supporting Online Learning. In K. Senthilkumar (Ed.), *AI-Assisted Library Reconstruction* (pp. 209–237). IGI Global. doi:10.4018/979-8-3693-2782-1.ch012

Moustapha, A., & Yusuf, B. (2023). Artificial intelligence adoption and utilization by librarians in university libraries in Kwara State, Nigeria. *Library Philosophy and Practice (e-journal)*, 7917. Retrieved from https://digitalcommons.unl.edu/libphilprac/7917

Rajkumar, N., Tabassum, H., Muthulingam, S., Mohanraj, A., Viji, C., Kumar, N., & Senthilkumar, K. R. (2024). Anticipated Requirements and Expectations in the Digital Library. In K. Senthilkumar (Ed.), *AI-Assisted Library Reconstruction* (pp. 1–20). IGI Global. doi:10.4018/979-8-3693-2782-1.ch001

Senthilkumar, K. (Ed.). (2024). *AI-Assisted Library Reconstruction*. IGI Global. doi:10.4018/979-8-3693-2782-1

Senthilkumar, K. R. (2024). Revolutionizing thrust manufacturing. In *Advances in computational intelligence and robotics book series* (pp. 80–93). doi:10.4018/979-8-3693-2615-2.ch005

Senthilkumar, K. R., Jagajeevan, R., & Sangeetha, S. (2024). Impact of AI on Library and Information Science in Higher Institutions in India: A Comprehensive Analysis of Technological Integration and Educational Implications. In K. Senthilkumar (Ed.), *AI-Assisted Library Reconstruction* (pp. 21–33). IGI Global. doi:10.4018/979-8-3693-2782-1.ch002

Sivaraj, P., Madhan, V., Mallika, V., & Senthilkumar, K. R. (2024). Enhancing Library Services Through Optimization Algorithms and Data Analytics: Enhancing Library Services Mathematical Model. In K. Senthilkumar (Ed.), *AI-Assisted Library Reconstruction* (pp. 290–306). IGI Global. doi:10.4018/979-8-3693-2782-1.ch016

Subaveerapandiyan, A., & Gozali, A. (2024). AI in Indian Libraries: Prospects and Perceptions from Library Professionals. *Open Information Science*, *8*(1). doi:10.1515/opis-2022-0164

Subaveerapandiyan. (2023). Application of Artificial Intelligence (AI) In Libraries and Its Impact on Library Operations Review. *Library Philosophy and Practice (e-journal)*, 7828. Retrieved from https://digitalcommons.unl.edu/libphilprac/7828

Vasishta, P., Dhingra, N., & Vasishta, S. (2024). Application of artificial intelligence in libraries: A bibliometric analysis and visualization of research activities. *Library Hi Tech*. Advance online publication. doi:10.1108/LHT-12-2023-0589

Wheatley, A., & Hervieux, S. (2019). Artificial Intelligence in Academic Libraries: An Environmental Scan. *Information Services & Use*, *39*(4), 347–356. doi:10.3233/ISU-190065

Yu, K. (2019). The Application of Artificial Intelligence in Smart Library. Academic Press.

Chapter 21
AI Insights Deciphering India's Ascendancy Through the Digital Library:
Navigating the Digital Realm India's Odyssey Towards Information Equity and Technological Eminence

B. Velmurugan
https://orcid.org/0000-0003-4513-0178
NPR College of Engineering and Technology, India

S. Dharmalingam
Chettinad College of Engineering and Technology, India

K. Binith Muthukrishnan
https://orcid.org/0000-0002-9854-2785
NPR College of Engineering and Technology, India

K. R. Senthilkumar
https://orcid.org/0000-0001-7426-5376
Sri Krishna Arts and Science College, India

ABSTRACT

India's trajectory toward digital eminence is intricately woven into the fabric of its burgeoning digital library ecosystem. Through the lens of artificial intelligence (AI) insights, this chapter delineates the pivotal role of digital libraries in India's ascent within the global digital milieu. At the heart of this exploration lies the profound impact of digital libraries as reservoirs of knowledge, catalyzing innovation, and fostering inclusive growth. By employing a multifaceted analysis, the authors uncover the transformative potential inherent in these repositories, elucidating their capacity to democratize access to information, propel research and education, and underpin socioeconomic advancement.

DOI: 10.4018/979-8-3693-5593-0.ch021

INTRODUCTION

In an era defined by rapid technological advancement and digital transformation, India stands poised at the forefront of a digital revolution. At the heart of this transformation lies the proliferation of digital libraries, emerging as indispensable repositories of knowledge and catalysts for societal progress. Leveraging Artificial Intelligence (AI) insights, this paper endeavors to unravel the intricate tapestry of India's ascendancy through its digital library ecosystem (K. Senthilkumar & Maniiarsan, 2020).

India's journey towards digital eminence is underpinned by a relentless pursuit of knowledge democratization and technological innovation. As a nation endowed with a rich cultural heritage and a burgeoning knowledge economy, India recognizes the pivotal role of digital libraries in driving inclusive growth, fostering innovation, and nurturing a knowledge-driven society. At the intersection of technology, policy, and collaboration, India's digital libraries represent the fulcrum of its digital aspirations, serving as enablers of empowerment, progress, and global leadership (K. R. Senthilkumar, 2019).

In this introductory section, we embark on a journey to decipher the multifaceted dimensions of India's digital library landscape. We delve into the significance of digital libraries as agents of change, illuminating their transformative potential in reshaping the socioeconomic fabric of India. Through a comprehensive analysis, we navigate the evolution of India's digital library ecosystem, tracing its roots from the early endeavors to the contemporary initiatives driving the nation towards information equity and technological eminence (Marty et al., 2023).

Furthermore, we underscore the pivotal role of AI in unraveling insights and unlocking the latent potential of digital libraries. By harnessing AI algorithms for data curation, knowledge discovery, and personalized learning, India's digital libraries are poised to transcend traditional boundaries, democratizing access to information and fostering a culture of lifelong learning. Against this backdrop, we set the stage for a deeper exploration of India's digital library landscape, illuminating the path forward for leveraging digital repositories as instruments of empowerment, progress, and global leadership in the digital age (Guo et al., 2023).

Global Setting

The International Monetary Fund (IMF) anticipates one-third of the world to be in recession in 2023. The World Bank's latest Global Economic Prospects (GEP), released on January 10, 2023, projects a prolonged slowdown in the global economy, with growth estimated at 2.2% – the third-lowest in three decades. The Food and Agriculture Organization (FAO) Food Price Index declined for the ninth consecutive month in December 2022, primarily due to decreases in vegetable oil prices and cereals. Crude oil prices averaged US$ 80.9 per barrel in December, down from US$ 91.1 in November. In the Euro area, inflation decreased to 9.2% in December 2022 from 10.1% in November 2022. The global economic outlook remains uncertain (D. K. Senthilkumar, 2024).

Growth and GDP

The advance GDP estimates for the year 2022-23 indicate a growth rate of around 7%, with expectations of GDP growth ranging from 6.0% to 6.8% in 2023-24. This outlook is contingent on the trajectory of global economic and political developments. The projections align broadly with estimates from multilateral agencies such as the World Bank, the IMF, the Asian Development Bank (ADB), and the

Reserve Bank of India (RBI). Optimistic growth forecasts are driven by several positive factors, including a rebound in private consumption, increased Capital Expenditure (Capex), widespread vaccination coverage, the return of migrant workers to construction sites, strengthened corporate balance sheets, and well-capitalized public sector banks facilitating credit supply (Shams et al., 2024).

Additional support for economic growth stems from the expansion of public digital platforms and transformative initiatives such as PM GatiShakti, the National Logistics Policy, and Production-Linked Incentive schemes aimed at boosting manufacturing output. India stands out among major economies, maintaining an expansionary Composite Purchasing Managers' Index (PMI) reading in December 2022. The services PMI recorded its highest expansion in six months, driven by an increase in new business (Aliouat et al., 2023).

Despite the triple challenges of COVID-19, the Russian-Ukraine conflict, and global central bank policy rate hikes, resulting in the appreciation of the US Dollar and widening Current Account Deficits (CAD) in net importing economies, global agencies consistently project India as the fastest-growing major economy, with an anticipated growth range of 6.5-7.0% in Financial Year 2023-24 (Manfletti et al., 2023).

Strengths of the Indian Economy

As per the Economic Survey 2022-2023, the Central Government's Capital Expenditure (Capex) surged by 63.4% during the initial eight months of FY23, emerging as a significant driver of the current year's Indian economy. Anticipated is a sustained rise in private Capex, supported by strengthened corporate balance sheets. The credit growth to Micro, Small, and Medium Enterprises (MSME) recorded an impressive average of over 30.6% from January to November 2022, propelled by the extended Emergency Credit Linked Guarantee Scheme (ECLGS). Additionally, the overall bank credit witnessed an uptick, influenced by borrowers shifting from volatile bond markets and external commercial borrowings toward banks. A robust credit growth is anticipated in FY24 if inflation subsides, and the real cost of credit remains stable (Ge et al., 2023).

The Mahatma Gandhi National Rural Employment Guarantee Scheme (MGNREGS) has played a pivotal role in providing direct employment in rural areas and indirectly facilitating income diversification for rural households. Schemes like PM-Kisan and PM Garib Kalyan Yojana have contributed to ensuring food security, an impact acknowledged by the United Nations Development Programme (UNDP). The National Family Health Survey (NFHS) results from FY16 to FY20 depict improvements in rural welfare indicators, encompassing gender, fertility rate, household amenities, and women empowerment (Gazzawe & Albahar, 2024).

Inflation, Current Account Deficit (CAD), and Global Slowdown

India's inflation rate moderated to 5.7% in December 2022, primarily driven by a significant reduction in food inflation. The average Wholesale Price Index stood at 11.5%, while the Consumer Price Index was 6.8% for April-December 2022. Government and RBI measures, along with a decline in global commodity prices, have succeeded in bringing retail inflation below the RBI upper tolerance target in November 2022. Despite the Indian rupee depreciating by 0.8% against the US dollar in December 2022, it remains relatively resilient compared to other currencies. The challenges of a depreciating rupee persist, especially with potential further increases in US Federal Reserve policy rates (D. K. Senthilkumar, 2024).

RBI projects headline inflation at 6.8% in FY23, slightly outside its target range. Challenges such as increased commodity prices due to European strife, widening CAD, and a global economic slowdown may pose concerns for the Indian economy. The CAD widening to 4.4% of the GDP in the quarter ending September 2022 may persist due to elevated global commodity prices and the continued strong growth momentum of the Indian economy. Global growth is projected to decline in 2023, impacting the global market size, which may affect India's exports. While slowing demand might lower global commodity prices, potential risks to India's CAD in FY24 need close monitoring. The rate hike by the US Federal Reserve and the associated capital flow may influence the US dollar's appreciation and lead to Current Account Deficit widening and inflationary pressures in net importing economies. The possibility of financial contagion from advanced economies, where non-financial sector debt has risen significantly, adds to the downside risks to the global economic outlook (K. Senthilkumar & Maniiarsan, 2020).

India's Economic Strength and Drivers of Growth

The challenges stemming from the Reserve Bank of India's monetary tightening, the expansion of the Current Account Deficit (CAD), and the sluggish growth in exports are primarily attributed to geopolitical tensions in Europe. These occurrences present potential drawbacks to the economic growth of India in FY23. The preliminary estimates, as per the National Statistical Office (NSO), anticipate growth within the range of 6.5-7.0%, a figure surpassing that of most major economies and marginally exceeding the average growth rate of the Indian economy in the decade preceding the pandemic.

Despite formidable global challenges and a more restrictive domestic monetary policy, India is poised to achieve a growth rate between 6.5% and 7.0%, even without the benefit of a base effect. This resilience underscores India's capacity to recover, rejuvenate, and re-energize its economic drivers. Notably, the domestic stimulus has seamlessly taken over from external stimuli, fostering a significant uptick in manufacturing and investment activities.

As the growth of exports moderated, a rebound in domestic consumption, particularly in contact-intensive services like trade, hotels, and transport, propelled India's economic growth. The expanded capital budget (Capex) of the central government and public sector enterprises has significantly boosted construction activity in FY23. Direct tax revenue collections, GST collections, and private sector investment have all exhibited buoyancy, with the fiscal deficit target for this financial year expected to be met.

The general increase in export demand, rebound in consumption, and public Capex have collectively contributed to the revival of corporate investment and manufacturing activities. The banking sector has responded adeptly to the demand for credit, with credit growth moving into double digits across most sectors (Rezaei et al., 2023).

In terms of employment, the Periodic Labour Force Survey indicates a rise in employment levels in the current financial year. The urban unemployment rate has declined, accompanied by an improvement

Table 1. Growth rate of the India economy

Sr. No.	Sector of the Economy	Growth rate of GVA at Basic Prices 2022-23
1	Agriculture and Allied Activities	3.50%
2	Industrial Sector	4.10%
3	Services	9.10%

Table 2. Tax revenue collections, GST collections, and private sector investment

S. No.	Sectors	2021-22 Actuals	2022-23 Budget Estimates	2022-23 Revised Estimates	2023-24 Budget Estimates
1	Pension	198946	207132	244780	234359
2	Defence	366546	385370	409500	432720
3	Subsidy				
4	Fertilizer	153758	105222	225220	175100
5	Food	288969	206831	287194	197350
6	Petroleum	3423	5813	9171	2257
7	Agriculture & Allied Activities	76492	83521	76279	84214
8	PM Kisan	66825	68000	60000	60000
9	Commerce & Industry	47068	53116	37540	48169
10	Development of North East	2653	2800	2755	5892
11	Education	80352	104278	99881	112899
12	Energy	53696	49220	70936	94915
13	External Affairs	14146	17250	16973	18050
14	Finance	57364	21354	17908	13574
15	Health	84091	86606	77351	88956
16	Home Affairs	112301	127020	124872	134917
17	Interest	805499	940651	940651	1079971
18	IT & Telecom	25053	79887	74106	93478
19	Others	108447	113301	108102	120524
20	Planning & Statistics	3753	5720	6209	6268
21	Rural & Development	228760	206293	243317	238204
22	Scientific Department	27772	30571	25626	32225
23	Social Welfare	40595	51780	46502	55080
24	Tax Administration of which transfer to	17744	171677	177343	194749
25	GST Compensation Fund	110795	120000	130000	145000
26	Transfer to States	274580	334339	270936	324641
27	Transport	332238	351851	390496	517034
28	Union Territories	56490	58757	69040	61118
29	Urban Development	106840	76549	74546	76432
	Grand Total	**3793801**	**3944909**	**4187232**	**4503097**

in the Labour Force Participation Rate (LFPR). The MSME sector, particularly micro-enterprises, has received substantial support through schemes like ECLGS, leading to increased GST payments and showcasing the financial resilience of small businesses.

Looking ahead to 2023-24, India's recovery from the pandemic is expected to continue, supported by robust domestic demand and increased capital investment. Signs of a new private sector capital formation cycle are emerging, complemented by a substantial rise in government capital expenditure. Structural reforms, including the Goods and Services Tax and the Insolvency and Bankruptcy Code, have enhanced economic efficiency and transparency.

While strong domestic demand may raise India's total import bill and widen the Current Account Deficit (CAD), challenges such as subdued export growth and potential depreciation of the Indian currency are acknowledged. The Union Budget for 2023-24 envisions India as a technology-driven and knowledge-based economy, emphasizing economic empowerment, skill development, tourism, and green growth. The budget reflects a strong commitment to economic growth through increased infrastructure investment, with capital expenditure rising significantly over the previous fiscal year (Ge et al., 2023).

Global Economy and Challenges

1. Challenges faced by the global economy that will impact the growth and development of the Indian economy include:
2. Disruptions caused by COVID-19 in various economies.
3. The Russian-Ukraine conflict and its adverse effects, including disruptions in the supply chain, particularly of essential commodities like food, fuel, and fertilizer, leading to inflationary pressures.
4. Synchronized policy rate hikes by central banks across economies to combat inflation, resulting in the appreciation of the US Dollar and widening Current Account Deficits (CAD) in net importing nations.
5. The possibility of global stagflation and countries seeking to safeguard their economic interests, slowing down cross-border trade and affecting overall growth.
6. China's substantial slowdown prompted by its policies.
7. Challenges to growth arising from the loss of education and income-earning opportunities during the pandemic.

Potential Positive Factors Contributing to India's Growth Include

1. Limited health and economic consequences for the rest of the world stemming from the ongoing surge in Covid-19 infections in China, allowing for the continued normalization of supply chains.
2. Inflationary pressures resulting from the reopening of China's economy proving to be neither significant nor enduring.
3. Recessionary trends in major Advanced Economies (AEs) prompting a halt in monetary tightening and a resurgence of capital flows to India, coupled with a stable domestic inflation rate below 6 percent.
4. This scenario fostering increased confidence among investors and offering additional momentum to private sector investment.

CONCLUSION

India's journey towards digital ascendancy through its digital library ecosystem epitomizes the nation's steadfast commitment to knowledge democratization, innovation, and inclusive growth. Throughout this discourse, we have unveiled the transformative potential of digital libraries as catalysts for societal progress, leveraging AI insights to decipher the multifaceted dimensions of India's digital landscape.

At its core, India's digital library ecosystem embodies the principles of information equity and technological empowerment. By democratizing access to knowledge, India's digital libraries transcend geographic and socioeconomic barriers, fostering a culture of intellectual exploration and lifelong learning. Through initiatives such as the National Digital Library and Digital India, India has pioneered efforts to bridge the digital divide, ensuring that every citizen has the opportunity to harness the power of information for personal and societal advancement (Zhang et al., 2024).

Moreover, India's digital libraries serve as crucibles for innovation, catalyzing cross-disciplinary research and collaboration. By leveraging AI-driven analytics and data-driven insights, these repositories fuel advancements in fields ranging from healthcare to agriculture, driving technological progress and economic competitiveness. Through open access initiatives and collaborative partnerships, India's digital library ecosystem fosters a culture of innovation, propelling the nation towards global leadership in the digital age.

As India continues its journey towards digital eminence, the role of digital libraries as enablers of inclusive growth and societal development cannot be overstated. By fostering collaboration between government agencies, academic institutions, and private enterprises, India's digital libraries amplify their impact, driving collective efforts towards a knowledge-driven society. Through continuous innovation and strategic investments, India is poised to unlock the full potential of its digital library ecosystem, ushering in an era of unparalleled opportunity and progress (Gupta et al., 2023).

In conclusion, India's ascendancy through its digital library ecosystem symbolizes the nation's unwavering resolve to harness the power of information for the greater good. By embracing AI-driven insights and fostering collaboration, India is poised to chart a course towards a future where knowledge knows no bounds, and every citizen has the opportunity to thrive in the digital age. As we look towards the horizon, the trajectory of India's digital journey serves as a testament to the transformative potential of digital libraries in shaping a brighter, more inclusive future for generations to come (D. K. Senthilkumar, 2024).

REFERENCES

Aliouat, A., Kouadria, N., Maimour, M., Harize, S., & Doghmane, N. (2023). Region-of-interest based video coding strategy for rate/energy-constrained smart surveillance systems using WMSNs. *Ad Hoc Networks*, *140*, 103076. doi:10.1016/j.adhoc.2022.103076

Gazzawe, F., & Albahar, M. (2024). Reducing traffic congestion in makkah during Hajj through the use of AI technology. *Heliyon*, *10*(1), e23304–e23304. doi:10.1016/j.heliyon.2023.e23304 PMID:38187331

Ge, L., Dan, D., Koo, K. Y., & Chen, Y. (2023). An improved system for long-term monitoring of full-bridge traffic load distribution on long-span bridges. *Structures, 54*, 1076–1089. https://doi.org/https://doi.org/10.1016/j.istruc.2023.05.103

Guo, F., Wang, Y., & Qian, Y. (2023). Real-time dense traffic detection using lightweight backbone and improved path aggregation feature pyramid network. *Journal of Industrial Information Integration*, *31*, 100427. doi:10.1016/j.jii.2022.100427

Gupta, M., Miglani, H., Deo, P., & Barhatte, A. (2023). Real-time traffic control and monitoring. *E-Prime - Advances in Electrical Engineering, Electronics and Energy, 5*, 100211. https://doi.org/https://doi.org/10.1016/j.prime.2023.100211

Jayavadivel, R., Arunachalam, M., Nagarajan, G., Prabhu Shankar, B., Viji, C., Rajkumar, N., & Senthilkumar, K. R. (2024). Historical Overview of AI Adoption in Libraries. In K. Senthilkumar (Ed.), *AI-Assisted Library Reconstruction* (pp. 267–289). IGI Global. doi:10.4018/979-8-3693-2782-1.ch015

Kumar, N., Antoniraj, S., Jayanthi, S., Mirdula, S., Selvaraj, S., Rajkumar, N., & Senthilkumar, K. R. (2024). Educational Technology and Libraries Supporting Online Learning. In K. Senthilkumar (Ed.), *AI-Assisted Library Reconstruction* (pp. 209–237). IGI Global. doi:10.4018/979-8-3693-2782-1.ch012

Manfletti, C., Guimarães, M., & Soares, C. (2023). AI for space traffic management. *The Journal of Space Safety Engineering*, *10*(4), 495–504. doi:10.1016/j.jsse.2023.08.007

Marty, J.-Y., Bonnal, C., Faucher, P., & Francillout, L. (2023). Space traffic management as a necessity for future orbital operations a French perspective. *Acta Astronautica*, *202*, 278–282. doi:10.1016/j.actaastro.2022.09.051

Rajkumar, N., Tabassum, H., Muthulingam, S., Mohanraj, A., Viji, C., Kumar, N., & Senthilkumar, K. R. (2024). Anticipated Requirements and Expectations in the Digital Library. In K. Senthilkumar (Ed.), *AI-Assisted Library Reconstruction* (pp. 1–20). IGI Global. doi:10.4018/979-8-3693-2782-1.ch001

Rezaei, M., Azarmi, M., & Mir, F. M. P. (2023). 3D-Net: Monocular 3D object recognition for traffic monitoring. *Expert Systems with Applications*, *227*, 120253. https://doi.org/https://doi.org/10.1016/j.eswa.2023.120253. doi:10.1016/j.eswa.2023.120253

Senthilkumar, D. K. (2024). Revolutionizing Thrust Manufacturing. Advances in Computational Intelligence and Robotics Book Series. In D. Sathiesh (Ed.), *Using Real-Time Data and AI for Thrust Manufacturing* (1st ed., pp. 80–93). IGI. doi:10.4018/979-8-3693-2615-2.ch005

Senthilkumar, K. (Ed.). (2024). *AI-Assisted Library Reconstruction*. IGI Global. doi:10.4018/979-8-3693-2782-1

Senthilkumar, K., & Maniiarsan, P. (2020). *Comparison of E- Resources with their Usage Statistics in Southern Region*. Academic Press.

Senthilkumar, K. R. (2019). *User pattern of Libraries by students of Government Colleges in Tamil nadu: A study*. Library Philosophy and Practice.

Senthilkumar, K. R. (2024). Revolutionizing thrust manufacturing. In *Advances in computational intelligence and robotics book series* (pp. 80–93). doi:10.4018/979-8-3693-2615-2.ch005

Senthilkumar, K. R., Jagajeevan, R., & Sangeetha, S. (2024). Impact of AI on Library and Information Science in Higher Institutions in India: A Comprehensive Analysis of Technological Integration and Educational Implications. In K. Senthilkumar (Ed.), *AI-Assisted Library Reconstruction* (pp. 21–33). IGI Global. doi:10.4018/979-8-3693-2782-1.ch002

Shams, M. Y., Tarek, Z., El-kenawy, E.-S. M., Eid, M. M., & Elshewey, A. M. (2024). Predicting Gross Domestic Product (GDP) using a PC-LSTM-RNN model in urban profiling areas. *Computational Urban Science*, *4*(1), 3. Advance online publication. doi:10.1007/s43762-024-00116-2

Sivaraj, P., Madhan, V., Mallika, V., & Senthilkumar, K. R. (2024). Enhancing Library Services Through Optimization Algorithms and Data Analytics: Enhancing Library Services Mathematical Model. In K. Senthilkumar (Ed.), *AI-Assisted Library Reconstruction* (pp. 290–306). IGI Global. doi:10.4018/979-8-3693-2782-1.ch016

Zhang, J., Cheng, Y., Zhang, J., & Wu, Z. (2024). A spatiotemporal distribution identification method of vehicle weights on bridges by integrating traffic video and toll station data. *Journal of Intelligent Transportation Systems*. https://doi.org/https://doi.org/10.1080/15472450.2024.2312810

Compilation of References

. Ryll, L., Barton, M. E., Zhang, B. Z., McWaters, R. J., Schizas, E., Hao, R., ... Yerolemou, N. (2020). Transforming paradigms: A global AI in financial services survey. Academic Press.

Abayomi, O. K., Adenekan, F. N., Abayomi, A., Ajayi, T. A., & Aderonke, A. O. (2020). Awareness and Perception of the Artificial Intelligence in the Management of University Libraries in Nigeria. *Journal of Interlibrary Loan, Document Delivery & Information Supply*, *29*(1–2), 13–28. doi:10.1080/1072303X.2021.1918602

Abram, S. (2019). *Robots in libraries: Technology trends that aren't that out-there anymore!* https://lucidea.com/blog/robots-in-libraries/

Adeniran, O. A., & Ademilokun, O. O. (2022). Artificial intelligence applications in libraries: A review of the literature. *International Journal of Information and Communication Technology*, *16*(2), 221–237.

Adie, S., & Ajao, O. M. (2021). Application of artificial intelligence in information retrieval systems: A review. *International Journal of Library and Information Science Studies*, *12*(3), 105–121.

Adie, S., & Ajao, O. M. (2022). Artificial intelligence applications in academic libraries: A systematic review of the literature. *Library Hi Tech*, *40*(2), 301–324.

Aithal, S., & Aithal, P. S. (2023). Effects of AI-based ChatGPT on higher education libraries. *International Journal of Management, Technology, and Social Sciences*, *8*(2), 95–108. doi:10.47992/IJMTS.2581.6012.0272

Aizenberg, E., & van den Hoven, J. (2020). Designing for human rights in AI. *Big Data & Society*, *7*(2). doi:10.1177/2053951720949566

Ali, M. Y., Naeem, S. B., Bhatti, R., & Richardson, J. (2022). Artificial intelligence application in university libraries of Pakistan: SWOT analysis and implications. *Global Knowledge, Memory and Communication*. . doi:10.1108/GKMC-12-2021-0203

Ali, M. Y., Naeem, S. B., & Bhatti, R. (2020). Artificial intelligence tools and perspectives of university librarians: An overview. *Business Information Review*, *37*(3), 116–124. doi:10.1177/0266382120952016

Aliouat, A., Kouadria, N., Maimour, M., Harize, S., & Doghmane, N. (2023). Region-of-interest based video coding strategy for rate/energy-constrained smart surveillance systems using WMSNs. *Ad Hoc Networks*, *140*, 103076. doi:10.1016/j.adhoc.2022.103076

Aloisi, A., & De Stefano, V. (2023). Between risk mitigation and labour rights enforcement: Assessing the transatlantic race to govern AI-driven decision-making through a comparative lens. *European Labour Law Journal*, *14*(2), 283–307. doi:10.1177/20319525231167982

Compilation of References

Alowais, S. A., Alghamdi, S. S., Alsuhebany, N., Alqahtani, T., Alshaya, A. I., Almohareb, S. N., Aldairem, A., Alrashed, M., Bin Saleh, K., Badreldin, H. A., Al Yami, M. S., Al Harbi, S., & Albekairy, A. M. (2023). Revolutionizing healthcare: The role of artificial intelligence in clinical practice. *BMC Medical Education*, 23(1), 689. doi:10.1186/s12909-023-04698-z PMID:37740191

Alpert, L. I. (2016). *Washington Post to cover every major race on election day with help of artificial.* intelligence.www.wsj.com/articles/washington-post-to-cover-every-race-on-election-day-with-the-helpof-artificial-intelligence-1476871202

Anderson, K. (2022). *Disability rights and digital technology: The global impact of the UN convention on the rights of persons with disabilities.* Lexington Books.

Anis, M. (2023). Leveraging Artificial Intelligence for Inclusive English Language Teaching: Strategies And Implications For Learner Diversity. *Journal of Multidisciplinary Educational Research*, 12(6).

Arya, H., & Mishra, P. (2011). Twitter: A new tool for academic libraries. *Journal of Advancements in Library Sciences*, 1(2), 11–17.

Asemi, A. & Asemi, A (2018). Artificial intelligence (AI) application in library systems in Iran: A taxonomy study. *Library Philosophy and Practice (e-journal)*, 7(9), 1-10.

Asemi, A., & Asemi, A. (2018). Artificial Intelligence (AI) Application in Library Systems in Iran: A Taxonomy Study. *Library Philosophy and Practice (e-journal).* https://digitalcommons.unl.edu/libphilprac/1840

Asemi, A., & Asemi, A. (2018). Artificial intelligence (AI) application in library systems in Iran: A taxonomy study. *Library Philosophy and Practice (e-journal).* https://digitalcommons.unl.edu/libphilprac/1840/

Asemi, A., &Asemi, A. (2018). Artificial Intelligence (AI) application in Library Systems in Iran: A taxonomy study. *Library Philosophy and Practice*, 2.

Asemi, A., Ko, I., & Nowkarizi, M. (2020). Application of Natural Language Processing in Library Cataloging: A Review. *Library Philosophy and Practice.*

Asemi, A., & Asemi, N. (2018). Intelligent library technologies: A review of knowledge-based assistance in library services. *International Journal of Information Science and Management*, 16(2), 91–108.

Asemi, A., Ko, A., & Nowkarizi, M. (2020, June 30). Intelligent libraries: A review on expert systems, artificial intelligence, and robot. *Library Hi Tech*, 39(2), 412–434. doi:10.1108/LHT-02-2020-0038

Awasthi, S. (2023). The Role of ChatGPT in Enhancing Financial Literacy and Education. *Journal of Applied Management-Jidnyasa*, 13-18.

Ayyadevara, R. (2018). Machine learning: Unveiling patterns in big data. *Journal of Artificial Intelligence Research*, 15(1), 102–120.Godfrey C (2008) Second life: A virtual world for libraries. *RSR. Reference Services Review*, 36(4), 433–439.

Bagchi, M. (2020). Conceptualizing a library chatbot using open-source conversational artificial intelligence. *DESIDOC Journal of Library and Information Technology*, 40(6), 329–333. doi:10.14429/djlit.40.06.15611

Bailey, C. W., Jr. (1991). Intelligent library systems: artificial intelligence technology and library automation systems. *Advances in Library Automation and Networking, 4.* Retrieved May 17, 2017, from http://eprints.rclis.org/4891/1/intlibs.pdf

Bali, M. M. E. I., Kumalasani, M. P., & Yunilasari, D. (2022). Artificial Intelligence in Higher Education: Intelligence dynamics between educators and students. *Journal of Innovation in Educational and Cultural Research*, 3(2), 146–152. doi:10.46843/jiecr.v3i2.88

Banerji, B., & Feroz, M. A. (2024). Elements of AI Ethical Regulatory Framework and SDGs. In *Exploring Ethical Dimensions of Environmental Sustainability and Use of AI* (pp. 126–139). IGI Global. doi:10.4018/979-8-3693-0892-9.ch007

Barsha, S., & Munshi, S. A. (2024). Implementing artificial intelligence in library services: A review of current prospects and challenges of developing countries. *Library Hi Tech News*, *41*(1), 7–10. doi:10.1108/LHTN-07-2023-0126

Bedi, G., & Sharma, R. (2021). Emerging trends in artificial intelligence (AI) and its applications in libraries: A review. *International Journal of Information Technology and Management*, *20*(2), 567–583.

Behan, J., & Keeffe, O. (2006). The development of an intelligent library assistant robot. In *Proceedings of the IASTED international conference on artificial intelligence and applications* (pp. 474–479). Academic Press.

Belgibaev, B., Mansurova, M., Abdrakhim, S., & Ormanbekova, A. (2024). Smart traffic lights with video vision based on a control minicomputer in Kazakhstani megacities. *Procedia Computer Science*, *231*, 792–797. doi:10.1016/j.procs.2023.12.136

Bello-Orgaz, G., & Camacho, D. (2021). The ethics of AI in digital libraries: A review. *The Journal of Documentation*, *77*(6), 1311–1331.

Bhattacharya, C., & Sinha, M. (2022). The role of artificial intelligence in banking for leveraging customer experience. *Australasian Accounting. Business and Finance Journal*, *16*(5), 89–105.

Bhutoria, A. (2022). Personalized education and artificial intelligence in the United States, China, and India: A systematic review using a human-in-the-loop model. *Computers and Education: Artificial Intelligence*, *3*, 100068. doi:10.1016/j.caeai.2022.100068

Bishnoi, L., & Narayan Singh, S. (2018). Artificial Intelligence Techniques Used In Medical Sciences: A Review. *2018 8th International Conference on Cloud Computing, Data Science & Engineering (Confluence)*, 1–8. 10.1109/CONFLUENCE.2018.8442729

Blakemore, E. (2016). *High tech shelf help: Singapore's library robot*. https://www.libraryjournal.com/?detailStory=high-tech-shelfhelp-singapores-library-robot

Borgohain, D. J., Bhardwaj, R. K., & Verma, M. K. (2024). Mapping the literature on the application of artificial intelligence in libraries (AAIL): A scientometric analysis. *Library Hi Tech*, *42*(1), 149–179. doi:10.1108/LHT-07-2022-0331

Bozkurt. (2023). https://medium.com/@ayhanbzkrt/chatgpt-user-guide-for-libraries-c09667745a8

Bozkurt, A., Karadeniz, A., Baneres, D., Guerrero-Roldán, A. E., & Rodríguez, M. E. (2021). Artificial Intelligence and Reflections from Educational Landscape: A Review of AI Studies in Half a Century. *Sustainability (Basel)*, *13*(2), 2. Advance online publication. doi:10.3390/su13020800

Brady, L. (2024). ChatGPT in medical libraries, possibilities and future directions: An integrative review. *Health Information and Libraries Journal*, *41*(1), 4–15. Advance online publication. doi:10.1111/hir.12518 PMID:38200693

Brown, A. (2022). Enhancing Library Services through AI-Powered Virtual Reality. *Journal of Library Technology*, *35*(2), 134–150.

Brown, C., Li, J., & Smith, A. (2021). Improving search accuracy in library catalogs using natural language processing. *Journal of Information Science*, *47*(6), 731–745.

Brown, L. M. (2022). Gendered artificial intelligence in libraries: Opportunities to deconstruct sexism and gender binarism. *Journal of Library Administration*, *62*(1), 19–30. doi:10.1080/01930826.2021.2006979

Compilation of References

Burtsev, M., Seliverstov, A., Airapetyan, R., Arkhipov, M., Baymurzina, D., Bushkov, N., ... Zaynutdinov, M. (2018, July). Deeppavlov: Open-source library for dialogue systems. In *Proceedings of ACL 2018, System Demonstrations* (pp. 122-127). 10.18653/v1/P18-4021

Cavedon, L., & Jatowt, A. (2020). Ethical aspects of digital libraries. *Journal of the Association for Information Science and Technology, 71*(1), 6–7.

Chang, M., & Wu, Y. (2024). The role of ethics in AI-driven digital library development: A conceptual framework. *The Journal of Documentation, 80*(2), 396–412.

Chen. (2023). Chat GPT and Its Possible Impact on Library Reference Services. *Internet Reference Services Quarterly, 27*(2), 121-129.

Chen, H., & Wu, Y. (2023). Automated Metadata Generation for Digital Collections: A Comparative Study of AI Techniques. *The Journal of Documentation, 79*(6), 1245–1260.

Chen, J., & ... . (2019). Personalized Book Recommendation System Based on Machine Learning in Library. *Journal of Library and Information Science, 45*(2), 123–136.

Chen, L. (2022). *Designing accessible libraries: Best practices and innovative approaches*. Morgan & Claypool Publishers.

Chen, M., & Wang, L. (2024). AI Literacy Education: Curriculum Development and Implementation. *Computers & Education, 40*(2), 98–115.

Chen, M., & Wang, L. (2024). Deep Learning Approaches for Content Recommendations. *Neural Networks, 40*(2), 98–115.

Chen, M., & Wang, L. (2024). Enhancing Content Recommendation Systems Using AI with Natural Language Processing. *Journal of Natural Language Engineering, 45*(4), 312–328.

Chen, Q., & Liu, W. (2023). AI-Driven Quality Control in Digital Library Collections. *Journal of Digital Information Management, 21*(2), 102342.

Chen, R., & Wang, L. (2022). Content Recommendation Systems Using AI in Digital Libraries. *International Journal on Digital Libraries, 45*(4), 312–328.

Chen, R., & Wang, L. (2022). Integrating AI Literacy across Disciplines: Interdisciplinary Perspectives. *Journal of Interdisciplinary Studies in Education, 45*(4), 312–328.

Chen, X., Xie, H., Zou, D., & Hwang, G.-J. (2020). Application and theory gaps during the rise of Artificial Intelligence in Education. *Computers and Education: Artificial Intelligence, 1*, 100002. doi:10.1016/j.caeai.2020.100002

Chen, X., & Zhang, L. (2023). Chatbots in Libraries: Enhancing Patron Services with AI Technology. *Journal of Academic Librarianship, 49*(3), 102964.

Chen, X., & Zhang, Y. (2023). AI-Powered Knowledge Discovery Systems for Library Collections: A Case Study. *Journal of Knowledge Management, 27*(5), 102768.

Chen, X., Zhang, Y., & Liu, Y. (2021). AI-powered library services: A literature review. *International Journal of Library Science, 22*(2), 145–158.

Chen, Y., & Huang, M. (2023). Ethical implications of AI in academic libraries: A content analysis. *Journal of Academic Librarianship, 49*(3), 102358.

Chen, Y., & Wang, H. (2023). Blockchain Technology for Secure and Transparent Library Transactions. *Library Hi Tech, 41*(4), 612–628.

Chen, Z., & Zhang, H. (2024). AI-driven digital libraries: Ethical considerations and guidelines. *Library Trends*, *72*(1), 104–123.

Chiancone, C. (2023, August 4). *The Library of the Future: AI in Public Libraries.* https://www.linkedin.com/pulse/library-future-ai-public-libraries-chris-chiancone/

Choi, I., & Kim, W. C. (2023). Enhancing financial literacy in South Korea: Integrating AI and data visualization to understand financial instruments' interdependencies. *Societal Impacts*, *1*(1-2), 100024. doi:10.1016/j.socimp.2023.100024

Cillo, P., & Zilinski, L. (2022). Ethical implications of AI applications in libraries. *Library Hi Tech*, *40*(3), 546–562.

Coleman, C. N. (2017). *Artificial intelligence and the library of the future revisited.* https://library.stanford.edu/blogs/digital-library-blog/2017/11/artificial-intelligence-and-library-future-revisited/

Corke, P. (2013). *Robotics, vision and control: Fundamental algorithms in MATLAB.* Springer.

Cotera, M. (2018). *We embrace digital innovation: IE University Library reinventing higher education.* 4th Lebanese Library Association Conference "Innovative Libraries: Paths to the future", in collaboration with IFLA Asia Oceania Section, Lebanon.

Cox, A. M., Pinfield, S., & Rutter, S. (2019). The intelligent library: Thought leaders' views on the likely impact of artificial intelligence on academic libraries. *Library Hi Tech*, *37*(3), 418–435. doi:10.1108/LHT-08-2018-0105

Croft, B. W., Metzler, D., & Strohman, T. (2015). *Search engines: information retrieval in practice.* Pearson Education, Inc. Retrieved June 16, 2019, from https://ciir.cs.umass.edu/downloads/SEIRiP.pdf

Culotta, A., & Mattei, N. (2024). Use Open Source for Safer Generative AI Experiments. *MIT Sloan Management Review*, *65*(2), 11–12. https://www.scopus.com/inward/record.uri?eid=2-s2.0-85183135558&partnerID=40&md5=f295b2a7b4e2a4261c695df98f73fc81

DasR. K.IslamM. S. U. (2021). *Application of Artificial Intelligence and Machine Learning in Libraries: A Systematic Review.* doi:10.48550/ARXIV.2112.04573

Davis, W. (2023). *Universal design in the digital world: A practical guide.* Elsevier.

De Sarkar, T. (2023). Implementing robotics in library services. *Library Hi Tech News*, *40*(1), 8–12. doi:10.1108/LHTN-11-2022-0123

Deng, Y., Xia, C. S., Peng, H., Yang, C., & Zhang, L. (2023). *Large Language Models are Zero-Shot Fuzzers: Fuzzing Deep-Learning Libraries via Large Language Models.* Academic Press.

Dennis, M. J., & Aizenberg, E. (2022). The Ethics of AI in Human Resources. *Ethics and Information Technology*, *24*(3), 25. doi:10.1007/s10676-022-09653-y

Divayana, D. G. H., Ariawan, I. P. W., Sugiarta, W., & Artanayasa, I. W. (2015). Digital library of expert system based at Indonesia Technology University. *International Journal of Advanced Research in Artificial Intelligence*, *4*(3), 1–8.

Eberhart, G. M. (2019). *An AI lab in a library: Why artificial intelligence matters.* American Libraries. Retrieved June 27, 2019, from https://americanlibrariesmagazine.org/blogs/the-scoop/ai-lab-library/

El Shazly, R. (2021). Effects of artificial intelligence on English speaking anxiety and speaking performance: A case study. *Expert Systems: International Journal of Knowledge Engineering and Neural Networks*, *38*(3), e12667. doi:10.1111/exsy.12667

Compilation of References

Elhajjar, S., Karam, S., & Borna, S. (2020, November 3). Artificial intelligence in marketing education programs. *Marketing Education Review*, *31*(1), 2–13. doi:10.1080/10528008.2020.1835492

Eslit, E. R. (2023). Voyaging Beyond Chalkboards: Unleashing Tomorrow's Minds through AI-Driven Frontiers in Literature and Language Education. Academic Press.

Ex Libris. (2019). *How AI can enhance the value of research libraries*. Retrieved October 4,2019, www.libraryjournal.com/?detailStory=how-ai-can-enhancethe-value-of-research-libraries

Fakhri, P. S., Asghari, O., Sarspy, S., Marand, M. B., Moshaver, P., & Trik, M. (2023). A fuzzy decision-making system for video tracking with multiple objects in non-stationary conditions. *Heliyon*, *9*(11), e22156. doi:10.1016/j.heliyon.2023.e22156 PMID:38034808

Farney, T. (2020). Library technology: Innovating technologies, services, and practices. *College & Undergraduate Libraries*, *27*(2–4), 51–55. doi:10.1080/10691316.2020.1952776

Felzmann, H., Fosch-Villaronga, E., Lutz, C., & Tamò-Larrieux, A. (2020). Towards Transparency by Design for Artificial Intelligence. *Science and Engineering Ethics*, *26*(6), 3333–3361. doi:10.1007/s11948-020-00276-4 PMID:33196975

Ferguson, I. A., & Durfee, E. H. (1998, October). Artificial intelligence in digital libraries: Moving from chaos to (more) order. *International Journal on Digital Libraries*, *2*(1), 1–2. doi:10.1007/s007990050032

Fine, A. (2017). *Artificially intelligent math for school educators*. https://districtadministration.com/artificially-intelligent-math-forschool-educators

Fukuda-Parr, S., & Gibbons, E. (2021). Emerging Consensus on 'Ethical AI': Human Rights Critique of Stakeholder Guidelines. *Global Policy*, *12*(S6), 32–44. doi:10.1111/1758-5899.12965

Gale, W. G., & Levine, R. (2011). Financial literacy: What works? How could it be more effective? *How could it be more effective*.

Garai-Fodor, M., Varga, J., & Csiszárik-Kocsir, Á. (2022, March). Generation-specific perceptions of financial literacy and digital solutions. In *2022 IEEE 20th Jubilee World Symposium on Applied Machine Intelligence and Informatics (SAMI)* (pp. 193-200). IEEE. 10.1109/SAMI54271.2022.9780717

Garcia, C., & Martinez, A. (2023). Autonomous Inventory Management Systems for Libraries using RFID and AI. *Library Resources & Technical Services*, *67*(2), 65–78.

Garcia, E., & Rodriguez, M. (2022). Content Recommendation Systems Using AI for Social Media Platforms. *Journal of Social Media Analytics*, *38*(3), 189–204.

Garcia, E., & Rodriguez, M. (2022). Fostering AI Literacy through Informal Learning Environments. *Journal of Informal Learning*, *38*(3), 189–204.

Garcia, F., & Martinez, S. (2023). AI Literacy for Workforce Development: Vocational Education and Training Programs. *Journal of Vocational Education and Training*, *20*(1), 56–72.

Garcia, F., & Martinez, S. (2023). Visual Content Recommendation Systems Using AI. *Journal of Visual Communication and Image Representation*, *38*(3), 189–204.

Garcia-Febo, L. (2019). Exploring AI: How libraries are starting to apply artificial intelligence in their work. American Libraries. https://americanlibrariesmagazine.org/2019/03/01/exploring-ai/

Gazzawe, F., & Albahar, M. (2024). Reducing traffic congestion in makkah during Hajj through the use of AI technology. *Heliyon*, *10*(1), e23304–e23304. doi:10.1016/j.heliyon.2023.e23304 PMID:38187331

Ge, L., Dan, D., Koo, K. Y., & Chen, Y. (2023). An improved system for long-term monitoring of full-bridge traffic load distribution on long-span bridges. *Structures, 54*, 1076–1089. https://doi.org/https://doi.org/10.1016/j.istruc.2023.05.103

George, D. A. S., George, A. S. H., & Martin, A. S. G. (2023). ChatGPT and the Future of Work: A Comprehensive Analysis of AI's Impact on Jobs and Employment. *Partners Universal International Innovation Journal, 1*(3), 3. Advance online publication. doi:10.5281/zenodo.8076921

Gilbert, R. (2019). Inclusive design for a digital world: Designing with accessibility in mind. Academic Press.

Goli, M., Sahu, A. K., Bag, S., & Dhamija, P. (2023, February 24). Users' acceptance of artificial intelligence-based chatbots: An empirical study. *International Journal of Technology and Human Interaction, 19*(1), 1–18. doi:10.4018/IJTHI.318481

Gozalo-Brizuela, R., & Garrido-Merchan, E. C. (2023). ChatGPT is not all you need. *A State of the Art Review of large Generative AI models* (arXiv:2301.04655). arXiv. http://arxiv.org/abs/2301.04655

Grimes, N., & Porter, W. (2023). Closing the digital divide through digital equity: The role of libraries and librarians. *Public Library Quarterly*, 1–32. doi:10.1080/01616846.2023.2251348

Gujral, M., Smith, J., Johnson, A., Martin, R., Wilson, S., & Davis, L. (2019). Chatbot applications in libraries: A literature review. *International Journal of Information Science and Management, 17*(2), 87–102.

Guo, H., & Polak, P. (2021). Artificial intelligence and financial technology FinTech: How AI is being used under the pandemic in 2020. *The fourth industrial revolution: implementation of artificial intelligence for growing business success*, 169-186.

Guo, F., Wang, Y., & Qian, Y. (2023). Real-time dense traffic detection using lightweight backbone and improved path aggregation feature pyramid network. *Journal of Industrial Information Integration, 31*, 100427. doi:10.1016/j.jii.2022.100427

Guo, J., & Zhu, X. (2024). Ethical considerations in AI implementation for digital libraries: A case study of algorithmic bias. *The Journal of Documentation, 80*(4), 783–799.

Gupta, M., Miglani, H., Deo, P., & Barhatte, A. (2023). Real-time traffic control and monitoring. *E-Prime - Advances in Electrical Engineering, Electronics and Energy, 5*, 100211. https://doi.org/https://doi.org/10.1016/j.prime.2023.100211

Gupta, M., & Kumar, S. (2024). AI Literacy for Lifelong Learning: Continuing Education and Professional Development Programs. *Lifelong Learning in Europe, 45*(2), 98–115.

Gupta, M., & Kumar, S. (2024). Federated Learning for Privacy-Preserving Content Recommendations. *Journal of Parallel and Distributed Computing, 45*(2), 98–115.

Gupta, P. (2023). *Technology-enabled innovations for accessibility in library services: Emerging research and opportunities*. Information Science Reference.

Gustavsson, J., & Hedlund, M. (2011). The art of writing & speaking, https://www.svet.lu.se/sites/svet.lu.se/en/files/art-of-writingspeaking-2011.pdf

Habbal, A., Ali, M. K., & Abuzaraida, M. A. (2024). Artificial Intelligence Trust, Risk and Security Management (AI TRiSM): Frameworks, applications, challenges and future research directions. *Expert Systems with Applications, 240*, 122442. doi:10.1016/j.eswa.2023.122442

Haffenden, C., Fano, E., Malmsten, M., & Börjeson, L. (2023). Making and using AI in the library: Creating a BERT model at the national library of Sweden. *College & Research Libraries*, *84*(1). Advance online publication. doi:10.5860/crl.84.1.30

Hagendorff, T. (2020). The ethics of AI ethics–An evaluation of guidelines. *Minds and Machines*, *30*(1), 99–120. doi:10.1007/s11023-020-09517-8

Haleem, A., Javaid, M., & Khan, I. H. (2019). Current status and applications of Artificial Intelligence (AI) in medical field: An overview. *Current Medicine Research and Practice*, *9*(6), 231–237. doi:10.1016/j.cmrp.2019.11.005

Hamad, F., Al-Fadel, M., & Fakhouri, H. (2022). The provision of smart service at academic libraries and associated challenges. *Journal of Librarianship and Information Science*, 096100062211141. Advance online publication. doi:10.1177/09610006221114173

Haney, B. S. (2018). The Perils & Promises of Artificial General Intelligence. SSRN *Electronic Journal*. doi:10.2139/ssrn.3261254

Hao, J., & Zhang, H. (2020). The ethical challenges of using AI in education. *International Journal of Information and Education Technology (IJIET)*, *10*(8), 575–580.

Harisanty, D., Anna, N. E. V., Putri, T. E., Firdaus, A. A., & Noor Azizi, N. A. (2022). Leaders, practitioners and scientists' awareness of artificial intelligence in libraries: A pilot study. *Library Hi Tech*. Advance online publication. doi:10.1108/LHT-10-2021-0356

Hashimoto, D. A., Rosman, G., Rus, D., & Meireles, O. R. (2018, July). Artificial Intelligence in Surgery: Promises and Perils. *Annals of Surgery*, *268*(1), 70–76. doi:10.1097/SLA.0000000000002693 PMID:29389679

Hastungkara, D. P., & Triastuti, E. (2019). Application of e-learning and artificial intelligence in education systems in Indonesia. *Anglo-Saxon*, *10*(2), 117-133.

Heilinger, J.-C. (2022). The Ethics of AI Ethics. A Constructive Critique. *Philosophy & Technology*, *35*(3), 61. doi:10.1007/s13347-022-00557-9

Hepper, E. G., Gramzow, R. H., & Sedikides, C. (2010). Individual differences in self-enhancement and self-protection strategies: An integrative analysis. *Journal of Personality*, *78*(2), 781–814. doi:10.1111/j.1467-6494.2010.00633.x PMID:20433637

Herrlich, H. (2023, May 23). *The Future of Libraries: AI and Machine learning – Fordham Library News*. https://librarynews.blog.fordham.edu/2023/05/23/the-future-of-libraries-ai-and-machine-learning/

Hervieux, S., & Wheatley, A. (2021). Perceptions of artificial intelligence: A survey of academic librarians in Canada and the United States. *Journal of Academic Librarianship*, *47*(1), 102270. doi:10.1016/j.acalib.2020.102270

He, Y., Jiang, Y., Song, X., & Xie, Y. (2020). Artificial intelligence for library service innovation: A review. *Journal of Information Science and Technology*, *16*(2), 220–232.

Hirsch, T., & Hofer, B. (2022). Using textual bug reports to predict the fault category of software bugs. *Array (New York, N.Y.)*, *15*, 100189. doi:10.1016/j.array.2022.100189

Hodonu-Wusu, J. O. (2024). The rise of artificial intelligence in libraries: The ethical and equitable methodologies, and prospects for empowering library users. *AI and Ethics*. Advance online publication. doi:10.1007/s43681-024-00432-7

Huang, Y.-H. (2022). Exploring the implementation of artificial intelligence applications among academic libraries in Taiwan. *Library Hi Tech*. Advance online publication. doi:10.1108/LHT-03-2022-0159

Hung, A., Parker, A. M., & Yoong, J. (2009). Defining and measuring financial literacy. Academic Press.

Hussain, A. (2020). Cutting edge. In Advances in library and information science (ALIS) book series (pp. 16–27). doi:10.4018/978-1-7998-1482-5.ch002

Hussain, S. (2022). Transforming library services in the age of modern information technology. *Journal of Library Innovation*, *14*(3), 45–62.

Hwang, G.-J., & Chang, C.-Y. (2021). A review of opportunities and challenges of chatbots in education. *Interactive Learning Environments*, 1–14. doi:10.1080/10494820.2021.1952615

Jaillant, L., & Rees, A. (2023). Applying AI to digital archives: Trust, collaboration and shared professional ethics. *Digital Scholarship in the Humanities*, *38*(2), 571–585. doi:10.1093/llc/fqac073

Jange, S. (2015, January). Innovative services and practices in academic libraries. *2015 4th International Symposium on Emerging Trends and Technologies in Libraries and Information Services*. 10.1109/ETTLIS.2015.7048194

Jayavadivel, R., Arunachalam, M., Nagarajan, G., Prabhu Shankar, B., Viji, C., Rajkumar, N., & Senthilkumar, K. R. (2024). Historical Overview of AI Adoption in Libraries. In K. Senthilkumar (Ed.), *AI-Assisted Library Reconstruction* (pp. 267–289). IGI Global. doi:10.4018/979-8-3693-2782-1.ch015

Jiang, Q., Zak, L., Leshem, S., Rampa, P., Howle, S., Green, H. N., & Iqbal, T. (2023, April). Embodied AI for Financial Literacy Social Robots. In *2023 Systems and Information Engineering Design Symposium (SIEDS)* (pp. 220-225). IEEE. 10.1109/SIEDS58326.2023.10137791

Jobin, A., Ienca, M., & Vayena, E. (2021). The global landscape of AI ethics guidelines. *Nature Machine Intelligence*, *3*(6), 486–495.

Johnson, B. (2019). Enhancing user engagement in public libraries through AI chatbots. *Public Library Quarterly*, *38*(2), 143–156.

Johnson, K., & Anderson, J. (2023). Enhancing User Experience in Digital Libraries through AI-Powered Recommender Systems. *Information Technology and Libraries*, *42*(2), 32–45.

Johnson, L., & … . (2018). Virtual Reality Library Orientation: A Case Study. *Journal of Academic Librarianship*, *44*(3), 332–337.

Jones, M. (1985). Applications of Artificial Intelligence within Education. *Computers & Mathematics with Applications*, *11*(5), 517-526.

Jones, K. S., & Smith, A. J. (2022). Ethical considerations in AI-driven digital library development. *The Journal of Documentation*, *78*(1), 226–244.

Jones, K., & White, E. (2023). AI Literacy Programs for K-12 Education: A Systematic Review. *Educational Technology Research and Development*, *28*(3), 215–230.

Jones, K., & White, E. (2023). Hybrid Content Recommendation Systems Incorporating AI Techniques. *Journal of Intelligent Information Systems*, *44*(2), 30–45.

Jones, L., & Smith, J. (2023). AI-Powered Chatbots for Library Reference Services. *Journal of Information Science*, *45*(1), 76–89.

Julakanti, S. (2023). The Pandemic's Impact on the Intersections of Financial Literacy, AI, and Behavioral Economics. *Journal of Student Research*, *12*(4). Advance online publication. doi:10.47611/jsrhs.v12i4.5453

Compilation of References

Kai-jun, Y., Gong, R., Sun, L., & Jiang, C. (2019, January 1). The application of artificial intelligence in smart library. doi:10.2991/icoi-19.2019.124

Kamal, M., Bhat, S. A., & Wani, G. M. (2020). Role of academic libraries in providing personalized services in the era of the digital world. *International Journal of Innovative Technology and Exploring Engineering, 9*(4S), 1067–1072.

Kavoliūnaitė-Ragauskienė, E. (2024). Right to Privacy and Data Protection Concerns Raised by the Development and Usage of Face Recognition Technologies in the European Union. *Journal of Human Rights Practice*. Advance online publication. doi:10.1093/jhuman/huad065

Kellam, L. M., & Thompson, K. (Eds.). (2016). Databrarianship: The academic data librarian in theory and practice. Association of College and Research Libraries, a division of the American Library Association.

Khang, A., Shah, V., & Rani, S. (Eds.). (2023). *Handbook of Research on AI-Based Technologies and Applications in the Era of the Metaverse*. IGI Global. doi:10.4018/978-1-6684-8851-5

Khan, R., Gupta, N., Sinhababu, A., & Chakravarty, R. (2023). Impact of Conversational and Generative AI Systems on Libraries: A Use Case Large Language Model (LLM). *Science & Technology Libraries*, 1–15. doi:10.1080/0194262X.2023.2254814

Khanzode, K. C. A., & Sarode, R. D. (2020). Advantages and disadvantages of artificial intelligence and machine learning: A literature review. *International Journal of Library and Information Science*.

Kim, D. S. (2006, July). A study on introducing six sigma theory in the library for service competitiveness enhancement. In *Proceedings of the World Library and Information Congress: 72nd IFLA General Conference and Council, Seoul, Korea* (pp. 20-24). Academic Press.

Kim, H., & Lee, J. (2024). Ethical implications of AI-driven digital library development: A meta-analysis. *International Journal of Digital Library Management*.

Kim, A., & Lee, J. (2024). AI Literacy for Citizen Science: Engaging Communities in Scientific Inquiry. *Citizen Science: Theory and Practice, 38*(2), 98–115.

Kim, A., & Lee, J. (2024). Temporal Content Recommendation Systems Using AI. *Journal of Information Science, 38*(2), 98–115.

Kim, D., & Choi, E. (2023). Data Mining Techniques for User Behavior Analysis in Digital Libraries. *Journal of Information Retrieval Research, 16*(3), 102845.

Kim, E., & Park, J. (2022). AI Literacy and Media Literacy: Intersections and Synergies in Educational Programs. *Media Education Research Journal, 38*(3), 189–204.

Kim, E., & Park, J. (2022). Deep Learning-based Content Recommendation Systems Using AI. *Journal of Deep Learning Technologies, 45*(2), 98–115.

Kim, H., & Jung, S. (2023). AI-Driven Citation Analysis for Collection Development in Academic Libraries. *Journal of Librarianship and Information Science, 55*(2), 321–335.

Kim, H., Lee, J., & Park, S. (2022). Context-Aware Content Recommendation Systems Using AI. *ACM Transactions on Information Systems, 45*(4), 123–140.

Kim, H., Lee, J., & Park, S. (2022). Teaching AI Literacy: Best Practices and Challenges. *Journal of Educational Technology & Society, 45*(4), 312–328.

Kim, H., & Park, J. (2023). Culturally Responsive AI Literacy Education: Considerations and Recommendations. *Cultural Studies of Science Education, 20*(1), 56–72.

Kim, H., & Park, J. (2023). Real-time Content Recommendation Systems Using AI. *Journal of Real-Time Systems, 20*(1), 56–72.

Kim, J. (2023). *The future of accessibility in international higher education*. Routledge.

Kim, J. Y., & Park, Y. J. (2022). Artificial intelligence and library services: A review of research trends. *Journal of Korean Library and Information Science Society, 56*(2), 101–122.

Kim, J., & Lee, E. (2023). Incorporating AI Ethics into Educational Programs: A Critical Pedagogical Approach. *Journal of Educational Ethics and Philosophy, 38*(3), 189–204.

Kim, J., & Lee, E. (2023). Mobile Content Recommendation Systems Using AI. *Mobile Information Systems, 38*(3), 189–204.

Kim, S., & Lee, J. (2022). Content Recommendation Systems Using AI: A Comprehensive Review. *Information Processing & Management, 58*(2), 87–102.

Kim, Y., & Park, J. (2023). Ethical guidelines for AI implementation in digital libraries: A comparative study. *Journal of the American Society for Information Science and Technology, 74*(2), 278–292.

Kim, Y., & Park, S. (2023). Knowledge Graphs in Library Cataloging: A Review of AI Techniques. *Cataloging & Classification Quarterly, 61*(1), 67–82.

Kitchin, R. (2014). Big data, new epistemologies and paradigm shifts. *Big Data & Society, 1*(1). doi:10.1177/2053951714528481

Kling, R., & Elliott, M. (1994). Digital library design for organizational usability. *ACM SIGGROUP Bulletin, 15*(2), 59–70. doi:10.1145/192611.192746

Koltay, T. (2019). Accepted and emerging roles of academic libraries in supporting research 2.0. *Journal of Academic Librarianship, 45*(2), 75–80. doi:10.1016/j.acalib.2019.01.001

Kong, H., Yun, W., Joo, W., Kim, J. H., Kim, K. K., Moon, I. C., & Kim, W. C. (2022). Constructing a personalized recommender system for life insurance products with machine-learning techniques. *International Journal of Intelligent Systems in Accounting Finance & Management, 29*(4), 242–253. doi:10.1002/isaf.1523

Koskelainen, T., Kalmi, P., Scornavacca, E., & Vartiainen, T. (2023). Financial literacy in the digital age—A research agenda. *The Journal of Consumer Affairs, 57*(1), 507–528. doi:10.1111/joca.12510

Kotios, D., Makridis, G., Fatouros, G., & Kyriazis, D. (2022). Deep learning enhancing banking services: A hybrid transaction classification and cash flow prediction approach. *Journal of Big Data, 9*(1), 100. doi:10.1186/s40537-022-00651-x PMID:36213092

Kruse, L., Wunderlich, N., & Beck, R. (2019). Artificial intelligence for the financial services industry: What challenges organizations to succeed. Academic Press.

Kulkarni, S. (2023). *Machine-Learning-Assisted Recommendation System for Financial Organizations* (Doctoral dissertation, Westcliff University).

Kumar, D., & Suthar, N. (2024). Ethical and legal challenges of AI in marketing: An exploration of solutions. *Journal of Information, Communication and Ethics in Society*. doi:10.1108/JICES-05-2023-0068

Kumar, N., Antoniraj, S., Jayanthi, S., Mirdula, S., Selvaraj, S., Rajkumar, N., & Senthilkumar, K. R. (2024). Educational Technology and Libraries Supporting Online Learning. In K. Senthilkumar (Ed.), *AI-Assisted Library Reconstruction* (pp. 209–237). IGI Global. doi:10.4018/979-8-3693-2782-1.ch012

Kumar, N., & Singh, S. (2022). Content Recommendation Systems Using AI for Health and Wellness Applications. *Journal of Health Informatics*, *38*(2), 98–115.

Kurshan, E., Shen, H., & Chen, J. (2020, October). Towards self-regulating AI: Challenges and opportunities of AI model governance in financial services. In *Proceedings of the First ACM International Conference on AI in Finance* (pp. 1-8). 10.1145/3383455.3422564

Larivière, V., Haustein, S., & Mongeon, P. (2015). The oligopoly of academic publishers in the digital era. *PLoS One*, *10*(6), e0127502. doi:10.1371/journal.pone.0127502 PMID:26061978

Latte, A., & Bankapur, V. M. (2022) Evaluation of Web Content of Selected Private Medical College Libraries in Karnataka. *Journal of Library Development, 8*(2). http://hdl.handle.net/10760/43684

Lee, A. S., Babenko, O., George, M., & Daniels, V. (2022, September 6). The promises and perils of remote proctoring using artificial intelligence. *Canadian Medical Education Journal*. Advance online publication. doi:10.36834/cmej.74299 PMID:37304635

Lee, D., & Park, H. (2024). Multi-criteria Content Recommendation Systems Using AI. *Journal of Multi-Criteria Decision Analysis*, *20*(1), 56–72.

Lee, H. W. (2019). Applying online educational technology to foster financial literacy: Financial-institution leaders' insights. *The Qualitative Report*, *24*(10), 2625–2654. doi:10.46743/2160-3715/2019.3605

Lee, H., & Kim, J. (2022). AI Literacy for Health Education: Promoting Health Literacy in the Digital Age. *Health Education & Behavior*, *45*(4), 312–328.

Lee, H., & Kim, J. (2022). Robust Content Recommendation Systems Using AI. *Journal of Systems and Software*, *45*(4), 312–328.

Lee, H., & Kim, S. (2023). Personalized Recommendation Systems in Library Collections: A Review of Emerging AI Techniques. *Library Hi Tech*, *41*(2), 305–321.

Lee, J., & Kim, M. (2023). AI-Driven Preservation Strategies for Digital Libraries. Preservation. *Digital Technology & Culture*, *52*(3), 102664.

Lei, X., Fathi, J., Noorbakhsh, S., & Rahimi, M. (2022). The impact of mobile-assisted language learning on English as a foreign language learners' vocabulary learning attitudes and self-regulatory capacity. *Frontiers in Psychology*, *13*, 872922. doi:10.3389/fpsyg.2022.872922 PMID:35800918

Leskovec, J., Rajaraman, A., & Ullman, J. D. (2014). *Mining of massive datasets*. Cambridge University Press. doi:10.1017/CBO9781139924801

Levantesi, S., & Zacchia, G. (2021). Machine learning and financial literacy: An exploration of factors influencing financial knowledge in Italy. *Journal of Risk and Financial Management*, *14*(3), 120. doi:10.3390/jrfm14030120

Levine, G. S. (2004). Global simulation: A student-centered, task-based format for intermediate foreign language courses. *Foreign Language Annals*, *37*(1), 26–36. doi:10.1111/j.1944-9720.2004.tb02170.x

Liang, J. C., Hwang, G. J., Chen, M. R. A., & Darmawansah, D. (2021). Roles and research foci of artificial intelligence in language education: An integrated bibliographic analysis and systematic review approach. *Interactive Learning Environments*, *31*(7), 4270–4296. doi:10.1080/10494820.2021.1958348

LibLime. (2023, December 4). *Revolutionizing Library Cataloging with Artificial Intelligence (AI)*. https://www.linkedin.com/pulse/revolutionizing-library-cataloging-artificial-intelligence-ai-coo9c

Li, J., & Zhao, X. (2018). The impact of AI-powered recommendation systems on user satisfaction in academic libraries. *Journal of Academic Librarianship*, *44*(3), 301–309.

Lin, T., & Liu, Q. (2024). Ethical challenges in AI implementation for digital libraries: Insights from a case study. *Information Processing & Management*, *60*(2), 102655.

Liu, C., & Chang, J. (2023). The ethics of AI in digital libraries: A case study of privacy concerns. *Library Hi Tech*, *41*(1), 32–49.

Liu, G. (2011). The application of intelligent agents in libraries: A survey. *Program*, *45*(1), 78–97. doi:10.1108/00330331111107411

Liu, Q., & Chen, H. (2024). Ethical dimensions of AI implementation in digital libraries: A comparative analysis. *Journal of the American Society for Information Science and Technology*.

Liu, X., & Wu, Z. (2023). Leveraging Natural Language Processing for Semantic Enrichment in Digital Libraries. *Journal of the Association for Information Science and Technology*, *74*(6), 1350–1365.

Liu, Y., & Zhang, Q. (2023). AI-Enabled Data Fusion for Cross-Domain Information Integration in Libraries. *Information Fusion*, *78*, 85–98.

Li, X., & Zhang, Q. (2023). Reinforcement Learning for Optimal Resource Allocation in Library Operations. *Information Processing & Management*, *59*(2), 102765.

Li, Y., Lee, K. H., & Hsieh, L. (2021). Ethical issues in AI-driven digital libraries. In *International Conference on Information* (pp. 84-95). Springer.

Li, Y., & Yang, J. (2023). AI-Powered Virtual Assistants for Reference Services in Libraries. *RSR. Reference Services Review*, *51*(2), 102598.

Loncar, M., Schams, W., & Liang, J. S. (2023). Multiple technologies, multiple sources: Trends and analyses of the literature on technology-mediated feedback for L2 English writing published from 2015-2019. *Computer Assisted Language Learning*, *36*(4), 722–784. doi:10.1080/09588221.2021.1943452

Lund, B. D., & Wang, T. (2023). Chatting about ChatGPT: How may AI and GPT impact academia and libraries? *Library Hi Tech News*, *40*(3), 26–29. doi:10.1108/LHTN-01-2023-0009

Lupton, M. (2020). Artificial intelligence in libraries: Implications for ethics, bias and the future of librarianship. *Library & Information Science Research*, *42*(3), 232–243.

Lusardi, A., & Mitchell, O. S. (2011). Financial literacy around the world: An overview. *Journal of Pension Economics and Finance*, *10*(4), 497–508. doi:10.1017/S1474747211000448 PMID:28553190

Mahmood, K., & Richardson, J. V. Jr. (2013, August 2). Impact of Web 2.0 technologies on academic libraries: A survey of ARL libraries. *The Electronic Library*, *31*(4), 508–520. doi:10.1108/EL-04-2011-0068

Makhija, P., Chacko, E., & Sinha, M. (2021). Transforming Financial Sector Through Financial Literacy and Fintech Revolution. *Financial Inclusion in Emerging Markets: A Road Map for Sustainable Growth*, 239-255.

Compilation of References

Makri, S., & Warwick, C. (2020). Ethical implications of AI in academic libraries. *Journal of Academic Librarianship*, *46*(2), 102146.

Mallikarjuna, A., & Prabhakar, N. (2021). Impact of Artificial Intelligence (AI) applications on academic libraries. Pearl. *Journal of Library and Information Science*, *15*(1), 46–52. doi:10.5958/0975-6922.2021.00006.1

Malpani, A. (1999). Health library in India works to empower patients. *BMJ (Clinical Research Ed.)*, *319*(7212), 785–785. doi:10.1136/bmj.319.7212.785 PMID:10488022

Mandell, L. (2008). Financial literacy of high school students. In *Handbook of consumer finance research* (pp. 163–183). Springer New York. doi:10.1007/978-0-387-75734-6_10

Mandell, L., & Klein, L. S. (2009). The impact of financial literacy education on subsequent financial behavior. *Financial Counseling and Planning*, *20*(1).

Manfletti, C., Guimarães, M., & Soares, C. (2023). AI for space traffic management. *The Journal of Space Safety Engineering*, *10*(4), 495–504. doi:10.1016/j.jsse.2023.08.007

Manser Payne, E. H., Peltier, J., & Barger, V. A. (2021). Enhancing the value co-creation process: Artificial intelligence and mobile banking service platforms. *Journal of Research in Interactive Marketing*, *15*(1), 68–85. doi:10.1108/JRIM-10-2020-0214

Mao, Y., & Shi-Kupfer, K. (2023). Online public discourse on artificial intelligence and ethics in China: Context, content, and implications. *AI & Society*, *38*(1), 373–389. doi:10.1007/s00146-021-01309-7 PMID:34803237

Mardanghom, R., & Sandal, H. (2019). *Artificial intelligence in financial services: an analysis of the AI technology and the potential applications, implications, and risks it may propagate in financial services* (Master's thesis).

Marty, J.-Y., Bonnal, C., Faucher, P., & Francillout, L. (2023). Space traffic management as a necessity for future orbital operations a French perspective. *Acta Astronautica*, *202*, 278–282. doi:10.1016/j.actaastro.2022.09.051

Massis, B. (2018, July 9). Artificial intelligence arrives in the library. *Information and Learning Science*, *119*(7/8), 456–459. doi:10.1108/ILS-02-2018-0011

Mazurek, G. (2023). Artificial Intelligence, Law, and Ethics (Polish Text). *Krytyka Prawa. Niezalezne Studia and Prawem*, *2023*, 7.

McCorduck, P. (2004). Machines who think. *Artificial Intelligence*, 340–400.

Mckie, I. A. S., & Narayan, B. (2019). Enhancing the academic library experience with chatbots: An exploration of research and implications for practice. *Journal of the Australian Library and Information Association*, *68*(3), 268–277. doi:10.1080/24750158.2019.1611694

Micheli, M., Gevaert, C. M., Carman, M., Craglia, M., Daemen, E., Ibrahim, R. E., Kotsev, A., Mohamed-Ghouse, Z., Schade, S., Schneider, I., Shanley, L. A., Tartaro, A., & Vespe, M. (2022). AI ethics and data governance in the geospatial domain of Digital Earth. *Big Data & Society*, *9*(2). doi:10.1177/20539517221138767

Misra, S. K., Sharma, S. K., Gupta, S., & Das, S. (2023). A framework to overcome challenges to the adoption of artificial intelligence in Indian Government Organizations. *Technological Forecasting and Social Change*, *194*, 122721. doi:10.1016/j.techfore.2023.122721

Mittelstadt, B. (2021). Ethics of AI in Libraries: Navigating Opportunities, Risks, and Responsibilities. In *Proceedings of the International Conference on Theory and Practice of Digital Libraries* (pp. 321-335). Springer.

Miu, C., Gopurathingal, J., Thota, V., Thompson, M., van Beek, N., Kuczynski, J., ... Iqbal, T. (2022, April). A financial literacy ai-enabled voice assistant system for educational use. In *2022 Systems and Information Engineering Design Symposium (SIEDS)* (pp. 345-350). IEEE. 10.1109/SIEDS55548.2022.9799370

Mizrahi, K. G., & Sarit, K. (2024). A Human-Centered Approach to AI Governance: Operationalizing Human Rights through Citizen Participation. In *Human-Centered AI*. Chapman and Hall/CRC.

Mogali, D. S. S. (2014). *Artificial Intelligence and its Applications in Libraries.* https://www.researchgate.net/publication/287878456

Mogali, S. S. (2014, February). Artificial Intelligence and its applications in libraries. *Bilingual International Conference on Information Technology: Yesterday, Today and Tomorrow*.

Mogali, S. S. (2015). Artificial intelligence and it's applications in libraries. *University of Agricultural Science Krishinagar Journal, 3*(1), 1–11.

Mohanraj, A., Viji, C., Varadarajan, M. N., Kalpana, C., Shankar, B., Jayavadivel, R., Rajkumar, N., & Jagajeevan, R. (2024). *Privacy and Security in Digital Libraries.* doi:10.4018/979-8-3693-2782-1.ch006

Moustapha, A., & Yusuf, B. (2023). Artificial intelligence adoption and utilization by librarians in university libraries in Kwara State, Nigeria. *Library Philosophy and Practice (e-journal), 7917*. Retrieved from https://digitalcommons.unl.edu/libphilprac/7917

Moybeka, A. M., Syariatin, N., Tatipang, D. P., Mushthoza, D. A., Dewi, N. P. J. L., & Tineh, S. (2023). Artificial Intelligence and English Classroom: The Implications of AI Toward EFL Students' Motivation. *Edumaspul: Jurnal Pendidikan, 7*(2), 2444–2454. doi:10.33487/edumaspul.v7i2.6669

Murgatroyd, S. (2024, February 25). Artificial Intelligence and future of higher education. *Revista Paraguya Education a Distancia, 5*(1), 4–11. doi:10.56152/reped2024-vol5num1-art1

Murphy, D. (2015). *Robotics and the human touch in libraries and museums.* Available online https://slis.simmons.edu/blogs/unbound/2015/04/06/robotics-and-the-human-touch-in-libraries-and-museums/

Murugesan, R., & Manohar, V. (2019). Ai in financial sector–a driver to financial literacy. *Shanlax International Journal of Commerce, 7*(3), 66–70. doi:10.34293/commerce.v7i3.477

Naik, P., Keshava, & Khan, K. M. (2019). User's perception on e-resource services: a case study of yenepoya institute of technology library. *National Conference: Knowledge Organization in Academic Libraries (I-KOAL)-2019*.

Natarajan, M., & Velmurugan, T. (2022). Implementation of Artificial Intelligence in Libraries: A Systematic Review. *International Journal of Library and Information Science, 14*(1), 1–14.

Nguyen, C., & Tran, T. (2023). AI Literacy and Digital Citizenship: Empowering Students for Lee, D., & Park, H. (2024). "Addressing AI Bias in Educational Programs: Equity, Diversity, and Inclusion Perspectives. *Equity & Excellence in Education, 45*(2), 98–115.

Nguyen, C., & Tran, T. (2023). Location-based Content Recommendation Systems Using AI. *Journal of Location Based Services, 38*(3), 189–204.

Nguyen, J., & Tran, L. (2024). Content Recommendation Systems Using AI for Cultural Heritage. *Journal of Cultural Heritage, 20*(1), 56–72.

Nguyen, L., & Tran, T. (2023). AI Literacy Initiatives in Higher Education: Case Studies and Lessons Learned. *The Journal of Higher Education, 18*(4), 231–246.

Nguyen, L., & Tran, T. (2023). Semantic Web Technologies for Content Recommendation Systems Using AI. *Journal of Web Semantics*, *38*(3), 189–204.

Nguyen, L., & Tran, T. (2024). Semantic Content Recommendation Systems Using AI. *Information Sciences*, *45*(2), 98–115.

Nissim, G., & Simon, T. (2021). The future of labor unions in the age of automation and at the dawn of AI. *Technology in Society*, *67*, 101732. doi:10.1016/j.techsoc.2021.101732

Niszczota, P., & Abbas, S. (2023). GPT has become financially literate: Insights from financial literacy tests of GPT and a preliminary test of how people use it as a source of advice. *Finance Research Letters*, *58*, 104333. doi:10.1016/j.frl.2023.104333

Noh, Y. (2022). A study on the discussion on Library 5.0 and the generation of Library 1.0 to Library 5.0. *Journal of Librarianship and Information Science*. Advance online publication. doi:10.1177/09610006221106183

Ocaña-Fernández, Valenzuela-Fernández, Y., & Garro-Aburto, L. A. (2019). Artificial Intelligence and Its Implications in Higher Education. *J. Educ. Psychol. Propos. Represent*, *7*, 553–568.

Odeyemi, S. O. (2019). *Robots in Nigerian academic libraries: Investigating infrastructural readiness and potential for library services in information technology satellite meeting "Robots in libraries: challenge or opportunity?"* Technical University of Applied Sciences. https://creativecommons.org/licenses/by/4.0

Olendorf, R., & Wang, Y. (2017). Big Data in Libraries. In S. C. Suh & T. Anthony (Eds.), *Big Data and Visual Analytics* (pp. 191–202). Springer International Publishing. doi:10.1007/978-3-319-63917-8_11

Oliver, J. C., Kollen, C., Hickson, B., & Rios, F. (2019). Data science support at the academic library. *Journal of Library Administration*, *59*(3), 241–257. doi:10.1080/01930826.2019.1583015

Olubiyo, P. O., & Awoyemi, R. A. (2021). Automation of Academic Libraries in Nigeria: Issues and Practices. *Library Philosophy and Practice (e-journal)*, *5613*. https://digitalcommons.unl.edu/libphilprac/5613

Omame, I. M., & Alex-Nmecha, J. C. (2020). Artificial Intelligence in Libraries. In N. E. Osuigwe (Ed.), Advances in Library and Information Science (pp. 120–144). IGI Global. doi:10.4018/978-1-7998-1116-9.ch008

Osei-Mensah, C. Y., & Osei-Mensah, F. Y. (2021). Artificial intelligence (AI) in libraries: Applications, benefits, and challenges. *Library Hi Tech*, *39*(3), 425–442.

Ostertag, E., Hendler, J., Diaz, R. P., & Braun, C. (1992). Computing similarity in a reuse library system: An AI-based approach. *ACM Transactions on Software Engineering and Methodology*, *1*(3), 205–228. doi:10.1145/131736.131739

PandaS.HasanS.KaurN. (2024). Enhancing Library 5.0: Leveraging cloud and FoG computing for intelligent services and resource management. *ResearchGate*. doi:10.6084/m9.figshare.25231316.v1

Panda, S., & Kaur, N. (2023). Exploring the viability of ChatGPT as an alternative to traditional chatbot systems in library and information centers. *Library Hi Tech News*, *40*(3), 22–25. doi:10.1108/LHTN-02-2023-0032

Panda, S., & Kaur, N. (2023). Revolutionizing language processing in libraries with SheetGPT: An integration of Google Sheet and ChatGPT plugin. *Library Hi Tech News*. Advance online publication. doi:10.1108/LHTN-03-2023-0051

Panos, G. A., & Wilson, J. O. (2020). Financial literacy and responsible finance in the FinTech era: Capabilities and challenges. *European Journal of Finance*, *26*(4-5), 297–301. doi:10.1080/1351847X.2020.1717569

Parkar, R., Payare, Y., Mithari, K., Nambiar, J., & Gupta, J. (2021, July 1). AI and web-based interactive college enquiry chatbot. *2021 13th International Conference on Electronics, Computers and Artificial Intelligence (ECAI)*. 10.1109/ECAI52376.2021.9515065

Park, C.-W., Seo, S. W., Kang, N., Ko, B., Choi, B. W., Park, C., Chang, D. K., Kim, H., Kim, H., Lee, H., Jang, J., Ye, J. C., Jeon, J. H., Seo, J. B., Kim, K. J., Jung, K.-H., Kim, N., Paek, S., Shin, S.-Y., ... Yoon, H.-J. (2020). Artificial Intelligence in Health Care: Current Applications and Issues. *Journal of Korean Medical Science*, *35*(42), e379. doi:10.3346/jkms.2020.35.e379 PMID:33140591

Park, H., & Kim, J. (2023). AI Literacy for Special Education: Adaptive Strategies and Inclusive Practices. *Journal of Special Education Technology*, *20*(1), 56–72.

Park, H., & Kim, J. (2023). Graph-based Content Recommendation Systems Using AI. *Journal of Graph Algorithms and Applications*, *20*(1), 56–72.

Park, J., & Choi, H. (2023). Predictive Analytics for Library Collection Development: A Case Study of AI Applications. *Collection Management*, *48*(1/2), 65–79.

Park, J., & Lee, S. (2023). AI-Driven Decision Support Systems for Library Management. *Library Leadership & Management*, *37*(4), 213–227.

Patel, A. J., & Williams, E. R. (Eds.). (2024). *Case studies on accessibility and inclusion in the digital age*. ALA Editions.

Patel, A., & Gupta, S. (2023). Enhancing AI Literacy: Strategies and Approaches in Educational Programs. *International Journal of Artificial Intelligence in Education*, *28*(2), 87–102.

Patel, A., & Gupta, S. (2023). Personalized Content Recommendations Using AI Techniques. *Expert Systems with Applications*, *45*(4), 312–328.

Patel, B., & Shah, R. (2022). Global Perspectives on AI Literacy Education: Comparative Studies and Cross-Cultural Experiences. *Compare: A Journal of Comparative Education*, *45*(4), 312–328.

Patel, B., & Shah, R. (2022). Interactive Content Recommendation Systems Using AI. *International Journal of Human-Computer Interaction*, *45*(4), 312–328.

Patel, I., & Shah, K. (2023). Dynamic Content Recommendation Systems Using AI. *Journal of Dynamic Decision Making*, *38*(3), 189–204.

Patel, K., & Gupta, S. (2022). Privacy-Preserving Content Recommendation Systems Using AI. *Journal of Privacy Preserving Machine Learning*, *45*(2), 98–115.

Patel, S., & Patel, J. (2024). Designing Online Courses for AI Literacy: Pedagogical Strategies and Technologies. *Online Learning : the Official Journal of the Online Learning Consortium*, *45*(2), 98–115.

Paul, J., Ueno, A., & Dennis, C. (2023). ChatGPT and consumers: Benefits, pitfalls and future research agenda. *International Journal of Consumer Studies*, *47*(4), 1213–1225. doi:10.1111/ijcs.12928

Pavlik, J. V. (2023). Collaborating with Chat GPT: Considering the implications education. *Journalism and Mass Communication Educator*, *78*(1). doi:10.1177/10776958221149577

Pence, H. E. (2022). Future of artificial intelligence in libraries. *The Reference Librarian*, *63*(4), 133–143. doi:10.1080/02763877.2022.2140741

Pflanzer, M., Dubljević, V., Bauer, W. A., Orcutt, D., List, G., & Singh, M. P. (2023). Embedding AI in society: Ethics, policy, governance, and impacts. *AI & Society*, *38*(4), 1267–1271. doi:10.1007/s00146-023-01704-2

Pikhart, M. (2020). Intelligent information processing for language education: The use of artificial intelligence in language learning apps. In *24th International Conference on Knowledge-Based and Intelligent Information & Engineering Systems, Procedia Computer Science* (No. 176, pp. 1412–1419). Academic Press.

Pisoni, G., & Díaz-Rodríguez, N. (2023). Responsible and human centric AI-based insurance advisors. *Information Processing & Management, 60*(3), 103273. doi:10.1016/j.ipm.2023.103273

Pokrovskaya, A. (2024). The role of AI in protecting intellectual property rights on e-commerce marketplaces. *Russian Law Journal, 12*(1), Article 1. https://russianlawjournal.org/index.php/journal/article/view/3673

Popkova, E. G., & Gulzat, K. (2020). Technological Revolution in the 21st Century: Digital Society vs. Artificial Intelligence. In E. G. Popkova & B. S. Sergi (Eds.), *The 21st Century from the Positions of Modern Science: Intellectual, Digital and Innovative Aspects* (Vol. 91, pp. 339–345). Springer International Publishing. doi:10.1007/978-3-030-32015-7_38

Pramanik, A., Sarkar, S., & Pal, S. K. (2023). Video surveillance-based fall detection system using object-level feature thresholding and Z−numbers. *Knowledge-Based Systems, 280*, 110992. doi:10.1016/j.knosys.2023.110992

Provost, F., & Fawcett, T. (2013). *Data science for business: What you need to know about data mining and data-analytic thinking*. O'Reilly Media, Inc.

Radford, A., Narasimhan, K., Salimans, T., & Sutskever, I. (2018). *Improving language understanding by generative pre-training*. Retrieved from https://www.cs.ubc.ca/~amuham01/LING530/papers/radford2018improving.pdf

Raed, R.A., Tidjon, L. N., Rombaut, B., Khomh, F., & Hassan, A. E. (2022). *An Empirical Study of Library Usage and Dependency in Deep Learning Frameworks*. Academic Press.

Rajkumar, N., Tabassum, H., Muthulingam, S., Mohanraj, A., Viji, C., Kumar, N., & Senthilkumar, K. R. (2024). Anticipated Requirements and Expectations in the Digital Library. In K. Senthilkumar (Ed.), *AI-Assisted Library Reconstruction* (pp. 1–20). IGI Global. doi:10.4018/979-8-3693-2782-1.ch001

Rego Rodríguez, F. A., Germán Flores, L., & Vitón-Castillo, A. A. (2022). Artificial intelligence and machine learning: Present and future applications in health sciences. *Seminars in Medical Writing and Education, 1*, 9. doi:10.56294/mw20229

Remund, D. L. (2010). Financial literacy explicated: The case for a clearer definition in an increasingly complex economy. *The Journal of Consumer Affairs, 44*(2), 276–295. doi:10.1111/j.1745-6606.2010.01169.x

Rezaei, M., Azarmi, M., & Mir, F. M. P. (2023). 3D-Net: Monocular 3D object recognition for traffic monitoring. *Expert Systems with Applications, 227*, 120253. https://doi.org/https://doi.org/10.1016/j.eswa.2023.120253. doi:10.1016/j.eswa.2023.120253

Richey, R. G. Jr, Chowdhury, S., Davis-Sramek, B., Giannakis, M., & Dwivedi, Y. K. (2023). Artificial intelligence in logistics and supply chain management: A primer and roadmap for research. *Journal of Business Logistics, 44*(4), 532–549. doi:10.1111/jbl.12364

Robinson R.N. (2018). Artificial Intelligence: Its importance, challenges and applications in Nigeria. *Direct Research Journal of Engineering and Information Technology, 5*(5), 36 – 41.

Rodgers, W., Murray, J. M., Stefanidis, A., Degbey, W. Y., & Tarba, S. Y. (2023). An artificial intelligence algorithmic approach to ethical decision-making in human resource management processes. *Human Resource Management Review, 33*(1), 100925. doi:10.1016/j.hrmr.2022.100925

Rodrigues, R. (2020). Legal and human rights issues of AI: Gaps, challenges and vulnerabilities. *Journal of Responsible Technology, 4*, 100005. doi:10.1016/j.jrt.2020.100005

Rodriguez, A., & Perez, R. (2023). Sentiment Analysis in Library User Feedback: A Case Study of AI Applications. *Library & Information Science Research, 45*(3), 102435.

Rodriguez, M., & Hernandez, P. (2023). Deep Learning for Metadata Enhancement: A Case Study in Library Cataloging. *Cataloging & Classification Quarterly, 61*(3), 234–248.

Rodriguez, S. (2023). *Inclusive technology for libraries: Enhancing user experience.* Chandos Publishing.

Roll, I., & Wylie, R. (2016). Evolution and Revolution in Artificial Intelligence in Education. *International Journal of Artificial Intelligence in Education, 26*(2), 582–599. doi:10.1007/s40593-016-0110-3

Rubin, V. L., Chen, Y., & Thorimbert, L. M. (2010). Artificially intelligent conversational agents in libraries. *Library Hi Tech, 28*(4), 496–522. doi:10.1108/07378831011096196

Ryan, M. (2020). Ethical considerations for AI in libraries. *Library Hi Tech, 38*(4), 856–868.

Saeidnia, H. R. (2023). Ethical artificial intelligence (AI): Confronting bias and discrimination in the library and information industry. *Library Hi Tech News.* Advance online publication. doi:10.1108/LHTN-10-2023-0182

Sanji, M., Behzadi, H., & Gomroki, G. (2022). Chatbot: An intelligent tool for libraries. *Library Hi Tech News, 39*(3), 17–20. doi:10.1108/LHTN-01-2021-0002

Schiff, D., Biddle, J., Borenstein, J., & Laas, K. (2020). What's Next for AI Ethics, Policy, and Governance? A Global Overview. *Proceedings of the AAAI/ACM Conference on AI, Ethics, and Society*, 153–158. 10.1145/3375627.3375804

Sellamuthu, S., Vaddadi, S. A., Venkata, S., Petwal, H., Hosur, R., Mandala, V., Dhanapal, R., & singh, J. (2023). AI-based recommendation model for effective decision to maximise ROI. *Soft Computing*, 1–10. doi:10.1007/s00500-023-08731-7

Senthilkumar, K., & Maniiarsan, P. (2020). *Comparison of E- Resources with their Usage Statistics in Southern Region.* Academic Press.

Senthilkumar, K. (Ed.). (2024). *AI-Assisted Library Reconstruction.* IGI Global. doi:10.4018/979-8-3693-2782-1

Senthilkumar, K. R. (2019). *User pattern of Libraries by students of Government Colleges in Tamil nadu: A study.* Library Philosophy and Practice.

Senthilkumar, K. R. (2024). Revolutionizing thrust manufacturing. In *Advances in computational intelligence and robotics book series* (pp. 80–93). doi:10.4018/979-8-3693-2615-2.ch005

Senthilkumar, K. R., Jagajeevan, R., & Sangeetha, S. (2024). Impact of AI on Library and Information Science in Higher Institutions in India: A Comprehensive Analysis of Technological Integration and Educational Implications. In K. Senthilkumar (Ed.), *AI-Assisted Library Reconstruction* (pp. 21–33). IGI Global. doi:10.4018/979-8-3693-2782-1.ch002

Serafini, L., & Bouquet, P. (2004). Comparing formal theories of context in AI. *Artificial Intelligence, 155*(1–2), 41–67. doi:10.1016/j.artint.2003.11.001

Shams, M. Y., Tarek, Z., El-kenawy, E.-S. M., Eid, M. M., & Elshewey, A. M. (2024). Predicting Gross Domestic Product (GDP) using a PC-LSTM-RNN model in urban profiling areas. *Computational Urban Science, 4*(1), 3. Advance online publication. doi:10.1007/s43762-024-00116-2

Sharma, R., Kumar, A., & Singh, S. (2022). Content Recommendation Systems Using AI in E-Commerce. *IEEE Transactions on Knowledge and Data Engineering, 38*(3), 189–204.

Sharma, R., Kumar, A., & Singh, S. (2022). Empowering Educators with AI Literacy: Professional Development Programs. *Journal of Digital Learning in Teacher Education, 38*(3), 189–204.

She, L., Waheed, H., Lim, W. M., & Sahar, E. (2022). Young adults' financial well-being: Current insights and future directions. *International Journal of Bank Marketing, 41*(2), 333–368. doi:10.1108/IJBM-04-2022-0147

Compilation of References

Shen, Y., & Li, X. (2023). Ethical considerations in AI-driven digital library development: A Delphi study. *Journal of Librarianship and Information Science*.

Shiddiqi, A. M., Yogatama, E. D., & Navastara, D. A. (2023). Resource-aware video streaming (RAViS) framework for object detection system using deep learning algorithm. *MethodsX, 11*, 102285. doi:10.1016/j.mex.2023.102285 PMID:37533793

Shrivastava, R., & Mahajan, P. (2016, April 2). Artificial Intelligence Research in India: A Scientometric Analysis. *Science & Technology Libraries, 35*(2), 136–151. doi:10.1080/0194262X.2016.1181023

Silva, D. (2023, July 22). Optimizing website user Experience: How AI personalization algorithms drive conversion rates. *Medium*. https://uxplanet.org/optimizing-website-user-experience-how-ai-personalization-algorithms-drive-conversion-rates-6bcc63fa366d

Silva, S. M. D. (1997). A Review of Expert Systems in Library and Information Science. *Malaysian Journal of Library and Information Science, 2*(2), 57–92.

Singh, A., & Sharma, S. (2024). Adaptive Content Recommendation Systems Using AI. *ACM Transactions on Intelligent Systems and Technology, 38*(2), 98–115.

Singh, A., & Sharma, S. (2024). Assessing AI Literacy: Evaluation Frameworks and Tools. *Assessment & Evaluation in Higher Education, 38*(2), 98–115.

Singh, G., & Kumar, A. (2024). AI Literacy for Sustainable Development: Environmental Education Initiatives. *Environmental Education Research, 38*(2), 98–115.

Singh, G., & Kumar, A. (2024). Content Recommendation Systems Using AI for Educational Platforms. *Journal of Educational Technology & Society, 38*(2), 98–115.

Singh, R. (2023). Artificial intelligence and accessibility: Challenges and opportunities. *Journal of Technology and Inclusion, 12*(1), 45–62.

Sisman-Ugur, S., & Kurubacak, G. (Eds.). (2019). *Handbook of Research on Learning in the Age of Transhumanism*. IGI Global. doi:10.4018/978-1-5225-8431-5

Sivaraj, P., Madhan, V., Mallika, V., & Senthilkumar, K. R. (2024). Enhancing Library Services Through Optimization Algorithms and Data Analytics: Enhancing Library Services Mathematical Model. In K. Senthilkumar (Ed.), *AI-Assisted Library Reconstruction* (pp. 290–306). IGI Global. doi:10.4018/979-8-3693-2782-1.ch016

Smith, J., & Johnson, L. (2021). Artificial intelligence for accessibility: Advancing inclusivity with AI. Academic Press.

Smith, A. B. (2020). Emerging AI Technologies for Libraries. *Journal of Library Innovation, 12*(2), 45–58.

Smith, A., Johnson, B., & Brown, C. (2020). The role of artificial intelligence in automating library operations. *Library Trends, 68*(4), 512–528.

Smith, E., & Johnson, M. (2023). AI-Enabled Data Visualization Tools for Library Analytics. *Journal of Academic Librarianship, 49*(5), 102991.

Smith, J. (2022). Leveraging Emerging AI Technologies to Enhance Library Services. *Journal of Library Innovation, 44*(2), 112–125.

Smith, J., & Johnson, A. (2022). Educational Programs for AI Literacy: A Comprehensive Review. *Journal of Educational Technology Research, 16*(3), 201–218.

Smith, J., & Johnson, M. (2021). Personalized Recommendations in Libraries: A Case Study of AI-Powered Systems. *Library Trends, 69*(3), 345–360.

Smith, K., & Johnson, L. (2022). AI Literacy for Parents and Guardians: Family Education Programs. *Journal of Family and Consumer Sciences Education, 38*(3), 189–204.

Smith, K., & Johnson, L. (2022). Neighborhood-Based Methods for Content Recommendations Using AI. *Journal of Ambient Intelligence and Humanized Computing, 38*(3), 189–204.

Song, Z., Mellon, G., & Shen, Z. (2020). Relationship between racial bias exposure, financial literacy, and entrepreneurial intention: An empirical investigation. *Journal of Artificial Intelligence and Machine Learning in Management, 4*(1), 42–55.

Soria, V. (2020). Applying Natural Language Processing to Library Metadata Enrichment: A Case Study. *Library Resources & Technical Services, 64*(3), 144–156.

Strubell, E., Ganesh, A., & McCallum, A. (2019). Energy and policy considerations for deep learning in NLP. *Proceedings of the Annual Meeting of the Association for Computational Linguistics, 57*, 3645-3650.

Subaveerap, I. A. (2023). Application of Artificial Intelligence (AI) In Libraries and Its Impact on Library Operations Review. *Library Philosophy and Practice (e-journal). 7828*. https://digitalcommons.unl.edu/libphilprac/7828

Subaveerapandiyan. (2023). Application of Artificial Intelligence (AI) In Libraries and Its Impact on Library Operations Review. *Library Philosophy and Practice (e-journal)*, 7828. Retrieved from https://digitalcommons.unl.edu/libphilprac/7828

Subaveerapandiyan, A., & Gozali, A. (2024). AI in Indian Libraries: Prospects and Perceptions from Library Professionals. *Open Information Science, 8*(1). doi:10.1515/opis-2022-0164

Suryakant, K. B. (2013). Present Status of Library Collection, Staffing Pattern and Services Provided by the Dental College Libraries in Karnataka: A Study. *International Journal of Information Dissemination and Technology, 3*.

Tang, A., Li, K.-K., Kwok, K. O., Cao, L., Luong, S., & Tam, W. (2023). The importance of transparency: Declaring the use of generative artificial intelligence (AI) in academic writing. *Journal of Nursing Scholarship*. Advance online publication. doi:10.1111/jnu.12938 PMID:37904646

Tan, L., & Chen, Q. (2023). Ethical considerations in AI implementation for digital libraries: A systematic literature review. *Journal of Information Science, 49*(1), 77–94.

Tavakoli, M., Faraji, A., Vrolijk, J., Molavi, M., Mol, S. T., & Kismihók, G. (2022). An AI-based open recommender system for personalized labor market driven education. *Advanced Engineering Informatics, 52*, 101508. doi:10.1016/j.aei.2021.101508

Tenda, E. D., Henrina, J., Setiadharma, A., Aristy, D. J., Romadhon, P. Z., Thahadian, H. F., Mahdi, B. A., Adhikara, I. M., Marfiani, E., Suryantoro, S. D., Yunus, R. E., & Yusuf, P. A. (2024). Derivation and validation of novel integrated inpatient mortality prediction score for COVID-19 (IMPACT) using clinical, laboratory, and AI—processed radiological parameter upon admission: A multicentre study. *Scientific Reports, 14*(1), 2149. Advance online publication. doi:10.1038/s41598-023-50564-9 PMID:38272920

The University of Queensland. (2023). https://guides.library.uq.edu.au/referencing/chatgpt-and-generative-ai-tools

Thompson, B. (2022). *AI for good: Harnessing artificial intelligence for better accessibility*. MIT Press.

Vadari, S., & Malladi, C. (2024). Generative Knowledge Management for Financial Inclusion Through Financial Literacy: A Systematic Review. *IUP Journal of Knowledge Management, 22*(1).

Compilation of References

Van De Sompel, H., Nelson, M. L., Sanderson, R., Balakireva, L. L., Shankar, H., & Meehan, M. (2004). Analyzing the persistence of references in web resources. *D-Lib Magazine : the Magazine of the Digital Library Forum*, *10*(9).

Vasishta, P., Dhingra, N., & Vasishta, S. (2024). Application of artificial intelligence in libraries: A bibliometric analysis and visualisation of research activities. *Library Hi Tech*. Advance online publication. doi:10.1108/LHT-12-2023-0589

Verma, M. (2023). Novel study on AI-based chatbot (ChatGPT) impacts on the traditional library management. *International Journal of Trend in Scientific Research and Development*, *7*(1), 961–964.

Vidhate, S., Badgujar, A., Patil, N., & Pawar, R. (2019). *A Review on Library Automation Using Artificial Intelligence*. Academic Press.

Vijay Kumar, V. M., & Senthil Kumar, J. P. (2023). Insights on financial literacy: A bibliometric analysis. *Managerial Finance*, *49*(7), 1169–1201. doi:10.1108/MF-08-2022-0371

Vijayakumar, S., & Sheshadri, K. N. (2019). Applications of Artificial Intelligence in Academic Libraries. *International Journal on Computer Science and Engineering*, 7.

Viji, C., Najmusher, H., Rajkumar, N., Mohanraj, A., Nachiappan, B., Neelakandan, C., & Jagajeevan, R. (2024). *Intelligent Library Management Using Radio Frequency Identification.*, doi:10.4018/979-8-3693-2782-1.ch007

Wang, H., & Li, Y. (2023). Reinforcement Learning for Automated Collection Development in Libraries. *Library Acquisitions: Practice & Theory*, *47*(3), 102758.

Wang, H., & Zheng, L. (2023). *Ethical issues in AI-driven digital library development: A qualitative analysis*. International Journal of Digital Library Services.

Wang, J., Hu, F., Abbas, G., Albekairi, M., & Rashid, N. (2024). Enhancing image categorization with the quantized object recognition model in surveillance systems. *Expert Systems with Applications*, *238*, 122240. doi:10.1016/j.eswa.2023.122240

Wang, L., & Chen, Z. (2023). Intelligent Document Clustering for Information Organization in Digital Libraries. *Journal of Information Science*, *49*(1), 45–59.

Wang, L., & Liu, Q. (2023). Intelligent Tutoring Systems for Information Literacy Instruction in Libraries. *Journal of Education for Library and Information Science*, *64*(2), 102954.

Wang, Q., & Huang, Y. (2023). AI-Driven Text Mining for Information Extraction in Digital Libraries. *The Journal of Documentation*, *79*(4), 812–828.

Wang, X., Sun, Z., Chehri, A., Jeon, G., & Song, Y. (2024). Deep learning and multi-modal fusion for real-time multi-object tracking: Algorithms, challenges, datasets, and comparative study. *Information Fusion*, *105*, 102247. doi:10.1016/j.inffus.2024.102247

Wang, Y., & Liu, S. (2022). Application of Machine Learning in Library Circulation Services: A Case Study of Predictive Analysis. *Library Management*, *43*(1/2), 78–91.

Wang, Z., & Liu, Y. (2024). AI ethics in digital libraries: A scoping review. *The Journal of Documentation*, *80*(3), 616–632.

Wang, Z., & Zhang, X. (2023). Machine Translation for Multilingual Access to Library Resources. *International Journal of Translation, Interpretation, and Applied Linguistics*, *5*(1), 32–46.

Wei, L. (2023). Artificial intelligence in language instruction: Impact on English learning achievement, L2 motivation, and self-regulated learning. *Frontiers in Psychology*, *14*, 1261955. doi:10.3389/fpsyg.2023.1261955 PMID:38023040

Wheatley, A., & Hervieux, S. (2020). Artificial intelligence in academic libraries: An environmental scan. *Information Services & Use*, *39*(4), 347–356. doi:10.3233/ISU-190065

Williamson, S. M., & Prybutok, V. (2024). Balancing Privacy and Progress: A Review of Privacy Challenges, Systemic Oversight, and Patient Perceptions in AI-Driven Healthcare. *Applied Sciences (Basel, Switzerland)*, *14*(2), 2. Advance online publication. doi:10.3390/app14020675

Wilson, H. L., & Peterson, M. (Eds.). (2024). *Accessibility, user experience, and usability in information technologies*. IGI Global.

Winkler, B., & Kiszl, P. (2022). Views of academic library directors on artificial intelligence: A representative survey in Hungary. *New Review of Academic Librarianship*, *28*(3), 256–278. doi:10.1080/13614533.2021.1930076

Wójcik, M. (2023). Areas and contexts of the use of robotics in libraries: An overview of the applied solutions and a discussion of prospects. *Library Hi Tech*. Advance online publication. doi:10.1108/LHT-10-2022-0487

Wu, H., Ma, Y., Xiang, Z., Yang, C., & He, K. (2022). A spatial–temporal graph neural network framework for automated software bug triaging. *Knowledge-Based Systems*, *241*, 108308. doi:10.1016/j.knosys.2022.108308

Wu, J., Williams, K. M., Chen, H. H., Khabsa, M., Caragea, C., Tuarob, S., ... Giles, C. L. (2015). Citeseerx: Ai in a digital library search engine. *AI Magazine*, *36*(3), 35–48. doi:10.1609/aimag.v36i3.2601

Wu, W., & He, S. (2022). Ethical considerations in implementing AI technologies in digital libraries: A literature review. *Journal of Data and Information Science*.

Xiao, J. J. (2016). *Handbook of consumer finance research*. Springer. doi:10.1007/978-3-319-28887-1

Xu, M., & Wang, X. (2024). Ethical considerations in AI implementation for digital libraries: A case study of user perceptions. *Information Research*, *29*(2).

Yang, L., & Wang, Y. (2024). The ethics of AI in digital libraries: Perspectives from library professionals. *Journal of Librarianship and Information Science*.

Yang, S., Kanan, T., & Fox, E. (2010). Digital library educational module development strategies and sustainable enhancement by the community. *Research and Advanced Technology for Digital Libraries: 14th European Conference, ECDL 2010, Glasgow, UK, September 6-10, 2010 Proceedings*, *14*, 514–517.

Yang, S., & Zhang, X. (2022). Ethical considerations in AI implementation for digital libraries: A survey. *Information Processing & Management*, *59*(5), 102803.

Yi, Z. (2021). Research on intelligent service mode of digital library based on data intelligence. *4th International Conference on Advanced Electronic Materials, Computers and Software Engineering (AEMCSE)*, 942–945. 10.1109/AEMCSE51986.2021.00192

Yu, K. (2019). *The Application of Artificial Intelligence in Smart Library*. Academic Press.

YuadiI.SighA. R.NihayaU. (2024). Text Recognition for Library Collection in Different Light Conditions. *TEM Journal*, 266–276. https://doi.org/ doi:10.18421/TEM131-28

Zhang, J., Cheng, Y., Zhang, J., & Wu, Z. (2024). A spatiotemporal distribution identification method of vehicle weights on bridges by integrating traffic video and toll station data. *Journal of Intelligent Transportation Systems*. https://doi.org/https://doi.org/10.1080/15472450.2024.2312810

Compilation of References

Zhang, L., Guo, W., Zhang, Y., Liu, S., Zhu, Z., Guo, M., Song, W., Chen, Z., Yang, Y., Pu, Y., Ding, S., Zhang, J., Liu, L., & Zhao, Q. (2023). Modern Technologies and Solutions to Enhance Surveillance and Response Systems for Emerging Zoonotic Diseases. *Science in One Health*, 100061. https://doi.org/https://doi.org/10.1016/j.soh.2023.100061

Zhang, Y., & Wang, W. (2024). Ethical considerations in AI implementation for digital libraries: An empirical study. Journal of Information Science and Technology.

Zhang, H. (2021). Implementation of Robotic Shelf Reading in an Academic Library. *College & Research Libraries*, *82*(4), 523–537.

Zhang, H., & Chen, L. (2023). Neural Networks for Image Recognition in Library Digital Collections. *The Journal of Imaging Science and Technology*, *67*(4), 409–423.

Zhang, H., & Wang, L. (2023). Recommender Systems for Academic Libraries: A Comparative Analysis of AI Algorithms. *Journal of Academic Librarianship*, *49*(6), 102996.

Zhang, K., & Aslan, A. B. (2021). AI technologies for education: Recent research & future directions. *Computers and Education: Artificial Intelligence*, *2*, 100025. doi:10.1016/j.caeai.2021.100025

Zhang, M., & Wu, H. (2024). AI ethics in digital libraries: A bibliometric analysis. *Journal of Informetrics*, *18*(2), 101253.

Zhao, J., & Li, H. (2024). Exploring ethical implications of AI-driven digital library development: A survey of users' perspectives. *Library Management*, *45*(2), 123–139.

Zhao, Z., Zhu, J., Jiao, P., Wang, J., Zhang, X., Lu, X., & Zhang, Y. (2024). Hybrid-FHR: A multi-modal AI approach for automated fetal acidosis diagnosis. *BMC Medical Informatics and Decision Making*, *24*(1), 19. Advance online publication. doi:10.1186/s12911-024-02423-4 PMID:38247009

Zhou, X., Chen, Z., Jin, X., & Wang, W. Y. (2021). HULK: An energy efficiency benchmark platform for responsible natural language processing. *Proceedings of the Conference of the European Chapter of the Association for Computational Linguistics: System Demonstrations*, *16*, 329-336.

Zohny, H., McMillan, J., & King, M. (2023). Ethics of generative AI. *Journal of Medical Ethics*, *49*(2), 79–80. doi:10.1136/jme-2023-108909 PMID:36693706

About the Contributors

KR. Senthilkumar working as a Librarian in Sri Krishna Arts and Science College, Coimbatore. His most notable contributions to the field of E- Library and the Development of Library Web page. His research interests span both bibliometrics and Web 2.0. Much of his work has been on improving the understanding, design, and performance of Information systems, mainly through the application of E- Library, Survey, and Compare evaluation. In the Information Science arena, he has worked on TN Public Online Library. He has explored the presence and implications of self-similarity and heavy-tailed distributions in Open Source Journals. He has also investigated the implications of Web workloads for the design of scalable and no cost-effective Web Pages. In addition, he has made numerous contributions to research papers like Journals, Conference and Book Chapters.

* * *

Subaveerapandiyan A. was formerly employed as a Junior Professional Assistant at Bennett University in India. His academic journey is marked by acquiring dual master's degrees in Library and Information Science and English Language and Literature. His research pursuits encompass various subjects, notably digital literacy, research data management, Artificial Intelligence, and scholarly communication. His scholarly contributions are substantial, encompassing the publication of over 40 research papers. Recognising his exceptional research in LIS, he was received by the Society for the Advancement of Library and Information Science Dr M Tamizchelvan Memorial National Special Appreciation and Meritorious Award as a young professional in 2021.

Mohammed Gulzar Ahmed has been working as Principal & Dean in Yenepoya Pharmacy College & Research Centre (Yenepoya Deemed to University), Mangalore, Karnataka, India. He has 22 years of teaching and 3 years of Research experience. He has achieved 150+ publications of International and national accredited reputed journals (Scopus, WOS, UGC). He has knowledge in Novel drug delivery, nanotechnology, targeted drug Delivery & Stability Studies. He has Published 7 patents, 3 book chapters & 4 Books. He has fetched DST-SERB CRG grant, few seed grants from Yenepoya & RGUHS university. He has successfully guided 3 PhD's, 25 M.Pharm & Co guided 15 MDS. Currently 8 PhD candidates and 1 M.Pharm candidate are working under his guidance. He has awarded with Best Researcher, Best Paper and Good Teacher by the university.

Lalitha B. received her B.E degree and M.E degree from Anna University. She has 15 years of teaching experience. She has published 15 research papers in International Journals in the area of Power Electronics, Renewable Energy, Control Systems, Machine Learning and Internet of Things. She is a member of ISTE and IEEE.

About the Contributors

Anold Chama is a Library Officer in the Ministry of Home Affairs and Internal Security under the Department of National Archives' Library Unit. He is a candidate of Bachelor's program of Library and Information Science with Public Administration at the University of Zambia. Academic pursuits align with a keen interest in Artificial Intelligence, Digital Literacy, and Educational Technology. Navigating the evolving landscape of information science, he contributes to the advancement of library services.

Solomon Paul Raj D. is an esteemed Assistant Professor of English at Sri Krishnan Arts and Science College, bringing with him a decade of dedicated experience in the field of education. He is a distinguished scholar with a TESOL certification authorized by Trinity College London, underscoring his expertise in teaching English to speakers of other languages. Dr. Raj has an impressive array of Scopus-indexed publications, with his research primarily focused on English Language Teaching (ELT), Artificial Intelligence (AI), and deep learning. His work in integrating technology with language teaching methodologies has contributed significantly to the advancement of ELT, making him a respected figure in academic and research circles.

Hmalatha Gunasekaran received her Ph.D in Information and Communication Engineering from Anna University, Chennai, India. She has more than 18 years of teaching experience and her area of interest is Deep Learning, Big Data and Data Mining..

Je Joseph is an ardent learner of CHRIST University School of Business management doing his honours degree in management.

Jya K. is working as Assistant Professor of English in Sri Krishna Arts and Science College, Coimbatore holding five years of experience in teaching and mentoring students. She possesses a strong academic background, having earned a doctoral degree in English Literature at Bishop Heber College, Trichy. In addition to her teaching responsibilities, she is an active member of the academic communities, such as ELT@I and ELTIF. She has presented more than six of her research papers at various conferences and published nearly twelve papers in National and International Conferences. She has acted as a resource person in an International Conference and attended two events as a Guest Speaker. She has contributed her service as one of the editorial members in an International Journal "Language, Education and Culture Research".

Aandraj K. C. serves as a Documentation Assist -I at the Library and Documentation Centre of The Kerala Minerals and Metals Ltd in Kollam, Kerala. He holds a B.Sc, MLiSc & M.Phil, along with UGC NET and a Part-Time Ph.D Research scholar, Madurai Kamaraj University, Madurai, (Under the guidance of Dr. S Aravind, Librarian & Head, GTN Arts College, Dindugal) With a career spanning 16 years in managing information in libraries. He has co author book in library science and published 15 Conference papers.

Judeson Antony Kovilpillai has 6 years of experience as an Assistant Professor, and he is passionate about teaching in the fields of Industry 4.0, Embedded Systems, Internet of Things (IoT), Artificial Intelligence (AI), and Machine Learning (ML). Prof. Judeson holds a Ph.D. degree with the title "Investigations on machine learning and deep learning techniques for machinery fault diagnosis and tile defect detection in cyber-physical systems" from Anna University, Chennai. His thesis aims to make significant contributions to the advancement of fault diagnosis techniques in cyber-physical systems, bridging the gap between theory and practical applications. In addition to his academic expertise, Prof. Judeson has shown a strong commitment to continuous learning and professional development. He has completed 38 certification courses across various disciplines on platforms like NPTEL, BEC-Business English Certification, Coursera, Udemy, and Achology. Notably, he also gained valuable experience as a Research Intern during his post-graduation at the Healthcare and Technology Innovation Centre, IIT Madras.

Madhuri Kumari is a PhD Scholar (Pursuing) at the School of Library and Information Science at the Central University of Gujarat in India. She completed her Graduation in BSc Zoology (Hon) at Vinoba Bhave University, India. She completed her Bachelor's and Master's in Library and Information Science at Indira Gandhi National Open University, India. She is NETJRF (National Eligibility Test Junior Research Fellowship) under UGC. Her PhD research aims to assess the library websites of Indian academic institutes through content analysis. She is trying to spot content and library services available on academic library websites through the content analysis method. Through Web Analytics trying to give insight about library visibility over the World Wide Web. Her research interest lies in the field of Bibliometrics, Digital Library, Research Data Management, and Evaluation of Library Websites. She has published two peer-reviewed articles: "Awareness of Predatory Journals in Library and Information Science Faculties in India" and "Library Websites of Institutes of National Importance: A Content Study". Presented a paper at an international conference on "Statistical Tools and Techniques for Research Data Analysis". She has an intermediate level of expertise in software LMS Koha, MS Word, MS Excel, VOSviwer, Biblioshiny and SPSS. She has also worked as a volunteer in various events conducted in her department. She has some interest in writing poems and painting. She has also been active in sports and played volleyball at the national level in school.

Vdhya M. is currently working in Sri Krishna Arts and Science College, total experience is 10 years, published more than 25 journal.

P. Murugesan is currently working as professor in Mechanical Engineering at KSR College of Engineering. He has more than 25 years of experience in teaching profession. He published 75 international journal publications and received the award from the professional societies like ISTE, IE and SAMP as a best secretary award .He supervised the 26 UG projects, 12 PG projects and one PhD thesis.

Srumathy N. has completed her B. Sc and B. Ed under Bharathiyar University. Currently She is doing her post graduation in Mathematics.

Mgeshkumar Naarayanasamy Varadarajanis a senior IT professional having 21 years of comprehensive Development, Testing and DevOps experience, which includes Analysis, Architecture, Development, Solutions, Migrations and Quality Control with good understanding of the entire Software Development Life Cycle and Software Testing Life Cycle Rich experience in Program Management, Change Management, Release Management and Project Management with detailed planning, scheduling, progress monitoring and delivery Worked internationally, Hands-on experience and having expert domain knowledge in Banking and Finance (USA & Singapore), Health Care (USA), Telecom (UK), Retail (India), and Government (UK).

About the Contributors

Balusamy Nachiappan is an experienced IT professional with a strong background in object-oriented software development, design, and architecture. Certified as a Salesforce System Architect and Salesforce Application Architect, Balusamy specializes in banking, including investment banking and core banking, with international exposure. With extensive experience in the travel domain, including airlines, ship & cargo industries, Balusamy also has proficiency in supply chain management and real estate. With a solid track record of over a decade in product development across various sectors, Balusamy is proficient in Waterfall, V Model, and Agile-Scrum methodologies, and holds extensive onsite exposure in the US, Japan, the UK, and Qatar.

Jgajeevan R. holds a diverse academic background with qualifications including a B.Com., MBA, M.Phil., and a PhD, which he earned in the field of HR from Bharathiar School of Management & Entrepreneurial Development, Bharathiar University in Coimbatore. He embarked on his professional journey as a Marketing Executive for a satellite channel and later transitioned to the computer hardware marketing sector as a Business Development Executive. His career took an educational turn when he joined Sri Krishna Arts & Science College and VLB Janakiammal College of Arts & Science as a lecturer. Subsequently, he served as a lecturer at Kongunadu Arts & Science College before advancing to the position of Head of the Management department. His longest tenure was at PSG Institute of Management, where he dedicated 17 years of service until 2022.

Kavitha R. is presently working as Assistant Librarian cum Assistant Professor, Department of Library and Information Science, Mother Teresa Women's University, Kodaikanal, India. Formerly, she was working as Assistant assistant professor in Library and Information Science, Annamalai University, Annamalainagar. She is qualified with M.A.,(Eco), MLIS., M.Phil., Ph.D, She has presented a number of articles in various conferences. 21 papers in various national and International conferences, 39 Research articles were published in International Journals and Editor book Chapters . She has attended 14 workshops and seminars and published, Five Books with ISBN. She acted as resource person and Rapporteur in many conferences and seminars. She was honoured with "Noolagakkalaimani" award in 2019 and "Noolagar Chemmal" award in 2020. She is one of the translators in IGNOU- Swayam courses in 2020. At present, she is guiding 4 Ph.D's. One of the members of the Academic Library Association – Tamilnadu & Kerala, the Madras Library Association, the Library Professionals Association (LPA), the Professional Membership of Institute of Scholars(InSc) and Indian Academic Researcher Association(IARA).

S Radhakrishnan holds a Doctorate in Management, an MBA, an MPhil, and is NET and DTT qualified. Currently serving as an Associate Professor in the Department of Management Studies at Debre Berhan University in Debre Berhan, Ethiopia, he brings over 23 years of teaching expertise and boasts a decade of practical experience in the industry. He has contributed his skills in various international locations, including China, Bangladesh, Hong Kong, Zambia, and multiple regions within Ethiopia.

N. Rajkumar is an Associate Professor in the Department of Computer Science and Engineering. He earned his Ph.D. in Information and Communication Engineering from Anna University, Chennai. With a rich experience of 15 years in the realm of technical education, he has made substantial contributions to the academic arena. His research background is highly commendable, encompassing over 20 publications in esteemed international journals, coupled with numerous presentations at both international and national conferences. Moreover, he actively engages as a member of prestigious professional societies such as ISTE, IAENG, and CSTA. His primary areas of interest comprise Software Engineering, Computer Networks, Internet of Things, and Machine Learning.

Aravind S. is serving as a Librarian and Head, Central Library & Department of Library and Information Science, G.T.N. Arts College (Autonomous), Dindigul, Tamil Nadu, India. He is qualified with B.A., (RIM), B.L.I.Sc., M.L.I.Sc, M.Phil., M.B.A., M.Sc.,(IT), PhD.,(LIS). He has presented 54 articles in various national and international conferences and 50 research articles in reputed national and international Journals. He is establishing his role in article publishing, paper presentations in seminars and workshops, and publishing 14 books with ISBNs. He is serving as an editorial board member in Nineteen International Journals. He has organised many more conferences, workshops, seminars, and FDPs. At present, he is supervising 4 Ph.D. scholars, with 4 already awarded their degrees. He has submitted project proposals for DST-SERB and DST grants in 2024. He has received National Best Librarian Award from Madras Library Association on 2019 and Mayas Research (P) Ltd on 2019 and Best Librarian Award from Academic Library Association Tamil Nadu in 2022. He is one of the translators in IGNOU- Swayam courses in 2020 He has visited abroad like Malaysia, Singapore, Thailand, Sri Lanka, France, Greece, Dubai, Bahrain and Lebanon for paper presentation and tour.

Drga Devi S. has earned her M.Sc. and M.Phil. degrees from Bharathiar University. Currently, she is pursuing her Ph.D. and has authored several research articles and book chapters. She serves as an Assistant Professor in the Department of Mathematics at SKASC

Hnry Kishore S. is an Associate Professor and Head of the English Department at Sri Krishna Arts and Science College in Coimbatore, India. He boasts an impressive academic background in English Literature, Mass Communication & Journalism, Philosophy, Linguistics, and Psychology. This includes a Ph.D. in English, multiple Master's degrees, as well as prestigious certifications in English language assessment and training. Dr. Kishore is a prolific scholar with publications spanning English literature, comparative literature, and critical theory. His work explores themes ranging from Shakespeare and Arthur Miller to ecocriticism, postcolonialism, and the influence of philosophy on literature.

Areen Taj, currently working as Librarian at Yenepoya Pharmacy College and Research Centre, and also currently she is pursuing Ph.D. at the Central University of Gujarat in Gandhinagar, completed her Master's degree in Library and Information Science from the University of Mysore in 2016. Following this, she undertook a library traineeship at the esteemed Indian Institute of Management Ahmedabad (IIM-A) during the academic year 2016-17. She then served as a Project Assistant for NAAC and NIRF projects at the Information and Library Network (INFLIBNET) Centre in Gandhinagar, Gujarat. she has also successfully cleared the UGC-NET and K-SET examinations in Library and Information Science. Additionally, she holds a Diploma in Computer Application (DCA). With a keen interest in teaching and learning, she has contributed to scholarly publications, including one article in a UGC-Care listed journal and four papers presented at national and international conferences. Her research interests encompass Digital Library, Digitalization, Discovery, Access, and long-term Digital Preservation of library resources, LIS Metrics, ICT, Web 2.0 Technologies, and Scholarly Communication. Currently, she serves as a librarian at our college.

About the Contributors

Delma Thaliyan is a member of the faculty of CHRIST UNIVERSITY, Banglore. She is a multifaceted professional with an ardent interest in the overall development of students and in domain of management education. With 20 years of excellent experience in academics and industry with relevant knowledge and delivery skills, she expanded her research interests in Diversity and Inclusion, Happiness and wellbeing which glossed in to several publication in national and international Journals of repute. She is a corporate trainer in the area of performance management and an ardent researcher who received her doctoral degree in management in the year 2020.

C. Viji holds the position of Associate Professor in the Department of Computer Science and Engineering, Alliance University, Bangalore. She accomplished her Ph.D. in Information and Communication Engineering from Anna University, Chennai. She expertise in the realm of technical education has resulted in noteworthy contributions to the academic sphere. Her research background is indeed impressive, encompassing over 10 publications in esteemed international journals, along with numerous presentations at both international and national conferences. Furthermore, she actively engages as a member of renowned professional societies such as IAENG and CSTA. Her primary areas of interest span Software Engineering, Internet of Things, Networks, and Machine Learning.

Index

A

Access and Library Services 24
Adaptability 72, 164, 166, 169, 174, 240, 248, 266, 283
AI Challenges 39, 72
AI Ethics 1-2, 4-16, 18-23, 28, 58, 87, 99-102, 104-106, 139-141, 147, 150, 153
AI in Libraries 26-27, 34-35, 44, 51, 53-54, 57-58, 60, 68, 90, 105, 108, 115, 117-118, 136, 166, 186, 199, 201, 208-210, 221, 274
AI Technologies 3-4, 20-21, 23, 25, 28, 34-35, 44, 47-48, 51-52, 54-56, 58, 60, 63-64, 68, 86, 90, 96-98, 100, 105, 108-109, 111, 115, 118, 126, 130, 132, 134-137, 143, 152, 166, 180, 189-192, 196, 199, 204, 211, 215-219, 221-224, 227-232, 238, 240, 246-250, 267-269, 273, 277, 281-283
AI-Based Recommendation Systems 235-236, 238-240
AI-Driven Language Enhancement 238, 244-251
AI-Driven Libraries 56-58, 61, 272-274
Algorithmic Approaches 47
Algorithmic Bias 4, 51, 54-55, 57, 60, 63, 65, 85, 104, 146, 191, 199, 201, 210, 227, 231, 281-282
Approaches 21, 52, 78, 91-92, 107-108, 110, 112, 117-118, 124, 151, 153, 157, 174, 179, 207, 216, 224, 229-230, 235, 248, 265-266, 279-280
Artificial Intelligence (AI) 1-2, 24-25, 34, 36, 39, 45, 47-52, 54, 56-58, 60, 62-64, 71, 85, 107, 109, 111-118, 120, 125, 134-135, 137, 141-142, 144-146, 148-151, 155, 173, 178-179, 186-188, 190, 193, 195-198, 201-204, 207-208, 210, 212, 214, 216-217, 219, 221, 223, 226, 228-232, 235, 239, 244, 251, 253-254, 267, 272-277, 279-286

B

Bibliometric Analysis 1-2, 4, 18, 20, 38, 106, 234, 284
Big Data 11, 21-22, 26, 28, 35-36, 69, 124, 187, 195, 242, 260, 270

C

Cataloguing 26-27, 33, 39, 41, 48-50, 107, 109, 255-256, 268, 270
Challenges 1-3, 18-30, 34-35, 39, 43, 46-49, 51, 53-58, 60-61, 63, 65, 67, 70, 72, 76, 83, 90, 93, 95-96, 101, 103-104, 109, 112-113, 115, 136, 138, 143, 147-151, 153, 157-158, 162, 165-166, 179-180, 183-184, 186, 191-193, 196, 199, 208, 210-211, 215, 217-218, 220-223, 225-226, 230-232, 234-235, 240-242, 245-247, 249-251, 254, 269, 272-274, 277, 281-283, 287-288, 290
Chatbots 25-28, 34-35, 44, 52, 66, 68-70, 72-77, 79-81, 115, 117-119, 121, 125-126, 129-131, 178, 187-189, 192, 196, 200-201, 207, 210, 219, 229-230, 238, 268, 275, 277
ChatGPT Libraries 72-76, 79-81
Citation Metrics 4, 112
Collaborative Filtering Recommender Systems 155
Content Recommendation 155, 174-176, 191-192, 216, 272-273, 280
Content-Based Filtering 159-162, 168, 261, 264-266
Conversational AI 66, 72-81
Cultural Nuance 250
Curriculum 28-29, 118, 134, 137-138, 140, 145, 147, 152, 166, 229-230
Cutting-Edge NLP Techniques 254

D

Data Analytics 26, 28, 35, 37, 48, 58, 62-64, 83, 110, 118, 127, 132, 141, 148, 154, 159, 176, 191, 200, 210, 243, 253, 271-273, 275, 277, 283-284, 293
Data Mining 20, 115, 131, 187, 259-260, 270, 277, 283
Determinants 226, 228-229
Developers 3, 44, 72-78, 80-81, 99-102, 110, 220-221, 224, 240
Digital Age 34, 47-49, 52, 54, 56-58, 60-61, 81, 108, 112, 129-130, 146, 151, 153, 164, 186, 192,

Index

200, 202, 224, 233, 245, 250, 270, 272-274, 283, 286, 291

Digital Knowledge Access 272-275, 283

Digital Libraries 85-87, 90-101, 103-106, 116-117, 119, 124-125, 131-133, 139, 147, 153, 162, 174-175, 193, 196, 201, 204, 213, 217, 253, 275, 277-280, 285-286, 290-291

Digital Literacy 60, 108, 128, 197, 199, 220, 230, 237

Digital Transformation 47-48, 56, 286

Discovery 24-26, 29, 31-32, 34, 52, 54-56, 60, 64, 66-67, 109, 112, 115-116, 119, 123, 127, 129-130, 155-156, 159, 162, 164, 190, 196, 198, 238, 247-248, 259, 261-262, 270, 272-273, 275-276, 278, 280, 283, 286

E

Education 2-3, 23, 25, 29-30, 32, 34-35, 37, 45, 48, 51, 54, 64, 67, 69-70, 80, 82, 86-87, 90-92, 96, 99-103, 108, 117, 133-135, 137-148, 150-154, 166, 179-180, 182-185, 196, 198, 203, 209, 212, 224, 228-230, 232-233, 236-238, 240-241, 243, 249, 251-252, 269, 279, 285, 290

Educational Technology 61, 82, 96, 104, 131, 139, 152-154, 159, 175-176, 179, 212, 233, 242, 252, 270, 284, 292

Ethical Challenges 1-2, 18-21, 70, 104

Ethical Considerations 8, 18, 20-21, 27, 29, 35, 55-58, 60-61, 65, 68, 85, 94, 96, 104-106, 146, 186, 199, 247, 249-250, 273, 281, 283

F

Feature Extraction 159

Financial Education 229-230, 232, 235, 237-238, 240

Financial Literacy 226-241

Future Directions 23, 29, 34-35, 69, 150, 221, 232, 234, 240, 250

I

Impact of AI 7, 12, 37, 39, 43, 62, 71, 83, 97-98, 102, 108, 111, 116, 118-119, 132, 136, 154, 166, 176, 179, 184, 211, 221, 240, 243, 253, 271, 284, 292

Inclusive Growth 286, 290-291

India 1, 15, 24, 30, 36-37, 39, 47, 62-63, 71-72, 83, 85, 107, 118, 132, 136, 154, 166, 176, 178-179, 186, 191, 194-195, 214, 226, 235, 241, 243-244, 253-254, 271-273, 284-292

Information Access 33, 35, 44, 53, 193, 218, 236, 238, 244-247, 249-251, 270, 275

Information Literacy 25, 40, 49, 133, 197, 211, 219, 244-245

Information Management 47-52, 54, 56-58, 60-61, 130, 247, 254, 272-273

Information Retrieval 25, 27-28, 34, 39, 49-51, 53, 63-64, 66, 107-108, 113, 115, 117, 131, 186-187, 200, 202, 205, 212, 224, 244-245, 247-248, 250, 254-258, 262-263

Innovation 2, 19-20, 22, 25, 45, 47-51, 54, 60-61, 65, 70, 107, 110-113, 115, 130, 132, 135, 137, 139-141, 148-151, 171, 174, 185, 193, 199, 201, 211, 220-221, 223, 241, 247, 250, 253, 260, 267, 272-274, 285-286, 290-291

Integration and Customization 72

Intellectual Freedom 186, 192-193, 196, 200

Interfaces 48, 51-53, 56, 58, 60, 63-64, 67, 72-73, 76-77, 88, 90, 92-93, 99, 127-130, 204, 207, 211, 215-216, 219, 240, 244, 248, 250, 262

Interventions 27, 55, 226, 229-230, 232

K

Knowledge Democratization 285-286, 290

Knowledge Hubs 47, 223

Knowledge Management 115, 130, 234, 273

L

Language Comprehension 244

Learning and Teaching 134

Library 24-45, 47-72, 74-80, 82-83, 85-97, 99-102, 104-133, 136, 139, 141-142, 147, 153-154, 159, 162, 166, 171, 176-177, 186-189, 192-197, 199-224, 235-236, 238-256, 259-263, 267-268, 270-271, 273-276, 278-279, 281-286, 290-293

Library and AI 39

Library of the Future 61, 195, 212

Literacy 25, 27, 29, 35, 40, 48-49, 59-61, 108, 125, 128, 130, 133-139, 145-146, 151-154, 197, 199-200, 207, 209, 211, 219-220, 226-241, 244-245

M

Metadata Enhancement 127, 129, 132, 192

Metrics 4-7, 10-11, 13-14, 19, 65, 90, 107, 110-112, 127-128, 130, 160, 221, 236, 249, 266

Mobile Internet 195

N

Natural Language Processing (NLP) 49-50, 52-53, 55,

64-65, 80, 109, 115, 126, 129, 188-189, 191-192, 201, 209, 215, 238, 244-245, 247-248, 250, 254, 267, 279
Next-Generation Libraries 47-49, 51-54, 57-61, 107
NLP 39, 42, 49-50, 52-53, 55, 64-65, 80, 83, 109, 115, 117, 119, 126-127, 129, 188-189, 191-192, 201, 203, 209, 215, 238, 244-245, 247-248, 250, 254, 261-263, 267, 279
NLP in Library 39

O

Outcomes 3, 27, 88-92, 96, 101, 126, 140, 216, 218, 221-222, 226, 229, 231-232, 236, 239-240, 246, 260-261

P

Pedagogy 134
Personalization 50, 62, 65, 123, 135, 157, 161, 169, 172, 174, 248, 255, 261
Personalized Financial Services 235-236, 239-241
Physically Challenged 186-189
Privacy Concerns Fairness 85
Probabilistic Model 254

R

Recommendation Systems 48, 51, 53, 60, 66, 109, 112, 127, 131, 157-158, 164-168, 171-176, 186, 189-192, 203, 214-216, 219-220, 222-224, 235-236, 238-240, 244, 255, 261, 263-267, 272-273, 280
Recommender Systems 50, 53, 67, 131, 133, 155, 165
Referencing 5-6, 39, 83, 202
Remote Services 195, 203
Research 1-2, 4-8, 10, 12-16, 18-24, 26-36, 38, 40-48, 52, 58-59, 63-70, 72, 75, 78, 81, 103, 105, 108-109, 111-113, 115, 118, 128, 130-133, 135, 137, 139-141, 144-145, 149, 152-154, 166, 179-180, 185, 190-191, 194, 196-200, 203-204, 207, 209-210, 212, 216-219, 221-224, 233-234, 237, 240-244, 246-248, 250-254, 260, 268, 273-274, 278, 284-285, 291
Research Libraries 42, 45, 63-69, 113, 133, 212
Review 2, 21, 23-24, 26, 31, 35-36, 63, 69-70, 82, 97, 104-105, 113, 131-132, 135, 152, 154, 175, 179-180, 190, 193, 205, 216-217, 222, 226, 228, 234, 241, 243, 245-246, 251-253, 272-274, 282, 284

S

Scholarly Publications 1-2, 4, 59
Search 5, 25, 27-28, 31-32, 39, 41-42, 44, 50-56, 60, 64-67, 89, 91, 96, 102, 108, 111, 114, 116, 119-121, 123, 125, 128-130, 140, 189-190, 192, 195-196, 199-202, 204-206, 209-212, 214, 219, 222-223, 238, 244-245, 247-248, 250, 255-256, 258-259, 261-263, 267, 270, 272-273, 275-276, 280-283
Semantic Analysis 256, 275
Semantic Understanding 238, 245, 250, 262
Smart Cities 195, 203
Strategies 24, 34, 44, 47, 55, 57, 86-87, 90-91, 101-102, 107, 109, 117, 121, 126, 129-131, 140, 144, 147, 150, 152-153, 156-159, 163-164, 166-169, 171-174, 199-200, 204, 216, 227, 229-232, 237-238, 244-251, 253, 259-262, 265, 268

T

Tools 2, 5, 24-29, 32-35, 41-43, 51, 54, 57-58, 60, 64, 66-68, 73-75, 78-81, 109, 111, 119-120, 132, 139-140, 143-144, 154, 165, 178-179, 187, 190-191, 199-200, 206-207, 210, 214-216, 218, 220-224, 226, 228-232, 236-237, 241, 244-246, 266-267, 272, 275-280
Training 25, 29, 34, 40, 51, 54-59, 67-68, 78, 90-91, 100-103, 107-108, 110, 125, 134-135, 137-142, 144-148, 150-152, 188, 197, 199, 201, 204, 206, 216, 221-223, 228, 249, 259, 274, 282
Transparency 3-4, 21, 28, 34, 51, 53, 55-57, 60-61, 65, 67, 71, 85-90, 94, 96-98, 100, 103, 136, 146, 161, 164, 166, 173-174, 201, 209, 239-240, 249, 281, 290

U

User Experience 28, 33, 35, 39, 48-53, 58, 62, 68, 76, 78, 81, 107, 112, 117, 122, 131, 189-190, 192, 196, 199-201, 206, 209, 214, 216, 219, 221, 223-225, 238, 244-246, 248-249, 254, 262-263, 266, 268, 273, 275, 278, 280-283

V

Vector Space Model 254, 257

Y

Yenepoya (Deemed to be University) 24-25, 29
Yenepoya Central Library 24, 26, 28, 30-31, 34

Publishing Tomorrow's Research Today

Uncover Current Insights and Future Trends in Business & Management
with IGI Global's Cutting-Edge Recommended Books

Print Only, E-Book Only, or Print + E-Book.
Order direct through IGI Global's Online Bookstore at www.igi-global.com or through your preferred provider.

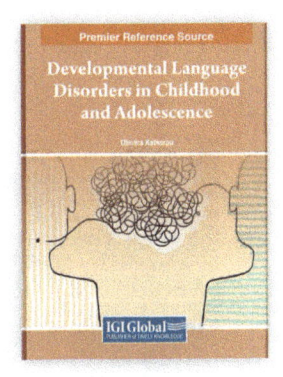

Developmental Language Disorders in Childhood and Adolescence
ISBN: 9798369306444
© 2023; 436 pp.
List Price: US$ **230**

The Sustainable Fintech Revolution: Building a Greener Future for Finance
ISBN: 9798369300084
© 2023; 358 pp.
List Price: US$ **250**

Cases on Enhancing Business Sustainability Through Knowledge Management Systems
ISBN: 9781668458594
© 2023; 366 pp.
List Price: US$ **240**

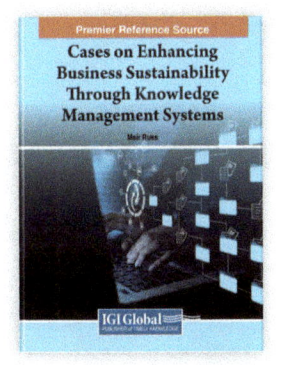

5G, Artificial Intelligence, and Next Generation Internet of Things: Digital Innovation For Green and Sustainable Economies
ISBN: 9781668486344
© 2023; 256 pp.
List Price: US$ **280**

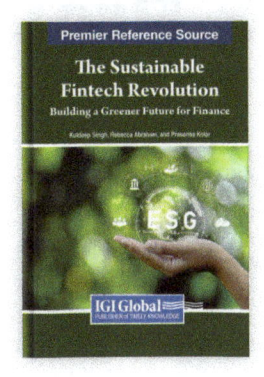

The Use of Artificial Intelligence in Digital Marketing: Competitive Strategies and Tactics
ISBN: 9781668493243
© 2024; 318 pp.
List Price: US$ **250**

AI and Emotional Intelligence for Modern Business Management: Bridging the Gap and Nurturing Success
ISBN: 9798369304181
© 2023; 415 pp.
List Price: US$ **250**

Do you want to stay current on the latest research trends, product announcements, news, and special offers?
Join IGI Global's mailing list to receive customized recommendations, exclusive discounts, and more.
Sign up at: www.igi-global.com/newsletters.

Scan the QR Code here to view more related titles in Business & Management.

www.igi-global.com | Sign up at www.igi-global.com/newsletters | facebook.com/igiglobal | twitter.com/igiglobal | linkedin.com/igiglobal

Ensure Quality Research is Introduced to the Academic Community

Become a Reviewer for IGI Global Authored Book Projects

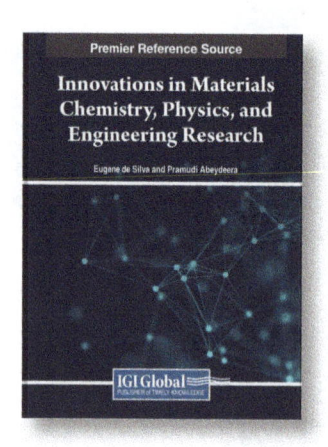

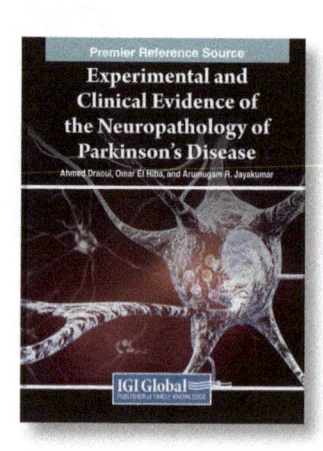

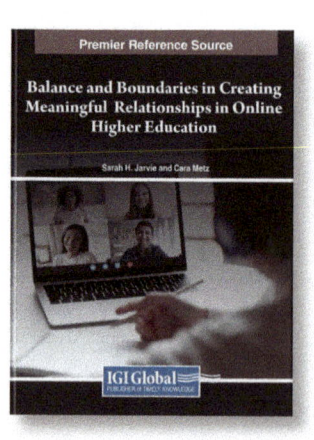

The overall success of an authored book project is dependent on quality and timely manuscript evaluations.

Applications and Inquiries may be sent to:
development@igi-global.com

Applicants must have a doctorate (or equivalent degree) as well as publishing, research, and reviewing experience. Authored Book Evaluators are appointed for one-year terms and are expected to complete at least three evaluations per term. Upon successful completion of this term, evaluators can be considered for an additional term.

If you have a colleague that may be interested in this opportunity, we encourage you to share this information with them.

IGI Global's Open Access Journal Program

Publishing Tomorrow's Research Today

Including Nearly 200 Peer-Reviewed, Gold (Full) Open Access Journals across IGI Global's Three Academic Subject Areas: Business & Management; Scientific, Technical, and Medical (STM); and Education

Consider Submitting Your Manuscript to One of These Nearly 200 Open Access Journals for to Increase Their Discoverability & Citation Impact

Web of Science Impact Factor	Journal
6.5	Journal of Organizational and End User Computing
4.7	Journal of Global Information Management
3.2	International Journal on Semantic Web and Information Systems
2.6	Journal of Database Management

Choosing IGI Global's Open Access Journal Program Can Greatly Increase the Reach of Your Research

Higher Usage
Open access papers are 2-3 times more likely to be read than non-open access papers.

Higher Download Rates
Open access papers benefit from 89% higher download rates than non-open access papers.

Higher Citation Rates
Open access papers are 47% more likely to be cited than non-open access papers.

Submitting an article to a journal offers an invaluable opportunity for you to share your work with the broader academic community, fostering knowledge dissemination and constructive feedback.

Submit an Article and Browse the IGI Global Call for Papers Pages

We can work with you to find the journal most well-suited for your next research manuscript. For open access publishing support, contact: journaleditor@igi-global.com

IGI Global e-Book Collection

Publishing Tomorrow's Research Today

Including Essential Reference Books Within Three Fundamental Academic Areas

Business & Management
Scientific, Technical, & Medical (STM)
Education

- Acquisition options include Perpetual, Subscription, and Read & Publish
- No Additional Charge for Multi-User Licensing
- No Maintenance, Hosting, or Archiving Fees
- Continually Enhanced Accessibility Compliance Features (WCAG)

| Over **150,000+** Chapters | Contributions From **200,000+** Scholars Worldwide | More Than **1,000,000+** Citations | Majority of e-Books Indexed in Web of Science & Scopus | Consists of Tomorrow's Research Available Today! |

Recommended Titles from our e-Book Collection

Innovation Capabilities and Entrepreneurial Opportunities of Smart Working
ISBN: 9781799887973

Advanced Applications of Generative AI and Natural Language Processing Models
ISBN: 9798369305027

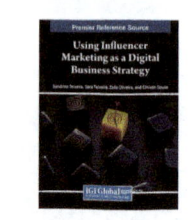

Using Influencer Marketing as a Digital Business Strategy
ISBN: 9798369305515

Human-Centered Approaches in Industry 5.0
ISBN: 9798369326473

Modeling and Monitoring Extreme Hydrometeorological Events
ISBN: 9781668487716

Data-Driven Intelligent Business Sustainability
ISBN: 9798369300497

Information Logistics for Organizational Empowerment and Effective Supply Chain Management
ISBN: 9798369301593

Data Envelopment Analysis (DEA) Methods for Maximizing Efficiency
ISBN: 9798369302552

Request More Information, or Recommend the IGI Global e-Book Collection to Your Institution's Librarian

For More Information or to Request a Free Trial, Contact IGI Global's e-Collections Team: eresources@igi-global.com | 1-866-342-6657 ext. 100 | 717-533-8845 ext. 100

Are You Ready to Publish Your Research?

IGI Global — Publishing Tomorrow's Research Today

IGI Global offers book authorship and editorship opportunities across three major subject areas, including Business, STM, and Education.

Benefits of Publishing with IGI Global:

- Free one-on-one editorial and promotional support.
- Expedited publishing timelines that can take your book from start to finish in less than one (1) year.
- Choose from a variety of formats, including Edited and Authored References, Handbooks of Research, Encyclopedias, and Research Insights.
- Utilize IGI Global's eEditorial Discovery® submission system in support of conducting the submission and double-blind peer review process.
- IGI Global maintains a strict adherence to ethical practices due in part to our full membership with the Committee on Publication Ethics (COPE).
- Indexing potential in prestigious indices such as Scopus®, Web of Science™, PsycINFO®, and ERIC – Education Resources Information Center.
- Ability to connect your ORCID iD to your IGI Global publications.
- Earn honorariums and royalties on your full book publications as well as complimentary content and exclusive discounts.

Join Your Colleagues from Prestigious Institutions, Including:

- Australian National University
- Massachusetts Institute of Technology
- Johns Hopkins University
- Tsinghua University
- Harvard University
- Columbia University in the City of New York

Learn More at: www.igi-global.com/publish
or Contact IGI Global's Aquisitions Team at: acquisition@igi-global.com

Individual Article & Chapter Downloads
US$ 37.50/each

Easily Identify, Acquire, and Utilize Published Peer-Reviewed Findings in Support of Your Current Research

- Browse Over **170,000+ Articles & Chapters**
- **Accurate & Advanced** Search
- Affordably Acquire **International Research**
- **Instantly Access** Your Content
- Benefit from the **InfoSci® Platform Features**

THE UNIVERSITY of NORTH CAROLINA at CHAPEL HILL

" *It really provides* **an excellent entry into the research literature of the field**. *It presents a manageable number of* **highly relevant sources** *on topics of interest to a wide range of researchers. The sources are* **scholarly, but also accessible** *to 'practitioners'.* "

- Ms. Lisa Stimatz, MLS, University of North Carolina at Chapel Hill, USA

IGI Global Proudly Partners with eContent Pro® International

Editorial Services

Providing you with High-Quality, Affordable, and Expeditious Editorial Support from Manuscript Development to Publication

Copy Editing & Proofreading

Perfect your research paper before publication. Our expert editors will correct faulty spelling, grammar, punctuation, and word usage.

Scientific & Scholarly Editing

Increase your chances of being published. Our expert editors will aid in strengthening the quality of your research before submission.

Figure, Table, Chart & Equation Conversions

Enhance the visual elements of your research. Let our professional designers produce or correct your figures before final submission.

Journal Recommendation

Save time and money when you rely on our expert journal selectors to provide you with a comprehensive journal recommendation report.

Order now to receive an automatic **10% Academic Discount** on all your editorial needs.

Scan the QR Code to Learn More

Upload Your Manuscript, Select Your Desired Editorial Service, and Receive a Free Instant Quote

Email: customerservice@econtentpro.com

econtentpro.com